THE
FASCIST ECONOMY
IN NORWAY

THE
FASCIST ECONOMY
IN NORWAY

BY

ALAN S. MILWARD

OXFORD
AT THE CLARENDON PRESS
1972

Oxford University Press, Ely House, London W. 1

GLASGOW NEW YORK TORONTO MELBOURNE WELLINGTON
CAPE TOWN IBADAN NAIROBI DAR ES SALAAM LUSAKA ADDIS ABABA
DELHI BOMBAY CALCUTTA MADRAS KARACHI LAHORE DACCA
KUALA LUMPUR SINGAPORE HONG KONG TOKYO

PRINTED IN GREAT BRITAIN
AT THE UNIVERSITY PRESS, OXFORD
BY VIVIAN RIDLER
PRINTER TO THE UNIVERSITY

PREFACE

THIS book is intended as a study of German economic policy in Norway from 1940 to 1945, of its results, and of the light it throws on fascism. It is based on the archives of the Economic Department of the Reichskommissariat in Norway, a source previously almost entirely unused. My pleasure in being the first person to use it was alloyed by thoughts of the injustice that the better part of it should have been retained in Britain where no one realized its true importance. Nor, indeed, did I for many years although for a long time I had been aware of its existence. Happily my work, if it achieves nothing else, has at least been the cause of these papers being returned to Norway, their rightful and proper home. Had they been there before, Norwegian historians would no doubt have produced better books than this. I can assure them, however, that my work does not aim at being definitive. It is exploratory and there is plenty of room for subsequent explorers.

One of my main purposes in writing this book was to provide a sequel to my earlier study of the German occupation of France. I was disappointed that German economic policy in France revealed only indirectly German plans for Europe as a whole and therefore chose to write about a smaller power and one whose position in German eyes was much less ambivalent. I thought a study of Norway would test some of the conclusions in my study of France and I think it is fair to say that this book is much more revealing about the fascist New Order than the earlier one. It has, as well, a further dimension of economic interest. Norway seemed to me to be, of all the occupied economies, the most open and the most dependent on international factor mobility and thus the least well suited to incorporation in the fascist system. The problem of exploitation by the conqueror was also more difficult in a country with so few resources of its own. Such were my reasons in choosing this topic. Whatever the result, I cannot be accused of adding to the torrent of books on familiar subjects. Very few books exist in the English language about the economy or history of Norway. I am glad to have added one to the list.

Something of the history of the archives of the Economic Section of the Reichskommissariat is explained in the Note on Sources. I have also used papers of other ministries and official bodies, particularly of the *Reichsministerium für Bewaffnung und Munition* and the *Reichsluftfahrtministerium.* Certain files of the *Volkswirtschaftsabteilung* of I. G. Farben, of A/S Nordag, of the *Reichsamt für wehrwirtschaftliche Planung*, of *Deutsche Handelskammer in Norwegen*, and of Field Marshal Eberhard Milch also proved very useful. So did certain published sources. These are listed in the Note on Sources. The recent economic history of Norway has been well served by the publications of the Norwegian Statistical Central Office, no less during the war than for other periods, and I have drawn heavily on their works.

I would like to express my thanks to those who have helped and encouraged me with my work. Mr. Helge Paulsen made his knowledge of the Reichskommissariat papers in the Riksarkivet freely available to me. It was very great, since he had himself worked on the same subject. I am very grateful to him for making my visits to Hovedøya so agreeable. Professor S. B. Saul made time at short notice to read the first draft of the manuscript and his many suggestions improved it very much. The friendly help and archival skills of Miss Angela Raspin of the Foreign Documents Centre of the Imperial War Museum have saved me countless hours. In the midst of apparent chaos she has located all kinds of documents that I could never have found and drawn my attention to many others that I would not otherwise have known about. The Committee on International Studies of Stanford University contributed generously, enabling me to visit both Germany and Norway and paying the cost of typing the manuscript. My thanks also to Dr. Dagfinn Mannsåker, who made the resources of the Riksarkivet freely available to me and was so kind on my visits there, to Mrs. Sharon Lavorel for her help with the manuscript, to Professor W. N. Medlicott, Mrs. Agnes Peterson, Professor M. Skodvin, Christopher and Anne-Marie Smout, Mr. B. Soan, and Dipl. Ing. A. Speer. Readers owe a debt to my wife, who has deleted some passages of remarkable boredom, which I, spending my life in universities, could not reasonably be expected to detect. Those that remain are, like the mistakes, my own.

There can be few cities in the world which shelter so many curious and interesting people as San Francisco and it would be unfair not to acknowledge a place where you can buy learned books at two o'clock in the morning.

A.S.M.

San Francisco, July 1970

CONTENTS

LIST OF TABLES

LIST OF ABBREVIATIONS

Abt.	Abteilung
Aktstykker	*Aktstykker om den tyske finanspolitikk i Norge*, ed. S. Hartmann and J. Vogt (Oslo, 1958)
B.A.	Bundesarchiv
B.R.T.	British registered tons
D.G.E.P.	*Documents on German Foreign Policy, 1918–1945*
F.D.	Foreign Document
Gbm.	Generalbevollmächtigter
Hauptabt. Volkswi.	Hauptabteilung Volkswirtschaft
I.M.T.	*Trial of the Major War Criminals before the International Military Tribunal*
Mbh. in F.	Militärbefehlshaber in Frankreich
N.D.	Nuremberg Document
N.T.L.L.	National Technological Lending Library
R.A.	Riksarkivet
Rk.	Reichskommissar für die besetzten norwegischen Gebiete
Rk.f.d.See.	Reichskommissar für die Seeschiffahrt
Rlm.	Reichsluftfahrtministerium
Rm.f.B.u.M.	Reichsministerium für Bewaffnung und Munition
Rm.f.R.u.Kp.	Reichsministerium für Rüstungs- und Kriegsproduktion
Rwm.	Reichswirtschaftsministerium
Wi.Rü.Amt.	Wirtschafts- und Rüstungsamt

Unless otherwise indicated 'ton' is used to mean 'metric ton'

I

NATIONAL SOCIALISM AND NASJONAL SAMLING

WERE Norway now one of the world's poorest, rather than one of the world's richest, countries no economist would be very optimistic about its future. Its forbidding terrain, infertile soils, and harsh climate, its relative lack of mineral resources, the fierce attachment to tradition and locality of its inhabitants, and their remote situation on the northern bounds of the inhabited world, would all be considered severe obstacles to economic development. Such they were for most of the nineteenth century while Norway remained a poor country of fishermen and peasants. The industrial revolution in Norway took place in those two decades before the First World War when capital, labour, and entrepreneurial talent crossed international frontiers with a readiness which has never been recaptured. No country shared more happily in these developments than Norway. The inhabitants were few in number and an extraordinarily high proportion of them took advantage of that same ease of mobility which brought capital to Norway, to leave for the United States. Although complaints that Norway was becoming a virtual colony of more-developed countries were not unknown, Norway avoided the imperialistic aspects of the international economy more successfully than other developing lands at the time, partly because the small population and its high rate of emigration made an increase in *per capita* incomes much easier than elsewhere and partly because of the whole-hearted participation in the international economy of Norwegian entrepreneurs and labour. The carriage of goods between economies far removed from Norway's own soon attracted Norwegian businessmen, and shipping became Norway's major industry. No country in the world has depended more successfully on the international economy for its own domestic development for where, in more recent times, small populations have become very rich through foreign trade it has been due to the export of one primary product only, as in the cases of Kuwait, Bahrein, or Nauru.

Such was Norway's singularity, a singularity it preserved in an increasingly hostile economic environment until the German invasion in April 1940 incorporated the country into an economic system which was intended to exist as far as possible on a self-sufficient basis and which was designed by the sworn enemies of all those principles of economic liberalism which had been so widely accepted in Norway. Not universally accepted, however; there had always been a strain of opposition to the activities of foreign capitalists in Norway. Nevertheless, few countries have manifested so weak an intellectual opposition to capitalist economic development. For Norway the German invasion was therefore much more than an occupation by a foreign army, it was a subjection to a political, economic, and intellectual system which was the absolute opposite of that under which the country had flourished.

The political events which accompanied the German invasion of Norway were so strange and complicated that they have already been the theme of historians, official and unofficial.[1] What remains to discover about them is only the detail which, as is proper to the activities of conspirators and revolutionaries, remains in some instances obscure. The broad lines of political activity in Norway during the occupation have also been explored and nothing is likely to be changed by future historians apart from the inevitable process of reinterpretation to suit the changing interests of other generations.[2] None the less, the precise political and economic intentions of the German occupiers have not been thoroughly explored. It may still be asked, 'Why study German economic policy in so small an economy and so unimportant a country?' There are two reasons why such a study is of particular value.

In the first place Norway was the one occupied territory to be ruled almost throughout the occupation by a government that has usually been regarded by historians as indubitably fascist. This distinction may be slightly artificial, partly because the definition of fascist has recently been the object of a lot of well-justified argument, some of the protagonists, for instance, maintaining that the Hungarian government was fascist in nature throughout the occupation of that country. The greater element of artificiality lies in the fact that the occupying power was the ultimately effective ruler whatever the nature of the domestic government. Nevertheless, the author's earlier study of German economic policy in occupied France has shown that the lack of agreement between the occupying power and the French government did in fact seriously affect what Germany could do, even though the Vichy governments were very weak.[3] In the case of a country like Norway where the occupying power could rule through a government of its own political persuasion, there did exist, at least in

[1] M. Skodvin, *Striden om okkupasjonstyret i Norge fram til 25 September 1940* (Oslo, 1956); H. Boehm, *Norwegen zwischen England und Deutschland* (Lüneburg, 1956); C.-A. Gemzell, *Raeder, Hitler und Skandinavien. Der Kampf für einen maritimen Operationsplan* (Lund, 1965); J. Andenaes, O. Riste, and M. Skodvin, *Norway and the Second World War* (Oslo, 1966) is a useful summary in English.

[2] T. C. Wyller, *Fra okkupasjonárenes maktkamp* (Oslo, 1953); *Nyordning og motstand, en framstilling og en analyse av organisasjones politiske funksjon under den tyske okkupasjonen* (Oslo, 1958); S. Kjeldstadli, *Hjemmestyrkene* (Oslo, 1958).

[3] A. S. Milward, *The New Order and the French Economy* (Oxford, 1970).

theory, the chance of a more outright assertion and implementation of fascist economic principles.

This was the more likely because it becomes clear from any study of German policy in Norway that that country was to be much more completely integrated into the New Order than was France. The precise final intentions of the German occupiers in France remain curiously obscure in many respects. France was to be incorporated into the New Order in a wholly subordinate position. But how much territory would have been actually annexed? And what sort of political and economic sanctions would Germany have retained? It seems clear that opinion in the German government on these questions changed several times during the course of the war.

As far as Norway was concerned this was not the case. Although the main reason for the invasion and occupation of that country, at the time, was a strategic one, the origins of National Socialist interest in it were in the first place racial and in the second place economic. Norway was regarded as a Germanic country and therefore a better proposition for total integration into the New Order than France. The social structure of the country, embodying, as it did, a large sector of relatively poorly rewarded peasants and fishermen, seemed to offer great opportunities to a fascist party bent on mounting a political campaign against the liberal businessmen and socialist trade unions who had hitherto disputed the political control of the country. Furthermore, the relative lack of complexity of the economy seemed to make it more susceptible of incorporation within the framework of economic reconstruction which Germany hoped to erect in Europe than a complex economy, both liberal and imperialist in nature, such as that of France.

The nature and scope of German economic plans for Europe, the New Order, have not been as yet satisfactorily defined. Indeed their definition can but wait upon more studies of occupation policy. Only by such studies can the present theoretical assessments, which are based on every side on a large measure of political prejudice, be replaced by a juster and more exact appreciation of the New Order. Nevertheless, because it is necessary to explain what is to come, it may be permissible to summarize very briefly the general aims of German economic policy in Europe in the Second World War.

The New Order was an attempt to create within the confines of Europe a *Großraumwirtschaft*, an economy sufficiently autarkic to enable Europe to exist without dependence on other areas either for raw materials or markets. The core of this *Großraumwirtschaft* would be the German manufacturing area in the centre of Europe, including Alsace, Lorraine, Bohemia, Moravia, the Austrian territories, and the whole of Silesia. The peripheral areas would be suppliers of foodstuffs and raw materials and purchasers of manufactures. Within this general conception there were inevitably many exceptions, but making allowance for the special position of Italy and for the fact that the intentions of the occupiers in European Russia were to concentrate on its agricultural potential, the conception was not un-realizable. It was a policy which could restore the status of a great power to Germany and at the same time satisfy the ideological aspirations of its rulers. In fact on all the details of this economic policy there was much argument in Germany. In particular the ruling groups in Germany were divided as to the degree of economic dynamism which such a policy implied. It was supported by many business groups because of its advantages to German manufacturing industry for which it was in some ways but a continuation of their historic struggle for resources and markets. For many revolutionary fascists, however, it was an economic policy whose final aim was not dynamism but social stability.[1] These disputes took place over the occupation of Norway no less than over that of other countries. In spite of these profound differences in German intentions the essential aim of German economic policy remained to make the Norwegian economy both a fascist economy and a part of the peripheral ring of fascist Europe.

Although Norway was still in many respects an underdeveloped economy in 1939, and thus apparently not too unfitted for its allotted place in the New Order, it will be seen that in fact it was to prove extremely difficult to assimilate. The main reasons for this were economic. But any examination of the economic failures of German policy in Norway must also take into consideration the failure to integrate the country politically with the New Order. Norway was distinguished from all other western occupied terri-tories by the extent to which its wartime government shared the ideological assumptions of its conquerors. Whether initiated by Nasjonal Samling or by the German occupiers the economic policies pursued during the occupation were fascist in conception and application. In spite of this, scarcely any support for fascism ever developed in Norway and political opinion remained resolutely opposed to German economic policy.

To explain this paradox it is necessary to narrate briefly the circum-stances surrounding the rise to power of Nasjonal Samling and its leader, Quisling. For in part it was these circumstances that meant that from the moment of the invasion Nasjonal Samling was the helpless prisoner of the National Socialist Party and its representatives in Norway. That fascist parties disagreed on policy should cause no surprise. The road to fascism always proceeded by way of most intense nationalism. Where fascist parties came to power they occasionally thwarted the wishes of the German occupiers in the course of defending their own national interests. In Norway even this was scarcely true. Although there were disputes on economic

---

[1] A. S. Milward, 'French Labour and the German Economy, 1942–1945: An Essay on the Nature of the Fascist New Order', in *Economic History Review*, 2nd series, xxiii (1970).

policy between the Norwegian and German fascist parties, some of them bitter, in every case the German will prevailed. The reason for this lay in the abject terms on which Norwegian fascism was allowed into power.

This was partly due to the intrigues which Quisling pursued before, during, and after the invasion. Their result was to deliver him and his party into the hands of the National Socialist Party while destroying any small degree of independence of action Nasjonal Samling may have originally had. But the starting-point of these intrigues was the extreme weakness of Nasjonal Samling within Norway. In the general election of 1936 the party obtained only 1·8 per cent of the total vote. From that point onwards its electoral fortunes declined. It could therefore never face the Germans as representative of any sizeable body of Norwegian political opinion. Two things accounted for Nasjonal Samling's position, therefore, the series of political mistakes made by Quisling in the hope of becoming a national leader and, once he had become leader, the fact that his party proved so little representative, so ill-organized, and so ridden by petty intrigue that the German administration could not be induced to take its views very seriously. Fundamentally it was dependent on the strength of the German armed forces and the administrative expertise of the National Socialist Party to keep power.

It is of course absurd to suppose that Nasjonal Samling was a parliamentary party in the sense that other Norwegian political parties were. Its final ambitions were not parliamentary, it believed neither in democracy nor in compromise. It was a fascist revolutionary party and as such part of a pan-European movement. With reason its leaders believed that its European significance was greater than its Norwegian significance. They loathed Norwegian politicians for playing what they considered a parochial game in a remote corner of the map while they themselves were at grips with the more vital questions of European society. But it should be firmly noted that their speculations in this wider game were in no sense supported by those whose interests they claimed to represent. Beyond question Nasjonal Samling was the least supported of all fascist parties to come to power. And it was its contempt for the more normal roots of political strength that delivered it through conspiracy into the hands of the vastly more powerful German party.

The National Socialist Party paid little attention to Nasjonal Samling after its foundation in 1933. This is the clearest indication of how unimportant it actually was, for in its symbolism, in its choice of initials, and in the date of its foundation Nasjonal Samling proclaimed its inspiration from the German rather than the Italian pattern of fascism. Quisling himself could perfectly fairly claim to be one of the founding fathers of fascism, but it was the seizure of power by the National Socialist Party in Germany in 1933 which seemed to clothe the bare bones of his dream with the flesh of reality. The indifference to Nasjonal Samling in German party ranks is the more noteworthy because of the unsullied 'Germandom' of the Norwegian people.

It was this racial affinity between the two peoples which interested important circles of the National Socialist Party in Norway, if not in Nasjonal Samling. In 1921 German businessmen in Lübeck had founded an organization, Nordische Gesellschaft, with the purpose of reopening extensive cultural relations with Scandinavia. That organization had more than a hint of geopolitics about it.[1] Its magazine, *Ostsee-Rundschau*, founded in 1929, belongs to those early conceptions of European *Großraum-politik* which were to be transmitted through the writings of geopoliticians into fascist ideology. This organization, like many similar in Germany, needed only an administrative reorganization and a touch of ideological stiffening to enable it to play its part in the structure of the fascist state. The task of so incorporating it, of bringing it into the process of *Gleichschaltung*, fell to that section of the National Socialist Party organization which was most interested in Scandinavian affairs on ideological grounds, the Außenpolitisches Amt (Foreign Policy Office) of Alfred Rosenberg.

Rosenberg's interpretation of European history was so entirely racial that it was inevitable that he should think of the Scandinavian people as 'natural' allies of Germany against the Slav menace. The Baltic peoples, he believed, were bound together in an inescapably common destiny of the blood.[2] Such sentiments were echoed more or less exactly in Quisling's own interpretation of history. As a first-hand witness of the Russian revolution and later in his capacity as a relief organizer in many parts of the Soviet Union, Quisling had developed an almost completely racial explanation of communism and, like Rosenberg, he believed that the future salvation of Europe would only really be assured by a large measure of racial change.

The 'Nordic principle' which Quisling believed existed in the composition of Europe as a whole, thanks to the wanderings and colonizing efforts of the Vikings, was also, he believed, present in Russia which had been colonized by Viking traders. Communism represented the triumph, perhaps only temporary, of an inferior racial strain over this 'Nordic principle',

---

[1] There is an article by its *Geschäftsführer*, who survived the *Machtübernahme*, Dr. Ernst Timm, 'Wirtschaft und Verkehr in nordeuropäischen Raum', p. 565, in H. F. Blunck (ed.), *Die nordische Welt, Geschichte, Wesen und Bedeutung der nordischen Völker* (Berlin, 1937).

[2] A. Rosenberg, *Der Mythus des zwanzigsten Jahrhunderts. Eine Wertung der seelisch-geistigen Gestaltenkämpfe unserer Zeit*, 105–6 edition (Munich, 1937), p. 115. This is, of course, Rosenberg's best-known work, but the same theme recurs elsewhere. See his *Tradition und Gegenwart, Reden und Aufsätze, 1936–1940* (Munich, 1943), pp. 330, 422. This was edited by his private secretary, Thilo von Trotha, who also had a particular interest in 'Nordic culture'. See also, Nordische Gesellschaft, *Nordisches Schicksal Europas* (Lübeck, 1939), which contains an essay of the same title by Rosenberg.

an 'Eastern-Asiatic' revolt against civilization as a whole. 'But men's ideas, religion, language, learning, art, and institutions are all forms under which the spirit of race expresses itself.' Race—the inherited physical and mental constitution of a people—is also to a certain extent the vehicle of a particular philosophy of life. A typical illustration of this may be seen in the spread of Protestantism, which practically coincides with the distribution of the Nordic race.

There is little doubt that Socialism—apart from its adherents among the Jewish intelligentsia—is mainly prevalent in the short-skulled Alpine race, which includes the bulk of the lower classes in Central Europe and the majority of the original Slav inhabitants of Eastern Europe. In the case of Bolshevism, we find that this revolutionary development of Socialism exists as a mass-movement precisely in those parts of Russia where there is most Asiatic blood in the Slav population. Bolshevism might be described as an Asiatic-Slav movement led by Jewish minds.[1]

This conception of an economic and political destiny of race, developed quite separately, although out of the same events, as that of Rosenberg. The destiny in either case was the same, a triumph of 'Germandom', in Rosenberg's words, or, in Quisling's words, of 'The Nordic Principle'.[2]

Nevertheless, one often sees really fine types in the Russian villages—men who remind one of the best type of peasant in the Norwegian highlands, and sometimes have quite a Viking air about them. What I myself have seen of the Russian peasants has given me a great liking for them and belief in them. Their influence, and the contribution they may make as a vital source of racial renewal, will decide the future of the Russian people.[3]

It might therefore have been thought that the consequence of the taking over of Nordische Gesellschaft by the Außenpolitisches Amt would soon lead to relations between the National Socialist Party and Nasjonal Samling. That there is no evidence that it did so is indicative of the feebleness of the Norwegian party and, also, perhaps, of a certain doubt as to its ideological soundness on other matters, a doubt never entirely to be resolved.

The businessmen of Nordische Gesellschaft were subordinated after 1933 to the chairmanship of Friedrich Hildebrandt, Reichsstatthalter of Mecklenburg.[4] Hildebrandt was an expert on peasant affairs and found the

---

[1] V. A. L. J. Quisling, *Russland og vi*, trans., *Russia and Ourselves* (London, 1931), p. 146.

[2] For a clear exposition of Quisling's philosophical standpoint see H.-D. Loock, *Quisling, Rosenberg und Terboven* (Stuttgart, 1970).

[3] V. A. L. J. Quisling, *Russia and Ourselves*, p. 27.

[4] H. A. Jacobsen, *Nationalsozialistische Außenpolitik, 1933–38* (Frankfurt am Main, 1968), pp. 483 ff.

lack of ideological conviction in his new charge displeasing.[1] He resigned his position in August 1934 and was succeeded by Hinrich Lohse, Gauleiter of Schleswig-Holstein. Lohse only took the job on condition of not being bothered with it very much and served mainly as a figurehead. The influences on Nordische Gesellschaft were thus contradictory, on the one hand the older pan-European businessman's view and on the other the more ardently fascist and anti-capitalist view. Its periodicals and publications reflect this uneasy alliance, an alliance which was, of course, at the root of the National Socialist Party's power in Germany. *Ostsee-Rundschau* gave space to the conventional business reports on Scandinavian economies, to the older geopolitical school of writing, and to the more specifically fascist geopolitics of Werner Daitz.[2] Daitz had been Hildebrandt's main rival for control of Nordische Gesellschaft in 1933 but the matter had been decided against him. He continued to write in its publications.[3] He lectured on his theories at the annual assembly of Nordische Gesellschaft in 1935 and in 1937. The same contradictions are apparent in the annual economic reports of the Gesellschaft, only after the outbreak of war do they take on an unmitigatedly fascist character.[4]

Vikings played as large a part in Daitz's thought as they did in Quisling's or Rosenberg's. The Hanseatic towns, Lübeck in particular, he saw as the living symbol of German Vikingdom. Nordic man, in his 'pure' state, was always a conqueror; the Vikings were the 'purest' expression of Germandom. In his work, too, appears the theme that all Baltic peoples were bound together in an inescapably common destiny. This was also the view of Thilo von Trotha whose influence on the affairs of Außenpolitisches Amt was considerable in its early stages. The day would come, von Trotha believed, when even Britain would be forced to abandon her liberal conceptions of international trade in favour of a *Großraumwirtschaft*. The countries most to suffer would be Denmark and Norway whose exports were so specifically aimed at the British market. Economic

---

[1] See his pamphlet: F. Hildebrandt, *Nationalsozialismus und Landarbeiterschaft*, Nationalsozialistische Bibliothek, vol. 17 (Munich, 1930), particularly his denunciation of business trusts, p. 13.

[2] Daitz formulated the conception of a *Großeuropa* based on racial affinity, on blood rather than on economic geography, introducing a further development into the original German conception of that idea. W. Daitz, *Der Weg zur völkischen Wirtschaft und zur europäischen Großraumwirtschaft* (Dresden, 1938), reissued as *Der Weg zur Volkswirtschaft, Großraumwirtschaft und Großraumpolitik* (Dresden, 1943).

[3] Daitz, 'Deutsche Ostraumpolitik' in *Ostsee-Rundschau* (1933); 'Der nordische Charakter des Dritten Reiches' in *Lübeckische Blätter*, xi (1935).

[4] They had been published since 1926 by the Press Bureau under Walter Zimmerman: Reichskontor der Nordischen Gesellschaft, *Die Wirtschaft der nördlichen Länder* (Lübeck, 1938) is still mainly conventional capitalist reporting of certain economic indicators; idem, *Nordeuropa und das Reich kriegswirtschaftlich gesehen* (Lübeck, 1940) is a curious transitional mixture; idem, *Deutschland und der Norden. Gemeinsame Wege zur Kontinentalwirtschaft* (Lübeck, 1941) has jettisoned the businessman's idiom completely in favour of fascist theories of economic reconstruction.

developments would finally bring about what should happen through racial affinity.[1]

If Außenpolitisches Amt hoped through the medium of Nordische Gesellschaft to bring about Norway's allegiance to the New Economic Order by the development there of a political party favourable to German intentions, their efforts were a total failure in the 1930s. It is interesting that Norway, a country which seemed in many ways to have a history and a social structure which might lead to the development of a minority fascist party of some size, remained resolutely 'liberal' in the 1930s. The poorest sections of Norwegian society, the peasants and agricultural workers, had formed their own political party after the First World War and carried on a lively opposition both to the liberal ascendancy and to the powerful and wealthy labour unions which remained allied for a long time to the communist International. Quisling had tried to create a fascist party from this peasant party and had served in its first government as Minister of Defence. The experiment had been a total failure. This failure can scarcely be attributed to the supposedly individualistic, and therefore, presumably, liberal traits with which most writers claim Norwegians to have been imbued from birth by the nature of their country. Rather it should be attributed to the failure of the Norwegian peasant party to take as strong an anti-capitalist position as its fellows in Italy, Germany, and the Balkans and to the absence of any support for this particular aspect of anti-capitalism from the socialist groups. Norwegian socialism and communism were based very firmly on an industrial proletariat and a strict allegiance to Marx; they lacked that anarchist and populist support which might have detached itself and gone over to a fascist party as it did in Italy and Spain. The Norwegian Labour Party was every inch a product of Norway's industrial revolution. A highly organized body with a firm political ambition, it relied on a relatively prosperous and powerful group in Norwegian society, the industrial workers, and was more homogeneous in its political structure than weaker socialist parties elsewhere.

Peasant politics in Norway tended to seek the support of the older conservative parties throughout the inter-war period, for those traditional conservative forces seemed to have a position of greater strength than the small and heterogeneous band of militant counter-revolutionaries whose conviction that anti-communism demanded a revolutionary overthrow of the parliamentary system was looked at askance by most right-wing circles. It should be remembered that the origins of Norway's national independence in modern times lay in a constitutional assembly. That link between parliamentarism and nationalism had never been broken. The struggle for national independence from Sweden in 1906, had harked back to the Constitutional Assembly at Eidsvold in 1814 which had first

[1] H. A. Jacobsen, op. cit., p. 488.

declared the Kingdom of Norway 'free, independent, indivisible and inalienable'. King Haakon, whom the moderate constitutionalists had sought to make the symbol of Norway's independence in 1906, still reigned in 1940. For all the apparent advantages of Norway's social structure to a potential fascist party, such a party could only with enormous difficulty overcome the fact that Norway's democratic constitution retained nationalist emotion firmly behind it, however international the scope of the country's economy. The monarchy's symbolical position was greatly reinforced by the attacks on the constitution; the result of the German invasion was to make it stronger than ever.

Rosenberg's efforts were not concentrated uniquely on Nasjonal Samling in spite of the close similarity in the evolution of his own ideas and those of Quisling. Initially the National Socialist Party showed just as great an interest in the more conservative elements which supported Nasjonal Samling rather than owed it automatic allegiance. The political writer, Hermann Harris Aall, who was later to become a member of Nasjonal Samling and to be elevated to the dignified rank of professor by Quisling, typifies the links between extreme Norwegian and German antiliberalism which already existed while the young Quisling was developing his own more revolutionary ideas in his various official and unofficial posts in Soviet Russia in the 1920s. Aall had taken a strong stand against the international aspects of Norway's existence before the First World War and during that war had sprung into prominence as a critic of the allied infringement of Norwegian neutrality and Norway's apparent subservience in the face of this infringement. His popularity as a writer in Germany therefore dated from 1918, his political stance was anti-British and as rabidly anti-communist as Quisling's. The anti-British aspect of his writing took the form of a rather vague attack on materialism and liberal capitalism. These elements, but much more the conception of a racial tie between Norway and Germany, led to a revival of interest in his work in Germany after 1933.[1] Nevertheless, Aall was more a follower of the geopolitical school than a fascist; witness his great admiration for the Swedish geopolitical scholar Kjellen. His writing in the inter-war period was mainly confined to problems of neutrality and only after the occupation of Norway did he appear with a defence of Nasjonal Samling.[2] It was he who was to

[1] H. H. Aall, *Das Schicksal des Nordens. Eine europäische Frage* (Weimar, 1918), p. 348. 'It is a political error if a people does not seize its own individuality. No overriding economic speculation nor whipped-up public opinion can expunge the fact that the Norwegian people in the most important aspects of life—through descent, cultural and geographical, belongs to the German race.'

[2] See his works: *The Neutral Investigation of the Causes of Wars. An Essay Concerning the Politics of War of the Great Powers and the Policy of Small Nations* (Oslo, 1923), is an attack on the Treaty of Versailles; *Verdensdespotiet og havets frihet*, trans. *Weltherrschaft und die Rechtlosigkeit der Meere* (Essen, 1940) is an attack on the Comintern and the League of Nations and a long essay on the international law of neutrality; *Er Norge et fritt*

represent for Admiral Canaris one of the future hopes for an anti-communist Europe not dominated by the National Socialist Party. Alfred Mjøen, the Norwegian eugenicist, also spoke several times in Germany under the auspices of Nordische Gesellschaft. Like Aall's, his popularity in Germany also dated from the First World War when he had defended German occupation policy in Poland mainly on the grounds that the Poles were an inferior race and the German race was Europe's bulwark against such contamination.[1]

Nasjonal Samling was reduced to begging for recognition from the National Socialist Party and to trying to divert some of their funds into its own chest to support a newspaper. The foundations of its ultimate political subjection had already been laid. Quisling may have met Rosenberg in 1934, but the meeting did not benefit Nasjonal Samling.[2] Quisling's attempts to attract the favourable attention of the German government

---

land? (Oslo, 1940) is a discussion of Norway's legal status under occupation; *Norges politiske nyreisning* (Oslo, 1941) is an attempt to set Nasjonal Samling within a historical framework of the European rejection of liberalism; *Nasjonalt livssyn og verdenspolitik* (Oslo, 1942) is an attempt to set this rejection of liberalism in Norway in a framework formed by the events of the First World War, thus completing the cycle of his thought and establishing a satisfactory harmony of evolution between the development of his own thought and that of his country to the same point—'To supplant liberalism and Bolshevism in Norway by a National Socialist new order of nordic spirit; a league between the Germanic people and agreement in Europe; German-European Co-operation in tidying up and reconstructing the Russian area', *Nasjonalt livssyn og verdenspolitik*, p. 360.

[1] A. Mjøen, *Germanen oder Slaven? Die Mongolisierung Europas. Eindrücke eines Neutralen von einer Reise an die Ostfront und zu Hindenburg* (Berlin, 1917). See particularly p. 75. Mjøen, however, was no National Socialist. Not *all* racial mixtures were bad, he believed (although most were degenerate). The mixture of German and Jew was a good one, it made the Jew get up earlier in the morning (p. 65). Mjøen was responsible for the 'Eugenic Programme of the Norwegian Committee for Race Hygiene', presented at various eugenics congresses and particularly discussed at Paris in 1913. His institute in Oslo, Vinderen Biologiske Laboratorium, published a eugenics journal with the title *Den nordiske race*, and he himself published articles on racial crossing in several European countries. See 'Delinquenza e genio alla luce della biologia' in *Atti del Primo Congresso Italiano di Eugenetica Sociale* (Milan 1924); 'Die Bedeutung der Kollateralen für den Begabungsgrad der Kinder' in *Verhandlungen des V. internationalen Kongreßes für Vererbungswissenschaft* (Berlin, 1927); and 'Rassenkreuzung beim Menschen' in *Volk und Rasse. Illustrierte Vierteljahrschrift für deutsches Volkstum*, ii (1929).

[2] For all the staid nature of his outward appearance Quisling lived the life of an international revolutionary conspirator and it is therefore quite likely that the true facts of that life will prove to be more complicated than they at present seem, repeated often enough from the same limited number of sources. A remarkable number of question marks still hover around the established version of his career. One reason for the number of uneasy suspicions which are attached to this version is the persistence with which he has been denigrated in most post-war writing, a pointless attitude towards one who was, in any case, of very limited ability. Books by his admirers have only deepened the confusion about the facts of his life. See, in that respect, R. Hewins, *Quisling, Prophet Without Honour* (London, 1965) and H. F. Knudsen, *Jeg var Quislings sekretaer* (Copenhagen, 1951), trans. *I Was Quisling's Secretary* (London, 1967). The 'official' account of his life in *Norsk biografisk leksikon* is very hostile and not very enlightening. The best account by far is H.-D. Loock, *Quisling, Rosenberg und Terboven*.

bore no fruit until 1939. Even in that year his success was preceded by a most fulsome letter begging for introductions which might well have had less effect than it did had not the approaching war focused attention more sharply on the question of Norway's strategic position.

The chief intermediary between Quisling and Rosenberg was a Norwegian businessman, a member of Nasjonal Samling, living in Dresden, Albert Viljam Hagelin, later to be one of Quisling's cabinet ministers. He had a distant connection with Göring and had had some contacts with the Rosenberg group. Through him Quisling met Rosenberg on a visit to Berlin in June 1939, and at last was able to establish Nasjonal Samling as the main channel for National Socialist funds and political activity in Norway. In December 1939 Quisling was again in Germany. By this time the existence of naval plans for an attack on Norway, both on the British and on the German side, made him, whatever his political position in his own country, a much more important figure in Germany. He met Rosenberg again and, as a result of what passed, he and Hagelin were taken to meet Grand-Admiral Raeder, Commander-in-Chief of the Navy.[1]

A plan to invade Norway had been pressed hard by the naval general staff from the opening of the war because they were afraid that a British occupation of that country would confine them to a hopelessly defensive strategy akin to that forced on them in the First World War. Their interest thus coincided with Rosenberg's views on the nature of the coming struggle and both navy and Außenpolitisches Amt saw a valuable tool in Quisling. Quisling apparently told both Raeder and Rosenberg that in the event of a British invasion, which did not seem likely, Nasjonal Samling would be able to turn over certain key installations to German forces who might wish to make a preventive landing. Alternatively Nasjonal Samling could seize power and invite the Germans to defend the country. Were they practical proposals they would greatly strengthen Raeder's case for an action against Norway. Raeder's summing-up of the meeting was that if Hitler received 'a favourable impression' the High Command should co-operate with Quisling in preparing plans for invasion and occupation either with the consent of a Norwegian government or without.[2]

Hitler then received Quisling and Hagelin, apparently on 18 December. Quisling handed Hitler a memorandum on the need for unity among Germanic peoples. Hitler, apart from a cautious opening monologue on the strategic situation, was more or less silent. The result of the meeting was that the High Command was instructed to prepare contingency plans.[3]

[1] A. Rosenberg, *Das politische Tagebuch Alfred Rosenbergs aus den Jahren 1934/35, und 1939/40*, ed. H.-G. Seraphim (Göttingen, 1956), Quellensammlung zur Kulturgeschichte, No. 8, p. 91.
[2] Ibid., p. 94.   [3] C.-A. Gemzell, *Raeder, Hitler und Skandinavien*, p. 273.

On 19 December there was a further meeting when Quisling was assured that in the event of a British attack help would be forthcoming. Whatever effect these meetings had on subsequent military events, and that may well not have been very great, for Nasjonal Samling they were crucial. Quisling had taken the first and irrevocable steps to subjecting his party to German tutelage. If Nasjonal Samling were to seize power and reorganize the country theirs would be a *Machtübernahme* actively supported and even organized from outside the country. In that respect they might have claimed only to be following the example of the Austrian National Socialist Party, but in Austria the fascist movement, for all the great help it received both from Germany and from Italy, also drew on a deep well of popular support in the country itself.

Selected members of Nasjonal Samling would be sent to Germany where they would be trained to take part in a *coup d'état*, if the need for one arose, by members of the National Socialist Party. Such a coup would require the support of units of the German armed forces. Without such support it could never be successful, a fact recognized by both parties to the plan.[1] Hans Scheidt, Amtsleiter in the Außenpolitisches Amt, accompanied Quisling back to Oslo to help in the necessary organization.[2] The German Foreign Office, it appears, had no knowledge of what was afoot. It was a purely party matter. For his own party the political consequences of Quisling's actions were inescapable.

Hitler had shown a certain scepticism about the ability of Nasjonal Samling to organize such a coup. Reports on the strength and finances of the party suggested that its earlier neglect by the German party had not been entirely unjustified. It had, for Rosenberg, the great advantage of fitting in with his own ideological conceptions. It needed but a little ideological stuffing and a lot of organizational stiffening to become as effective a disciple of the National Socialist Party as the Sudeten German People's Party had become two years previously. The German armed forces were clearly not impressed by these plans. Their own planning seems to have concentrated almost entirely on the study of a more conventional invasion which would assume the opposition of the Norwegian government.[3] These more realistic plans which excluded the idea of a *coup d'état* came to dominate German policy except in the circle of Außenpolitisches Amt.

By the end of January 1940 the plans had taken definitive shape as operation *Weserübung*. On 21 February mounting fear of Allied intervention

---

[1] A. Rosenberg, *Das politische Tagebuch*, p. 195.

[2] See his later report on the situation in Norway: N.D., PS-947.

[3] The planning of the invasion is discussed in W. Hubatsch, *Die deutsche Besetzung von Dänemark und Norwegen, 1940*, Göttinger Beiträge für Gegenwartsfragen, 5 (Göttingen, 1952); C.-A. Gemzell, *Raeder, Hitler und Skandinavien*; and T. K. Derry, *The Campaign in Norway*, Official History of the Second World War, Military Series (London, 1952).

in the Russo-Finnish War caused the plans to be speeded up and General Niklaus von Falkenhorst, who was to serve throughout the war as Commander-in-Chief in Norway, was put in charge of the operation. In fact the Russo-Finnish armistice agreement, signed on 12 March, deprived both Britain and Germany of any public excuse for armed intervention in Scandinavia. For Britain the event was decisive since her invasion plan was contingent on a welcome from the Norwegian government. In Germany, however, after some hesitation, it was decided to let *Weserübung* go ahead. The plan was ready and Norway had assumed a vital strategic importance, for one reason because of the iron-ore traffic down the Norwegian coast.[1] It was a small country, entirely Germanic, with a certain number of valuable resources. The decision was therefore taken to incorporate it forcibly into the New European Order. On 2 April the die was cast. Norway would be invaded in the night of 8–9 April.[2]

When the invasion took place Außenpolitisches Amt decided to stage the *coup d'état* for which they had originally hoped. Scheidt and Hagelin arrived in Oslo to persuade Quisling to implement the original plan before any alternative arrangements for the government of the country should be made by the military or the foreign ministry. Quisling presumably decided that the moment had arrived for him when the tide in his affairs, 'taken at the flood, leads on to fortune'. With help from Scheidt he took possession of the broadcasting studio in Oslo and announced the formation of a Nasjonal Samling government. These events took the German ambassador even more by surprise than the Norwegian government, which had fled the city. Their result was to ruin whatever chance might have existed for an understanding between the German and Norwegian governments and to strengthen the Norwegian will to resist. They threatened to turn a brilliantly conceived amphibious surprise attack into a military campaign which might cause the postponement of the planned invasion of France.[3]

In Norway, as everywhere, there were much narrower limits to the

---

[1] The British plan to invade Norway had been based on the mistaken idea that interrupting this traffic would cripple the German economy, see Sir Winston Churchill, *The Second World War*, vol. i, p. 420. The question is analysed in R. Karlbom, 'Sweden's Iron-Ore Exports to Germany, 1933–44', *Scandinavian Economic History Review*, xiii. 1 (1965); J.-J. Jäger, 'Sweden's Iron Ore Exports to Germany 1933–1944', ibid. xv. 1 and 2 (1967); A. S. Milward, 'Could Sweden have Stopped the Second World War?', ibid.

[2] The day after the final decision was made, one of the most unsatisfactorily explained of all Quisling's activities occurred. He travelled to Copenhagen for secret conversations with a German intelligence officer, Colonel Hans Piekenbrock. Piekenbrock was apparently instructed to discover certain details of Norway's naval defences. It has never been seriously suggested that these details were of especial military value. It is difficult to believe, however, that a man like Quisling, who had had a successful career as an Army officer, did not understand the import of this meeting.

[3] There is a large and repetitious literature about the smallest details of the military events. The most useful items are O. Lindbäck-Larsen, *Krigen i Norge, 1940* (Oslo, 1965); W. Hubatsch, op. cit.; T. K. Derry, op. cit.; J. Mordal, *la campagne de Norvège* (Paris, 1949); and B. Ash, *Norway, 1940* (London, 1964).

degree to which Hitler was prepared to sacrifice ideological consistency to expediency than historians have generally supposed. He remained in this case loyal to his political convictions and instructed Ambassador Bräuer that whatever settlement was reached with the Norwegian government it must recognize the new importance of Quisling and Nasjonal Samling. Theodor Habicht, who had been the chief link between the Austrian and German National Socialist parties, was sent to Oslo to help the Foreign Service arrive at a suitable arrangement. Unfortunately for German policy Nasjonal Samling fulfilled the prophecies of the most sceptical of the National Socialists. Two of those whom Quisling named to his cabinet refused publicly to serve, including the anti-communist agitator, Major Hvoslef. Norwegian government and society more or less ignored the existence of a government based on so tiny a minority of the population. Except where the Nygardsvold cabinet, in its frantic search for a safe resting place, exerted temporary authority, the executive power was actually wielded by the German armed forces from the moment of invasion.[1]

This absurd failure of Nasjonal Samling ended its last chance of ever achieving any independence from the National Socialist Party. Bräuer, with the encouragement of his government, negotiated an agreement with more prominent and more respectable conservative and judicial circles in Oslo to form an Administrative Council (Administrajonsrådet). The council came into being on 15 April and Quisling was removed to the sidelines. He was, on Hitler's instructions, to be 'given an honourable position' and 'held in reserve'. Bräuer led Hitler to believe that Administrajonsrådet would actually be a recognized government which could replace Rosenberg's abortive experiment with Nasjonal Samling and have the further advantage of not raising the awkward issue of ultimate sovereignty. In the event King Haakon VII refused to recognize Administrajonsrådet as being anything but what its name suggested, an administrative committee. Quisling had been rejected by Germany in favour of an expedient which was no more satisfactory.

The outcome was that Hitler took the last logical step open to him. Nasjonal Samling had failed. The more orthodox methods of diplomacy had failed. Norway would now be handed over to the National Socialist Party itself under whose guidance and control Nasjonal Samling would be educated and organized into a fascist party truly fit to lead the Norwegian *Volk*. That the experiment with Administrajonsrådet had never been anything but a short-term expedient and that Hitler's intention from the

---

[1] For the trials and tribulations of the Nygardsvold government see C. J. Hambro, *I Saw It Happen in Norway* (London, 1940); D. Lehmkuhl, *Journey to London* (London, 1945); H. Koht, *Norway, Neutral and Divided* (New York, 1941); idem, *For fred og fridom i krigstid* (Oslo, 1957); T. Lie, *Med England i ildlinjen* (Oslo, 1956).

outset was to create a fascist Scandinavia is confirmed by Hitler himself during a discussion on the Scandinavian question in Führer Headquarters in March 1942. After dinner Hitler expressed himself as follows:

He was glad that the Dutch Queen Wilhelmina had fled and did not constitute, by her presence, like the Belgian King Leopold, a factor that one must take account of. It could consequently be all fairly much the same to us what the Japanese planned for the Dutch colonial Empire. And in particular Queen Wilhelmina did not disturb the concentration of the German world as did the Danish and Swedish kings who carried on in such a way that they became primeval and got in the way of everything. As far as Denmark was concerned, either in the short-run or the long-run a solution had to be sought in the personality of Claussen [the Danish fascist leader], all the more so since the support of Mussert in Holland and Quisling in Norway had shown itself as correct.[1]

Bräuer was dismissed in disgrace; Habicht also was recalled. On 14 April Hitler named the Gauleiter of Essen, Josef Terboven, as Reichskommissar für die besetzten norwegischen Gebiete (for Occupied Norwegian Territory). Ten days later Terboven took up office bringing with him the nucleus of the Reichskommissariat which was to rule Norway and educate Nasjonal Samling for five years.

There can be no doubt that Skodvin is quite justified in seeing the most sinister implications for Norway's future both in the choice of the word 'Reichskommissariat' and in the appointment of Terboven as its head.[2] Bohemia and Moravia had been placed under a Reichs Protector and the decree appointing him had served in some ways as a model for that making Terboven Reichskommissar.[3] Terboven was virtually in the same position as a minister of the Reich, he stood directly under the Führer from whom alone he received orders. The arrangement was the more drastic in as much as *Weserübung* had been a project organized and controlled throughout by the Wehrmacht. General von Falkenhorst retained full powers in the military sphere but the administration of the country, with that one reservation, was transferred entirely to an administrative machine recruited from within the National Socialist Party.

The search for a political solution in France after the defeat and occupation of that country always stopped short of this final conception. It is still not clear, and was probably not clear at the time, even to Hitler, what French territories Germany would have annexed in any peace treaty. There were serious objections, political, economic, and racial to France's incorporation in the New Order in any form except as an independent, although wholly subordinate, state. None of these objections

---

[1] H. Picker, *Hitlers Tischgespräche in Führerhauptquartier, 1941–42*, ed. G. R. Ritter (Bonn, 1951), pp. 57–8.
[2] M. Skodvin, *Striden om okkupasjonsstyret i Norge*, pp. 196 ff.
[3] It is printed in full in M. Skodvin, op. cit., pp. 200–1.

carried weight in the case of Norway. Rosenberg's idea of a common destiny of the blood was to be at last fulfilled, if not quite in the way he had foreseen. France's place in the New Order was never determined.[1] Norway's was determined at the moment of Terboven's appointment. Nor was her entry into the New Order to be a gradual absorption. She was to be provided from the start with a German fascist government to compensate for the inadequacy of her own fascist party.

The subsequent history of Nasjonal Samling's struggles to shake off the yoke of the National Socialist Party is interesting but less relevant. Economic policy, like all other aspects of policy, was decided in the Reichskommissariat. The Norwegian cabinet seldom was able to do more than act as a vehicle for transmitting these decisions to the general machinery of government. There were differences between the two parties on economic affairs, but their policies had a broad degree of similarity which only lessened as Germany's economic position became more desperate. In any case the extreme political weakness of Nasjonal Samling in the country prevented it from ever being able to pose as the champion of national sentiment against German oppression.

This political weakness continued through the occupation period. In spite of a good deal of admonition and practical help in organization from the National Socialist Party, Nasjonal Samling never made any really worthwhile progress in recruitment or in local party organization. There were 26,178 party members in December 1940 and 42,920 in April 1942. After that point the increase of membership was very slight and in 1943 the total membership began to decline. Its upper echelons were little better organized than its lower. It suffered from that malady which seems to affect all very small political parties, squalid intrigue between persons. It never had sufficient funds or sufficient organization to operate on an effective level in the numerous isolated localities where Norwegian political opinion was formed. For all its public cant about attachment to the soil and the locality it became very much an Oslo party and it was in the capital that its recruiting drive was most successful. In Norwegian political life this was a grave weakness. Wyller has shown how political opinion in Norway crystallized during the war around the existing groups and associations in Norwegian life, and through these groups a certain modified liberal view of existence was defended against the fascist attack.[2] The group organizations which fascism hoped would be the starting-place for a national conversion away from the creed of internationalist individualism in fact became a bulwark of anti-fascism.

[1] See the discussion in E. Jäckel, *Frankreich in Hitler's Europa* (Stuttgart, 1967), pp. 46 ff.
[2] T. C. Wyller, *Nyordning og motstand, en framstilling og en analyse av organisasjones politiske funksjon under den tyske okkupasjonen.*

Fascism proved to have no economic appeal to the Norwegian people. Rather its appeal was to a small coterie of intellectuals, administrators, minor businessmen, and policemen. Hagelin, who was an unscrupulous general dealer, was all too typical of its leading personnel. Anti-materialist thought did not prevent substantial personal profits accruing to many others. Frederick Prytz, later Minister of Finance, had been Quisling's business partner in Russia in the 1920s. Part of his fortune had come through black market money deals with Persian businessmen. Alf Whist, the last Nasjonal Samling Minister of Trade, Industry, Handicrafts, and Fishing, had made a fortune in marine insurance; more than anyone he was a representative of that 'international finance capital' which Norwegian, like other fascisms, denounced. Nor could Norwegian fascism gain any popular foothold by the politics of anti-semitism. Jews had not been allowed into Norway until the mid nineteenth century. There were few there and the positions they held made it very difficult to represent them either as the leaders of socialist conspiracy or of international capitalism. Anti-semitism therefore had to remain in Norway a merely intellectual standpoint without much practical application.

There is, indeed, more than a suspicion that Quisling himself had not entirely thrown off the shackles of liberal individualist thought, increasing even further the doubts as to whether Nasjonal Samling was really entitled to participate equally in the same revolution as National Socialism. Hitler's reservations about him partly turned on his 'bourgeois' nature, more prone to compromise than the Führer himself. Like Nansen, Quisling had seen a ray of hope in Russia in the early 1920s with the introduction of the New Economic Policy.[1] Stolypin, he believed, could have saved Russia from the Bolshevik Revolution.[2] His dismissal meant that in the end Communism had helped the 'lazy, weak-kneed' peasant against his more efficient competitor.[3] The 'Nordic principle' which he so much emphasized appears in his work as a highly individualistic principle. It is not entirely surprising that he should have had so many business friends.

It did not take long for Terboven to become thoroughly pessimistic about the value of Quisling and Nasjonal Samling to the fascist movement. He had himself been in the National Socialist Party from its early days. His studies had been interrupted by the First World War in which he served as a gunner. He joined the party after the war while employed as a bank clerk in Essen and rose to political prominence as a leader of the opposition to the French forces during their occupation of the Ruhr. In the party's darkest days after the failure of the Munich *Putsch* and during

[1] It is time that the political career of Nansen was explored in greater detail than it has been. Prytz was, of course, a 'Nepman'.
[2] V. A. L. J. Quisling, *Russland og vi*, p. 81.   [3] Ibid., p. 88.

Hitler's imprisonment, Terboven had been a local organizer in the Ruhr. He had been one of the local leaders of the large Ruhr Gau created by Goebbels in 1925 in an attempt to change party policy from the lines laid down by Hitler and the Munich leaders.[1] He had climbed a long, steep, and arduous path to revolution with the National Socialist Party. Is it surprising that he should have found Nasjonal Samling's idea of a revolution naïve?

He therefore tried to induce Quisling to accept, if only temporarily, some more traditional elements of the Norwegian political scene. Quisling's unwillingness led only to greater humiliation for himself and his party. Terboven planned to replace Administrajonsrådet by a new governing council, the Riksråd, which would be sanctioned by the remaining members of the Storting. Nasjonal Samling's opposition to these vestiges of parliamentarianism meant that only one of their members, Axel Stang (later a conspicuous failure as Minister of Sport), was named to the Riksråd. In June their party funds were seized. Quisling was deposed as party leader by the Reichskommissar who appointed in his stead Jonas Lie, the Minister of Justice, whom he may have met while Lie was serving on the International Police Commission during the Saarland plebiscite. Quisling left for Germany where he remained for a month.[2] Finally, as a result of agitation by his friends he was given an audience by Hitler on 18 August. At this meeting Hitler reasserted his faith in a fascist Norway. 'A new, young Norway would learn to understand this and for him a young Norway was only thinkable under the leadership of Nasjonal Samling and indissolubly tied to Quisling's own person.'[3]

From this moment there was increasing pressure on Terboven to permit more Nasjonal Samling members in the government. This he did by ending the constitutional wrangle on 25 September. Administrajonsrådet disappeared and in its place appeared Nasjonal Samling whose government, to emphasize its subordinate position, was called the 'Council of Commissioner Ministers'. One year later they became full ministers. On 1 February 1942 they became a 'national government' and Quisling joined his ministers in the cabinet chamber as 'Minister-President'. The titles scarcely mattered. Events and the weakness of Nasjonal Samling meant that the country was governed by the decrees of the Reichskommissar. Nor did the legal status of the occupying power in international law change.[4]

---

[1] *Das Tagebuch von Joseph Goebbels, 1925/26*, ed. H. Heiber, Schriftenreihe der Vierteljahrshefte für Zeitgeschichte, 1 (Stuttgart, 1961), trans. *The Early Goebbels Diaries: 1925/26*, ed. H. Heiber (London, 1962); P. Hüttenberger, *Die Gauleiter; Studie zum Wandel des Machtgefüges in der NSDAP*, Schriftenreihe der Vierteljahrshefte für Zeitgeschichte, 19 (Stuttgart, 1969), pp. 35–9.

[2] It has never been discovered what exactly happened to him.   [3] N.D. NG–2948.

[4] W. Herdeg, *Grundzüge der deutschen Besetzungsverwaltung in den west- und nordeuropäischen Ländern während des zweiten Weltkrieges*, Studien des Instituts für Besatzungsfragen in Tübingen zu den deutschen Besetzungen im 2. Weltkrieg, 1 (Tübingen, 1953), pp. 45–6.

The Reichskommissariat was a less complicated structure than the military government of France. It contained five main divisions, of which the second, the Main Department for the Economy (Hauptabteilung Wirtschaft) was the largest.[1] The first head of this division was Karl Eugen Dellenbusch whom Terboven recruited from the Reichs Ministry of the Interior (Reichsministerium des Innern). Dellenbusch returned to Germany in June 1941.[2] This economic department was much more complicated than the other sections. Even at this early stage Germany's economic ambitions in Norway were foreshadowed by these administrative arrangements. The Main Department for the Economy was divided into eight sub-departments. The most important was the first, the Department for the Economy (Abteilung Wirtschaft). It held a general control over the execution of economic policy and was responsible for welding the many decisions reached in various departments in Oslo and Berlin, or by Hitler or Terboven, into a unified policy. Its head was Carlo Otte, a Hamburg senator and economic adviser to the Hamburg Gau. Otte was one of the inner circle of advisers around Karl Kaufmann, Gauleiter of Hamburg. When Kaufmann became Reichskommissar for Shipping (Reichskommissar für die Seeschiffahrt) in May 1942 Otte was appointed in addition his 'Beauftragte' in Norway.

The other departments had a more detailed task in particular sectors of the Norwegian economy. The second department was for social policy, a field in which Norway was thought to lag far behind Germany and where considerable changes were foreseen. There was a separate department for the establishment and supervision of prices (Preisbildung und Preis-überwachung) which also indicated the specific aims of the New Order. Other than these departments there were separate departments for those sectors of the Norwegian economy which were to have a particular importance for German plans, agriculture, fishing, shipping, forestry, and transport. These eight sub-departments represented a more detailed and complex administrative structure for the economy than was devised in any other branch of the administration. No other of the five Main Departments of the Reichskommissariat had more than two sub-departments.

There was one further organization which concerned itself with German economic policy in Norway, the German Chamber of Commerce in Norway (Deutsche Handelskammer in Norwegen). Although similar organizations existed in other European lands and played an important part in implementing German trade policies in the thirties, Norway had

[1] M. Skodvin, op. cit., p. 193.
[2] H. Paulsen, 'Reichskommissariat og "motytelsene" under riksrådsforhandlingene', in Studier i norsk samtids-historie, Norge og den 2 verdenskrig: *1940 — Fra nøytral til okkupert*, p. 342.

been far enough out of the German orbit for there never to have existed such a body there. From an early date the German administration exercised pressure on the Norwegians to allow the founding of a Chamber of Commerce in Norway. It was opened on 19 November 1940 in a ceremony attended by Kehrl and by Koppenberg and at which Secretary of State Landfried made a speech of some importance vaguely outlining German economic plans.[1] At that time there were about 800 members. By July 1943 the membership had grown to 1,600 of whom 1,000 were Norwegians.[2] It meddled scarcely at all in official policy although it followed it and executed it carefully, keeping a careful check, for example, on Jewish businesses in Norway. Its main function was a forum where German and Norwegian businessmen could meet and in which the German viewpoint could be assiduously advanced.

The Reichskommissariat and its satellite represented a more complex economic policy body than that which Nasjonal Samling imposed on the normal working of the civil service. The Council of Commissioner Ministers contained a Minister for Shipping, K. Irgens, a former member of the Norwegian court circle. In addition it had both a Minister of Labour and a Minister of Social Affairs, T. Hustad and Professor B. Meidell. Their functions were quite separate. Meidell's task was to spread the revolutionary gospel and begin the reconversion of Norwegian society. Hustad's job was to deal with the trade unions, that is to say to squash the main source of opposition to the regime. The Ministry of Trade and Industry and the Ministry of Agriculture were not controlled by members of Nasjonal Samling, although T. J. Fretheim, the Minister of Agriculture, did not differ greatly from the party line. Nor was the Ministry of Finance under control of the party.

Before Quisling himself joined the government officially in January 1942 he tried to force Terboven to reduce the size of the Reichskommissariat. But his negotiations were unsuccessful and the ceremony formally installing a Norwegian government in power once more made very little real difference to the balance of political power although it created a lot of new administrative difficulties for the Reichskommissariat whose final powers of decision had to be exercised in a much less direct way. The only Nasjonal Samling minister not to be retained in the new government was Meidell. Fretheim had now joined the party, so the Ministry of Agriculture was also under Nasjonal Samling control. But the biggest change was that the new constitution permitted Nasjonal Samling to take over those economic ministries previously outside their reach. The civil

[1] R. A. Deutsche Handelskammer in Norwegen, E21, (løpe 153), 'Bericht über die Gründung der deutschen Handelskammer in Norwegen', 19 November 1940.
[2] R. A. Deutsche Handelskammer in Norwegen, I80, 'Gesamtüberblick über die Arbeit der Deutschen Handelskammer in Norwegen' (n.d.)

servants who had been in charge of the Ministry of Trade and Industry (which now included handicrafts and fishing) and the Ministry of Finance were subordinated to Nasjonal Samling ministers. Eivind Blehr became Minister of Trade and Industry. He was later replaced by Alf Whist. Quisling's former business colleague and dabbler in Russian affairs, Frederick Prytz, became Minister of Finance.

The political subjection of Nasjonal Samling and its administrative dependence on the Reichskommissariat may seem to make it unnecessary to bother very much about its economic ideas. In a general way this is true. Economic policy in Norway between 1940 and 1945 was almost entirely the creation of the Reichskommissariat. Like all economic policy in occupied areas during that period it was dictated by two primary considerations, the course of the German war economy and the course of the war. Yet one particular interest attaches to the economic policy of Nasjonal Samling and that, once again, is its subservience to the intellectual leadership of the National Socialist Party. In fact Quisling had little interest in economic ideas and the economic policy of himself and his followers, even had they been free to follow it, would still have been a copy of that of the German party. At every turn of its history Nasjonal Samling found itself pilfering the intellectual baggage of other fascist parties. The evolution of its economic policy was no exception to this. The party programme had much to say about economic affairs. It started from the assumption that the institutions of the liberal state were an institutionalization of the class struggle because of their 'horizontal' nature. Society thus existed in a perpetually inharmonious condition in which repression fought against revolution. Only by the reconstruction of society along 'vertical' lines of organization could this be changed. Even the delegates to the main governing assembly should be chosen as occupational delegates representing the various 'vertical' interests of society.[1] In general, economic policy would be determined within a more harmonious political framework. But the methods for achieving this harmony would not be uniquely political, certain specific economic reforms were necessary.

The sixth point of the programme was that public finances would be more rigorously controlled and the tax system simplified into one unified tax whose burden would fall equally on the various geographical areas of the country.[2] This was no more than the common stuff of Norwegian conservatism but later points were specifically fascist even though derivative. 'Everyone has the right and the duty to work,' declared point eight, 'everyone is to perform bodily or spiritually honourable work.' The

[1] See the exposition in T. C. Wyller, *Frå okkupasjonsårenes maktkamp* (Oslo, 1953), pp. 10 ff.
[2] Nasjonal Samling's programme was printed in much of their literature for it had the same symbolism as the German National Socialist Workers' Party's 'unalterable' programme. See, for example, Nasjonal Samling, *Årbok 1942*, pp. 27 ff.

following points indicated how this was to be achieved. All the resources of the country would be developed by a national control of the economy which would leave undisturbed the rights of private property and private enterprise. The laws governing employers and workers, 'work-givers', and 'work-takers' as they were called following the usual fascist terminology, would be changed to give 'a greater sense of personal responsibility' to both. The laws governing financial institutions and companies would be changed in the same sense. Lock-outs and strikes would be illegal.

There were also specific clauses dealing with the financial system. There was to be a 'rational currency system'. The main aspect of its rationality would be its stability. To achieve this the banking system would be centralized and reconstructed. Credit would be made available throughout the economy, not merely to large firms but to small businessmen as well. Unemployment would not be tolerated. Capital would be considered as a national resource, to be deployed as fully as all others. Proper controls would ensure that this process did not reduce the value of savings, old-age pensions, or life insurances.

There was in all this, as in the economic programmes of the fascist governments in Germany and Italy, a heavy emphasis on the 'reality' of certain phenomena. Work was seen as the 'real' basis of the economy together with tangible physical resources. 'National socialism works with the reality of living things.'[1] Unreal things were the international financial arrangements which had proved so unsuccessful in the inter-war period and the financial speculation common to capitalist economies. The intention was to break with the long history of 'materialist' policies, whether of the right or left, and reconstitute Norwegian society in a more stable form.

Quisling provided a simpler gloss on the party programme in 1941.

The main reforms against capitalism and communism are:

1. A better distribution of private property and the attempt to create private property for as many Norwegians as possible.

2. The employment of capital and money as the servant of business life and the needs of the people.

3. Development of agriculture and the reversal of the excess settlement of country people in the towns.

4. A new framework of business and professional life.

5. Complete utilization of the country's resources.[2]

There was nothing in this of any originality. Less revolutionary in tone than most of Hitler's speeches on his party's programme, it was, nevertheless,

[1] R. J. Fuglesang and O. Kolby, *Nasjonal-økonomisk nyordning* (Oslo, 1944), p. 6.

[2] V. A. L. J. Quisling, *Norges frihet og selvstendighet. Artikler og taler 9 april 1940–23 juni 1941* (Oslo, 1942), 'Nasjonalt forfall og nasjonal gjenreisning', speech in Colosseum, 12 March 1941.

a resounding echo of events in National Socialist Germany.[1] This is the more apparent if the implications of Nasjonal Samling's programme are considered. The attack on materialism led to a brand of anti-capitalism which both in policy and language duplicated almost exactly that of Gottfried Feder who had compiled the 'unalterable' programme of the National Socialist Workers' Party. The emphasis on autarkic development and full employment in spite of the international economic conjuncture meant that Norway would be driven into the larger European autarkic area of the New Order, the German *Großraumwirtschaft*. This was a destiny which Quisling seems to have accepted freely and happily for his country although it implied utter subordination to German economic objectives. Nasjonal Samling's ultimate objective, total social stability, was so like that of the National Socialists that every device which the fascist revolution in Germany used to attain this aim was incorporated in Nasjonal Samling's own programme for Norway in the hope that it would work there also.

Norway, Quisling wrote after the 1937 elections, had chosen 'Marx and Mammon'.[2]

Liberalism and Marxism [he declared in 1941], the Anglo-Jewish and Russo-Jewish materialistic world systems, that is what the Norwegian leaders had to offer to thirsty souls when the new national day of work should have begun. Borrowed and objectionable foreign ideas, which did not accord with northern particularities and were also in themselves basically false and wrong, made our leaders speak of freedom and democracy, but they meant by those words London and Marx and their own Mammon-interests.[3]

The attack on capitalism was directed against 'big finance' and was strikingly reminiscent of the National Socialist Party's early attacks on department stores. It was directed towards liberating capital on easier terms for smaller businessmen. As in Germany and Italy the whole emphasis of the party programme was on the use of capital rather than on its ownership. For Norway, adherence to the fascist order in Europe would mean adherence to a world where international capitalist exploitation would no longer determine the pattern of internal economic development and militate against the interests of Norway's own entrepreneurs.

It means freedom from the yoke of capitalism. And that is not just a phrase. We all know, or at any rate ought to know, that 'capitalism'—international finance capital and its representatives here in Norway—has prevented the

[1] There is an interesting study of the party's early history: H.-O. Brevig, *NS—fra parti til sekt* (Oslo, 1970).

[2] V. A. L. J. Quisling, *Quisling har sagt. Citater fra taler og avisartikler* (Oslo, 1940), article in *Fritt Folk*, 23 October 1937.

[3] Idem, 'Nasjonal forfall og nasjonal gjenreisning', speech in Colosseum, 12 March 1941.

utilization of those riches which rest in our mountains, our waterfalls, in the seas, and the large areas of uncultivated lands.

What has prevented their utilization?

What has created chronic unemployment in our country where there should be an endless amount of positive labour to perform?

The capitalist system. The old parties were, each in its own way, a tool of this economic system with its struggle between special interests, and finally each and every one nothing but the wage slave of international Jewish finance.[1]

The individual rights guaranteed by democracy were no more than an encouragement to individual irresponsibility, an irresponsibility to the national state. The only specifically Norwegian element in Quisling's attacks on capitalism was his belief that Norway, as a relatively undeveloped country, was being kept deliberately in a state of economic subjection by capitalist imperialism. 'Democracy and its economic liberalism has become a gigantic international system of booty that rested originally on industry and large landownership, then later on the power of finance.'[2] The cure for this was an attack on the banking and credit system which would force it to deploy capital in the common interest.

It is at this point that Nasjonal Samling reveals its extraordinarily derivative quality, for not only were these ideas copied directly from Feder's programme for the National Socialist Party, but the slogan used as a rallying-cry was also copied. Speaking to handicraft workers in 1941, Quisling decried the tendency of capitalism to create monopolies which in themselves became a cause of social revolution. Bank credit should be made available to handicraft workers through a reconstructed guild organization. 'That will create the basis for a new social conception, for a conception expressed in the familiar phrase: common use before individual use (fellesnytten foran egennytten).'[3] Or as the last point of the National Socialist Party had it, 'Gemeinnutz vor Eigennutz'.

Fundamentally such a policy required a spiritual conversion of the population from materialist egoism to a more fascist way of thinking. The similarity of such an experience in all countries was no doubt the main reason for Quisling's adherence to the New Order; the Norwegian fascist revolution would need to shelter within the bounds of the European fascist revolution. But it also is clear that Quisling believed certain economic advantages would accrue to Norway other than those derived from the spiritual rebirth of the population. The *Großraumwirtschaft*, he believed, would be a more equitable system for the future development of Norway.

---

[1] Idem, *For Norges frihet og selvstendighet*, speech on 26 September 1940.
[2] Idem, article in *Fritt Folk*, 3 December 1938.
[3] Idem, *Tale til norges håndverkere, 9 September 1941*.

His adherence to it was not simply the result of the political situation in which he came to power, a concession to the tremendous economic and political power of the conqueror, but a long-considered policy.

Even in his book, written several years before the founding of Nasjonal Samling, he had taken such a position.

> From another point of view, the following consideration is of interest. The world is tending towards unity. Within this organization of humanity, a process of crystallization is taking place, not only into great, but into world powers—'Empires', of which Russia is one. And the remarkable fact is that Russia occupies just such a central position as regards the world powers over the whole globe, as Germany occupies amongst the great national powers of Europe.[1]

The *Großraumwirtschaft* was merely the admission of the 'reality' of such developments. In 1936 he had advocated a policy of autarkic development in Norway within the framework of a planned Germanic international trading system.[2] Britain's persistence in siding with Mammon left no alternative but the German *Großraumwirtschaft*. Whether such an alternative exactly met point 29 in the party programme—'Goods which can certainly be produced in sufficient numbers in the country should not be imported from abroad'—was no doubt not worth too close an examination.

The advantages of the fascist trading system were a recurrent theme of the speeches and writings of Gulbrand Lunde.[3] Even in 1935 he had hoped to push Norway more closely into the network of German clearing agreements and away from the atmosphere of 'liberal speculation'. At a meeting of journalists in Venice in 1942 he celebrated his success.

> Our industries, our branches of the fishery and our shipping will, for example, be guaranteed large and stable markets in spite of increased world competition. I can reveal that in the framework of the New Order a large industrial project, which will make possible to our country a certain yearly export of several hundred million kroner, is, amongst other things, in preparation, and the whole thing from a single product of which the raw materials and the productive power—hitherto unutilized—were and are present in Norwegian nature. I could cite other similar examples of the ways in which the European New Order is to the advantage of Norway but I would like to limit myself in this place to the remark that economic circumstances of this kind and the fact that the internal development of the country will no longer be disturbed by party

---

[1] V. A. L. J. Quisling, *Russia and Ourselves*, p. 179.

[2] Idem, 'Et Nordisk verdenssamband mellem skandinaver, briter, tyskere og andre nordiske folk', in *Fritt Folk*, 29 June 1936. See *Quisling har sagt—II. Ti års kamp mot katastrofepolitikken* (Oslo, 1941).

[3] G. Lunde, article in *Vestlandets Avis*, 15 January 1935. See G. Lunde, *Kampen for Norge. Skrifter, foredrag og avisartikler 1933–1940*, ii (Oslo, 1941), 154 ff.

politics, the hunt for capital, and labour conflicts, together will increase Norway's economic strength and will create a growing natural standard of living.[1]

That the purpose of stable markets was to guarantee the perpetual security of the fascist revolution and that that revolution was in itself a search for social stability was readily admitted by its Norwegian proponents. 'A strong and healthy nation', said Lunde, would be the best defence against 'the red plague'.[1] 'A revolutionary earthquake of the kind which did not lay the Russian peasant cottages in ruins, would completely shatter a western community and turn it into a desert', wrote Quisling.[2] To reconstruct the inherently revolutionary society which had emerged from the French Revolution so that it could attain a point of stability it was necessary to alter the path of Norwegian economic and social development. This, again, took the form of copying German policies. It involved retaining a large peasant sector in the economy and protecting it from the harsh winds of economic change by a variety of legal and economic devices. Such a policy had, relatively, greater importance for the economy as a whole in Norway than in Germany, but there was no mistaking its origins.

It was the peasant who would be the chief beneficiary of fascist economic policy.

I appeal to you, Norwegian peasant, who in spite of all still occupy your own ground and hearth as a free man. You surely believe that you will never receive a sufficient payment for your goods, the number of restrictions and compulsory regulations seems exceedingly high to you at this time. But in Russia Bolshevism took land and hearth away from the peasants and hunted millions and millions of them to death. In the years 1932–3 alone Stalin caused six million peasants to starve to death in order to press the whole peasant estate in this way into the slavery of the communist communal enterprises. . . .[3]

The agricultural policies of Nasjonal Samling had therefore a deeper dimension than the attempts of Norwegian governments in the 1930s to grow more food. And in this deeper dimension they corresponded exactly with the aims of German policy. A reduction of the peasants' burden of debt, an extension of agricultural credit to him on easy terms, an absolute security of tenure and an increase in the amount of land cultivated, all these public aims of Nasjonal Samling attracted the enthusiastic support of the German administration.[4]

[1] 'Die Rede des Ministers Gulbrand Lunde auf dem Venediger Journalistenkongress 1942', in *Die Nationale Revolution in Norwegen* (Oslo, 1944), pp. 101–2. The reference is to the aluminium plan. See Chapter VII.

[2] V. A. L. J. Quisling, *Russia and Ourselves*, p. 164.

[3] Idem, speech on 1 February 1943. *Die Nationale Revolution in Norwegen*, p. 120.

[4] F. Thrana, 'Odels-og gjeldspolitikk,' in Nasjonal Samling, *Nasjonalverket. Det nye Norge* (Oslo, 1941).

The old German ideals and ideas still live today among the peasantry, especially in the valleys. The Norwegian peasant was always proud of being a peasant. He was never a serf, and the old German odel-law still survives in Norway today because no democracy ever succeeded in extirpating this idea so deeply rooted in the consciousness of the Norwegian people.[1]

'History teaches us', wrote Quisling, who was inordinately fond of lecturing his people,

that an independent and self-sufficient agriculture is the soundest basis for the community of the people, the state, and the general welfare, and that neglect of arable farming leads to the collapse of the country. And if one class of the working people inside the community needs protective measures by the state to be saved from being exploited in this mercantilist period it is the peasants who have been brought into so serious an economic situation.[2]

After the creation of Nasjonal Samling Quisling lectured the peasants on their failure to respond to his earlier approaches. 'Sooner or later a choice will have to be made between the different social systems and their consequences: between liberalism which forcibly leads to the suppression of the peasantry, and the new social system which wants to build a peasants' and workers' state on a national and social basis.'[3]

Derivative though Nasjonal Samling's policies were they were in no way opportunist. Their similarity to those of the National Socialist German Workers' Party stemmed from a common view of the world and the economy, from an agreement at a profound level on the nature of society and its destiny. If Quisling copied from the National Socialists it was because they were more successful than his own party and more likely to achieve this international destiny. Quisling's anger at being accused of opportunism at his trial was well-justified. His last words at that trial were a defence of his own intellectual consistency and, albeit that they reflect only too accurately how much greater was his own estimation of himself than other peoples', they are an honest statement of his position.

Nasjonal Samling's programme, which is not a copy of that of the Germans— I had already worked it out in Russia in 1918— was an attempt to reflect practical love for one's neighbours—which turned out in this way. But the programme in itself is a step in that direction. It is this I have laboured for. It is this I have attempted to pave the way for and I know the recognition will grow constantly through what is happening in the world today. I thought during that time in Russia I would get support and I discussed it with the Bolshevik leaders in the Ukraine—the materialistic basis of communism, whose economic principles in themselves are not at all unjustifiable as to industry, etc., to raise this to a spiritual

[1] G. Lunde, *Rede des Ministers Dr. Gulbrand Lunde vor dem Deutschen Auslandswissenschaftlichen Institut der Universität Berlin*, 15 October 1941.

[2] V. A. L. J. Quisling, article in *Nationen*, 27 February 1933.

[3] Idem, article in *Nasjonal Samling*, 21 June 1934.

level. I have discussed it with the Germans. I have told Hitler that National Socialism in Germany is materialistic and they wouldn't survive, they'll founder on it. 'Blut und Boden', that is only a disguised materialism and materialism leads only to total egoism in its final consequences.[1]

The German invasion provided Quisling with the opportunity to spread more widely in Norway the spiritual conversion of himself and his small band of brothers. The economic policy of Nasjonal Samling was only a means to this end. For Germany the existence of Nasjonal Samling meant that Norway could be governed through an agent and a party which welcomed the New Order and all it stood for. But German economic policy had empirical short-term aims that had to take precedence over these more spiritual matters.

[1] *Straffesak mot Vidkun A. L. J. Quisling* (Oslo, 1946), p. 460.

II

THE NATURE OF THE NORWEGIAN ECONOMY

IT is habitual among writers on Norway to account for the curiosities of the economic development of that country by its geographical peculiarities and its mountainous terrain. What most dominated Norwegian development, however, was the smallness of the population, the proximity of rapidly industrializing societies with which that population maintained close trading connections, and the marked difference between the earlier history of the country and that of most other European lands. This difference meant that those obstacles to commercial and industrial development associated with the great estates and the *ancien régime* were much less present in Norway. When the great European estates were being formed in the ninth century and serfdom was spreading, the inhabitants of Norway were traders through all the waterways of northern and eastern Europe. The society which subsequently emerged in Norway was a peasant freeholding society. Although therefore the country was still very poor and backward in the early nineteenth century, it did not have those social obstacles to development associated with the survival in other European lands of great agricultural estates and quasi-feudal economic relationships. The obstacles to economic development in Norway were economic ones, more easily overcome, shortage of capital, shortage of raw materials, and ignorance. All were, in fact, overcome by close contact with neighbouring societies many of which were in the full spate of industrial development.

Poverty and remoteness delayed the process of industrialization until the late nineteenth century. Even in 1860, for example, Norway had only 68 kilometres of railway when other lands such as Spain and the Habsburg Empire had laid the basis of a national network.[1] But in the three decades before the First World War the industrial revolution in Norway transformed the country into a richer and more developed land than either of those countries. Foreign capital took advantage of the relative lack of obstacles to industrialization and supplied the deficiencies which would otherwise have existed, extensive involvement in foreign trade provided the raw materials which were lacking, and certain resources, in particular water power for the production of electric current, were cheaper and more

[1] Statistisk Sentralbyrå, *Historisk Statistikk 1968*, p. 410.

exploitable in Norway than elsewhere. The population was not large; an extraordinarily high proportion of the inhabitants emigrated to the United States, and with rapid economic development *per capita* incomes also rose rapidly. The social effects of industrialization on Norway were less traumatic than in most other European lands because the social structure was already so different before the process began and for that reason the process was itself more rapid. It did, however, depend on relative freedom of entry for foreign capital and on a sensitivity to the international economy and its opportunities which was not without danger.

There is no intention here to argue that no other path of economic development was open to Norway. Inevitably, in a country with so short a recent history of national independence and yet so long a consciousness of national difference, economic development of this type soon raised the issue of whether Norway could survive economically as a genuinely independent power. The independence which accompanied adherence to these liberal principles seemed to many to be in fact only a spurious independence. All proposals for changing the nature of society proceeded, by a much shorter series of logical steps than in a more complex economy, to proposals for sacrificing some degree of national sovereignty. Quisling's yearning for the German *Großraumwirtschaft* was but an expression of his fundamental aim, to change the nature of Norwegian society.

But it must be allowed that for a country like Norway in the nineteenth century the range of economic choice was exceedingly limited. This may readily be seen from the compromises with the international economy which the Norwegian socialist and communist parties were early obliged to make in their doctrines. Nasjonal Samling, being more absolutely anti-liberal in its ideology than the left-wing parties, did not make those compromises. In so far as it was entitled to take itself seriously it drew its strength from the apparent failure of the international economy in the inter-war period to sustain Norway's economic development in the way it had previously done. The accusations of 'treason' which were so freely bandied about between the extreme right and left wings of Norwegian political life in that period are a symptom of the search for an extra-national solution on both sides. Any over-all view of the Norwegian economy by the 1920s will show that an effective abandonment of the liberal system by that time would have had to be total to be successful. The compromise made by the Norwegian socialists was an acceptance of the extreme difficulty of introducing any basically different order of economic existence into a country so tied, for good or bad, to the international economy. Nasjonal Samling was far less aware of the immense problems involved in the abandonment of a path of development not so much recently chosen as haphazardly followed from the very beginning of Norway's independent national existence.

Although the state of the international conjuncture in the period between the wars did modify to some extent the extreme *laissez-faire* nature of the Norwegian economy, when it was so suddenly and violently incorporated into the fascist trading system in April 1940 it was still the most dependent of all European economies on the international economy. In spite of the smallness of the population there was no economy which it was more difficult to incorporate into the *Großraumwirtschaft*. For Norway, the invasion and occupation were a total break with her historical and economic past. For Germany, they were the source of endless economic difficulties.

The salient feature of the Norwegian economy, that which made it so difficult a morsel for the *Großraumwirtschaft* to digest, was the immense importance of its overseas trade in relation to the total income of the country. Exemplifying those disadvantages of international specialization criticized by fascist economic theorists, Norway was the least self-sufficient of all European economies. No country had so high a value of imports per inhabitant, and only Sweden had a higher value of exports per inhabitant. The value of total international trade per inhabitant was higher in Norway than in all other European countries. But the size of the shipping fleet was even greater than this might indicate. The fourth largest fleet in the world, it was exceeded only by that of vastly more populous countries. The country received its imports through a far-flung, complicated mesh of international trade, and paid for them in part through an almost equally wide distribution of exports, in part through its invisible earnings in shipping services by a merchant fleet which carried a significant proportion of the world's trade. The existence of so high a standard of living in Norway had come to depend on the existence of those very economic arrangements which the *Großraumwirtschaft* was intended to replace.

TABLE I. *Value of International Trade per Inhabitant in Various Countries, 1938**

(gold Norwegian kroner)

Country	Value of *per capita* imports	Value of *per capita* exports
Norway	222	146
Sweden	183	162
United Kingdom	195	107
Germany	72	66
Italy	30	28

* F.D. 5347/45, I. G. Farbenindustrie, Volkswirtschaftliche Abteilung, Vowi. 3901, 'Wirtschaftsbericht Norwegen'.

An over-all view of the Norwegian economy will show that the fierce pace of industrialization had far from eliminated the traditional peasant farming and fishing. Rather the industrial revolution had created an industrial sector of the Norwegian economy, a very modern and prosperous sector, within the framework of a much poorer and more traditional agricultural sector which had remained an important branch of the economy. The largest single occupational group in the economy were those dependent on agriculture, fishing, and forestry, the traditional occupations of the peasantry. These occupations still accounted for one-third of the total employment in Norway, considerably more than the contribution made by industrial employment. The share of the Gross Domestic Product contributed by this farming and fishing sector, however, was in no way proportionate to its size.

TABLE 2. *Gross Domestic Product of Norway by Category of Employment, 1930 and 1939**

(absolute figures at current prices)

Category of employment	1930		1939	
	Million kroner	Per cent	Million kroner	Per cent
Agriculture, forestry, fishing, and whaling	731	16·6	719	11·4
Mining, manufacturing, construction, electricity, gas, and water	1,327	30·1	2,103	33·5
Transport and communication	558	12·7	968	15·4
Trade, banking, and insurance	745	16·9	1,158	18·4
Other private and public services	1,050	23·7	1,336	21·3

* J. Bjerke, *Some Aspects of Long-term Economic Growth of Norway Since 1865*. Paper presented to the Sixth European Conference of the International Association for Research in Income and Wealth, Portoroz, Yugoslavia, 1959, p. 43.

The last census of employment in Norway before the war was in 1930. It has therefore only a limited value in a comparison with the figures for Gross Domestic Product, the more so as unemployment was extremely high in that year. Even so, the distribution of employment revealed in that year provides a reasonable case for believing the extraordinarily small contribution to the Gross Domestic Product made by the older sector of the economy and testifies to the dual nature of the Norwegian economy.

In fact, according to Bjerke's calculations, the contribution of the agricultural sector to the Gross Domestic Product fell from 16·6 per cent in 1930 to 11·4 per cent in 1939, while that of industry rose from 30·1 per cent to 33·5 per cent. It is likely, therefore, that the relative contribution per employed person in the two sectors was becoming even more unequal in that time.

Both these sectors, the industrial and agricultural, were deeply involved in Norway's international commerce. Before the beginnings of industrialization in Norway the mercantile marine had already become very large; in 1850 it was the sixth largest in the world.[1] Although the foundation of this merchant navy was not really a result of Norway's own trade, it is still remarkable to what extent Norway was a trading nation before the

TABLE 3. *Distribution of the Population of Norway by Employment, 1930**

Category	Actually employed	Normally employed	Normally employed as a percentage of whole labour force
Agriculture, forestry	336,364	838,848	29·9
Fishing	75,977	196,772	7·0
Industry, handicraft	309,813	774,031	27·5
Trade and commerce	145,839	285,555	10·1
Transport	103,422	272,805	9·7

* Statistisk Sentralbyrå, *Foreløbige resultater av folketellingen i Norge/ desember 1930.*

industrial revolution. Wood and fish, two of the basic goods of Norway's peasant economy, were her two staple exports and their absolute importance did not diminish in the twentieth century. On the eve of the Second World War Norway even developed some insignificant agricultural exports. The agricultural sector was therefore an integral part of Norway's trading links. The industrial sector was not, as many fascist writers suggested, foisted upon an otherwise self-sufficient economy by foreign exploiters.

The Norwegian trading fleet in 1939 amounted to 4,737,555 B.R.T., about 7 per cent of the world's total fleet. It was roughly the size of that of Japan and clearly exceeded in size only by the fleets of the United Kingdom and the United States. In terms of shipping tonnage per inhabitant, therefore, Norway far outdistanced all other economies. In addition the Norwegian fleet could fairly claim to be one of the most modern in the world; 45 per cent of the tonnage was less than ten years old.[2] This was a reversal of the historical pattern. Before 1914 Norway's merchant fleet had been essentially a fleet of tramp steamers, with a heavy preponderance of aging steamships. Most shipping firms had been small, lacking the capital to invest in more modern vessels. About one-half of the Norwegian tonnage was sunk in the First World War. The fleet that emerged from

[1] Ø. Lorentzen, *Norway, Norwegian Shipping and the War* (New York, 1942).
[2] Statistisk Sentralbyrå, *Norske skip i utenriksfart 1938 og 1939*, Norges offisielle statistikk, x. 101 (Oslo, 1946), p. 6.

reconstruction was very different from the old one. Not only was it preponderantly a fleet of modern motor ships, it was also a highly specialized fleet. The credit for building these specialized ships was usually provided by foreign industry and they were very frequently built abroad. Norwegian shipyards could not build ships over 10,000 tons dead weight and their total capacity was very small. The contribution of the Norwegian economy was therefore the knowledge of the shipping business and the crew. In this way many of the American oil companies found it cheaper to rely on Norwegian-owned and -operated tanker fleets and to lend the capital for their construction. A considerable part of Norway's foreign debt at the end of the 1930s was still represented by these ships' mortgages.

Although oil tankers constituted 37 per cent of the total merchant fleet, it was still large enough to encompass almost every variety of shipping.[1] Norwegian ships played a big part in the grain trade from Montreal to Europe and in the Scandinavian wood trade. The actual coasting trade of Norway itself, although vital to the country's existence, was relatively insignificant in international terms. The port of Oslo accounted for almost one-half of the total imports by value in 1939 and Oslo, Bergen, Trondheim, and Stavanger together accounted for about 70 per cent. The same four ports were responsible for only 40 per cent of the export trade by value, but that was due to the special role of the iron-ore port of Narvik. The Swedish railway system crossed the Norwegian frontier so that iron ore from the mines of northern Sweden could be exported in winter from an ice-free port when the Swedish ports on the Gulf of Bothnia were no longer accessible. In 1938 7,620,000 tons of ore were exported from Narvik. The vital role of Norway's fleet was not to carry Norwegian trade, no matter how important to the nation, but to earn sufficient income to enable Norway to run a heavy trading deficit and a balance-of-payments surplus. It was the earnings from shipping services that paid for the exceptionally large *per capita* imports into Norway and thus sustained the high standard of living there. Although in the 1930s attempts were made, by encouraging a greater production of food in Norway, to reduce the size of the import surplus, they were unsuccessful due to the volume of other imports that came into the country with returning prosperity in 1937 and 1938. Even the heavy import surplus occasioned by stockpiling in 1939 could be paid off by shipping earnings, which both in 1938 and 1939 were roughly the equivalent of the deficit on the balance of visible trade.

The components of Norway's visible trade were complex. No other country in Europe was so dependent on food imports and especially on imports of bread grain. The composition of Norwegian imports was heavily biased toward foodstuffs, raw materials, and semi-manufactured goods.

[1] Ibid., pp. 8–11.

Some of the raw materials and semi-processed goods were re-exported after a further stage of manufacture in Norway. This was true of many treated metal ores imported into Norway for smelting. The importance of finished manufactured goods both in Norway's import and export trade was relatively small. Not only was the composition of Norwegian trade

TABLE 4. *Development of Norwegian Imports and Exports 1926-39**

(000 current kroner)

Year	Imports	Exports	Import surplus
1926–30†	1,046,151	723,148	323,003
1931–5†	755,851	555,301	200,550
1936	926,982	685,169	241,813
1937	1,292,717	823,258	469,459
1938	1,192,650	786,529	406,121
1939	1,366,230	807,548	558,682

* Statistisk Sentralbyrå, *Norges handel 1939*, Norges offisielle statistikk, ix. 198 (Oslo, 1940), p. 6.
† Yearly average.

TABLE 5. *Norwegian Balance of Payments, 1938 and 1939**

(000,000 current kroner)

	1938	1939
Balance of visible trade	−406	−558
Sale of whale oil abroad	+28	+24
Earnings from shipping	+420	+550
Interest and dividends	−60	−57
Income from transit of goods	+18	+19
Income from foreign transport	+78	+49
Miscellaneous income	+15	+21
Balance	+93	+36

* Statistisk Sentralbyrå, *Statistisk årbok*, 1938, 1939.

complex, its distribution was widespread. Norwegian exporters had sought markets in the most distant lands and the population drew its daily bread, and industry its material inputs, from equally distant lands.

Three branches of the Norwegian export trade dominated all others in the 1930s, the export of wood products, wood pulp, and paper, the export of fish, and the export of processed metal ores and metals. The third of these was typically the result of the kind of industrialization which had taken place in Norway, for the metals were frequently not derived from

Norway's own ore resources. In fact the export of untreated metal ores was fourth in importance in Norway's export trade. In 1939 the first three of these categories each represented roughly 20 per cent of the value of Norwegian exports. Raw materials and semi-manufactured goods constituted over 40 per cent of imports by value in the same year, foodstuffs accounted for 15 per cent, machinery and production goods for 14 per cent, and clothing for 10·7 per cent.

TABLE 6. *The Composition of Norway's Exports and Imports, 1926-39**

(percentage total value)

	1926–30 (average)	1931–5 (average)	1936	1937	1938	1939
Exports						
Wood products, wood pulp, paper, etc.	26·8	23·6	22·1	24·3	21·8	21·5
Ores and unprocessed metals	4·6	5·6	7·1	6·5	7·9	7·3
Processed and prepared metals	12·8	17·2	18·3	19·2	19·4	20·0
Fish products	25·6	23·7	21·5	19·3	18·9	20·7
Imports						
Foodstuffs	23·2	20·0	15·7	14·8	15·7	15·2
Clothing and textiles	13·2	13·8	12·8	10·5	10·9	10·7
Raw materials and semi-manufactured goods	36·5	40·2	42·9	43·1	39·5	42·8
Ships	11·4	7·7	7·1	11·3	12·6	10·0
Machinery and production goods	8·8	10·8	14·1	13·4	14·3	14·0

* Statistisk Sentralbyrå, *Norges handel*, Norges offisielle statistikk, viii. 42; viii. 75; viii. 104; viii. 138; viii. 172; ix. 2; ix. 12; ix. 35; ix. 58; ix. 86; ix. 114; ix. 138; ix. 173; ix. 198.

Of the actual value of Norwegian exports in 1938, 786·5 million kroner, the three main groups accounted for 452·4 million kroner. The value of ore exports was 49·1 million kroner. Three other items made a significant contribution to the total. The export of chemical fertilizer brought in 53·4 million kroner, of skins and hides 49·1 million kroner, and of fish oil and animal fats 44·5 million kroner. Of the total value of imports in 1938, 1,192·6 million kroner, ships accounted for 150·7 million kroner, ores, coal, coke, stone, and earths for 136·1 million kroner, and textiles and textile products for 104·5 million kroner. The other important categories were machinery (94·1 million kroner), fats, oils, and rubber (83·6 million kroner), metal goods (81·2 million kroner), and grains and grain products (79·6 million kroner).

These are in some cases very large categories. To get a more accurate conception of the specific trading problems with which Norway was faced after 1940 it is necessary to look at the customs records which give trading figures by tonnage. From Tables 7 and 8 certain other important aspects of Norway's international dependence stand out. First should be

TABLE 7. *Norway's Main Exports, 1938 and 1939**

(tons)

Item	1938	1939
Iron ore (including concentrate)	1,497,140	1,182,125
Pyrites	654,956	653,962
Ferrous alloys	101,235	—
Aluminium	28,579	24,084
Ferrous silicon	32,932	40,989
Sulphur	76,631	83,746
Zinc	44,353	39,848
Copper ore	21,748	15,896
Wood pulp (damp weight)	503,633	454,898
Paper and cardboard	255,754	326,321
Cellulose (dry weight)	245,470	302,987
Timber	235,432†	288,294†
Fresh herring	96,116	121,474
Herring meal and fish meal	79,297	55,124
Fresh fish (other than herring)	23,769	32,575
Tørfisk and *klippfisk*	67,440	55,562
Salt fish (other than herring)	5,887	10,761
Salt herring	33,585	38,538
Canned fish	26,419	36,111
Fish oils, cod-liver oil, other fats	446,959‡	594,115‡
Fertilizers	456,963	471,443
Chemicals	53,437	73,691

* Statistisk Sentralbyrå, *Norges handel*, Norges offisielle statistikk, ix. 173; ix. 198.
† Cubic metres.
‡ Hectolitres.

noted the dependence on imported coal. For all the development of hydro-electric power in Norway coal remained a vitally important industrial and domestic fuel. The Norwegian railway system was almost completely dependent on coal imports. Secondly should be noted the large quantities of imported fodders. Norwegian agriculture was essentially a livestock agriculture. The arable resources of the land were extended in providing even the meagre proportion of domestic food requirements which they supplied. Food for livestock had to be imported on a large scale. Thirdly should be noted the large imports of ore, the basis of much of Norway's industry. Fourthly appears the number of specialized industrial processes dependent on the availability of cheap electric current—the manufacture of aluminium, of high-grade nitrogenous fertilizer, of ferro-alloys, and of zinc, all of which were heavily geared towards the export market.

The distribution of Norway's trade shows that the rise of the fascist trading bloc in Europe had not fundamentally altered Norway's pattern of trade. A study of Tables 9 and 10 will show that in the 1930s Norway

TABLE 8. *Norway's Main Imports, 1938 and 1939**

(tons)

Item	1938	1939
Fat	71,208	100,411
Wheat	164,733	252,787
Rye	131,391	139,289
Wheat flour	40,990	39,319
Fruit	49,516	49,039
Sugar	96,657	99,916
Syrup	18,360	17,020
Bran	54,796	59,269
Maize	148,273	134,173
Oil cake	77,883	88,827
Fertilizer	143,390	117,663
Oil seeds	102,424	92,525
Chemicals	44,897	57,391
Iron and steel	220,943	351,507
Manganese ore	124,361	103,543
Chromium ore	50,022	19,579
Bauxite	25,942	32,696
Alumina	43,737	45,639
Coal	2,269,849	2,736,188
Crude oil	595,052	699,270
Machinery†	100,639	115,246

* Statistisk Sentralbyrå, *Norges handel*, Norges offisielle statistikk, ix. 173; ix. 198.
† 1,000 kroner, corrected prices.

had not been brought any closer to integration in the *Großraumwirtschaft*. Rather the development of the *Großraumwirtschaft* had moved Norwegian trade back into the sterling orbit. Certainly the proportion of Norwegian imports originating in Britain increased slightly over that period. While German trading policy was changing the whole pattern of trade of most of its neighbours and particularly of the states of eastern and south-eastern Europe it was having scarcely any effect on Norway. The diversity of Norwegian trade and the close and well-worn connections between Norwegian and British trading circles made it almost impossible for Germany to exercise on the Norwegian economy the economic pressure which she could bring to bear on others although there were many Norwegian exports of such strategic importance for Germany as to be

TABLE 9. *Norwegian Imports from Certain Countries, 1933–8**

(000,000 kroner)

Country of origin	1933		1934		1935		1936		1937		1938	
	Amount	%	Amount	%	Amount	%	Amount	%	Amount	%	Amount	%
Finland	3·7	0·6	3·9	0·5	4·6	0·6	5·7	0·6	18·1	1·4	5·8	0·5
Sweden	56·4	8·5	79·9	10·9	87·1	10·6	111·2	12·0	144·8	11·2	143·0	12·0
Denmark	31·9	4·8	41·9	5·7	53·1	6·4	50·7	5·5	78·7	6·1	62·9	5·3
United Kingdom	151·9	22·8	168·8	22·9	192·1	23·3	221·1	23·8	318·1	24·6	278·7	23·1
Germany†	139·4	21·0	140·7	19·1	142·9	17·3	155·4	16·8	213·0	16·5	206·1	17·3
Austria	2·3	0·3	2·5	0·3	4·3	0·5	5·2	0·6	6·4	0·5	··	··
France	20·5	3·1	22·5	3·1	34·1	4·2	36·2	3·9	48·6	3·8	39·5	3·3
Spain	15·4	2·3	14·8	2·0	13·3	1·6	11·7	1·3	6·9	0·5	5·5	0·5
Italy	9·9	1·5	10·7	1·5	11·4	1·4	3·9	0·4	14·1	1·1	22·5	1·9
Poland	17·5	2·6	13·4	1·8	18·1	2·2	20·9	2·3	22·8	1·8	19·3	1·6
U.S.S.R.	17·1	2·6	14·7	2·0	8·7	1·0	11·7	1·3	15·4	1·2	18·9	1·6
U.S.A.	46·1	6·9	63·9	8·6	72·5	8·8	90·9	9·8	120·0	9·3	129·3	10·8

* Statistisk Sentralbyrå, *Norges handel*, Norges offisielle statistikk, ix. 35; ix. 58; ix. 86; ix. 114; ix. 138; ix. 173; ix. 198.
† Including Austria after 1 July 1938.

TABLE 10. *Norwegian Exports to Certain Countries, 1933–8**

(000,000 kroner)

Country of destination	1933		1934		1935		1936		1937		1938	
	Amount	%	Amount	%	Amount	%	Amount	%	Amount	%	Amount	%
Finland	8·4	1·5	7·9	1·4	8·7	1·4	10·3	1·5	16·5	2·0	12·5	1·6
Sweden	38·0	6·8	43·6	7·5	53·1	8·8	57·8	8·4	70·6	8·6	71·9	9·2
Denmark	23·8	4·3	23·0	3·9	25·1	4·2	30·8	4·5	30·7	3·7	35·0	4·5
United Kingdom	113·9	20·4	140·3	24·3	164·9	27·3	180·8	26·4	235·9	28·7	220·5	28·0
Germany†	69·8	12·5	79·1	13·7	79·0	13·1	89·1	13·0	107·9	13·1	120·4	15·3
Austria	2·0	0·4	1·6	0·3	3·7	0·5	4·6	0·7	4·4	0·5	..	..
France	32·5	5·8	27·0	4·7	29·8	4·9	45·2	6·6	52·1	6·3	58·4	7·4
Spain	11·5	2·1	15·5	2·7	16·2	2·7	11·7	1·7	4·6	0·6	8·1	1·0
Italy	16·7	3·0	19·1	3·3	10·6	1·8	7·6	1·1	21·1	2·6	23·5	3·0
Poland	4·2	0·8	4·8	0·8	6·1	1·0	8·9	1·3	9·4	1·1	9·3	1·2
U.S.S.R.	20·4	3·7	8·4	1·5	4·7	0·8	1·4	0·2	1·2	0·2	7·3	0·9
U.S.A.	60·3	10·8	55·3	9·5	61·7	10·2	76·6	11·2	78·8	9·2	58·9	7·5

* Statistisk Sentralbyrå, *Norges handel*, Norges offisielle statistikk, ix. 35; ix. 58; ix. 86; ix. 114; ix. 138; ix. 173; ix. 198.
† Including Austria after 1 July 1938.

worth the offer of a guaranteed market. Although Norwegian exports to
Germany grew in the 1930s they did not grow at the expense of Norwegian exports to Britain, although they did so partly at the expense of
Norwegian exports to the United States. From the same tables it can be
seen that Norwegian imports came from three main sources, from Britain,
other Scandinavian countries, and Germany. Between them these three
sources of supply accounted for over half the value of total imports. They
were equally responsible for about one-half of total exports, although in
the case of exports Britain, which was taking about one-quarter of Norway's
exports by value, easily outdistanced the others.

Much of the domestic economy of Norway can be understood from this
survey of her external economic relations. The origins of her foreign
trade were her own domestic raw materials but the small size of the
domestic market had meant that the major industries had produced from
the outset for an export market. Such industries were modern and highly
capitalized, although the capital was still foreign to a great extent. About
654 million kroner of the public debt in 1938 was foreign debt. If foreign
capital holdings and land holdings were included the total would have
been about 2,356 million kroner.[1] This capital did not find its way to the
older sectors of the economy and the older trades, which consequently
remained under-capitalized and, for all their size, on rather uneasy
ground.

Most Norwegian farms were small peasant farms, a high proportion of
them very small. Only a few were exclusively farming concerns. The
majority had some woodland and many were also fishing concerns. In
their way of life and economic activity Norwegian peasants more resembled
the crofters of the Highlands of Scotland than the peasant farmers of
Denmark or Sweden. Their income was provided by a mixture of farming,
fishing, and forestry. Although there were a few big firms engaged in these
occupations a fair impression of the Norwegian economy can be gained
from considering these activities together as the agricultural foundation
of that economy. In 1929 there were 298,000 peasant farms: 200,000 of
these owned some woodland; 70,000 of the farmers were also fishermen;
20,000 were trappers and hunters.[2]

The same census gives a good indication of the prevalence of small
farms in Norway. From Table 11 it can be seen that over 80 per cent of
the farmed land in Norway was exploited by farms between 2 and 30
hectares in size. Almost one-half of the agricultural land was owned in
units of less than 10 hectares. The very large number of garden plots and
allotments represents the diversity of interest of the cultivators.

[1] F.D. 5347/45, I. G. Farben, 'Wirtschaftsbericht Norwegen'.
[2] H. Lufft, *Die Wirtschaft Dänemarks und Norwegens. Gestalt-Politik-Problematik*
(Berlin, 1942), p. 115.

In relation to the total land area of Norway, the area devoted to agricultural purposes was very small. In the 1930s, and even more after the German occupation, debate was widespread on how much of the surface of Norway could be employed for agricultural purposes. Those, both Norwegians and Germans, who criticized the openness of the Norwegian economy believed that it was possible to extend enormously the farmed

TABLE 11. *Number of Farms and Proportion of Land Area Used according to Size of Individual Farms, 1929*[*]

Size of holding (hectares)	No. of farms		Land area used	
	Total	%	Hectares	%
Below 0·2	68,247	22·87	5,905·7	0·8
0·2–0·5	21,563	7·23	6,640·3	0·9
0·5–1	27,696	9·28	16,759·4	2·1
1–2	48,294	16·19	54,067·9	7·0
2–5	74,662	25·02	175,643·4	22·6
5–10	36,968	12·39	195,200·9	25·2
10–30	19,214	6·44	254,302·4	32·8
30–50	1,392	0·47	46,729·0	6·0
50–100	292	0·10	16,439·3	2·1
Over 100	32	0·01	3,649·6	0·5
Totals	298,360	100·00	775,337·9	100·00

* Reichsministerium für Ernährung und Landwirtschaft, *Berichte über Landwirtschaft, Zeitschrift für Agrarpolitik und Landwirtschaft*, 'Die Landwirtschaft in Norwegen', Sonderheft 155 (Prague, 1942–3), p. 158.

surface of the country in spite of its northerly latitude. Whatever the possibilities for expanding agricultural output in this way it is worth remarking that Norway was the most sparsely populated country in mainland Europe. The two most northerly counties, Finnmark and Troms, which were accessible from the rest of the country only by sea, supported a mere 151,000 inhabitants.

The general aim of government policy, despite its many variations in the inter-war period, had been to increase the domestic production of food partly by increasing the efficiency of cultivation and partly by encouraging settlement and the opening-up of new farmland. Over 1,500 new peasant farms a year were created between 1906 and 1936. At the time of the invasion plans existed to create a further 20,000 farms over the subsequent decade. The new holdings were allocated with state subsidies to groups of settlers, mainly in the northern provinces, and the settlers were provided with interest-free loans for the first five years of their occupation. The financial operations were managed by a state-controlled bank founded expressly to encourage such settlement.

Courageous though such a policy was, its success in reducing Norway's import bill was not very great. The quantity of food produced in the inter-war period increased considerably, but only such as to keep pace with the increasing quantity consumed. The greatest success was in meat production and other animal products. In 1928 Norway was a net importer of these products. In the course of the next ten years very small export surpluses of some of these commodities occasionally became available. In this respect Norway was following, with some delay, a general trend towards specialization in animal products common to all Scandinavian lands. This trend had developed much earlier in Denmark and gone much further there. The greater part of the crop yield in all Scandinavian countries was used in animal husbandry and provided the basis of a production of animal foodstuffs great enough to form a large part of the world's export trade in such products.[1] Of this trade, however, Norway had but a very small part and the attempt to produce more bread grain for domestic consumption had been pursued throughout the thirties.

The main instrument of this policy had been the act of 1928 setting up a state monopoly, Statens Kornforretning, to purchase grain. By offering relatively higher prices for wheat than for other grains it was able to induce a marked increase in wheat production. The rigours of the climate seemed to restrict the area available for arable farming to a very small proportion of the total land and the growing of bread grains in larger quantities could only succeed at the cost of importing larger quantities of animal fodder. Of European countries only Iceland had a smaller proportion of her agricultural land devoted to arable farming. That this did not represent the impossibility of growing more grain in Norway but rather the uneconomic nature of the operation is obviously true, for it appears that in the mid nineteenth century about a third of the agricultural land was used for grain farming.[2] But for all the efforts of Statens Kornforretning the cultivation of grain in the wetter western valleys continued to decrease in the inter-war period. The increase in the total output of grain was due to the new farms created in the same period.[3] The area of Norway used for agricutural purposes was probably about 15 per cent of the total land surface, but to that should be added the pasturing of sheep in summer on natural heaths and the pasturing of reindeer on the Arctic lands. In any table of land utilization in Norway the major role is played by 'heathland'. But the definition of 'heathland' is marvellously flexible and in the thirties

[1] Delegations for the Promotion of Economic Cooperation Between the Northern Countries, *The Northern Countries in World Economy*, 2nd edn. (Helsinki, 1939), pp. 31 ff.
[2] Reichsministerium für Ernährung und Landwirtschaft, *Berichte über Landwirtschaft* p. 137.
[3] Ibid., p. 61.

there were several plans to use these 'heathlands' to more purpose, plans which were to be greatly encouraged by the German administration. The area actually devoted to arable cultivation may be seen in Table 12.

TABLE 12. *The Extent of Arable Cultivation in Norway, 1939**

	No. of hectares	Total
Grains:		
Wheat	41,213	
Rye	3,176	
Barley	46,774	
Oats	87,024	
Mixed grains	4,894	
Legumes	592	
Grain and legumes		183,674
Potatoes	50,693	
Root crops	22,543	
Other arable and garden crops	37,657	
Total arable and garden cultivation		294,567

* Reichsministerium für Ernährung und Landwirtschaft, *Berichte über Landwirtschaft*, p. 151.

The yields obtained from arable farming were roughly akin to those obtained in Germany. In view of the harshness of the climate there is thus no reason to suppose that Norwegian peasant farming was any less efficient than peasant farming elsewhere. But the effect of the climate was to limit the range of choice of crop available to the arable farmer and to cause a considerable variation in the size of the harvest. The arable harvests of the years before the war are shown in Table 13. It is clear that the increasing area devoted to wheat growing produced results but it should also be noticed that the production of root fodder did not increase and that the production of other grains did not significantly change, apart from rye which was following a much longer-term declining trend.

The production of oats was generally sufficient to satisfy domestic demand, but imports of all other grains were necessary. Almost 20 per cent of barley consumed was accounted for by imports, over half of which came from Denmark. The domestic rye harvest in 1939 was sufficient to meet only 4 per cent of the demand, 139,451 tons being imported. Over half of the imported quantity came from Argentina and the rest mainly from Russia and Canada. The eightfold increase in the average wheat harvest had been met by a fivefold increase in consumption in the same period. Between 75 and 80 per cent of the total consumption still had to be imported. In 1939 wheat imports were 292,106 tons, almost entirely from Canada and Argentina. The population was thus not only dependent almost entirely on imports for its bread but on imports from countries with whom all possibility of trade stopped after April 1940. The same situation in 1917 had led to a serious threat to the population when the government of the United States had threatened to cut off grain exports to Norway.[1]

TABLE 13. *Norwegian Arable Crop Harvests, 1929–39**

(000 tons)

Year	Wheat	Rye	Barley	Oats	Total grain	Potatoes	Root fodder
1929–31†	18·7	12·5	99·2	170·9	311·1	813·4	533·3
1932–4†	24·6	11·5	111·3	183·3	341·6	937·4	573·9
1935–7†	58·6	11·4	122·5	180·5	382·6	907·6	513·6
1938	71·8	11·0	124·3	196·7	414·5	937·6	500·5
1939	77·9	6·2	103·5	200·8	400·2	807·0	355·9

* Statistisk Sentralbyrå, *Statistisk-økonomisk oversikt over året 1939* (Oslo, 1940), p. 68.
† Annual average.

The more important part of Norwegian agriculture was animal farming. Milk production accounted for 41 per cent of the total value of agricultural production (526 million kroner).[2] A further 11 per cent was accounted for by beef production. From this may be seen the dominant importance of the problem of fodder in Norwegian farming. But it was not merely cattle which had to be fed throughout the long winter. The numbers of livestock of all kinds was relatively high. Table 14 shows that there was a cow to every other person in Norway and more poultry than people.

TABLE 14. *Numbers of Livestock in Norway, 1929 and 1939**

Types of animals	20 June 1929	20 June 1939
Horses	177,169	203,931
Cows†	1,224,182	1,455,016
Pigs	289,039	361,953
Sheep	1,533,015	1,743,802
Goats	323,677	248,916
Poultry (adult birds)	2,929,440	3,437,858

* Statistisk Sentralbyrå, *Statistisk-økonomisk oversikt over året 1939*, p. 69.
† In the general category of cows, dairy cows accounted for 755,135 on 20 June 1929, and 864,336 in 20 June 1939.

[1] See the letter in the Appendix of O. Riste, *The Neutral Ally: Norway's Relations with Belligerent Powers in the First World War* (Oslo, 1965), p. 233.
[2] Reichsministerium für Ernährung und Landwirtschaft, *Berichte über Landwirtschaft*, p. 87.

The importance of cattle in the Norwegian economy tended to increase in the inter-war period. The number of sheep in Norway, by contrast, had declined in the last fifty years of the nineteenth century although the demands they made on imported feed were less than those by cattle. On the eve of the invasion Norway had roughly the same population of sheep as in 1865.[1] The number of hens kept had quintupled since 1891.[2] In 1924 Norway first became self-sufficient in egg production and afterwards developed a small export trade. Poultry-keeping fitted easily into the social framework of the peasant farms, but the fodder was almost entirely imported. Imported fodder was also the basis of the increase in milk production from 281,434 tons in 1920 to 792,621 tons in 1939.[3]

TABLE 15. *Fodder Needs of Norwegian Livestock**

(in fodder units calculated in 1939)

Animals	Fodder units	
	Tons	%
Horses	418,900	13·8
Cows†	1,848,489	60·9
Sheep	307,645	10·1
Goats	42,015	1·4
Pigs	258,465	8·5
Poultry	159,003	5·2
Total tonnage	3,034,517	

* Reichsministerium für Ernährung und Landwirtschaft, *Berichte über Landwirtschaft*, p. 43.
† In the general category of cows, dairy cows accounted for 1,387,584 tons or 45·7 per cent fodder units.

TABLE 16. *Norway's Annual Fodder Requirements**

Types of fodder	Fodder units	
	Tons	%
Hay and straw	1,385,306	45·6
Root crops, potatoes, and silage	171,244	5·6
Domestic fodder grains and legumes	160,000	5·3
Skim milk	40,000	1·3
Herring and fish meal	35,000	1·2
Imported fodder	417,006	13·7
Heathland	828,270	27·3
Total tonnage	3,036,826	

* Reichsministerium für Ernährung und Landwirtschaft, *Berichte über Landwirtschaft*, p. 43.

[1] Reichsministerium für Ernährung und Landwirtschaft, *Berichte über Landwirtschaft*, p. 111.   [2] Ibid., p. 121.   [3] Ibid., p. 145.

On the whole Tables 15 and 16 indicate that it was the larger animals that were mainly responsible for the high consumption of fodder. But the size of the fodder input is no real indication of its cost. Poultry was dependent on more expensive imported fodders as also, to a less extent, were pigs. The insistence with which the German authorities were to pursue their plan of increasing the stock of sheep in Norway at the expense of other animals is also explicable on the basis of the information in tables; sheep were less demanding on imports than all livestock except pigs.

Norway was no more self-sufficient in animal products than she was in arable products. The consumption of milk and milk products and grain together accounted, on a calorific basis, for about a half of normal consumption. But the variety of the diet in Norway would have been quite insufficient had Norway been forced to rely on domestic food production. That is to say that, on a purely calorific calculation, if the Norwegians had eaten all their own fish instead of exporting it they could, technically, have been fed. But even this was no use as a basis for German planning after the occupation, for Norway's fish exports were regarded as vital to the welfare of the whole *Großraumwirtschaft*. Technically, Norway was self-sufficient in proteins and fats and needed only to import carbohydrates. In reality the situation with regard to fats was very different and the incorporation of Norway into the *Großraumwirtschaft* sharply exacerbated one of the most acute of Germany's supply problems.

Norway's apparent export surplus of fats was entirely based on the whaling industry. Most of the whale oil never arrived in Norway but was carried straight to foreign ports. It was a high-grade fat fetching a good price on the export market and in its stead Norway imported large quantities of cheaper vegetable fats to serve as the basis for soap and margarine production. In an average year Norway's imports of fats were only just below 200,000 tons. In war this exchange could not take place; the whales could not be caught and in any case the imports were not available.

Even after seven years of National Socialist government Germany was still dependent on foreign supply for about 44 per cent of her total fat requirements. As a consequence of the extension of German rule to the rest of the continent and of the imposition of the fascist trading system, in 1941–2 the share of calories contributed to the European food budget by edible fats had fallen from 13·5 to 9·5 per cent.[1] After 1936 Germany began to build up her whaling fleet by hiring Norwegian crews and ships and greatly increased her share in whale-oil output. At the same time about 100,000 tons of the whale oil produced by Norwegian ships was sold to Germany.[2] The elimination of whaling on any serious scale after 1939

[1] K. Brandt, *Fats and Oils in the War*, War–Peace Pamphlets No. 2, Food Research Institute, Stanford University (Stanford, 1943), p. 30.

[2] Idem, *The German Fat Plan and its Economic Setting*, Fats and Oils Studies No. 6, Food Research Institute, Stanford University (Stanford, 1938), p. 290.

was therefore not only a serious blow to Norway's food supply but to that of Germany as well. It made Norway dependent on Germany for a commodity which was in particularly short supply in the *Großraumwirtschaft* as a whole. Although the general level of consumption of fats in Norway before the war was rather higher than that in most west European countries this was in part due to the northerly climate.

Bearing in mind that the fats actually consumed in Norway were imported it can be said that with a 'normal' consumption of calories Norway imported foodstuffs corresponding to about 43 per cent of the total calorific consumption.[1] None of the pre-war emergency plans drawn up by the Government Dietary Committee ever considered the case when Norway would be completely severed from all foreign supply. No matter how much the domestic production and the consumption of fish, milk, potatoes, and other vegetables were increased there was no overcoming the final dependence on three imports in particular, bread grain, fodder, and sugar. On an average in the thirties about 800,000 tons of grain and fodder and 100,000 tons of sugar and syrup were imported annually. Bread-grain production could be increased domestically, but only at the expense of a proportionately greater reduction in the fodder crop. Sugar had to be imported. It was therefore only possible to alleviate Norway's dependence on imported food, not to eradicate it. No agricultural policy, however favourable to the Norwegian peasantry, would change the fact that in annexing Norway the *Großraumwirtschaft* had annexed an area which it had to supply with scarce foodstuffs in difficult circumstances. Of the 259 million kroner value of Norwegian imports from Germany in 1939 only 3·1 million kroner were represented by luxury goods, drinks, foodstuffs, tobacco, and fat.

In spite of government encouragement to food producers the basic problems of a peasant agriculture remained unresolved, especially as the peasant's other main products, wood and fish, were sold on an unfavourable international market. A heavy weight of rural indebtedness bore down on most cultivators. The Storting attempted to alleviate this burden by its laws of 1932. The volume of debt was written down to the value of the holding and the cultivator received from a special loan-bank a credit for reconstruction to the value of 30 per cent of his holding. The credit was free of interest for the first three years of its term and was subsequently subject to interest at 3 per cent. The original creditor was obliged to renounce interest for a five-year period and his rate of interest in the subsequent period was restricted by law.

The success of this legislation is difficult to measure as it was overtaken by events after 1940. The gross assets of farmers rose by 150 million kroner from January 1932 to January 1940. The part played in their

---

[1] K. Evang, 'Norway's Nutrition Problem', mimeograph (London, 1942).

composition by livestock and equipment rose over the same period from 12·2 per cent to 16 per cent, while the relationship of the size of their over-all debt to those assets declined by 5 per cent.[1] But even in 1940 only 11·7 per cent of farmers were free from debt. Sixty-six per cent of all farmers were still indebted to more than 30 per cent of their assets. They had 62·7 per cent of the gross total assets of cultivators and were responsible for 89 per cent of the total agricultural debt.[2] Twenty per cent of the farms were in debt for between half and three-quarters of their total value.

Both forestry and fishing were generally under-capitalized and for this reason, in spite of the abundance of coniferous timber and the seas which teemed with fish, both found it difficult to compete internationally. Unlike that of most European countries the central government had retained little control over the national forests. About 13 per cent of the total area of forest was state-owned. A lot of this national forest was either polar forest or in areas where transport was difficult due to the shortage of labour. Two and a half per cent of the total forest was former state forest now purchased by exploiting companies but under such terms that the state retained some controlling rights. Three per cent was owned by the parishes. The remaining forest, well over 80 per cent, was privately owned. Sixty-one per cent was owned by peasants, divided between over 200,000 separate owners. The average size of a peasant holding of forest was merely 23 hectares.[3] This pattern of division also meant that the state forestry service was rudimentary and that exploitation was haphazard. Some steps had been taken by a law of February 1932 to control felling more closely through a regional inspectorate and Local Forestry Boards, but it did little more than tinker with the problem which was deeply rooted in Norwegian social organization.

About one-fifth of the total quantity of wood felled was used for domestic fuel. Of the rest part went to sawmills to be exported as sawn timber but the larger part went as raw material to industries based on wood. The establishment of the first mechanical sawmill in Norway in 1860 had been followed in the space of six years by the establishment of the first wood-pulp plant and within fourteen years by the first sulphate cellulose plant. The sulphite process soon followed and Norway developed an important complex of paper and cellulose industries based on a raw material still largely in the control of peasant farmers. The inexactness of statistical information on timber felling, due to the large number of owners, and the lack of real central control, means that the final consumers of felled wood

[1] Statistisk Sentralbyrå, *Bøndenes bruttoformue og gjeld*, Norges offisielle statistikk, xi. 183 (Oslo, 1949).
[2] Ibid., p. 23, 'Antall bønder, deres bruttoformue og gjeld delt etter gjeldprosenten'.
[3] H. Lufft, *Die Wirtschaft Dänemarks und Norwegens*, p. 109.

are not easily identified. In the two years before the war, for which reasonably good statistical information is available, the proportion of felled coniferous timber going to sawmills varied between 33 per cent and 52 per cent of the total. In 1937–8 relatively high prices were offered for wood pulp, cellulose, and paper and relatively low prices for the same products in 1938–9. Making allowance for the vagueness of statistics on felling, the average annual quantity of timber felled over the period 1936–7 to 1940–1 was about 9,836,000 cubic metres.[1] This very large quantity was therefore being felled mostly by ill-paid casual seasonal labour, for whom this was a regular method of eking out agricultural incomes, or by small farmers themselves. Once the occupation brought a state of full employment to Norway, and a fairly profitable market for peasant farmers, very serious difficulties in Norwegian forestry were inevitable and, as a consequence, in all those important industries which depended on a constant wood supply.

If forestry was an ill-paid undertaking fishing was scarcely better. A host of small entrepreneurs with little capital eked out their income from other sources by fishing the rich waters off the coast. In the years 1931–4 the price per ton of fish caught was roughly 50 kroner, in Germany it was 150 kroner, in Britain 210 kroner.[2] Only a small part of this discrepancy can be explained by the distance of Norway from the world markets and the small size of her domestic market. Lack of capital meant that Norwegian fishermen were unable to escape from selling their more traditional cheaper products. At a time when other countries were steadily increasing the proportion of the total catch sold as fresh fish Norway was unable to do the same. In spite of this the fishing industry played a vital part in the functioning of the whole economy, as it had done throughout the country's history.[3]

The yearly catch of fish, about 1 million tons, was as large as that of almost any other country in the world, the *per capita* catch far higher than other lands. In 1939 fish were almost one-quarter of the total value of all Norwegian exports. About a quarter of a million people derived their income mainly from fishing and the fish-processing industry, the actual number employed as fishermen about 125,000. Over half the fishermen were from north Norway and a very high proportion of the total catch came from those remote provinces.

Herring and codfish were the most important catch, herring most important for their quantity and prevalence, codfish for their value. The

---

[1] Statistik Sentralbyrå, *Skogavvirking 1936/37–1945/46*, Norges offisielle statistikk, xi, 42 (Oslo, 1950).

[2] M. Horn, *Norwegen zwischen Krieg und Frieden* (Innsbruck, 1941), p. 125.

[3] See, for example, R. Østensjø, 'The Spring Herring Fishing and the Industrial Revolution in Western Norway in the Nineteenth Century', in *Scandinavian Economic History Review*, xi (1963).

so-called 'small herring' were found throughout the year in great numbers in inshore waters. 'Spring herring' and 'winter herring' were caught in larger shoals with more definite migratory habits.[1] In addition sprats (brisling) were taken in large numbers in Oslo Fjord and the fjords between Bergen and Stavanger. The deep-sea fishing industry for codfish had also its seasonal aspect. Its most remarkable feature was the great Lofoten fishery which coincided with the arrival of the cod in the Westfjord. The herring catch tended to average between 600,000 tons and 700,000 tons annually, the catch of codfish between 200,000 tons and 250,000 tons. Such averages hide the important fact that in both cases the general trend of the catches had been downwards for a long time.

In both cases the rate of return to the fisherman depended on the proportion of fresh fish to the total catch which could be marketed. The price paid for fish packed in ice remained relatively high while the prices paid for salted, dried, or tinned fish underwent a long and slow decline, no doubt attributable to the gradual improvement of diet in Europe. Since salted herring and dried fish, both *klippfisk* and *stockfisk*, had been a staple of the export trade for centuries, the problem was one of fundamental long-term adjustment to a changing international market. The importance of that international market was overriding. About one-third of the catch of cod was exported and well over half the herring catch. Even in 1937, as may be seen from Table 7, much less than half of the herring exported were exported as fresh fish. The rest were exported either as salted herring, herring meal for use as fertilizer, or tinned herring, brisling, or sild. With codfish the problem was more acute still; less than one-fifth of the sales were sales of fresh or frozen fish. Both *klippfisk* and *stockfisk* each accounted for a greater total weight of sales, although the price paid for each of these products scarcely justified the labour of the men or the expenditure on the boats. *Stockfisk*, dried on a wooden frame and unsalted, found their main market amongst consumers with low incomes in Italy and West Africa; *klippfisk*, dried on the rocks and salted, found more favour in Portugal, Spain, and South America. The three main markets for these products, apart from Italy, were West Africa, which imported 9,525 tons in 1938, Cuba, which imported 2,283 tons, and Argentina, which imported 2,191 tons.[2] All these markets were closed in 1940, making an increase in the proportion of cod sold as fresh fish an even more compelling necessity. Tinned fish consisted mostly of brisling, small herring, and sild. In this case the problem of export markets after the occupation was equally present; the United States and Britain had usually taken over half the total quantity of tinned fish exported. The Norwegian domestic market

[1] 'Winter herring' (*storsild*) were caught from January to April and were usually larger than 'spring herring' (*vårsild*).
[2] Statistisk Sentralbyrå, *Norges handel*, 1938.

was too small to affect this position in any material way; the fishing industry and its associated trades had been developed by the demands of foreign consumers.

Looking back to the First World War, Norway may have felt less apprehensive about the disruption to her fish trade. From the start of that war there had been an increasing demand for Norwegian fish bringing greater and greater prosperity to the fishermen. Germany's need being the greater the prices offered by her buyers in 1915 were higher. They were buying the fish 'off the hook' and by-passing the Norwegian dealers.[1] Even in peacetime conditions Germany was the most important purchaser of fresh fish. Certain branches of the export trade were less susceptible to disruption. Salted herring were widely sold but the two main purchasers were Sweden and Poland. Italy was the main buyer of other salted fish. The herring-meal export was concentrated almost entirely on Germany where it went some way to alleviate the acute fertilizer shortages caused by National Socialist policy. There existed therefore a certain coincidence of interest between Norway and Germany. Both parties stood to gain from a greater quantity of fresh fish being exported. The geographical character of the Norwegian fishing industry was such that this could only be achieved by the installation of freezing plant in some of the more remote towns in north Norway. As far as both the Norwegian and German administrations were concerned this had to be accompanied by a reorganization of the fishing industry.

TABLE 17. *Quantities of Fish and Fish Products Exported from Norway**

(000 tons)

Item	1929	1933	1935	1936	1937	1938	1939
Fresh herring	121·0	110·7	98·4	102·4	96·3	96·1	121·5
Other fresh fish	19·0	26·3	24·1	26·7	28·3	23·8	32·6
Stockfisk	38·1	26·5	22·0	19·8	33·8	{67.4	{55·6
Klippfisk	48·5	32·6	35·0	36·1	38·6		
Salted herring	95·4	60·4	35·2	54·0	48·8	33·6	38·5
Other salted fish	13·3	5·7	4·7	2·6	8·5	5·9	10·8
Tinned fish	36·8	..	34·7	37·8	36·3	26·4	36·1
Herring meal and fish meal	82·2	85·5	64·3	73·9	43·1	79·3	55·1

* Statistisk Sentralbyrå, *Norges handel*, Norges offisielle statistikk, viii. 138; ix. 35; ix. 86; ix. 114; ix. 138; ix. 173; ix. 198.

In addition to the very large fishing industry Norway had also developed the largest whaling industry in the world. After the international regulation

[1] O. Riste, *The Neutral Ally*, p. 97.

of the whaling trade Norway was left with the largest share. The whales were caught in the Antarctic by annual expeditions and treated by floating whaling factories. Of the thirty-six factories in 1938–9 thirteen were Norwegian.[1] The most important product was whale oil, a commodity which at the time of the First World War had been a low-grade industrial fat but, due to changes in technology, in particular the perfection of the hardening process, had become a highly priced constituent of margarine. The total production in 1937–8 was 168,000 tons, worth 44,600,000 kroner. After 1940 this valuable source of income was no longer available.

Apart from fish and wood all other Norwegian exports, except metal ores, were the result of modern developments. And even in the case of metal ores the modern development had quite eclipsed the traditional mining activities. Any survey of Norwegian industry is closely related to a study of the country's foreign trade. In 1938, 58·5 per cent of the total industrial share capital was in plant working almost entirely for export.[2] About a third of the net value of industrial production was exported. By the side of the industries working for the export market there existed consumer-goods industries catering mostly for the demand of the domestic market. They seldom completely satisfied domestic demand and the pattern of Norwegian industry was thus a curious mixture of extremely specialized modern manufacturing industry and the extractive industries more associated with underdeveloped economies. This pattern had been created by international demand for many of the more highly specialized industries had been sited in Norway by foreign capital to take advantage of the extremely cheap electric current made available through the exploitation of the country's most abundantly available resource, water power. The unimportance of the domestic market to Norwegian manufacturers is further emphasized by the extremely high ratio of production goods to consumer goods in total industrial production. Tables 18 and 19 show the relative importance of the different branches of industrial production.

The reserves of metal ores in Norway were of particular interest to the occupying power because in some cases they had already formed an important part of German supply for some time and because in other cases they were of especial value to the war economy. The development of the remote arctic mines of Sydvaranger had led to a great increase in the production of iron ore during the inter-war period. The output in 1938, almost $1\frac{1}{2}$ million tons, was half as high again as that in 1929. Although Norway had an iron industry of her own almost the whole of her iron ore output was exported. The Sydvaranger ores were of very low ferrous content, about 34 per cent, and needed to be enriched before using. Their

[1] K. Brandt, *Whaling and Whale Oil during World War II*, War–Peace Pamphlet, No. 11, Food Research Institute (Stanford, 1948).
[2] Reichskontor der Nordischen Gesellschaft, *Deutschland und der Norden*, p. 113.

TABLE 18. *Number of Employed Persons, Hours Worked, and Net Value of Production in Norwegian Industry, 1937 and 1938**

Branch of industry	Number employed		Hours worked		Net production value	
	1937	1938	1937	1938	1937	1938
	(000)		(00,000)		(00,000 kroner)	
Ore and metal production	11·5	12·4	26·6	28·8	102·3	111·8
Iron and metal industries	36·6	37·5	82·7	84·0	212·4	238·0
Chemical industry	4·3	4·2	9·8	9·9	67·4	76·7
Wood industry	12·6	12·7	27·5	27·3	53·9	49·3
Wooden goods and paper industry	16·2	15·0	39·3	33·5	121·2	95·3
Textile and clothing industry	26·5	26·5	57·2	55·2	110·2	110·1
Foodstuffs industry	16·2	16·0	31·8	31·3	216·8	225·2
Other industries:						
Earth and stone industries / Oil and fat / Electricity and gas / Leather and rubber / Bookbinding and printing	19·6	19·8	44·2	43·2	131·7	137·3
Industry totals	143·5	144·1	319·3	313·2	1,015·9	1,043·7

* Statistisk Sentralbyrå, *Norges industri, 1938, 1939,* Norges offisielle statistikk, ix. 188; x. 16.

TABLE 19. *Value of Paid-up Share Capital in some Branches of Norwegian Industry, 1937**

(00,000 kroner)

Industry	Value of share capital
Chemical industry	199·0
Wood pulp, cellulose, and paper	144·6
Mining and smelting	134·8
Foodstuffs	98·3
Iron and metal industries	93·3
Textile industry	43·4

* F.D. 5347/45, I. G. Farben, 'Wirtschaftsbericht Norwegen'.

advantage was their low phosphorous content and their accessibility from the sea. Of the total iron-ore exports in 1939, 1,182,125 tons, 74 per cent went to Germany. No other consumer was of any real importance. Although British and French capital had played a part in developing the older ore fields, the Sydvaranger field, whose production came to eclipse all others, had been developed by German capital for the German steel industry. On the eve of the war Vereinigte Stahlwerke still owned 43 per cent of the capital. The ore was exported from Kirkenes and joined the stream of iron-ore traffic down the Norwegian coast from Narvik to the Rhine.

The other iron-ore mines were all much smaller. The second largest, that of Fosdalens Bergverks A/S, near to Malm in Nord-Trøndelag, also had some German capital. It produced a much higher-grade ore with about 53 per cent ferrous content and employed about 300 workers compared to the 1,500 workers of Sydvaranger. The ore exported to Britain was produced exclusively by one company, the British-owned Dunderland Iron Ore Co. near Mo i Rana in Nordland whose whole production was shipped to the United Kingdom. There were many other deposits mined but all of them of little significance. The domestic iron industry drew its supply from the Rødsand mines at Nesset near Oslo, which was owned by the largest iron works, Christiania Spigerverk, and occasionally from the Søfestad mines in Nissedal in Telemark whose ownership was divided between German steel companies and the Norwegian state. The small Titania mines in Sogndal in Rogaland were more renowned for the type of ore they produced which was of particular rarity because of its high titanium content.

It will have been remarked that only about 100,000 tons of ore were retained in the country for iron manufacture there. The history of the Norwegian iron industry reflects sharply the advantages and disadvantages of so open an economy. Until the mid nineteenth century iron production based on the charcoal smelting process continued to increase in Norway. It was almost entirely eliminated in a few years by competition from cheap Bessemer steel from other European countries. In the early twentieth century iron production began again to increase, this time based on specialized electrical smelting processes. In 1939 the production of iron was 43,599 tons. This quantity would have sufficed to meet about one-third of the domestic demand but in fact over two-thirds of it was exported, mainly high-grade electro-iron, while the domestic consumption was met by the import of inferior grades. There were two firms engaged in this production, but much the most important was the Christiania Spigerverk in Oslo. In fact plans for the erection of a large steel works of a more conventional kind in the north of the country had been the subject of political discussion for some time. The minimum estimated cost of such a project, 40 million kroner, had always proved a deterrent although the weakness of the economy in the event of another European war continued to lend strength to the arguments of those who wished to create the works. The plans disappeared from sight and all discussion became pointless with the occupation.[1] The responsiveness of the iron industry to international opportunities and the extraordinarily complicated nature of its trading operations may be seen in Table 20.

TABLE 20. *Import and Export of Ores and Iron Manufactures in Norway**

Items	Imports				Exports			
	1937		1938		1937		1938	
	Amount	Total	Amount	Total	Amount	Total	Amount	Total
	(00,000 kroner)				(00,000 kroner)			
Manganese ore	8·0		8·9					
Chrome ore	3·0	11·0	4·8	13·7	..		..	
Iron ore	..		..		14·6		25·8	
Iron pyrites	..		..		11·9		11·5	
Abbrände	..		..		0·7	27·2	0·6	37·9
Iron and steel	50·9		32·3		7·4		9·2	
Iron alloys	0·5	51·4	0·4	32·7	43·7	51·1	31·8	41·0
Scrap	0·3		1·0		1·0		0·9	
Iron and steel goods	79·9	80·2	65·7	66·7	8·7	9·7	7·1	8·0
Totals		142·6		113·1		88·0		86·9

* Statistisk Sentralbyrå, *Norges handel*, Norges offisielle statistikk, ix. 138; ix. 173.

It will be seen from Table 20 that Norway's export of iron pyrites was scarcely less important than her export of iron ore. Although the origins of this export lay in the demand from large consumers of sulphuric acid and sulphur the deposits were also suitable for utilization as a source of raw material for iron. By roasting the pyrites to rid it of sulphur, iron oxide could be produced for the manufacture of pig-iron. Towards the end of the occupation the pyrites deposits became of extreme importance to Germany for this purpose. Norway produced over 1 million tons of pyrites a year in the two years before the occupation, of which only a small part was used in the domestic production of sulphur. Almost 70 per cent of the output was directly exported from the three main mining areas Haugesund, Trondheim, and Narvik. Most of it went to Germany and Sweden; 260,914 tons and 181,040 tons respectively in 1939.

Almost the whole of the quantity retained in Norway was turned into sulphur at the Orkla smelting works at Thamshavn near Trondheim. About 90 per cent of the sulphur produced was also exported mainly to

[1] A similar project was carried out at the end of the war when Norsk Jernverk was created at Mo i Rana. It would appear that the deciding factor for building the works was not merely the events of the war but also the arrival of free plant from Germany as reparations.

Finland and Sweden. For Germany the pyrites deposits had a double importance beyond their ultimate potential as a source of iron. They were a source of sulphur and a potential source of copper. In the First World War the most serious of the disputes between the British and Norwegian governments had come as the result of the British attempt to stop the export of Norwegian pyrites to Germany whether cupriferous or not.[1] Sulphur was an important raw material in the munitions industry and copper a valuable component of many munitions. The only real change in this situation since 1918 had been the increased importance of sulphur as a hardening agent in the synthetic-rubber industry. In both capacities, therefore, pyrites was of great importance to Germany, but the particularly marked shortages of copper which occurred in the rearmament boom persuaded German planners that it would be no bad thing if more of the Norwegian production could be diverted in that direction. The Orkla works produced about 18,000 tons of copper annually, about 5,000 tons from pyrites with a high copper content. As a part of greater-German copper production the Orkla smelting works would not be wholly insignificant although the composition and provenance of its raw materials, and the destination of its exports, would need to be altered. There were many other copper-ore mines in Norway but the production of copper from pyrites had led to the closing of them all apart from the state-owned Røros mine in Osterdal.

The smelting operations carried out at the Orkla works were equalled in scale by those at the Eitrheim works of the Norwegian Zinc Company at Odda in Hardaland. Both works were dependent on cheap electric current although Eitrheim, like Orkla, also partly used domestic raw materials, in this case from the Sulitjelma zinc-ore mines on the Swedish frontier east of Bodo. The Eitrheim smelters once again repeat the pattern of the Norwegian economy for the domestic mines supplied them with roughly 6,500 tons of zinc concentrate compared to 100,000 tons of zinc ore imported annually from Spain, Yugoslavia, Newfoundland, Mexico, and Argentina. As in other cases the zinc-smelting industry, although so heavily dependent on imported raw materials, produced for an international rather than a domestic market. Germany was the main consumer with France and Sweden also being large purchasers. The origin of both the Orkla and Eitrheim works was the availability of electric power.

The very small quantities of nickel ore mined had laid the origins of the electrolytic production of nickel in the town of Kristiansand and the subsequent varied development of electrical smelting there. In 1929 Canadian capital had established the Falconbridge works which, even more than the Orkla or Eitrheim works, could stand as the epitome of Norway's industrial economy. The works remained the most modern and efficient

[1] O. Riste, *The Neutral Ally*, pp. 112 ff.

plant of its kind in the world to the outbreak of war. The small nickel-ore mines in Norway, although partly responsible for the location of the works, ceased to have much significance. Ninety per cent of the input came as nickel mat from Canada and the works were really an extension of the Canadian nickel industry to a location where the cost of production was lower and whence certain export markets could more easily be reached. The Evje nickel mine near Kristiansand was rapidly nearing exhaustion. The consequence for Germany was that if she were to use the excellent Falconbridge facilities for the production of a metal so extremely valuable in a war economy she would most probably have to reopen the older Norwegian nickel mines or supply Norway from elsewhere.

The same complex of electrolytic processes had given rise to an important industry manufacturing a range of specialized ferrous alloys, mainly from imported materials. The main raw materials, besides iron ore, were manganese ore and chromium ore. Over 100,000 tons of manganese ore were imported in each of the two years before the war, from the U.S.S.R. and from the Gold Coast. The larger part went to the manufacture of ferro-manganese for export. Chromium-ore imports, 50,000 tons in 1938 and 19,600 tons in 1939, came from Turkey and Rhodesia and were used for the manufacture of ferrochrome. In this case Norway was directly competing with Germany for scarce raw materials but at the same time directing a large part of her export of these strategically valuable products back to Germany. The export trade in these ferrous alloys may be seen from Table 21. It depended, of course, on the freedom to import their constituents.

One branch of this complex of metal industries dependent on electric power, the aluminium industry, far surpassed all others both in peacetime importance and in its subsequent importance in the war. The manufacture of aluminium began in 1906 when the British Aluminium Company opened a subsidiary works on Stangfjord in Sogn og Fjordane. One year later they took over another works being built at Vikeland near Kristiansand by the Anglo-Norwegian Aluminium Company. The incentive for foreign capital to settle in Norway was once again the cheapness of hydro-electric power in an industry where the price of electricity was so large a constituent of the final cost. Both works were dependent on power stations also created by foreign capital. In 1912 a Norwegian company, Det Norske Nitrid A/S, was created with the intention of producing aluminium nitride, an intention soon abandoned in favour of aluminium itself. The company had two works, in Tyssedal in Hardaland and at Eydehavn in Aust Agder with a joint annual capacity of 16,000 tons production. The two earlier works remained smaller; Vikeland had an annual production capacity of 4,000 tons, Stangfjord of 1,000 tons. The Aluminium Company of Canada created through a subsidiary company the works at Høyanger on the

TABLE 21. *Export of Ferrous Alloys from Norway, 1938 and 1939*[*]

(tons)

Alloy	1938						1939					
	Total export	Germany	Britain	Belgium	Sweden	United States	Total export	Germany	Britain	Belgium	Sweden	United States
Ferrosilicon	32,900	12,600	14,300	1,800	..	..	41,000	13,100	16,600	3,300	..	..
Ferrochrome	11,600	4,300	4,200	..	1,400	..	15,700	4,400	7,400	..	2,100	..
Ferro-manganese	37,600	900	..	10,900	3,900	12,700	67,400	100	..	30,800	3,700	23,200
Ferrosilico-manganese	12,900	4,600	6,100	..	..	..	22,300	5,900	11,600	..	..	..
Other alloys	6,200	..	..	..	..	..	400	..	..	..	..	..
Totals	101,200						146,800					

[*] Statistisk Sentralbyrå, *Norges handel*, Norges offisielle statistikk, ix. 138; ix. 173.

THE NATURE OF THE NORWEGIAN ECONOMY

Sognfjord in Sogn og Fjordane with an annual capacity of 9,000 tons. Finally, in 1927 the Haugvik Smelterverk, also with a capacity of 9,000 tons, was founded at Glomfjord in Nordland.

The industry was almost entirely a producer of finished aluminium. It was heavily dependent on imports, not only for the raw material, bauxite, but also for the intermediate stage of manufacture, alumina. The smelters were all accessible by sea and the whole industry could fairly be categorized as a series of extensions of foreign aluminium industries into Norway so that they might complete the final stage of manufacture more cheaply, the opposite state of affairs to the usual charge made against economic imperialism. The importance of aluminium grew very rapidly in the 1930s, especially in Germany as a result of the rearmament drive. The output of the major industrial countries easily eclipsed Norway's 39,000 tons per annum potential capacity, but the factors that had induced foreign capital to create the industry were not changed by the occupation while the need for aluminium for aeroplane production increased. Of all Norwegian assets it was the one most coveted by Germany before the invasion and most clearly destined to play an important role in the new Europe.

The Høyanger works was the only smelting plant to have an alumina plant also.[1] The plant produced about 18,000 tons of alumina a year, just sufficient for the needs of Høyanger alone. Even there the industry was dependent on bauxite imports. In 1939 Norway imported 32,696 tons of bauxite and 45,639 tons of alumina. The aluminium produced was sold very widely. Japan had come to be the largest importer in the 1930s with Britain not far behind but the network of this trade covered the whole world in a most complex mesh. German plans therefore could only be put into practice by a complicated rearrangement of these lines of supply and distribution.

A certain number of rarer metallic ores found in Norway were also of importance to Germany. This was particularly the case with the molybdenum ore mined in the Knaben mine in Fjotland in Vest Agder. Although this mine produced only 3 to 4 per cent of the world's output this was almost the whole of the output in the German sphere of influence, 95 per cent of the world's supply coming from the United States and Mexico. There was one other very small Norwegian mine in operation near Bodo. The Knaben mine's output had long been divided between Germany and Sweden. Once German strategic plans miscarried and stockpiles of molybdenum began to diminish this one Norwegian mine was to be literally the only place from which the stockpiles could be effectively replenished and it came to have a stratetic importance out of all proportion to its size. The rutile deposits at Sogndal in Rogaland came to have an almost equally dramatic strategic role at the very end of the war. Rutile,

[1] Alumina is processed ore, the intermediate stage in the manufacture of aluminium.

the ore of titanium, had been mined only in Norway until the discoveries in Virginia at the start of the twentieth century.

The other major Norwegian exporting industries were those based on wood and chemicals, especially nitrogenous fertilizer. Only about a quarter of the wood consumed by Norwegian sawmills was for export. The saw-milling industry embraced as many as 880 firms with 14,000 workers. The more advanced wood-processing industries had few firms, employed 16,500 workers, and the annual value of their production was almost twice as great. The total annual output of wood pulp in 1938 was 888,870 tons (damp weight). The output of cellulose in the same year was 455,531 tons. It was mainly the pull of the British market that had created the wood-pulp industry and up to the occupation over 400,000 tons of pulp were exported annually to Britain. France and Belgium were the only other customers of any importance. There existed in Norway a very considerable industry and export trade which was not connected in any way with demand from Germany and which had no particular value as far as the *Großraumwirt-schaft* was concerned. The export of cellulose was more widely distributed although Britain and the United States were much larger purchasers than other nations. Nor did German demand have any greater part to play in the Norwegian paper and cardboard industries, whose annual production in 1938 amounted to 365,677 tons. Thus integration into the *Großraum-wirtschaft* threatened disaster to the most valuable of all Norway's ex-ports. For the total value of exports of wood and wood products in 1939 was 170 million kroner, almost 22 per cent of the total value of all exports.

Quite the opposite was the case with the Norwegian chemical and fertilizer industry. This industry had developed at a very early stage in Norway, again largely because of the availability of cheap electrical power. It was mainly associated with the most important of all Norway's industrial complexes, the Rjukan factories of Norsk Hydro-Elektrisk Kvaelstof A/S. These works had been created in 1905 through the discovery by Birkeland and Eyde of a method of fixing nitrogen by the generation of extremely high temperatures through the use of an electric arc. Subsequently the electrical works became amongst the largest in the world. Their chief product was a fertilizer, nitrate of lime, but they also produced a wide variety of other nitrogenous products, nitrate of soda, nitrate of ammonia, carbide, cyanamide, and silicum-carbide. 'Norges Salpeter' became the most sought-after high-grade fertilizer in international commerce. The total value of production of this and the other forms of nitrogeneous fertilizer was 61 million kroner in 1938. The original fertilizer plant and power stations at Rjukan had been amplified by developments elsewhere so that Norsk Hydro operated two fertilizer plants in Telemark, at Notodden and Porsgrund. Close to the Rjukan works was developed the world's largest hydrogen-producing factory. This was to become in the war the only plant capable of producing heavy water for Germany.[1]

These developments, no matter how important the role of Norwegian inventors, were no less dependent on foreign capital than the rest of Norway's industry. The Birkeland process for fixing nitrogen had been superseded in the inter-war period by the Haber-Bosch process developed in Germany by I. G. Farben and in 1928 Norsk Hydro, by an agreement with I. G. Farben, had leased patent rights on the new process. The majority of the share capital in 1939 was in the hands of the French chemical combine Établissements Kuhlmann, a firm closely associated with I. G. Farben in the chemical cartel. A further quarter of the share capital was directly owned by I. G. Farben itself. The only other producer of fertilizer and the only other chemical plant of any special significance in wartime was Odda Smeltverk. This belonged almost entirely to the British Oxygen Company. Its annual production amounted to 27,600 tons of calcium cyanamide and 30,400 tons of calcium carbide. Calcium carbide production was exported almost in its entirety to Britain, calcium cyanamide was exported principally to the Netherlands, Belgium, Britain, and Sweden. Of the more important fertilizers over 400,000 tons of calcium nitrate were exported in 1939, mainly to Denmark, Sweden, and the United States.

Little more needs to be said about the Norwegian manufacturing industry. The essential points are all too clear. It was highly dependent on international trade for the import of its raw materials and for its sales. Nor was this dependence particularly on trade with Germany or with countries in the German orbit. Norway had good industrial reasons to remain so firmly a part of the sterling bloc in the 1930s. To clinch the matter it is worth drawing attention to the almost total dependence on two other imports, crude oil and coal. The consumption of oil fuels was small enough, due to the small size of the population, not to cause the anxiety it caused elsewhere. Nevertheless every drop was imported. There was one refinery, set up near to Oslo by American capital to refine crude oil imported directly from Peru and Colombia. The annual consumption of benzine by road transport was 180,000 tons. The consumption of diesel oil and fuel oil was about 300,000 tons annually. To this should be added a product of an equally vital quality, the so-called 'solar-oil' which fuelled the fishing fleets in every village of western Norway.

No coal was mined on the Norwegian mainland. The arctic island of Spitzbergen (Svålbard) had good deposits which could only be exploited under most difficult conditions. Only between May and October could the coal mined there be transported to Norway. Two firms, Norwegian and

---

[1] D. Irving, *The Virus House: Germany's Atomic Research and Allied Counter-Measures* (London, 1967), contains a history of this development.

Russian, mined between 600,000 and 700,000 tons of coal there a year in the 1930s, of which about 300,000 tons were sold in Norway. This sufficed to satisfy a little over 10 per cent of annual domestic demand. To sustain the Norwegian economy, therefore, a constant traffic in coal from Europe was essential; 2,269,849 tons were imported in 1938 and half a million tons more than this in 1939. In addition between 600,000 and 800,000 tons of coke a year were imported in the 1930s.

The most obvious shortcoming of German economic policy in the years before the war had been its failure to make any successful inroads into this coal trade to Norway. It was this as much as any other trade which was responsible for sustaining the percentage of Norwegian imports from the non-German area. The reason lay in the high price of German coal. The trade with Britain was governed not only by long-standing commercial ties but by a quota agreement under which the British supplied 70 per cent of Norway's coal imports. But after the fulfilment of that quota German coal was still losing ground to Polish coal in supplying the remainder. In general Germany supplied about 500,000 tons of total Norwegian coal and coke imports. One immediate result of the occupation therefore was to face Germany with the necessity of undertaking the whole of this supply, without which the economy could function only at a very low level. In spite of the high proportion of motor vessels in the Norwegian merchant fleet 39 per cent of total coal consumption was accounted for by shipping, especially the network of coastal shipping on which the country depended for its communications. The railway network, in spite of the cheapness of electric current, was almost entirely operated by steam engines. Without supplies of both coal and oil the Norwegian communications system would literally come to a standstill.

This was the more important because of the extreme importance of those communications in so large a country with so many isolated communities and where much industrial activity took place at great distances from the main European markets. The journey from northern Norway to Oslo is the equivalent of the journey from Oslo to Naples; neither the road nor railway systems reached so far and the two northern counties had to be provisioned either by water or through Sweden. Furthermore there were a very large number of communities only accessible by water. The activities of Norway's shipbuilders were closely related to the necessity of supplying coastal shipping and other small craft. There were about a hundred ship-building firms; only about a dozen had more than purely local importance. Four shipyards each employed over a thousand workers. The total output of ships in 1938 was 51,714 B.R.T., of which 13,063 B.R.T. were for foreign customers. This might be compared with the fact that in the same year Norway placed 249,653 B.R.T. of new orders for shipping in foreign yards, over 100,000 B.R.T. of which were placed in Germany. In 1939 the quantity of orders placed abroad was even higher. About three-fifths of the steel plate used for shipbuilding had to be imported from Germany, a further one-fifth from elsewhere. The maintenance of the vital coastal fleet ultimately depended on these supplies of foreign steel.

The railway system went only as far northwards as Mosjoen. Troms and Finnmark were without railways except for the fourteen miles of Swedish railway system from the frontier to Narvik. The total length of the whole Norwegian railway network was only just over 4,000 kilometres. Stavanger, the fourth largest town in the country, remained unconnected to the capital city by rail. The railway ran from there to Flekkefjord, but between that town and Kristiansand the south coast was not served by rail. Only 59 kilometres of the whole system were double-tracked. The deficiencies of the railway system were scarcely compensated by the road system, hampered as it was by the mountainous nature of the country and the harsh winters. The improvement both of road and rail networks became one of the primary objectives of German policy after the occupation.

There could never be any doubt that the incorporation of Norway into the *Großraumwirtschaft* in the short run was an economic disadvantage, unless the Norwegian population was to have its high living standards reduced to those of mere animal survival. The growth of the economy since the mid nineteenth century had been due to an extraordinary openness and responsiveness to the opportunities of the international market. By occupying small corners in international trade, and by allowing such considerations to dictate the type of industrial development which took place, Norway had been able to increase very steeply the incomes of her extremely small population (although these incomes were in fact most unequally distributed). The lack of restrictions on foreign capital and foreign capitalists, the readiness to depend entirely on foreign trade for even the most vital of supplies, the extreme reliance of manufacturing industry on export markets, the large amounts of people and capital employed in the trading sector of the economy, and the willingness to allow the course of domestic social development to be dictated by the circumstances of the international conjuncture, all made the Norwegian economy the antithesis of the German *Großraumwirtschaft*.

There were of course commodities available in Norway which could in particular respects enhance the autarkic nature of that *Großraumwirtschaft* were Norway to be incorporated. And some of these commodities had an especial significance in a war economy. But Tables 9 and 10 show that the balance of trade between Norway and the *Großraumwirtschaft* countries was much more passive than that between Norway and her other trading partners. A deficit in trade of 70 million kroner in 1933 developed into a deficit of 85 million kroner by 1938. The stockpiling of 1939 caused this to grow to 142 million kroner. Effectively, Norway paid for her valuable imports from Germany by her network of international trade and shipping services. How was she to pay after April 1940 when so much of this trade was lopped off, and when, due to that severance, the need for imports from Germany became much greater? The strategic issues involved dominated these economic questions in all German planning. The naval staff assumed that somehow Norway would be supplied, that German producers would somehow be able to fill the space left by the elimination of British supply and that the Norwegian economy would somehow soon adapt itself to the new opportunities of a different system.

But to respond to these new opportunities, if such there were, was to deny the whole force of the historical development of the Norwegian economy. That, of course, was precisely what Quisling wanted. As far as the National Socialist Party was concerned they underestimated the impact of these changes on Norway because they had no clear understanding of the essential differences between the development of their own country and of Norway. Whether ignorance is so good an excuse for Nasjonal Samling is doubtful. Say rather that their excuse was the reckless abandon of those who could tolerate the existing system no longer and knew they had to destroy it. Witness Quisling's first conversation with Hitler. 'He [Hitler] then asked: "Councillor Quisling, if you approach me for help do you know that England will declare war on you?" Quisling: "Certainly, I know that and reckon that at the same time Norway's trade will be destroyed." '[1]

[1] *Das politische Tagebuch Alfred Rosenbergs*, p. 94.

III

GERMAN PLANS FOR NORWAY

THE first few months of the occupation were a period of buoyant enthusiasm for the German administration. The difficulties anticipated from the immediate shock of the war were less severe than the officials of the Reichskommissariat had feared. In this period the necessary plans were laid to transform the Norwegian economy so that it might take its place in the new Europe. The contrast with German policy in France is most marked. In that country the essence of economic policy was that the French economy should be *useful* to the German war effort. Beyond that certain policies met with more favour from the occupiers than others. The Vichy government's attempts at strengthening the position of the French peasantry were applauded, the same government's economic relationships with other countries brought angry opposition. But these were secondary issues to that of the economic usefulness of France to the German war economy. In Norway the contrary was the case.

There could be no question of exploiting Norway in the way as varied an economy as the French could be exploited. It is true Norway was an occupied territory rather than an ally and thus liable to pay occupation costs, and that those occupation costs were proportionately even more swingeing than in France. But the total received in occupation costs was extremely small compared with the total received from France. Norway's passive trade balance with Germany could only be worsened by the invasion and the country had to be supplied to an extent that was never necessary in France. It was not merely on these economic grounds that policy in Norway and France was so different; they were but a reflection of political realities. Norway was to be bound indissolubly to the greater German Reich, autonomous perhaps, if the rule of Nasjonal Samling could be considered autonomy, but in no sense independent. No historic great power but a small state with a suitable racial composition, Norway was to be transformed from a bastion of liberalism to a bastion of Germandom and fascism.

All German economic plans for Norway should be seen in this light, as plans for a long-term transformation of the economy and of society. Plans for France were merely short-term expedients, to keep milking the economy until the end of the war or the signing of a peace treaty. Those events would then determine France's place in the New Order. Norway's place was never in doubt, from the moment of the occupation she was to be an integral part of that New Order.

After the initial military successes in the west, when the possibilities of a customs union involving the conquered western territories were still very much alive, Norway was considered to belong firmly within any such arrangement. According to the Economic Policy Committee of the Foreign Office Norway was to be treated more or less as though it were German territory.[1] The obstacle to creating such a union was the great difference in price levels and structures between Germany and the other west European economies. When, however, the projects for an immediate customs union faded into the background, those for an eventual one remained alive. On 8 August 1940 a customs union between Germany and Norway was still 'planned'.[2] Some indication of the nature of this planning may be gained from Dr. Baudisch's remarks at the Reichskommissariat conference on 18 September. 'Shortly a central contracts office would be founded through which all German contracts would be coordinated. In that way it should be possible to arrive at a comparable price structure. . . .'[3]

The plans for a customs union never got very far and were only the scheme of one particular section of the German administration. There was, certainly in the early stages of the occupation of the western territories, a different view also present in sections of the German administration. Göring, for example, advocated a much more consciously fascist policy of ruthless exploitation in which the occupied territories were seen as sources of raw materials and labour, quarries from which Germany might take whatever she wanted for her own war effort. But whether the New Order was to be shaped by German businessmen in the image of a common market subjected entirely to German economic and political domination or in the image of a fascist bloc rejecting the ultimate economic aspirations of other western societies (and the issue between these two possibilities was never entirely settled in the course of the war), from the point of view of Norway's inclusion in the final plans it made no difference. Norway's economic fate depended on two things. Firstly it depended on the outcome of the war and, secondly, if Germany were the victor, it depended on who controlled the destiny of the German revolution.

That Norway was considered as essential to the purely fascist conception of the New Order as to the older conceptions is apparent from Göring's letter to Funk of 17 August. They were the two chief protagonists in the argument over policy in occupied territory. Indeed, due to the racial

[1] D.G.F.P., Series D, ix, No. 399.

[2] R.A., Rk., Abt. Finanzen 2500, 'Bericht über öffentliche Finanzwirtschaft', 8 August 1940.

[3] Ibid., 'Vermerk über die Besprechung bei Hauptabteilungsleiter Otte am 18 September 1940', 23 September 1940.

composition of its population it was considered perhaps even more essential to a purely fascist Europe.

I am totally in agreement with you [Göring wrote], that *during the war* the production of foodstuffs and important commodities for the war effort for the benefit of the German war economy according to the Four Year Plan targets, must be increased to the highest possible level in the area controlled by Germany. All the measures for this purpose which can still expect a genuine success must be pursued as far as possible. *As far as the period after the war is concerned* I also share your opinion that it is a matter of extending to the utmost the sphere of Germany's economic power in Europe and the rest of the world and of giving the German people the highest possible standard of living by complete measures of control appropriate to a war economy. . . . As I have already explained in the conference held at Karinhall on this question it is particularly important to me that even before the end of the war as intensive as possible a penetration of, in the first place, the Dutch and Belgian, but also the Norwegian and Danish, economies should be attempted by German capital on a very wide basis and in return it should be open to Dutch and Danish interests to participate economically and to place their capital in Germany with the aim of creating in the shortest time common economic links and connections of interest between Germany and these countries.[1]

Before the clearing arrangements of the New Order were completely settled Norway was included in the planned 'inner circle' of countries whose clearing would have always to pass through Berlin, a position also reserved for Belgium, Holland, Luxembourg, Denmark, and the General-Government.[2] There is good evidence that German plans wavered over the question of whether France should be brought into this inner circle after the war, but for Norway no such doubts existed. For, even if the more wholly exploitative policy were to be pursued in Norway, Göring could not be insensible to the advantages of a customs union for German capital penetration into the country.

One goal of German economic policy [said his earlier memorandum of 2 August], is the increase of German influence in foreign enterprises. Whether, and to what extent, the peace treaty will bring a transfer of interests, etc., cannot yet be foreseen. It is necessary, however, even now to take advantage of every opportunity in order to enable the German economy while the war is still on, to obtain entry into interesting business enterprises. . . .[3]

In this respect tariffs could only be a hindrance. 'The furthest possible demolition of tariffs is practically bringing in a situation that we are trying

[1] R.A., Rk. Diverse, Pakke 10, Hauptabt. Verwaltung, Göring to Funk, 6 August 1940, 17 August 1940 (VP 13875/5).
[2] Ibid., 'Ausbau des deutschen Clearingsystems zu einem europäischen Zentralclearing'.
[3] D.G.F.P., Series D, x, No. 278.

to create at least as far as the western territories are concerned for the future greater European economy.'[1]

At the founding of the German Chamber of Commerce on 19 November 1940 State Secretary Landfried of the Reichs Economic Ministry spoke in unambiguous terms about German policy.

We are convinced that in the modern world Europe has become too small for the perpetual economic struggle and strife between the individual national economies and that only out of the co-operation of all the peoples of the continent of Europe, out of the conscious agreement of the needs of one with those of another and out of the consequent unified planning for all peoples in a reciprocal give and take, can stem the flowering of economic life and the highest development.

The conception of the European *Großraum* tries to bring together the national economic strengths of the European peoples; it wishes to make Europe safe against crises and to secure it as far as possible against all disturbances from happenings in world politics.[2]

That Norway's role in these developments would have to be decided by the larger partner was made equally clear.

One could certainly continue to elaborate examples of the possible development of the Norwegian economy. I would not, however, wish to fall back on prophecies! One thing is clear: if one speaks today in Norway of coming industrialization one must also be aware that it can only be pursued in the framework of European co-operation and in every case only in the closest collaboration with Germany with a view to lasting success. We Germans see our task, in agreement with our partners the Italians, and in that respect might I once again particularly stress this, not only to enter the future greater European economic arena as the greatest potential purchasers and most productive suppliers, but we also want to guarantee the sound attempt at development of our trading partners. Norway, whose economy, due to a very small internal market and an uncertain foreign market, up to now has had a delicately-balanced industrial sector, will be able to develop its economic strength in future in unsuspected ways as a greater potential producer and a more valuable component of the European economy.[3]

The more detailed aspects of German economic policy in Norway, at least until 1942, all belong within the framework of the general aim, to bring about such economic changes in the country as would enable it to play its part in the New Order. That such an aim should have existed while Germany was at war with other more powerful nations is not really surprising. The war was never intended to be a long war involving any degree

[1] R.A., Rk. Diverse, Pakke 10, Beauftragte für die Vierjahresplan, 'Abbau der Zölle gegenüber Holland, Belgien und Norwegen sowie gegenüber dem besetzten französischen Gebiet', 31 August 1940.

[2] Reichskontor der Nordischen Gesellschaft, *Nordeuropa und das Reich*, p. 139.

[3] Ibid., p. 143.

of economic reorganization, but a series of short wars culminating in the final Blitzkrieg on Russia. Norway could make its contribution in cash and raw materials to those short campaigns, like all other occupied territories, but the essential thing was that when the war was over Norway would be able to take its place in the new Europe. The war would guarantee the success of the fascist revolution; the long-term objective was to win that revolution. In any case, to the short-term objective of winning the war Norway seemed to have less to contribute than other occupied areas.

When the war changed its nature in spring 1942 and Hitler's hopes of a war which would involve Germany in a relatively limited economic effort were shattered, these long-range plans for Norway began to diminish in importance. From the failure of the Blitzkrieg onwards the question of Norway's contribution to the war became more important. First priority in German economic planning began to be awarded to questions of survival. The yardstick to be applied to economic policy in Norway became the extent to which such policy could help Germany's survival. Grand conceptions paled and the details of daily output of a certain limited range of goods became more important.

These changes of policy in Norway, the relegation of long-term policy to a lower priority, were associated with changes in the administration of the war economy in Germany. In particular they were associated with the development of a powerful central authority, the Reichs Ministry for Armaments and Munitions (Reichsministerium für Bewaffnung und Munition), later the Reichs Ministry for War Production (Reichsministerium für Kriegsproduktion).[1] The growth of this ministry meant that the economic policies to be pursued in Norway were subject to a much tighter control from Berlin and in general that they were policies initiated by that ministry. Before that time, that is to say from April 1940 to spring 1942, policies were not subject to this control but had their origins in many different ministerial sources. There might therefore be reasonable grounds for dividing the German occupation of Norway into two parts, before the development of the Speer Ministry and afterwards. But this would obscure the fact that the original long-term policies continued as ultimate policy aims although they receded further and further from the realm of practical attainability. As far as the Speer Ministry is concerned its importance for Norway was to introduce a sharp element of realism into policy there, to rigidly lay down a narrow order of economic priorities. The original attempt at reconstructing the whole Norwegian economy was, however, never formally abandoned.

---

[1] For changes in policy in Germany see D. Eichholtz, *Geschichte der deutschen Kriegswirtschaft 1939–1945*, vol. 2, *1939–1941* (Berlin, 1969); G. Janssen, *Das Ministerium Speer. Deutschlands Rüstung in Krieg* (Berlin, 1968).

The task of carrying out this reconstruction fell to the Reichskommis-sariat which also played its part in initiating policy. But the origins of many of the economic policies were very diverse. They might be decisions representing the particular interests of German ministries. They might be the result of pressure brought by German firms on their own govern-ment. They might be the result of pressure brought by particular groups in the National Socialist Party. The Wehrmacht had their own plans for bases and roads in Norway and Hitler himself had a grandiose plan for joining Norway to the new Europe by a magnificent new road and railway system. Whatever their origins, until spring 1942 all plans were filtered through the Reichskommissariat and the enthusiasm or otherwise of that body for the plans determined the energy with which they were pursued.

It cannot be said that these plans amounted to a coherent economic programme. Nor were they formulated according to any sense of priorities. Priorities were determined by the occasional interventions of the Führer but more frequently by whether the Reichskommissariat was genuinely interested. The plans themselves reflected the compromises on which the German fascist government was itself based. They were partly in the interest of the great private firms who supported the regime, partly in the interests of the National Socialist Party, and partly in the interests of Hitler's strategic plans. They carried within them the struggle over the nature of capitalist development which was inherent in National Socialism. Essentially they represented the common denominator of economic and social agreement in Germany. Their relevance to Norwegian conditions was another matter.

A speech delivered in Norway in February 1944 by Dr. Georg Brinck-mann, 'business leader' of the German Chamber of Commerce, collected together the stray details of German economic policy in Norway.[1] In reality they were never so coherent but no doubt looking back from 1944 it seemed as though German policy had been following a straighter path than it had actually trodden. The development of certain industries, mining, electrometallurgy, and chemicals, the increase of electric power output, the growth in food production, the attempt to attain greater self-sufficiency—when all the elements were put together they took on the form of a development plan designed to cope with the new circumstances of international existence. In fact the origins of each element of policy were very diverse and their achievement depended often on administrative or financial hazard.

The guiding lines laid down by the Main Department for Economy give a general impression of how much of the range of economic policy was

---

[1] R.A., Deutsche Handelskammer in Norwegen, E40/14 (løpe nr. 207), 'Vortrag an der Armee-Waffenschule, Lillehammer, am 2 Februar 1944'.

initially the contribution of the Reichskommissariat. The Main Department was given four essential tasks at the beginning of its administration:

i. The immediate mobilization of economic strength for Germany and Norway. Getting closed firms under way again as well as reconstruction of those factories that have been damaged because of the war.
ii. Immediate organization of railway and ship transport that has also been brought to a standstill by the war.
iii. Reorientation of Norwegian economic thought. Retreat from the Anglophile attitude of individuals and incorporation of the Norwegian economy into a European economic policy under the leadership of Germany.
iv. Reorientation of foreign trade towards those countries still reachable, especially towards Germany and the rest of central Europe; tight control of imports and exports on foreign exchange grounds.[1]

What was involved in the longer-term aims was left vague although under this wide aegis the Reichskommissariat introduced a battery of economic controls far more sweeping than mere controls on foreign trade. But the economic controls introduced in Norway resembled those in other occupied countries and their starting-point was the controls in the German economy itself. The principles of price and wage control in Norway were derived from German wage and price controls. The purpose of these controls was as much the adaptation of the conquered territory to a war economy as its incorporation into the New Order. To achieve that incorporation policies at the same time more specific and more wide-ranging were to be pursued. What were the specific long-term aims of German economic policy in Norway?

The most obvious weakness of the Norwegian economy from the standpoint of the New Order was her heavy dependence on food imports. Norway's incorporation into the *Großraumwirtschaft* exaggerated one of its weaknesses, an inability to maintain the same standard of living without food imports. Even including European Russia within the new autarkic area food imports would still be essential until long-range planning could induce sufficient substitution of products and the concomitant changes in diet.[2] Of course the introduction of another 3 million consumers into these cosmic calculations did not greatly alter the equation. The Norwegian standard of living would, in any case, be reduced. The problem was not the number of Norwegians but the physical problem of supplying them. It was not only that new sources of supply had to be found within the *Großraumwirtschaft* but that the goods had to be transported to Norway. This problem was made much more acute by the size of the German army of occupation.

[1] F.D. 5325/45, Rk., 'Ein Jahr Reichskommissar für die besetzten norwegischen Gebiete'. Bericht der Hauptabteilung Volkswirtschaft, n.d.
[2] A. S. Milward, *The New Order and the French Economy*, pp. 26 ff.

But the size of Norway's food imports had a deeper significance than this for the National Socialist Party. What they admired in Norway was the existence of a large body of 'pure German' peasants. The peasantry had preserved intact its virtue and faithfully resisted the insidious influence of mercantile capital on the economy. Left to the tender economic mercies of the international market, however, that peasantry had seen its position continually weakened, its income driven down, its hold on the land reduced. Yet in the Norwegian as in the German peasantry lay the hope for a regeneration of Europe. From within the ranks of those uncorrupted by the materialist creeds of humanism and liberalism would be created a new élite, a new European man.[1] The social regeneration of Europe therefore implied a quite new economic framework for the Norwegian peasantry. They were to be rescued from the fate which had borne down on them for so long. From being in the most invidious position in Norwegian society, outmoded traditionalists and obstacles to progress, they were to occupy the most heroic, standard bearers not only of the new Norway but of the new Europe.

It was not uncommon among German writers on the peasant question to consider the Norwegian peasantry as less corrupted even than their German brethren. They had been less exposed to the contaminations of racial admixture. The proof of this was usually seen in the survival in Norway of odal tenures. Such tenures meant that land occupied for a sufficient period of time by one family could, even after it had been alienated, be bought back, within a certain period of time, at a customary and traditional price lower than its market value. This ancient tenure bore many resemblances to the system of inalienable *Erbhöfe* introduced in Germany after 1933. It was thought to represent a wholesome social arrangement which had unfortunately decayed in Germany. 'The odal law, the indissoluble connection of the blood with the soil, has become the firm basis of every nordic world configuration.'[2] The value of the peasantry in the reconstruction of European society was emphasized in the speeches at the meeting of Nordische Gesellschaft in 1939. 'For our present situation and for all the known past we must set it down as a fact that the peasantry is the fountain of youth of all the peoples of nordic race.' 'If the German people should not find the path to the consciousness of their peasanthood and at the same time to the peasant quality of their daily existence then we, the community of fate of the nordic peoples, would fight in the end a hopeless fight for the eternality of our blood.'[2]

The supposition that the Norwegian peasantry had suffered because of the openness of the Norwegian economy led easily enough to the

[1] On National Socialist peasant policy and its relevance to Norway, see W. Darré, *Das Bauerntum als Lebensquell der Nordischen Rasse* (Munich, 1929).

[2] K. Motz, 'Das Bauerntum. Die Grundlage der nordischen Völker', in Reichskontor der Nordischen Gesellschaft, *Nordisches Schicksal Europas, Beiträge zum nordischen Gedanken und zur deutsch-nordländischen Arbeit* (Lübeck, 1939), p. 46.

supposition that in a closed system far more of Norway would be cultivated and the output of food would be far higher. The calculations previously made about the possible extent of farming in Norway were rejected as the false thinking of the market place. It became a standard article of belief that in the new system large areas of hitherto uncultivated or unutilized land would be occupied by farmers.

There are too many people in the fishery. These men who have mostly been familiar with agricultural work, will partly be employed on the waste lands which are capable of being recovered and which await the plough. Thus, for example, a single district, Sorenskriveri in Vesteraalen has 50,000 hectares of land which could be recovered. On the island of Aud there are 25,000 hectares of heath of which 10,000 hectares are suitable for cultivation. On Langøya, on Hinnøya, and in many other districts, there are large contiguous areas which await the peasants. In other areas such as North Helgeland and in the Salten parishes the favourable lands for new cultivation are somewhat scattered. But even here there is plenty of room. . . . The district of Troms should, according to experts, take possession of 100,000 hectares of unused land. . . . Norway should not forget that in this creation of new farming land lies a huge educational value for wider circles of the nation. The practice of colonization was at all times a measure for the value of the productive potential and strength of a race.[1]

There will now be an energetic policy of extending the cultivated land, millions of kroner will be allocated annually to the creation of new farms and the same time the very important and completely unfruitful moorland areas of the country will be drained and ploughed.[2]

In Norway there are 800,000 hectares of available land capable of being cultivated of which 500,000 hectares alone are heathland. Theoretically, therefore, there exists the possibility of bringing about self-sufficiency of the country in all foodstuffs and fodder. In that respect a plan of heathland cultivation is now foreseen in co-operation with the Reich. This programme means a task which will take many decades.[3]

The origins of this plan were not German but Norwegian. In the inter-war period there had been no lack of voices advocating a greater utilization of Norway's land surface. Quisling's own argument that colonization in the north was necessary as a bulwark against Bolshevik barbarians was an extreme statement of a view that in less extreme fashion had always had a certain currency in Norwegian economic and strategic thinking. The plan for utilizing heathland was in fact prepared by Bjorne Sakshaug of Norges Vel, a semi-private concern which had grown out of the nineteenth-century interest in agricultural reform.[4] Under the auspices of the department of

[1] M. Horn, *Norwegen zwischen Krieg und Frieden* (Innsbruck, 1941), pp. 111–12.
[2] H. Poll, *Norwegen, Land-Menschen-Schicksal* (Oslo, 1942), pp. 140–1.
[3] F.D. 5325/45, Rk., 'Ein Jahr Reichskommissar . . ., Ernährung und Landwirtschaft'.
[4] B. Sakshaug, 'Die norwegische Weiderwirtschaft' in Reichsministerium für Ernährung und Landwirtschaft, *Berichte über Landwirtschaft*.

agriculture the plan, long mooted, was transformed into actual policy in summer 1940. As formulated it was a plan for using heathland to provide pasture. About 215,000 hectares were thought to be a sufficient addition to the available pasture. To prepare such an area would involve an expenditure of about 240 million kroner over a twenty-year period.

The idea of such a plan was to utilize heathland for summer pasture thereby reducing the extra fodder imports which would otherwise be necessary to maintain a greater quantity of livestock. At the same time some heathland would become arable land. The intention in 1941 was, for example, to convert 56,000 hectares of heath into ploughland. The Germans were caught in a trap caused by their own conception of Norwegian society. The more rational way to increase food output in Norway was to increase the amount of animal products. But did not the idea of a German peasantry imply arable culture? Ought not the extension of cultivation and colonization to be a vehicle for reducing Norway's dependence on imported bread grain? The marginal land which could be taken into utilization could obviously most easily be utilized as summer pasture. An increase in livestock on that basis meant a greater amount of fodder would be needed to keep animals alive in winter. More domestic fodder production was difficult to achieve except at the expense of more domestic bread-grain production. Hence the attempt to shift pre-war Norwegian plans for the extension of farming in the direction of the extension of arable farming.

The Norwegian government had itself considered in 1939 emergency plans for a situation where food and fodder were difficult to get in a European war.[1] The priority in their plans was placed, not on grain production, but on an increased yield of fish, potatoes, and other vegetables. The second priority was to maintain and, if possible, increase the output of milk, milk products, and other animal products.[2] The compulsory growing of grain in the First World War, seen in retrospect, had not achieved very satisfactory results and the Government Dietary Committee which formulated these contingency plans for a future war decided that it was not worth sacrificing the production of animal feed in order to increase the output of bread grain.

The Reichskommissariat, like the Dietary Committee, foresaw no possibility that Norway could soon be made self-sufficient in foodstuffs. But whereas the Dietary Committee's plans were based on the assumption that Norway had to adapt to a short-term disruption of its normal economic life, those of the Reichskommissariat were based on the idea of a long-term adaptation. It was important for them that Norway should approach a state of self-sufficiency as nearly as possible. This, and the whole economic complexion of the fascist movement, drove them in the

---

[1] They never drew up plans for a situation in which they might be totally blockaded.
[2] K. Evang, *Norway's Nutrition Problem*, p. 13.

direction of an extension of grain cultivation, whatever the economic cost of such a decision. The short-term plan was to hold imports of bread grain roughly at the level of pre-war imports of wheat and allow imports of fodder to rise to over 400,000 tons a year.[1] On the basis of such short-term plans arable land would still be a much smaller proportion of total agricultural land than in 1918. That proportion in 1918 had been 52 per cent, in 1941 it was intended to be 42 per cent.[2] The reconstruction of Norwegian agriculture was rather to be undertaken by longer-range plans covering almost all food and fodder products. It is within this whole complex of plans that the plan for extending cultivation and using heathland should be seen.

Some elements of the contingency plans of the Dietary Committee were preserved. The quantity of potatoes produced was to be increased, so that they might not only play an even greater part in Norwegian diet, but serve also as pig-food in the place of imported animal feed. The total area devoted to soft-fruit farming was to be increased and the quantity of vegetables produced would also increase. One way of achieving both these ends was to use forcing houses. A capital-investment programme to build forcing houses was to be promoted in northern Norway to ease the problems of supply there.

There were to be long-term fundamental readjustments in livestock economy. One method of reducing the imports of fodder would be to reduce the stock of poultry by one-half, that is to say to its level at the end of the First World War.[3] Drastic though such a measure was its usefulness as an import saver would still not be sufficient to achieve Germany's ends, for the greater consumers of imported fodder were the larger animals.[4] Maintaining the supply of milk, fat, and cheese appeared to put severe constraints on any policy of slaughtering cattle, but dairy cattle were responsible for about half the total consumption of fodder. Nevertheless, by a process of ruthless weeding-out it was proposed to slaughter about 10 per cent of the dairy cattle without substantially reducing the final output of dairy products.[5] Pig-keeping would be reduced to the level of an individual small-scale enterprise so that pigs could be fed on waste rather than on imported fodder. There would be a gradual movement away from bacon pigs to fat pigs.[6] All these reductions were to be compensated for by an increase in the stock of sheep, for they could more easily be fed on the extensive moors and heaths and would provide, apart from their meat, a valuable industrial raw material in their wool. 'Without any doubt', wrote T. Fretheim, the Minister of Agriculture, 'the rearing of sheep in

[1] F.D. 5325/45, 'Ein Jahr Reichskommissar'.
[2] Reichsministerium für Ernährung und Landwirtschaft, *Berichte über Landwirtschaft*, p. 48.   [3] F.D. 5325/45, 'Ein Jahr Reichskommissar'.
[4] See Table 15.   [5] F.D. 5325/45, 'Ein Jahr Reichskommissar' p. 46.
[6] Reichsministerium für Ernährung und Landwirtschaft, *Berichte über Landwirtschaft*, p. 11.

our country has a great future, as extensive and excellent sheep-moors are available.'[1] What had prevented this success in the inter-war period had been imports of cheap foreign wool. Now that these were not a factor the sheep population could again rise. 'In the year 1939 we had some 1·7 million sheep including lambs and rams and it will be possible in a certain period to double this number.'[1] What was envisaged was a five-year plan to raise the number of sheep to almost 4 million.[2]

Such a large number of sheep, however extensive the plans for heath-land improvement, would still make very heavy demands on winter fodder. A number of plans for improving the domestic fodder situation were there-fore proposed at the same time. The extension of fodder-storage capacity throughout the country and improved methods of using silage could partly alleviate the situation. A greater proportion of fish converted into fish meal and a better utilization of the tundra could have the same effect. But an essential adjunct to these plans was the plan to produce more cellulose fodder. This was a product which had been used in the First World War with some success. An agreement was signed with the cellulose industry in the winter of 1940 for the delivery of 100,000 tons of fodder, and this and fish meal were to serve as the basis for the new sheep-rearing programme.[3] It was hoped by these means to reduce fodder imports to roughly 70,000 tons a year. Thus there existed a precise plan for Norwegian agriculture set in a vaguer and more ambitious framework of social transformation.

In this division of interests with a corresponding division between labour and capital one is persuaded to see one of the grounds, and perhaps the strongest ground, for the latent situation of economic crisis in Norwegian agriculture. It could at any rate be possible that this fragmentation of activity itself is only a symptom of a much deeper spiritual and sociological situation of crisis: there simply is lacking a certain binding, incorporation and subordination of individuals to the whole. Each individual is thus insufficiently socially and nationally restrained.[4]

It was to this problem that the Reichskommissariat's more distant plans were applied.

The tax situation of agriculture as well as the question of debt will be reviewed after an inquiry. In that case whatever measures are necessary will start from the basic principle that the peasantry has to help itself and that support from the public purse should basically not be expected. In this respect the intention is declared to bring order into agricultural finance and credit, in order to carry through at some time the necessary measures relating to the debt situation and agriculture.[5]

---

[1] Reichsministerium für Ernährung und Landwirtschaft, *Berichte über Landwirtschaft*, p. 11.   [2] F.D. 5325/45, 'Ein Jahr Reichskommissar'.
[3] Reichsministerium für Ernährung und Landwirtschaft, *Berichte über Landwirtschaft*, p. 49.   [4] H. Lufft, op. cit. p. 116.   [5] F.D. 5325/45, 'Ein Jahr Reichskommissar'.

The method by which the peasant would help himself was to supply a guaranteed market at a price which was, theoretically, supposed to represent an increased return on his outlay.

Landrat Svensson, a most thoroughgoing S.S. ideologist, drafted the outlines of agricultural policy to be pursued in Norway in the harvest year 1942–3 for Richert, the head of the Department.[1] Svensson seems to have been the leading figure in agricultural planning throughout the occupation and it may be for that reason that German schemes for Norwegian agriculture took on always a broad ideological air whereas in other departments more immediate practical matters of economics could often eclipse the longer-term aims. The essential elements of policy were to remain unchanged in spite of the changing military picture. Ploughland was to be increased by a further 35,000 hectares. The proportion of it devoted to potatoes was to be increased. More fodder, more vegetables, and more fruit were to be grown. The number of sheep was to be further increased. The number of cattle was to be brought into closer conformity with the supply of fodder. The priorities in the programme were, however, almost all of a political kind, an increase in propaganda to the peasants, a mechanism for sending farmers to Germany for political and agricultural education, and a similar arrangement for bringing German experts to Norway.

German agricultural plans were not without elements of contradiction. The intention to use more fish meal as fertilizer was only reconcilable with the intention to use Norwegian fish to increase the self-sufficiency of the *Großraumwirtschaft* if the quantity of fish caught were to go up. It was the chief priority of the Department of Fisheries in the Reichskommissariat to increase the fish catch so that an even greater surplus would be available for the rest of Europe. 'To discover', as they put it in their report, 'the possibilities presenting themselves through the occupation for the creation of a greater space [*großräumigen*] economic policy for fish and to prepare its execution.'[2] Some steps had been taken in this matter even before the invasion. After long pressure on Norway to sign a bilateral trading agreement embodying specific dispositions for the disposal of her fish exports in regular quantity for a fixed price to the German market, Germany had had some success in February 1940. The German-Norwegian trade treaty of 26 February had increased the quantity of fish which Germany would guarantee to purchase. Under the terms of the treaty Germany provided a certain amount of capital help to the Norwegian fishing industry to enable it to meet this new demand. The biggest item in this help was the provision of a deep-freezing plant at Trondheim.[3]

[1] R.A., Rk., Abt. Ernährung und Landwirtschaft, Pakke 52b, 'Arbeitsplan 1942–43', 22 January 1942.　　[2] F.D. 5325/45, 'Ein Jahr Reichskommissar', 'Fischwirtschaft'.
[3] It arrived with the invasion fleet.

The invasion provided the opportunity to implement forcefully a policy which had previously depended on trading pressures. Norwegian fish would be used to diminish the protein deficiency of the *Großraumwirtschaft*. The herring fishery would become a vital part not only of Germany's food supply but of that of all central Europe. Both from the standpoint of exporters and importers the higher the proportion of fresh fish the better and it was to this purpose that German capital help was extended. More deep-freeze installations than sanctioned by the February trade treaty would now be installed. Since 1938 Germany had been taking a fixed quota of winter herring at a fixed price. After the occupation this quota system could easily be extended to the other catches. The first steps were taken immediately, with negotiations to obtain a fixed quota of small herring for the German canning industry which was fully employed fulfilling Wehrmacht contracts. But the ultimate intention was to increase the supply of fresh fish at the expense of canned, salted, or dried fish. The freezing installations would have to be sited for the most part in northern Norway. 'The increased total quantity [of fish] to be prepared because of the German invasion means an increase in labour possibilities and will make a denser settlement in north Norway possible, which seems necessary on the grounds of population policy for the protection of the Nordic-Germanic peoples in this space.'

It should be emphasized that although the plans to install freezing plants were something the fishing industry itself had long desired, Germany's main interest and first priority was an over-all increase in fish exports of all types. The canned-fish trade which had mainly been directed to the United States and Britain was now to be directed towards Germany. The export of fish meal, which had been mainly directed towards Germany, was to be increased in the long run, once the fodder shortages in Norway had been overcome. In the future the Reichskommissariat hoped that about 35,000 tons of fish meal could be exported annually to Germany.

As in agriculture, so in fishing, the ultimate intention was to tackle the problem from first principles and institute a thorough reorganization of the industry and a general improvement in the income and social position of the fishermen. They were singled out as one of the groups in Norwegian society whose standard of living would be increased while that of the rest of the country was being reduced. The fishermen could easily be seen as the embodiment of the Viking spirit, like the peasant a hard-working pure-blooded patriot who had fallen victim to the machinations of international finance capital. The German administration hoped to reconstruct the Norwegian fishing industry in the same way as they had their own Baltic fishing industry, leaving the fisherman as an independent peasant but providing greater capital both for his boat and for fish-processing industries to deal with his catch, thereby increasing his returns and liberating him from his exploiter. Whether he would relish his new-found independence at the expense of his older independence (which in fascist eyes was but a servitude) was not considered.

It is clear that developments involving so great a reorientation of Norwegian fishing can only proceed under German influence and German capital participation. The Norwegian economy can never produce enough capital strength to perform the great tasks which grow before it in the future. Nothing has yet been undertaken in this direction under the Norwegian government. One could even say that the present Norwegian economic policy with regard to fish has only falteringly confronted so naturally necessary a development. The law on concessions, which is still valid at present, on the basis of a narrow national economic standpoint prevents the necessary combination between Germany, as the chief consumer, and the Norwegian fishing economy.[1]

What this 'necessary combination' implied may be deduced from the plans mooted for the fish-canning industry.

It is intended to make an attack on the problem of this relatively tightly-organized industry. In that respect the intervention of German capital in this branch of the fishing economy would be particularly desirable. Only in that way can the sharp competition which is to be expected after the war between the German and Norwegian canning industries be avoided. In this competition the Norwegian industry would actually have the advantage thanks to its excellent quality.[1]

The Department of Fisheries complained that official policy concentrated too heavily on merely securing a sufficient quantity of fish for Germany.

They hope, however, that the present state of affairs will not continue after the end of the war. The control of the respective Norwegian government offices and the alteration of the law on concessions and of Norwegian company law in favour of necessary German capital participation will therefore become a special target in the next months.[1]

Where German plans were concerned with industry they were tinged with a different hue. The preservation of the fishermen and farmers had its counterpart in the strict limitations to be imposed on industrial development. Liberal economists considering the problems of Norwegian agriculture and fishing might well hope that the further development of the economy would reduce the numbers of people in these low-productivity occupations and move them to other sectors of employment where productivity was higher. To fascist economists, farmers and fishers represented the 'healthy' core of society. Their preservation had one other useful aspect. It fitted well with the German conception of the *Großraumwirtschaft*

---

[1] F.D. 5325/45, 'Ein Jahr Reichskommissar', 'Fischwirtschaft'.

as a central European industrial heartland surrounded by a periphery of primary producers.

It was therefore primary producers in Norway who were mainly to benefit from these arrangements. The proposals affecting them were not for more productivity but for more production, and the main mechanism for obtaining this would be higher wages. Norwegian wages were regarded as not 'organic'. They reflected, that is to say, the varying strengths of the wage earners, especially the extent of their unionization, rather than the true needs of society.[1] The German administration therefore pursued a deliberate policy of allowing inflation to continue at an increased rate after the invasion in order to reduce real wages while compensating those classes whom they particularly wished to favour by increasing their money wage proportionately to other groups.

As far as Norwegian industry was concerned it was in an ambivalent position in these over-all plans. All circles of German opinion were well aware that Norway could not be expected to play the almost completely agricultural role of a Romania or a Yugoslavia in the *Großraumwirtschaft*. Yet they were equally well aware that in no circumstances must Norwegian industry be allowed to challenge German production. The difficulty was to arrive at a settlement for Norwegian industry which retained its usefulness for Germany while confining it within safe bounds. In this respect the policy of the National Socialist Party had to take account of the attitudes of those large firms on which it depended for its strategic successes. German plans for Norwegian industry therefore better reveal the diversity of origin of the various programmes administered by the Reichskommissariat than do those for Norwegian agriculture.

The role of the larger German firms in the formation of the *Großraumwirtschaft* has been much discussed by those writers who have identified fascism as a particular stage in the development of capitalism.[2] Their work has shown the intimate connections that bound larger German firms to the economic policy of the government but has not succeeded in showing that in the last resort the policy of the National Socialist Party was the same as the policy of those firms. The way in which the real business interests of the firm most closely associated with the National Socialist government, I. G. Farben, were involved in Norwegian policy throws much light on

---

[1] F.D. 5325/45, Rk., Generalbericht der Hauptabt. Volkswirtschaft, 3-Jahresbericht de Gruppe Lohnpolitik und Arbeitsbedingungen, 17 February 1943.

[2] D. Eichholtz, *Geschichte der deutschen Kriegswirtschaft*; J. Kuczynski, *Studien zur Geschichte des deutschen Imperialismus*, 2 vols. (Berlin, 1948, 1950,); idem, *Studien zur Geschichte des staatsmonopolistischen Kapitalismus in Deutschland 1918 bis 1945* (Berlin, 1963); W. Schumann and G. Lozek, 'Die faschistische Okkupationspolitik im Spiegel der Historiographie der beiden deutschen Staaten' in *Zeitschrift für Geschichtswissenschaft*, xii (1964); *Der deutsche Imperialismus und der zweite Weltkrieg*, Materialien der wissenschaftlichen Konferenz der Kommission der Historiker der DDR und der UdSSR vom 14 Bis 19 Dezember 1959 in Berlin, 5 vols. (Berlin, 1960).

the nature of German policy. Other German firms had a greater role to play in Norway at times than I. G. Farben but their attitude does not appear to have been significantly different.

I. G. Farben's main hopes of profiting from the *Großraumwirtschaft* were in eastern and south-eastern Europe and in France.[1] Norway was very much a side issue apart from the activities of Norsk Hydro. These had a special significance at the outset for two reasons. Firstly Norsk Hydro was a producer of nitrogen and as such a direct competitor in one of I. G. Farben's more profitable activities, something which I. G. Farben no longer felt obliged to tolerate. Secondly the plans of the German Air Ministry for the extension of aluminium manufacture in Norway also involved Norsk Hydro in its capacity as one of the world's largest producers of electric current. As far as the aluminium manufacturing plans went I. G. Farben was mainly anxious that its interests in Norsk Hydro should not suffer through that company's inevitable involvement with other German firms. As far as the manufacture of nitrogen and nitrogenous fertilizers was concerned the political role of Norsk Hydro was very large, large enough to greatly increase I. G. Farben's interest in the concern. The general German plan was to use Norwegian fertilizer production to supply the agriculture of Denmark, Sweden, Finland, the Netherlands, and Belgium.[2] Even were the pre-war Norwegian exports to the United States and Egypt to be now considered as available for these countries the total was evidently not sufficient to fulfil German plans without a considerable increase in production.

I. G. Farben's response to the invitations of the Reichs Economic Ministry to submit industrial proposals for the *Großraumwirtschaft* was much faster in the case of the Balkan countries than in that of Norway.[3] They were even quicker to submit their proposals in the case of France, a country whose future role in the *Großraumwirtschaft* remained uncertain.[4]

[1] On the connections between I. G. Farben and the Four Year Plan see D. Petzina, *Autarkiepolitik im Dritten Reich. Der nationalsozialistische Vierjahresplan*, Schriftenreihe der Vierteljahrshefte für Zeitgeschichte, No. 16 (Stuttgart, 1968). On the connections between I. G. Farben and German occupation policy see H. Radandt, 'Die I. G. Farbenindustrie A. G. und Südosteuropa 1938 bis zum Ende des zweiten Weltkrieges', in *Jahrbuch für Wirtschaftsgeschichte*, vol. 1 (1967), and R. Schröder, 'Die Ausschussprotokolle der I. G. Farben als Quelle zur Betriebsgeschichtsforschung über die Zeit des Kapitalismus' in ibid.

[2] F.D. 5325/45, Rk., 'Ein Jahr Reichskommissar', 'Industriewirtschaft'.

[3] B.A., R 7 II 615 Rwm., II. Bg.; Der Leiter der Hauptabt. II to II. Bg. Gabel, 25 July 1940. 'After the end of the war we count on the fact that there will result a *Großraumwirtschaft* in Europe under German leadership.' The letter is one of several asking for firms to submit specific proposals.

[4] B.A., R 7 II 615 Rwm., II. Bg., Abt. Bergbau II. Bg. 8524/40, 31 July 1940. Here the countries listed as belonging to the future European *Großraumwirtschaft* are Norway, Sweden, Denmark, Finland, Belgium, The Netherlands, Luxembourg, the Protectorate, the General-Government, Slovakia, Hungary, Yugoslavia, Romania, Bulgaria, and, of course, Germany.

Their plans for France were submitted on 3 August 1940, literally as soon as they could be prepared. Their plans for Norway were not submitted until 8 May 1941.[1] Before that time the development of the aluminium programme had caused I. G. Farben to define its policy for its own private purposes and, indeed, that programme being so much bigger business than Norwegian chemical production, it had tended to push chemical plans into the background. Nevertheless, the proposals outlined by I. G. Farben indicate the clear purpose of reducing such industrial development as would be allowed to take place in Norway to the status of a subsidiary branch of German industry.

As far as most chemical products were concerned the Norwegian market was already supplied by German firms. Between 1931 and 1936 a subsidiary of Norsk Hydro, Norsk Tjaerprodukter, had made some inroads into the German dyestuffs market there, but, by an agreement between the parent company and I. G. Farben in 1936, its production had been suppressed in return for a payment of seven annual instalments of 20,000 kroner. Its demise left only the cellulose industries and the fertilizer industry as serious obstacles to German domination in that field. I. G. Farben recommended that all plans for the expansion of cellulose-based chemical industries in Norway be stopped, a recommendation which in the event was not at all acceptable to the German government because of the need to produce cellulose fodder in Norway.

If the available capacity of the Norwegian chemical industry, as far as it impinges on our interests, is to be primarily used to meet domestic demand then we would like to give expression to the expectation that a further development of the Norwegian chemical industry will only be undertaken with the agreement of those German chemical interests, including ourselves, which export to Norway, something, for example, that has happened for years in the field of nitrogen and is happening at the moment in the light metals field.[2]

Such an attitude fitted well with the Party's own view of the *Großraumwirtschaft* except where strategic necessities were overriding. There was in the last resort only the most limited harmony between the economic interests of the big firms and the economic interests of the National Socialist Party whose vigorous opposition to ideas of economic growth and dynamism found few echoes in the counsels of industrialists. But this final lack of agreement could not appear until the *Großraumwirtschaft* was completed. While it was being completed a genuine harmony of interest

---

[1] F.D. 2203/45, Bundle G, I. G. Farben, 'Vorschläge grundsätzlicher Art, die sich im deutsch-norwegischen Verhältnis hinsichtlich Produktion und Absatz ergeben'. See also, D. Eichholtz, 'Die I. G. Farben "Friedensplanung"', in *Jahrbuch für Wirtschaftsgeschichte*, vol. iii (1966).

[2] Ibid., 'Entwicklung und Stand unserer norwegischen Exportinteressen, gegliedert nach Verkaufsgebieten, sowie Wünsche spezieller Art für bestimmte Produktionsgebiete'.

did prevail. The larger firms stood to gain enormously from the forcible creation of a coming European market and lent enthusiastic support to party policy whatever their ultimate reservations. That harmony was only broken by the limited strategic necessities occasionally imposed on the National Socialist government by its own war plans. Certain industries in all occupied countries had a particular relevance to the German war economy. Such, for example, was the aluminium industry in Norway. Here German plans were so far-reaching that they will be considered separately in another chapter. It is necessary to remark, however, that they were not carried out without a considerable amount of dispute between the party and the German aluminium manufacturers. The aluminium industry was not the only Norwegian industry to fall into this category of special strategic value, although it was the most important of those that did. Where Norwegian industry had strategic importance, or where it could make some contribution to the future self-sufficiency of the *Großraumwirtschaft* that could not be made by Germany, the general principles of the New Order had to be infringed to permit development. Where the industry fell into neither of these categories its production was to be confined to the share of the domestic market which it had at the time of the occupation. In all these situations Norwegian industry was in a very weak position. Its defence was the Concessions Law and the desire of the Reichskommissariat to move slowly in its policy of integration. Where the strategic factor was of greater importance the Reichskommissariat had to behave less cautiously and it was, therefore, mainly in industries having a direct relevance to the German war economy that capital penetration took place. Nevertheless the *Großraumwirtschaft*, like the fascist revolution, was never completed. No doubt the capital penetration by German industry was but a foretaste of the completed New Order.

The industries of greatest strategic interest to Germany were the production of particular metallic ores and metals. In these areas the intention was to get Norwegian production going again as soon as possible, to develop it to the necessary level, and to make sure that it was carried on in the German interest. A case in point was the mining and treatment of Norwegian pyrites deposits.

German participation in Norwegian mines [wrote the Main Economic Department in November 1940], is making progress at present. Negotiations of the Gesellschaft für Langestätten-Forschung on the opening up of the large pyrites district of Grong by German–Norwegian co-operation have come to a conclusion. A research company, based on parity on each side, is to undertake a systematic search of the whole district to secure German influence over the large pyrites deposits. When fully in operation this mining area will have the largest production of all Norwegian pyrites mines and will give employment to an at present almost uninhabited part of Norway for several years. Securing this mining area means possessing the key position in Norwegian ore mines for several years.[1]

Control of the Grong orefield implied that the rest of Norway's pyrites deposits had to be controlled and utilized entirely according to the German point of view.

The increased demand for pyrites came from the demand of the artificial-rubber and artificial-textile industries, but the demand from copper manufacturers also remained high. Whereas in general it was true that 'Germany is therefore urgently dependent on every ton of pyrites from Norway, irrespective of whether the pyrites contains copper or not', the production of copper itself in Norway was of almost equal strategic interest.[2] Before the war the Orkla smelting works had consumed about 240,000 tons annually of the pyrites mined, out of a total output of about 750,000 tons, and produced about 80,000 tons per annum of pure sulphur. At full capacity, however, the works could produce about 120,000 tons of sulphur a year. A further third of the mined output of pyrites had been exported to Germany and about 180,000 to 190,000 tons annually to Sweden with smaller quantities to other West European industrial lands. At the same time the Orkla works had produced about 18,000 tons of copper annually, about 5,000 tons of which was produced from copper pyrites and the rest from copper ore. This was roughly the quantity of copper which Germany hoped to get annually from Norway, a quantity equivalent to about 6 per cent of greater German demand.[2] So that this would not denude Norway of copper herself it was decided to increase copper production there to 22,000 tons annually.

There was one copper-ore mine in Norway, that at Røros. It had stopped working in 1938 and German plans were to resume mining there to supply Norwegian smelters. This mine and other Norwegian copper-ore reserves which had acquired much greater value in the new situation became the target of German firms, especially the Mansfeld Konzern. On 22 December 1939 Director Klingspor of the Mansfeld Company, told S.S.-Oberführer Zimmerman, Reichs Commissioner for Metals (Reichsbeauftragter für Metalle) that Mansfeld expected as a matter of course to have special rights over foreign copper deposits. He particularly mentioned Norway in the conversation. At the beginning of 1940 Mansfeld secured an option on the north Norwegian copper deposits by the usual device of being appointed trustee (Treuhänder) of the company.[3]

[1] F.D. 5211/45, Rk., Abt. Wirtschaft, 'Führerbericht für die Zeit vom 16.9–15.11.1940', 18 November 1940.
[2] F.D. 5216/45, Wi. Rü. Amt., 'Die Wehrwirtschaft Norwegens'.
[3] H. Radandt, *Kriegsverbrecherkonzern Mansfeld. Die Rolle des Mansfeld-Konzerns bei der Vorbereitung und während des zweiten Weltkrieges* (Berlin, 1957), p. 226.

The intention was to get the Røros mine going again in three to four months. But the refining plant there would not be restored. 'It is not in German interests to reconstruct the copper-refining plant at Røros, in place of refined copper only blister copper should now be produced.'[1] In the summer of 1940 Mansfeld secured two further options on the control of copper ore, on the Helden and Saltdalen deposits. Director Klingspor personally reported on 3 August 1940 to the meeting of the directors of the *Kupfergesellschaft* on the good prospects in Norway. He drew particular attention to the Grong pyrites deposits. His hopes were to share the capital costs of exploitation with I. G. Farben which had first begun to survey the deposits in 1938. I. G. Farben was, however, mainly interested in a quick expansion of its ore supply, whereas the Grong deposits would not be workable for years and would require very heavy, although indubitably profitable, investment. The initial investment was too heavy for Mansfeld itself and some government help was necessary.[2] In the event it was the slowness with which the Reich provided that investment that was to nullify the Grong project, but the intention and the plan were there, they were deflected from their goal only by financial shortages.

German interest was not in finished copper but in copper ore for German makers.

It is even less desirable for Norway to reorganize the Falconbridge plant [the nickel and copper electrolysis works belonging to the Canadians] so that it produces the whole of the domestic demand for copper metal in its own country. Norwegian copper demand in completed goods and semi-manufactures comes to around 10,000 tons of copper annually. If this plan were carried out the German foundries would get 10,000 tons of copper for their supply and there would only remain for German consumption about 8,000 tons instead of 18,000 tons.

The main interest in both copper and nickel was to secure the raw material. The *Erzgesellschaft* began a study of the nickel deposits at Raana.[3] In 1941 Germany was interested in reopening the older nickel mines in Norway, one closed in 1917 and the other in 1921. The problem here of course was to keep the Falconbridges melters supplied for they had previously depended almost entirely on nickel mat imported from Canada.

Two other metallic ores, rutile and molybdenum, had a vital strategic importance. Molybdenum was the more important not only by virtue of the greater quantities in which it was used but also by virtue of the fact that of all the essential constituents of armaments steel it was the one that German metallurgists were least able to find effective substitutes for. With the closing of trade with the United States the Knaben mine became

[1] F.D. 5216/45, Wi. Rü. Amt., 'Die Wehrwirtschaft Norwegens'.
[2] H. Radandt, *Kriegsverbrecherkonzern Mansfeld*, p. 242.
[3] F.D. 5211/45, Rk., Abt. Wirtschaft, 'Führerbericht für die Zeit vom 16.9–15.11.1940', 18 November 1940.

effectively the sole source of German supply. The Finnish mines were still only in the early stages of development and suffered badly from the Russo-Finnish war. Any German ownership of the Knaben mine was made difficult by the fact that it was controlled by a Swedish firm, Axel Johnson. Nevertheless in 1942 the Krupp firm became trustees for the mining company and agreed with the Swedish owners on a partition of the output, 75 per cent to Germany and the rest to Sweden.[1] The rutile deposits in Sogndal were exploited by a joint German–Norwegian firm after 1940.

As for iron ore itself, the Dunderland iron-ore mines were taken from their British owners and handed over to a trustee, Dr. Dittmann of Vereinigte Stahlwerke. His commission was to repair the damage done in the fighting and modernize the whole works so that exports to Germany would rise.[2] At the same time the Krupp firm undertook a survey of the Elsfjord deposits, south of the Dunderland deposits, with the intention of opening mining there. There were even plans to increase the output of coal in Spitzbergen so as to economize on shipping space between Germany and Norway. With further exploration of the islands the Reichskommissariat was still hoping in 1941 that Spitzbergen's coal output could be doubled and Norway's dependence on imports reduced thereby to 75 per cent.

So much for raw materials. In this case what happened in Norway was akin to what happened in other occupied territories. Germany's need for metallic ores was very great, their price mounted very steeply and in order to secure supply German firms took advantage of the occupation to integrate vertically with their suppliers. The surveying of new fields and opening of new mines engaged German capital heavily from the invasion. 'The most important task of the Norwegian economy is the further development of ore mining.'[3] In the later stages of manufacture there was less interest.

There were, however, general plans for development in the Norwegian shipyards, in the artificial-textile industries, and in the wood-processing industries. Their origins were very different. Norway was intended to be the greatest naval base outside Germany, the outer bulwark of the new Europe. Trondheim in particular was to be rebuilt to twice its size as a centre for the German navy.[4] In the circumstances the German navy wished to extend the capacity of Norwegian shipyards. The plans for artificial textiles and cellulose were designed to reduce Norway's import dependence.

The plans for the expansion of shipbuilding in Norway were always

[1] J.-J. Jäger, *Die wirtschaftliche Abhängigkeit des Dritten Reiches vom Ausland dargestellt am Beispiel der Stahlindustrie* (Berlin, 1969), p. 286.
[2] F.D. 5211/45, Rk., Abt. Wirtschaft, 'Führerbericht für die Zeit vom 16.9–15.11.1940', 18 November 1940.
[3] Reichskontor der Nordischen Gesellschaft, *Nordeuropa und das Reich*, p. 117.
[4] A. Speer, *Erinnerungen* (Frankfurt am Main, 1969), p. 196.

thought of as a long-term project. The capital sums involved in both modernizing the yards and increasing their capacity would be very large. Again, time alone could produce the necessary increase in the number of skilled workers. The motive for this investment on the part of the navy was very strong, however, for until it took place the repair of any warship larger than a destroyer in Norway was really out of the question.

The projected increase in sheep stocks in Norway would produce a greater quantity of domestic raw material for the textile industry. But self-sufficiency could only come through a greater output of artificial silk and cellulose fibres. There was a special attraction in such a plan for German firms could take the opportunity of getting access to a relatively cheap raw-material supply while also securing a share of the Norwegian consumer market. The result was the founding of Norsk Cellulfabrik, Sarpsborg, A/S. It was sited to take advantage of the largest of the Norwegian cellulose plants, the Borregaard Company at Sarpsborg. That firm supplied 60 per cent of the capital. Twenty-six per cent of the capital was provided by Phrix-Verfahrensverwertungs AG, Hamburg, which in return for its artificial-fibre processes and technical help was able to get a guaranteed and much cheaper supply of cellulose for its subsidiary.[1] In autumn 1940 the cellulose producers in Norway, Sweden, and Finland entered into a general marketing agreement.

In this regard Norwegian wood was a valuable raw material. It was the basis of more cellulose, and thus of more fodder, as well as being indispensable for the enormous construction undertakings of the German armed forces and for the heating of their billets. It was its importance in all these ways which led the German administration to protect it by purchasing wood pulp from the producers whose market in Britain had closed. Contracts to the value of 100 million kroner were signed in 1940 for wood pulp and paper.[2] The Department of Agriculture prepared a scheme after the occupation for a much greater centralized control of Norwegian forestry to prevent indiscriminate felling by peasant owners and generally to remove many of the peasant's freedoms to use his wood as he wished. But this scheme remained a rather remote one as the day-to-day control of forestry remained in the hands of the Trade Department.[3]

It could be concluded that German plans for Norwegian industry were based wholly on the concepts of the *Großraumwirtschaft* except where

[1] O. Ulshöfer, *Einflußnahme auf Wirtschaftsunternehmungen in den besetzten nord-, west- und südosteuropäischen Ländern während des zweiten Weltkrieges insbesondere der Erwerb von Beteiligungen (Verflechtung)*, Institut für Besatzungsfragen, Studien zu den deustschen Besetzungen im 2. Weltkrieg, No. 15 (Tübingen, 1958), p. 102.

[2] Germany purchased on similar grounds quarried stone, in order to use it after the war 'for monuments', Reichskontor der Nordischen Gesellschaft, *Nordeuropa und das Reich*, p. 142.

[3] F. D. 5325/45, 'Ein Jahr Reichskommissar', 'Forst-und Holzwirtschaft und Jagdwesen.'

strategic necessity dictated otherwise. What is surprising is the faithfulness with which this comprehensive framework of economic thought was rendered into a similarly comprehensive plan. German proposals and intentions reached into every corner of Norwegian economic life. They could be seen at their most sweeping in the schemes for transmitting electric current to Germany and for redesigning the Norwegian transport system.

The huge plans to develop the Norwegian aluminium industry were designed to use one of Norway's few advantages, cheap electric power. They necessarily had to embrace at the same time an immense investment programme in power stations. The ultimate hope was that Norwegian electric power could be exported to Germany to feed manufacturing capacity there. Terboven was, throughout the occupation, chairman of a committee to develop Norwegian electric power and seems to have had a considerable personal interest in the affair. The main obstacle, theoretically, was the problem of getting the current across the Kattegat. In February 1944 these plans were still under consideration, as Dr. Brinckmann's speech at that time indicates.

The exceptionally low development costs of its water power and its utilization puts Norway beyond all competition amongst those countries in which the costs of power are decisive in production costs. . . . It is beyond question that the later continued control of water power will far exceed the country's needs. Because of that Norway will be in the position of being the most important European exporter of electricity.[1]

Both road and railway systems were to be immensely improved. The driving force was partly a strategic one; access to the naval and military bases in west Norway by land had to be improved on the grounds of military safety. General von Falkenhorst on 21 August 1940 ordered measures to increase the productivity of Norwegian railways by employing more locomotives, turning round the trains more quickly, and reducing the number of crossings.[2] But more important than this was Hitler's desire to see Norway properly joined to the German Empire. 'The development of roads and railway lines is therefore not just a subsidiary task but a present necessity for the further economic development of Norway in the interests of the continental-European *Großraum*.'[3] Two railway lines in particular were to be completed, the southern railway, which would join Stavanger to Oslo, and the northern railway to the Arctic lands. The ultimate destination of the northern railway varied but construction on the stretch

---

[1] R.A., Deutsche Handelskammer in Norwegen, E40/14 (løpe nr. 207), 'Vortrag an der Armee-Waffenschule'.
[2] R.A., Rk., Abt. Finanzen, Pakke 23, Der Wehrmachtbefehlshaber Norwegen, 'Forderungen an die norwegischen Staatsbahnen', 21 August 1940.
[3] R ichskontor der Nordischen Gesellschaft, *Nordeuropa und das Reich*, p. 121.

Mosjoen to Mo began at once. After that there were definite plans to continue to Bodø. Hitler from time to time mentioned Narvik as the ultimate destination. This project in itself was an enormously expensive business, the most costly by far of all the proposed German capital investments in the country. Yet it was no more than the fulfilment of a long-standing Norwegian plan. The Storting itself had decided on the completion of the northern railway in 1908 and the completion of the southern railway had been advocated in the Storting by Michelsen as early as 1894.[1] It was further planned to convert all the Norwegian track to standard gauge and to electrify the whole system. The motive of the electrification was once more to reduce the volume of sea traffic needed to keep the Norwegian economy going. The fact that the Norwegian railways had not been electrified was usually regarded by the German administration as a sinister conspiracy by British coal owners to retain their export markets.

As for the road network, the main project was a continuous main road penetrating into north Norway and linking Narvik and the counties of Troms and Finnmark to the south for the first time. In addition the roads leading westward, especially to Stavanger and Bergen, were to be widened and generally improved, for one reason so that military lorries could pass along them. This project too was enormously expensive but won great support no matter what its cost from the military and from the Führer. There seems no record of Hitler's personal support for the 'Nordstrasse' until 1942 but it was then so strong that it is difficult not to believe that this particular aspect of German plans for the Norwegian economy was not due to some long-cherished personal dream of the Führer from the start.

Up until the very moment of the collapse of the Reich itself Hitler continued to insist on the completion of the Norwegian railway system at whatever cost. The reasons were not strategic for it was repeatedly demonstrated by the generals that the Norland railway would be extraordinarily vulnerable to any attack from the sea. Nor were the reasons genuinely economic. The cost of iron ore hauled by rail from Narvik would have been much too high. Hitler had firmly decided that Norway was to be a permanent part of the German Empire whatever local autonomy it might have.

It is curious that an invasion whose main reason was strategic should have resulted in so many far-reaching plans. But once persuaded that the invasion of Norway was necessary on military and strategic grounds, Hitler determined to incorporate the territory permanently into the new system. There were also strategic grounds for this incorporation. By early August 1940 Hitler had already begun his plans to make Trondheim into

[1] M. Rudolph, 'Geographie der Landstrassen und Eisenbahnen von Norwegen', in *Petermanns Mitteilungen*, Ergänzungsband xliv (1929), Ergänzungsheft No. 206.

a major German naval base and there is evidence that Narvik was destined to fulfil a similar function. Trondheim was also to be a great Nordic cultural centre, rebuilt on a magnificent new scale.[1]

Were Norway to submit to German plans and embrace her fate she would have shared in the reorganization of Europe, although her share would scarcely have been significant. The assurances of a future role in the new Europe for which Laval so earnestly begged Hitler seem to have been bestowed more readily on Nasjonal Samling. Fretheim was the recipient of such information in June 1942.

During my last stay in Berlin in June of this year I also had an interview with representatives of the Ostministerium and of the Finance Division of Deutsche Bank. I received there an impression of the enormous task of planned reconstruction which will be carried out in the occupied territories of the Soviet Union. For these tasks very great quantities of labour and a great many skilled industrial workers are necessary. Also the whole agricultural economy will have to be reconstructed.[2]

In this industrial and agricultural reconstruction Norway would take part. In the first place a small number of agricultural experts would be sent to Russia to help in the reorientation of Russian agriculture. After that selected Norwegian peasants would be sent to Russia to study agricultural conditions there with a view to eventual settlement.

This was no chance impulse of policy. In January 1942 Svensson set out the way in which Norwegian peasants would be chosen. 'Selection of settlers: preparation of a selection of settlers for the German eastern space [den deutschen Ostraum] from N.S. youth organizations, land-youth, N.S. peasant groups, Norwegian legion, S.S.-Standorte Nordland, Hird, Womans'-Hird.'[3] Terboven had some inkling of where exactly in Russia Norwegian influence would be extended. The Kola peninsula and the Murman coast were to be considered a particular sphere of interest for Norway. Such ideas roughly coincided with older dreams of territorial expansion in Norwegian right-wing circles. Members of Nasjonal Samling and the Hird joined in the campaigns against the Soviet Union and in the plans for its dismemberment. But for most of the population such schemes were chimeras. Although conceived on a European scale and for European reasons German economic policy in Norway essentially took the form of a programme for domestic action.

To call the whole complex of German plans a programme is perhaps to exaggerate their coherence. That there was an over-all conception of what

---

[1] H. Paulsen, 'Reichskommissariat og "motytelsene" ', p. 336.

[2] R.A. Rk. Diverse, Pakke 70, 'Utsendelse av en norsk delegasjon til de besatte Ostland områder, samt planer til Norges medvirkning til oppbyggelsen av de besatte områder v/T Fjeld Fretheim, Handelsdepartementet', 9 July 1942.

[3] R.A., Rk., Abt. Ernährung und Landwirtschaft, Pakke 52b, 'Arbeitsplan 1942–43', 22 January 1942.

the Norwegian economy should be in order to best fit into the framework of the *Großraumwirtschaft* is clear. But there was no getting round the fact that Norway did not fit very well, that the main reason for the occupation was a strategic one. This inherent contradiction in German policy was never resolved. On the one hand, if Norway was to be successfully absorbed into the economic structure of the New Order it had to become far more self-sufficient. On the other hand, to defend it required a German armed force almost a half million strong, an addition of one-sixth to the population. It was this inherent contradiction of purpose which caused the confusion in German plans, for strategic necessity sometimes dictated a course of economic policy which scarcely seemed compatible with the ideal economic arrangements of the *Großraumwirtschaft*.

It was the opinion of the Wehrmacht in 1941 that

Norway is now in a position better to use its own internal riches through better economic and technical methods. In that way the country can provide a rich contribution to the European *Großraumwirtschaft*. The problems of its own economy lie directly in the field of organization, in the elimination of liberal economic policy which must dissolve in the face of planning and control for the benefit of the generality.[1]

But once these problems were solved what would be Norway's specific contribution?

In the first place stands the still unutilised energy of the country, the 85·8 per cent unutilized water power which puts Norway in first place in Europe. The water power still available is estimated at 12·1 million kilowatts. Here there should in future be still unimagined possibilities for the electro-chemical and electro-metallurgical industries. The German aluminium industry has already made a beginning with this. Technology is already so far developed that the key question of the source of energy is no longer decisive. Thus the cheap electric power derived from water in Norway can become an export good by means of long distance transmission across national frontiers.

The wealth of wood will find expression in the delivery of cellulose and paper, later in the delivery of building wood also.

The products of mining are very welcome in that form especially due to the shortage of rare metals and sulphur.

The fish catch can be used to supplement the food supply in even greater quantity. A condition for this however is that the necessary freezing plant and means of transport are provided.

The final verdict can therefore be summarized in this way, that in the future Norway must be in the position, from an economic viewpoint, to be able to surrender a great deal more that it has to keep for its own economy.[1]

With that verdict all branches of the German government, party, army, and industrialists, would have agreed. In part such a result could be achieved

---

[1] F.D. 5216/45, Wi.Rü.Amt., 'Die Wehrwirtschaft Norwegens'.

by simply milking the Norwegian economy. There were two strong objections to carrying such a policy too far. One was the Germanic nature of the country, it was not to be subjugated by the New Order but to be one of its main props. The other was the utter dependence of the Norwegian economy on its international connections; cut off from them there was little to milk. That final verdict therefore implied a programme of capital investment in Norway, not in the interests of the Norwegian economy but in the interests of Germany and the *Großraumwirtschaft*. Such a programme of capital investment clashed both with the demand for enormous *per capita* occupation costs and with the expensive business of maintaining a large army of occupation there.

These contradictions meant that the economic plans for Norway were far harder to implement than to formulate. And the more the war progressed the more difficult did their implementation become. Although German policy never lost sight of its ultimate goal until late in 1943 or even in 1944, it is almost the case that Norway was nearer to her future role in the New Order in the summer of 1940 than at any other time. From the autumn onwards the hard tooth of reality slowly gnawed away German plans until they eventually became unrecognizable.

IV

FINANCE AND THE ESTABLISHMENT OF
AN OCCUPATION POLICY

THE preparation of German plans for the Norwegian economy and their implementation continued throughout the long period of political uncertainty in the summer of 1940. Indeed, this uncertainty prevented the basic question of how these plans were to be financed from being asked. There was no official Norwegian government to whom the bill could be presented until Terboven's 'act of state' in September 1940. Before that both the armed forces and the civil administration in Norway indulged in heavy expenditure in accordance with their plans, although from the beginning of the occupation the Reichskommissariat was worried about the propensity of the military to assume that so large an army could live off a land with so few resources.

Anxiety about the state of the Norwegian economy increased throughout this period for two reasons. In the first place, the expected inflation which it had been hoped would be controlled at a suitable level proved much less controllable. In the second place, the Norwegian merchant marine went over almost entirely to the Allies. About 20 per cent of the total tonnage was seized in Norway or in Axis ports; the rest, ignoring directives from Nasjonal Samling, sailed for Allied ports. At one stroke the German administration was deprived of the lynchpin of the Norwegian economy. In retrospect no miscalculation in the German plans was more serious. As the war continued, the problem of supplying Norway became more and more difficult, imposing a heavier strain on German shipping. To the expected difficulty of creating a quite new pattern of foreign trade for Norway with its inevitable early scarcities was added the worse problem of a shortage of shipping space even for the trade which remained.

In April the Norwegian government in London began to organize the Norwegian Shipping and Trade Mission (Nortraship) to charter the merchant fleet to the Allied governments.[1] Periodically throughout the war, further vessels deserted the Axis cause for that of the Allies and, to make the German situation worse, many of those remaining were sunk. In April 1940 there were 4,486,063 dead-weight tons of Norwegian shipping sailing in the Allied cause. Furthermore, the Norwegian whaling fleet,

[1] N. Ørvik, *Norge i brennpunktet fra forhistorien til 9 april 1940*, vol. i, *Handelskrigen 1939-40* (Oslo, 1953), for the preliminary moves in this regard.

which had already sailed on its expedition for the 1939–40 season, did not return but put into Allied ports and sold its catch there. In subsequent years, by a series of daring operations, Germany was able to capture several of the factory ships, but the catch in wartime was too small to alleviate the acute problem of fat supply caused in Norway by the loss of these ships.

The shortage of supply in Norway and the deterioration of the economic position were masked by the inflation and by the vast construction programmes of the Wehrmacht, in itself one of the causes of that inflation. To meet the unprecedented strain on its public finances, the Norwegian government printed money, while the supply of goods was severely restricted by the loss of overseas trade. At the same time the heavy underemployment and unemployment which had both become endemic in the economy in the inter-war period began to dwindle to nothing as the advent of the Wehrmacht caused an enormous building boom. The high wages paid by the armed forces to attract labour to the remote sites where it was needed intensified the inflation.

By autumn 1940, therefore, Norway was heading towards a severe economic crisis which was made all the more acute by the prolonged political uncertainty. For until there was some workable governmental arrangement in Norway, Germany's intentions for the country could not be really discovered. The main cause of the crisis was the vast scope of German undertakings, both civil and military, in an economy so utterly disrupted, and the uncertainty as to who was ultimately to pay for these undertakings and how the money was to be found.

Most of this uncertainty must be attributed to a lack of direction from Berlin. The only previous act of occupation on such a scale had been in Poland. That could serve as no precedent for it was in part an annexation and, for the rest, there was no intention to preserve anything of the Polish economy but its agriculture. The administrative and economic arrangements there were quite unsuited to Norway. After the occupation of Belgium, the Netherlands, and Northern France, a 'system' of occupation arrangements was evolved which was also applied to Norway. The burdens imposed on those countries were then used as yardsticks to measure what could be imposed on the Norwegian economy. Before that, a wild optimism existed as to the amount of cash and resources which might be squeezed out of Norway. The construction of a set of general arrangements for the New Order therefore coincided in time with the construction of an official Norwegian government and the solution of the political crisis there.

These events also meant that there was both a European and a Norwegian framework within which the growing economic crisis in Norway could be tackled. Autumn 1940 was the period of basic decisions and the turning-point of German occupation policy in Norway. It was the period when what it was hoped to do began to be replaced by what could actually be done, a march towards reality that was to continue towards the end of the war. The decisions taken at that time created from rapidly developing chaos a fixed political and economic regime which was to last until the German surrender. But in their taking much of German planning and even more of German and Nasjonal Samling aspirations had to be temporily abandoned.

It is interesting to observe the cautious and eminently practical manner in which Terboven pursued his aims in Norway. His political sense told him that Quisling and Nasjonal Samling could expect little support from the Norwegian population, especially as they now appeared as the mere puppets of a foreign invader. While he was in sympathy with Nasjonal Samling's economic aims he was in complete disagreement as to the speed and manner with which they could be attained. Norway had to be made a secure part of the New Order with all possible speed; there was no hope that an internal social revolution could be achieved with the same speed. Since the transition in the economy due to the invasion was inevitably violently disruptive, Terboven was determined to pursue, on the domestic front, a cautiously sound economic policy and as accommodating as possible a political policy, within the limits laid down by Hitler's directives. Such an attitude led at once to troubles with Nasjonal Samling's more ambitious ideas.

Nasjonal Samling had placed great stress in their propaganda on changes in credit policy. Cheap money and an extensive public credit system were their remedies against agricultural depression and urban unemployment. The monetary advisers which Terboven brought with him to form the nucleus of the Reichskommissariat's financial department were, as befitted the policy he intended to pursue, men of great orthodoxy with little sympathy for Nasjonal Samling's schemes. Christian Breyhan, the Head of the Public Finance Section until the end of August 1940, came from the Reichs Finance Ministry, to which he returned. His successor Hans Korff, of Danish extraction, came originally from the same ministry. He it was who was to be the main force in shaping financial policy in Norway during the occupation. He later carried a joint responsibility as financial adviser to the German administration in Denmark. There seems no doubt that his influence on Terboven was very great and that it was in favour of Terboven's own cautious approach to the Norwegian economy.[1] Rudolf Sattler, a regional director of the Reichsbank, became Beauftragte des Reichskommissars bei der Norges Bank. He also had some responsibilities for monetary policy in Denmark. The general interest of these officials in maintaining the Norwegian currency on a sound foundation proceeded in the first place from their desire to see the New Europe organized on a viable basis, that is to say one on which Germany's wartime interests

[1] H. Paulsen, 'Reichskommissariat og "motytelsene" ', p. 291.

could be safely pursued. Nasjonal Samling was not to be allowed to disturb that basis.

The greater threat, however, came not from the Norwegian fascists' revolutionary aspirations but from the rapidly mounting volume of Wehrmacht expenditure, coupled to the financial demands of the rest of the many economic schemes for Norway now emanating from Germany. The extraordinarily rapid rise in expenditure in such uncertain political circumstances carried an extreme threat of inflation. Nothing could have been more disturbing to German plans. Although in certain respects German intentions were to change the relative distribution of rewards in Norwegian society and the social pattern that prevailed there, their intention was to do so by administrative fiat and under the strictest possible controls. An uncontrolled inflation, with the certainty of rapid social change which it would bring about, was the very opposite of what they wished. The fascist social order was immutable because it was both justly in accordance with human merit and non-materialist. The social order was fixed on principles in man rather than in economic life. Inflation attacked it at its most vulnerable point, especially in a country like Norway where the necessary 'spiritual' outlook had been far from inculcated into the general population. Orthodox financial administration and fascist ideology therefore spoke with the same voice in 1940 and could come to each other's aid in stabilizing the New Order.

There were also more limited economic reasons, although even these were ultimately related to these larger considerations, which dictated 'soundness'. The price and wage levels in the German economy itself were most precariously balanced and depended for that balance on a most rigid control of those prices in international trade which affected Germany. The initial impact of the war on that trade was to create a large number of scarcities, of raw materials and manufactures, and to stimulate an inflation in all economies through the increased price of imports. Although by the nature of their economic system German purchasers were very much protected from these international price movements, such protection would not be permanent in a prolonged war. There were a number of channels through which price inflation in an occupied country could still leak to Germany, however strictly controlled. The price of raw materials could not be held down to the point where producers would be too discouraged, payments and transfers between soldiers, administrators, and Germany could not be blocked. For this reason too, in Norway as elsewhere, the initial stages of the New Order dictated financial caution.

There is considerable evidence that in the first flush of success the German administration dreamed of a customs union embracing the most suitable territories for inclusion. The memorandum of Carl Clodius, Deputy head of the Economic Policy Department of the Foreign Office, on

30 May shows that the idea of a customs union between the occupied territories was still alive in policy considerations.[1] On 7 June a memorandum from the same department indicated that Norway was 'practically to be treated as home territory'.[2] The speech by Walther Funk, the Economics Minister, delivered on 26 July, seemed to put an end to this. Giving a survey of general considerations affecting the organization of the New Order he indicated that a customs union was undesirable on practical grounds, the difference in price levels being so great.[3] Obviously such considerations must have weighed very heavily with the German government for their own economic policies in the pre-war years had been to insulate the price level as far as possible from that prevailing in countries like Norway whose trading policies were more international.

In spite of Funk's speech, which was not so much a declaration of official policy as a contribution to an internal argument in the German administration, the idea that eventually there would be a customs union involving western European territories persisted. The public finance department of the Reichskommissariat reported on 8 August, 'The customs between Germany and Norway continue as before. A customs union is planned whose implementation however depends on major *economic* decisions.'[4] The same section reported in similar terms after a discussion with Otte on 18 September.[5] So long as such ideas persisted the top priority of the Finance Department of the Reichskommissariat would obviously have to be to control the level of prices in Norway as drastically as possible in order to maintain them somewhere near the German level.

Terboven's long-term aims were the transformation of Norwegian society but his immediate aims were less far-reaching. The Norwegian economy must be exploited by allowing the German clearing debt to Norway to mount higher without any real possibility of repayment, a policy followed very successfully in other occupied countries. This policy too demanded financial 'soundness' elsewhere in the economy. It also demanded that at first the clearing debt should not rise so high as to make such soundness seem pointless. The expenditure of the German army and administration in Norway had to be curbed so that a better-disguised policy of exploitation could be carried out, one which would avoid bringing chaos to the Norwegian economy at the outset.

This cautious policy was made more necessary by the rapidity of inflation in Norway after the occupation, a rapidity partly induced by the occupation itself. The invading armies in Norway, as elsewhere, brought their

[1] D.G.F.P., Ser. D, ix, No. 354.   [2] Ibid., No. 399.
[3] W. Funk, 'Wirtschaftliche Neuordnung Europas', in *Südost-Echo*, xxx, 26 July 1940.
[4] R.A., Rk., Abt. Finanzen 2500, 'Bericht über öffentliche Finanzwirtschaft', 8 August 1940.
[5] Ibid., 'Vermerk über die Besprechung bei Hauptabteilungsleiter Otte am 18 September 1940', 23 September 1940.

own money, the Reichskreditkassenschein. Its issue was stopped as soon as possible in June and the notes remaining in circulation gradually withdrawn in July through the Bank of Norway. But even when the Reichskreditkassenschein remained in circulation only in small quantities, it proved a potential source of inflation. Small numbers of these notes continued in circulation in other economies until 1943. In the final count the most inflationary aspect of the occupation was the determination of the Wehrmacht to pay for everything they wanted, no matter what the price, on the assumption that some financial mechanism, whether the Reichskreditkassenschein or the Bank of Norway notes made available to them, would be devised to cover the cost.

In an economy like that of France, the bilateral clearing arrangements imposed after the occupation were sufficiently one-sided to constitute by themselves economic exploitation on a grand scale. In Norway this was less the case, although even the Nasjonal Samling ministers recognized the disadvantages of such a system.[1] The pattern of financing the occupation was the same in both instances by direct payments through the central bank into accounts at the disposal of the army of occupation. The sums provided by the central bank in France were designated as 'occupation costs'. In Norway this designation was fraught with difficulties. It raised all the questions about the relationships of the Norwegian and German governments which were better left unraised, especially the question of whether Norway was in 'a state of war' with Germany. At the same time the clearing arrangements forced on most economies, including France and Norway, meant that Germany could use the sums provided through the central bank to pay for goods in the occupied territory while her own exports to that territory continued to diminish. After the Franco-German clearing treaty, trade flowed overwhelmingly in the German direction. In the case of Norway, where the economic value of the acquired territory could, at any rate in the short run, only be realized by supplying a number of essential imports, the credits established on the clearing balance were less one-sided. The element of exploitation lay less in the trading arrangements than in the sums demanded for support of the occupying forces. Although these sums were negligible compared to the 35,250 million Reichsmarks paid by France through the whole period of the occupation, on a *per capita* basis they represented a heavier burden on the population.

That is not to say that if there had been any danger of the clearing arrangements benefiting Norway more than Germany they would not have been changed. But in the first stages of the occupation, caution was the watchword. Too brutal a treatment would endanger not only the 'revolution' in Norway but the revolution in Germany as well. The question of

[1] R.A., Naeringsdept., Kasse 2; Avlevering fra Universitetsbiblioteket, 'Meddelelser fra Naeringsministeren, No. 2, 26 January 1944, "Sentralclearingen i Berlin" '.

how much Norway could pay could not be settled without regard to the financial policy by which the Norwegian government would ultimately provide these sums. The directors of Norges Bank were as afraid of inflation as Terboven. Their fear was that either the arrival in power of Nasjonal Samling would produce a burst of public spending in a difficult situation or that the ultimate defeat of that party would produce a social revolution of an equally undesirable kind. If the Wehrmacht in Norway grew in size, or even if it remained the same size but its demands got greater, as is the nature of armies of occupation, the volume of money in the economy would increase while shortages restricted the availability of goods. It was not unlikely that German policy might prove so harsh that loans would be difficult to obtain and the necessary payments only able to be made by the use of the government printing presses. The extensive array of physical controls over the economy which the Reichskommissariat was eventually to construct was as yet far from developed. The political intentions of the conqueror remained obscure. His economic intentions may well have seemed more revolutionary than they were, for, to the eyes of the central bank, fascism represented a social revolution which was all too visible and whose limitations were not so easily perceptible.

Everything therefore conspired towards an agreement between the Reichskommissariat and the Norwegian financial authorities to pursue a cautious financial policy. Their battles, although battles of rival national interest, were fought out within a very well-defined area, that of financial soundness and orthodoxy. The losers were Nasjonal Samling, whose plans for social reconstruction were based on the financial unorthodoxy of the early years of the German and Italian revolutions, and the Wehrmacht, who were faced with the fact that financial orthodoxy prevented their living off the country in the way it had previously been supposed, rather vaguely, that they would. The agreement also slowed down the vast economic plans and projects to reconstruct the Norwegian economy and make it more appropriate to the *Großraumwirtschaft*. If inflation was to be kept at bay, it was not possible to carry out all these projects and to support so large an armed force.

Two issues were involved which were not always clearly separated by the German administration. One was the actual physical capacity of the Norwegian economy to provide goods and services for the occupying power. Suppose Germany to do nothing but loot the Norwegian economy, how much could that economy provide and still maintain the Norwegian population? The 'occupation costs' which Germany demanded from other west European countries were far beyond the cost of maintaining the army and administration there, the extra sums represented the modern equivalent of booty. In none of these cases, however, was the ratio of troops to population anywhere near as high as it was in Norway and the question in the Norwegian case was whether the Norwegian economy could physically provide for the occupying forces. The other issue was a more purely financial one. If the method of maintaining the troops in Norway was simply to make Norway pay for them in cash it was possible to pursue a financial policy there which would have, perhaps, in the long run, serious economic effects, but which would provide a sum of money appropriate to German needs. Although that money ultimately would represent real Norwegian resources the correspondence was not so immediate, given the enormous powers of control in the hands of the occupying power, as immediately to endanger the economy. That there should have been confusion between these two issues is understandable. The intention to reconstruct the Norwegian economy in itself implied an investment programme which would theoretically have the effect of increasing Norway's physical capacity to contribute. That was in part what it was intended to do. But the implementation of that programme also led to a great increase in the amount of money in circulation in Norway, a factor which seemed to make it easier to increase the purely financial burdens on the Norwegian state. Indeed, the increase in money seemed to compel an increase in the so-called 'occupation costs' merely as an anti-inflationary measure. As the call on Germany's own resources became greater as the war progressed so did Germany's demands on Norway become more purely financial in nature and the demand for cash increased as the physical capacity to provide goods and services began to deteriorate.

On 1 July the newly formed Department of Finance had had conversations with their Norwegian counterparts in which they had proposed raising a loan of 200 million kroner to be included in the national budget for 1940–1.[1] The main considerations were that the Wehrmacht expenditure in establishing their troops in barracks in Norway, bound at first to be very heavy, would be covered and that the loan itself would be an anti-inflationary device mopping up purchasing power.[2] It appears that at that stage the Reichskommissar and his officials had little idea of how costly the Wehrmacht's activities would be and were hoping to cover in this way what they thought would be an extraordinary period of expenditure at the start of the occupation. More mature considerations of financial policy were evolved in Berlin in the same month.

It was made clear to Terboven that the Hague Conventions allowed Germany to demand occupation costs from Norway and that such a demand should now be presented to the Norwegian government.[3] In order to establish the level of these costs the Reichs Ministry of Finance requested a survey of the potentiality of the Norwegian economy. In the

[1] H. Paulsen, 'Reichskommissariat og "motytelsene" ', p. 292.
[2] R.A., Rk., Abt. Finanzen, 2500, 'Tätigkeitsbericht bis 6 Juli 1940', 6 July 1940.
[3] Ibid., 'Meine Dienstreise nach Berlin im Juli 1940', 22 July 1940.

discussions over the loan which Terboven had already requested as well as in the discussion over occupation costs it became clear that there could be no settlement without a political settlement first. The military raised some interesting questions when the matter of charging the occupation costs to the budget was presented to them. 'Can one speak of "occupation" if no official armistice has yet been concluded? Do you know if it is intended to conclude such an armistice with Norway before the peace settlement?'[1] The political settlement did not arrive until the autumn when Terboven finally extricated himself on Hitler's orders from the negotiations over the proposed Riksråd and accepted Nasjonal Samling as his collaborators. The political and financial settlements therefore became almost inextricably tangled after July giving rise to a long period of delay during which the level of expenditure soared to heights far beyond those which the Reichskommissariat had originally imagined.

When the Administrative Department of the Reichskommissariat raised the question at the end of July of whose responsibility it was to provide the 200 million kroner for the Wehrmacht barracks they were told that this matter had to await the formation of a new regime.[2] Terboven had already decided that in the interests of financial soundness this money and certain other administrative expenses would have to be covered by the Norwegian budget.[3] The Main Department for the Economy decided that the new Norwegian government, when formed, should be persuaded to show three-quarters of the total in the budget under the heading 'supply etc.' and to show the remaining 50 million kroner in an extraordinary budget as 'justice and police department, building works'.[4] The implications for Norway were that not only would taxation have to be increased to cover this sum but loans would have to be raised as well.

By September the Reichskommissariat were beginning to worry about the mounting level of expenditure. Korff took the view that even by that time such a level of expenditure was insupportable for the Norwegian budget.[5] When the Wehrmacht presented its financial demands to Terboven as part of the process of establishing how much the Norwegian government would have to make available, it was at once clear that if they were accepted it would be hopeless to expect them to be covered by loans and taxes in Norway. A conference held in Skaugum on 3 October to consider the demands to be laid before the Nasjonal Samling government only widened the breach between the Reichskommissariat and the military. After outlining the difficult economic problems in Norway which had not been anticipated in the formulation of German policy before the invasion,

[1] R.A., Rk. Diverse, Pakke 10, Breyhan to Reichsfinanzministerium, 24 July 1940.
[2] *Aktstykker*, No. 2.   [3] Ibid., No. 3.   [4] Ibid., No. 5.
[5] R.A., Rk., Abt. Finanzen 2500, 'Vermerk über die Bepsrechung', 23 September 1940.

Terboven indicated that the events of the occupation had already caused the note circulation in Norway to increase from 500 million kroner before the invasion to over 800 million kroner. In such circumstances maintaining the exchange at the new level was already very difficult.[1] The Wehrmacht had demanded further expenses of 1,500 million kroner to last to May 1941. 'The Norwegian area [Raum]', Terboven said, 'must do everything possible to support the German Wehrmacht strongly. There is, however, a limit. Therefore it must be clearly decided how much the Norwegian economy can still produce. The remainder will have to be provided from Germany if the Norwegian economy is not to become disorganized.'[2]

Norges Bank had not been so thoroughly subjected to the control of a commissar as the central banks of other occupied countries. Sattler's powers seem to have been rather less than those of his fellows elsewhere.[3] Norges Bank was not likely, however, to remonstrate too violently against a monetary policy probably more moderate than they had expected. Sattler supported Terboven's view strongly, taking the line that further possibilities of credit in the Norwegian economy were now very limited. 'In the Reich such an expansion of credit inside five months would be unthinkable. The Netherlands and France have not yielded as much, relatively, as Norway.'[4] Sattler and Terboven agreed on a limit of 500 million kroner more as the furthermost possibility, a limit quite unacceptable to the military. The military claim rested on the fact that the defence of the territory and the further prosecution of the war were the first claims on expenditure. That this might mean the postponement or the cancellation of the economic programme in Norway troubled them little. Their bland refusal to budge from a merely military standpoint meant that the whole issue would have to be settled in Berlin. 'With 500 million kroner the uppermost limit of the Wehrmacht's contribution is reached', said Terboven. 'The Wehrmacht must see this. It is no good Intendant-General Losch contenting himself with saying, "the Norskes will pay". It

---

[1] The official kroner-Reichsmark exchange rate had been fixed at 1·666 kroner to the Reichsmark. This was a 7 per cent mark-up on the previous official exchange rate of 1·78 kroner = 1 Reichsmark. No trade had, however, passed at the official pre-war exchange rate and there were no equilibrium exchange rates so that the change is difficult to measure. If we assume that the rate of 1·24 kroner = 1 Reichsmark, the rate at which a considerable amount of trade was done, was somewhere near an equilibrium rate, the over-valuation of the Reichsmark appears as about 34 per cent. This is rather less than its over-valuation in respect of the franc and roughly comparable to its over-valuation in respect of the Bohemian crown.

[2] R.A., Rk. Diverse, Pakke 10, Breyhan to Reichsfinanzministerium, 24 July 1940, No. 10.

[3] A. Emmendörfer, Geld- und Kreditaufsicht in den von Deutschland während des zweiten Weltkrieges besetzten Gebieten; eine völkerrechtliche Untersuchung über die geld- und kreditwirtschaftlichen Massnahmen deutscher Besatzungsbehörden, Studien des Instituts für Besatzungsfragen, No. 12 (Düsseldorf, 1957).

[4] Aktstykker, No. 10.

must be realized in the Wehrmacht that this goes no further. It is a wonder that it has succeeded so far.'[1]

There were two separate components of the problem of Wehrmacht expenditure, the food and shelter of the troops and the expenditure on construction work. The failure of the invasion force to occupy the country without a war meant that the size of the armed forces in Norway was much greater than had been originally intended. Preliminary studies by the army show that the problem of supply for the troops had been considered in relation to a Wehrmacht of 150,000 rather than 500,000.[2] These calculations were based on the assumption that most of the foodstuffs required would be supplied from Norway. The milk and cheese supply together with the total annual need of 3,180 tons of various fats would all be provided from Norwegian supply. The meat necessary to supply such an army, 14,150 tons, could not be obtained entirely from Norway, but by substituting a larger fish ration for the regulation meat ration, the meat demand could be reduced to 10,400 tons of which about one-half could be obtained in Norway. Eggs, fish, and potatoes would also be obtained in Norway. In some foods supply from Germany would still be necessary. The total annual demand for flour for such a force would be about 30,000 tons, far beyond the capacity of Norway. Sugar would have to be imported, adding a further 2,200 tons annually to Norway's sugar imports. Fresh vegetables, other than potatoes, would mostly come from Denmark and Germany.

As the Wehrmacht in Norway grew in size these decisions appear to have been adhered to in principle. As the size of the Wehrmacht in Norway increased, the problem of supplying it from Germany increased also. The pressure on Norwegian food supply was intense and eggs, for example, disappeared from the open market at an early stage of the occupation. The Reichskommissariat wanted the purchasing of food by the Wehrmacht to be part and parcel of the general system of economic controls and rationing. At the Skaugum meeting the idea was broached of proceeding in the way that the military administration in France had proceeded, by controlling the total distribution of all goods after a fixed levy had first been taken for Wehrmacht purposes or for export to Germany. In Norway, however, such a system meant a direct confrontation between the German civil and military authorities. Only the civil authorities could ultimately decide what size quota was available for German purposes and it was already clear that such decisions would mean a reduction of the levies which the Wehrmacht was already taking by the use of its massive purchasing power. Both von Falkenhorst and Terboven were sceptical of the value of such

[1] Ibid.
[2] F.D. 5361/45, O.K.H., 'Einzelheiten zur Wehrmachtsbedarfdeckung in Norwegen', 26 June 1940.

arrangements in solving the problem because of the sheer quantity of supply required by the Wehrmacht. The situation was the more intractable because Wehrmacht purchasing policy was governed by a Führer-order stipulating that in Norway stocks should be sufficient for one year's supply.

The biggest single item in military expenditure was the building of airfields which, undertaken on that scale before the war, would have represented a quite staggering public investment project for an economy such as that of Norway. It was this which even more than the problem of general Wehrmacht provisioning threatened to wreck the economic programme of the Reichskommissariat, for it competed not merely for the available cash but also for the available labour and raw materials.

One week after the Skaugum meeting, Terboven travelled to Berlin to take the matter to a higher level in the Reichs Economic Ministry with Minister Funk. The Minister of Finance, Schwerin von Krosigk, also attended together with State-Secretaries Landfried and Körner. Sattler and Otte accompanied Terboven and General von Hanneken represented the Wehrmacht's interests. Terboven refused to abandon his estimate of 550 million kroner, a sum based on the costs of the military personnel in Norway. Their consumption would have to be catered for by the Reich itself. The shortage of foreign supply meant that production in Norway had fallen rather than increased. To avert an economic disaster, the Wehrmacht must be provisioned from Germany and where it was more convenient in the case of certain goods to supply the troops out of Norwegian production the Norwegian deliveries should be properly compensated for through the clearing accounts by the delivery of German goods to Norway.

The feeling of the meeting in the Reichs Economic Ministry was overwhelmingly against the Wehrmacht. The Norwegian standard of living had to be reduced but only within the limits of political feasibility.

The occupied country [said Schwerin von Krosigk], must bear the costs. But more troops have now been stationed in Norway than the productive capacity of the country can cater for. If we maintain this demand the economy collapses and this collapse militates against our own interests. In Norway, as in France, we must arrive at a fixed contribution which will have to be decided without a special breakdown of the occupation costs. Expenditure over that must come from the Reich.[1]

Funk also took up the theme that the cost of the occupation must come in principle out of the Norwegian standard of living but that the present demands of the Wehrmacht were absurd. If they were accepted the private economy would stop functioning altogether, the workers would become

---

[1] *Aktstykker*, No. 11.

slaves and the whole country would work for the Wehrmacht. 'The standard of living', said Terboven, 'will be further reduced. That is politically
manageable to a certain degree, but I have carried through a cold revolution
and our friends, whom we have only just recently put in power for the
first time, are coming to us and saying, you are treating Norway worse
than France.'[1]

The meeting agreed to certain administrative changes. In the first place
there would be a contracts department staffed jointly by the Reichskommissariat and the Wehrmacht and linked with the Price Supervision
Department of the Reichskommissariat. This new department would
examine the questions of what contracts for Wehrmacht supply should be
put out in Norway and what prices the Wehrmacht should pay for goods.
At the same time the Wehrmacht would inquire what categories of supply
it might be able to obtain from Germany. It was also decided that the cost
of supplying the troops must be borne by Germany. The costs paid by
Norway would be limited to the 'personal' costs of the army of occupation.
Meanwhile the Norwegian government would be ordered to institute
a programme of anti-inflationary taxation to mop up the surplus purchasing
power in the economy. All these decisions, although bringing some order
out of disorder, ignored the fundamental question of how much the Norwegian economy could contribute and whether Terboven's estimate,
roughly coincidental with the 'personal' costs of the Wehrmacht, was justified. Funk proposed that Hans Kehrl, a departmental head of the Economic
Ministry, should investigate this issue and come to a final decision.[2]
Terboven was insistent that the investigation should be undertaken by the
Reichskommissariat. In the event it was a joint effort.

The inquiry was begun under Kehrl's supervision on the following day.
The general method of procedure was a comparison with the formal
occupation costs levied on other economies. Such comparisons showed
that the reproaches of Nasjonal Samling were perfectly justified, but they
were of less value in determining a final sum. If the total expenditure of
the Wehrmacht were to be covered from Norwegian payments, the *per
capita* burden on the population would have been well over one Reichsmark a day whereas the burden of paying the occupation costs implied
a daily *per capita* levy of 50 pfennigs on the population of France. The
occupation costs for Belgium and the Netherlands were less than for France.
If the burden on the Norwegian population were to be the same as that on
France that would imply payments of roughly 75 million kroner a month.
This sum was rejected by Sattler as too high on the practical grounds that
the Norwegian government could not provide more than 200 million

---

[1] Ibid.
[2] He was later to become head of the Planning Office (Planungsamt) in the Speer
Ministry.

kroner in its annual budget at the moment to cover the costs. Costs of 75 million kroner monthly until the end of May 1941 would represent 975 million kroner.

There were perfectly sound economic reasons for rejecting the figure of 75 million kroner monthly of which these practical considerations were but a symptom. However comparable the pre-war levels of *per capita* income in Norway and France the circumstances of the war made Norway a much poorer country since so large a proportion of her national income was represented by invisible earnings. In such calculations also some allowance has to be made for the absolute size of the occupied economy. The greater diversity of resources and productive capacity in the French economy allowed it far greater possibilities of substitution and a much more flexible capacity to respond to the peculiar wartime circumstances. Without making such allowances, the calculation becomes merely arbitrary. These considerations seem to have played no part in the German discussions but there was another consideration which did influence the meeting towards rejecting the conclusion of these calculations. Did not political considerations imply that Norway should be treated less harshly than France? The experts of the Reichs Economic Ministry and the Reichskommissariat agreed that the contribution which Norway could make in the budget should be 200 million kroner, the sum already demanded in the 1940–1 budget. Eventually the costs were fixed at 500 million kroner from 1 May 1940 to 31 May 1941.[1]

These calculations did nothing to cater for the possibility of increasing 'personal' costs of the Wehrmacht. They were an attempt to fix a maximum possible contribution from the Norwegian economy to the Wehrmacht. The hope was that these sums could be covered by Norwegian public finances leaving still plenty of scope for the Reichskommissariat's own economic programme which should in any case soon generate extra income for the Norwegian state. 'If the Norwegian state is to produce on its own account 500 million kroner until 31 May 1941 this contribution will be covered by the budget within two and a half years provided that from 1 June 1941 no further military costs are to be included in the budget.'[2] General von Falkenhorst asked in October for a contribution to the expenses of railway building and was firmly turned down. There could be no demands on public finances other than those decided.[3]

One result of the inflation was that the tax income of the Norwegian state increased considerably in the period after the invasion. In the first

[1] R.A., Rk. Abt. Finanzen 2500, 'Bericht über öffentliches Finanzwesen für die Zeit von 16 September bis 31 Oktober 1940', 29 October 1940.

[2] F.D. 5211/45, Rk., Abt. Wi., 'Führerbericht für die Zeit vom 16.9–15.11.1940', 18 November 1940.

[3] R.A., Rk., Abt. Finanzen 2500, 'Vermerk über die Besprechung bei Reichskommissar Terboven am 26 Oktober 1940', 29 October 1940.

quarter of the accounting year, July to September, it was 162,200,000 kroner as against the 130,400,000 kroner of the previous three months.[1] This increase hid the fact that the sources of tax income were changing with the new economic circumstances. The tax on commercial vehicles which had brought in 22,500,000 kroner in the previous accounting year was now, owing to the severe controls on the use of petrol, no longer bringing in a significant yield. Much more drastic was the reduction in income from customs duties, a state of affairs which might well prove permanent. There was therefore little ground for supposing that this improvement in revenue would be a long-term improvement.

In fact, in so far as it was merely the result of inflation it represented an unsound state of affairs, for already the Reichskommissariat had begun to introduce controls specifically designed to halt that inflation. The first measures of effective price control utilized in part such Norwegian machinery as already existed for that purpose. Since the law on trusts in 1926 there had been an authority, the Trustkontrollkontoret, whose task was to supervise cartel prices. These authorities seem not only to have agreed with German price policy but also to have provided the Reichskommissariat with much information on how a more extensive price control could be more effective.[2] These authorities were therefore coupled with the new Price Supervision Department of the Reichskommissariat in controlling the local authorities set up by the Decree on Price Control of 12 September 1940.[3] The evolution of price control in Norway during the occupation moved, with every legislative act, away from using the normal administrative organs of the country towards greater reliance on the Nasjonal Samling police and officials. The legislation of 12 September 1940 was not in fact very effective although its lack of effectiveness is not entirely to be blamed on slackness of enforcement but on the general economic situation. In 1941 a series of Control Boards was set up, one for each parish. The three members of the board were named by the Fylkesmann and were consumers and businessmen.[4] Although these changes were more effective they still had the ultimate weakness of relying for their execution on local officials who were often out of sympathy with German policy.

At the same time as these measures of price control were introduced, two other anti-inflationary policies were pursued, the institution of rationing and other controls on many foodstuffs and raw materials and the

[1] F.D. 5211/45, Rk., Abt. Wi. 'Führerbericht für die Zeit vom 16.9–15.11.1940', 18 November 1940.

[2] F.D. 5306/45, Rk., Gruppenleiter der Abt. Preisbildung und Preisüberwachung, 'Tätigkeitsbericht für den Zeitraum von Mai 1940 bis Ende 1942', 20 February 1943.

[3] F.D. 5225/45, Rk., 'Die gerechtliche Grundlage für die Preisregulierung, die Verordnung des Administrationsrats über Preisregulierung vom 12 September 1940'.

[4] Ibid., 'Die wichtigsten Preisgesetze und Verordnungen seit der Besetzung', Vorschriften für Kontrollämter, 29 December 1941.

increasing of taxation to soak up the excess purchasing power. Eggs, bacon, and meat were all given fixed prices and a complicated set of regulations was introduced determining the prices of wood.[1] At the same time administrative experiments in controlling those raw materials which were most likely to be in demand by Germany were begun. Usually their starting-point was a set of negotiations with the Norwegian government determining what preparation of total output would be available for German purposes. The remaining part was then either rationed or otherwise strictly allocated among Norwegian consumers. Such was the case with rubber, crude oil, leather, and steel before the end of November 1940.

The increases in taxation were closely connected with the problem of how to raise the 200 million kroner expenses to be shown in the Norwegian budget. As early as August the financial department had decided that taxes on income in Norway would eventually have to be increased. But since this meant a change in the whole tax structure it could not happen straight away.[2] Taxes on consumption were already as high as in Germany so it was necessary to go slowly. Once some degree of confidence had been built up that the occupiers were responsible men who, in the economic field at least, did not want to reduce Norway to the status of another General Government, it would be possible to use the money market to secure loans. But caution, and inflation, dictated that part of the effort of balancing the budget as nearly as possible should come from extra taxation. 'In view of these great inroads, the method of supplying the expenditure and the backing of these kroner requisitions had to be carefully manœuvered in the psychological area between the given possibilities, —the area of banking technique and that of exchange policy', as Sattler was later to express it.[3] In this respect German policy in Norway had one advantage over that in France, the absence of 'official' occupation costs. Those credits to the Wehrmacht which did not appear in the budget but only in other accounts were secret. The advantage was, again in Sattler's words, that this 'awakened on the Norwegian side, the hope that the Deutsche Bank would later accept responsibility for a great part of the Wehrmacht demands'.[3]

By October the turnover tax was nearer to 10 per cent than its preoccupation level of 6 per cent. Personal income taxes had reached a level of 30 per cent on the incomes of the unmarried, their highest level yet in Norway. The wartime taxes introduced by the Norwegian government

---

[1] F.D. 5211/45, Rk., Abt. Wi., 'Führerbericht', 18 November 1940.
[2] R.A., Rk., Abt. Finanzen 2500, 'Bericht über öffentliche Finanzwirtschaft', 8 August 1940.
[3] F.D. 5320/45, Rk., Abt. Beaufträgter bei der Norges Bank, 'Bericht über die Finanzierung der Deutschen Wehrmacht und des Reichskommissariats sowie über die Entwicklung des Geldkredit—und Währungswesens in der Zeit vom 8 April 1940 bis 31 Dezember 1942', 15 February 1943.

remained in force. The Reichskommissariat felt that it was unsafe to go beyond these levels at the time and hoped to raise the large sum left by public borrowing.

In the light of what was to occur later, not only in Norway but in other occupied countries, it is strange to reflect on the pessimism with which the possibility of raising loans was at first approached. The prevailing scarcity of goods in most occupied countries together with the irrepressible inflation, meant that in every case where a reasonable façade of governmental and constitutional respectability was maintained the public debt was eagerly taken up and even at times when it would have seemed that doubts as to the final outcome of the war would have caused the public to hold off. It will be seen from Tables 22 and 23 that the desire of the public in Norway to find an outlet for disposable liquid funds was as ready as elsewhere.

TABLE 22. *New Government Loans Issued, 1940–5**

(000,000 kroner)

Year	Long-term loan (Statsobligasjonslån)	Short-term loan (Statsveksellån)	Total
1940	75	. .	75
1941	200	604	804
1942	425	785	1,210
1943	300	498	798
1944	730	733	1,463
Jan.–Mar. 1945	400	268	668
Total	2,130	2,888	5,018

TABLE 23. *Long-term Government Borrowing in Norway, 1940–5**

Year	Interest rate (%)	Sum (000,000 kroner)	Time period (years)	Date of issue
1940	4	75	5	1 Nov. 1940
1941	3½	100	10	1 Apr. 1941
1941	3½	100	30	15 Dec. 1941
1942	3½	200	40	1 Apr. 1942
1942	3½	225	40	15 Nov. 1942
1943	. .	50	12	15 June 1943
1943	3½	150	40	15 June 1943
1943	2½	100	7	15 June 1943
1944	3½	300	40	1 Feb. 1944
1944	3½	300	40	1 July 1944
1944	2½	100	12	1 July 1944
1944	. .	30	12	1 Aug. 1944
1945	2½	100	12	1 Feb. 1945
1945	3½	300	40	1 Feb. 1945

* Statistisk Sentralbyrå, *Statistisk-økonomisk utsyn over krigsårene* (Oslo, 1945), p. 14.

The issue of the 4 per cent loan for 75 million kroner on 1 November was readily taken up. The plan of the Reichskommissariat was to watch the response to this issue of 100 million kroner.[1] The second issue was made on 1 April 1941. In the intervening period the growth of bank deposits was very rapid, especially that of savings-bank deposits. Table 24 might suggest that, once adequate control of available goods had been instituted, the Reichskommissariat's financial policy need not have been so cautious.

TABLE 24. *Bank Deposits, 1940–5**

(000,000 kroner)

Year	Deposits in joint-stock banks	Deposits in savings banks	Deposits with life insurance companies	Funds and other public institutions	Total
1940	52·6	6·7	4·0	..	..
1941	131·9	84·8	22·7	..	..
1942	195·3	187·1	88·6	..	..
1943	172·2	288·4	226·1	..	..
1944	322·4	450·7	326·5	233·3	1,332·9

* Statistisk Sentralbyrå, *Statistisk-økonomisk utsyn*, p. 15.

But the one compelling reason to caution was the constant rise in Wehrmacht expenditure. The decisions taken in Berlin on 9 and 10 October had only defended Terboven's position providing that a satisfactory method of providing the rest of the Wehrmacht costs was evolved. Until some concrete administrative arrangements had been made for that, the financial decisions relative to Norwegian public finances took place in the shelter of a flimsy administrative dam on the other side of which the tide of Wehrmacht expenditure rose to a level far beyond the sums spent by the Norwegian government. At the time of the Berlin meeting, the account for Wehrmacht expenditure in Norges Bank already stood at 800 million kroner.[2] By 10 November it stood at 1,200 million kroner.[1] By the end of September the note issue had increased by 56 per cent since the invasion. By 7 November it had increased by 72 per cent. Between 1933 and 1937, when the German economy was in full expansion from an extremely low level of activity, the note issue had increased by only 35 per cent. As matters stood, even if Terboven's policy could be sustained, there would be a substantial reduction in Norway's standard of living. 'The heavy demands on Norwegian finances will only be satisfied if there is a consequent lowering of the standard of living among the middle and lower groups.'[3] But if the dam burst a currency collapse was certain. If the

[1] F.D. 5211/45, Rk., Abt. Wi., 'Führerbericht', 18 November 1940.
[2] *Aktstykker*, No. 11.
[3] Ibid., No. 13.

demands of the armed forces continued to increase at the rate they had increased since the invasion, the sum required by the end of May 1941, when a further assessment of Norway's capacity to pay was to be made, would be 200,000 million kroner.

The permanent administrative changes introduced in relation to Wehrmacht purchases and contracts were of small consequence unless the problem as a whole were not dealt with. A Division of Public Contracts (Referat für öffentliche Aufträge) was set up in the Reichskommissariat to co-operate with the Central Supply Office of the Norwegian government. The nature and level of Wehrmacht contracts remained under the ultimate control of the Commander-in-Chief. These contracts were mostly for construction work and where the necessary supply of raw materials was to come from Norway, as, for example, in the case of concrete, it would be considered within the general system of allocation practised by the Reichskommissariat and the Norwegian government. 'Through this organization', the Reichskommissariat opined, 'we should be able to achieve a situation where a sufficient quantity of goods remains for civilian consumption and where the material needs of the Wehrmacht will be satisfied as far as possible by supply from the Reich.'[1] That is to say that the Reichskommissariat would decide the over-all quantity of materials available and allocate a certain portion to the Wehrmacht, forcing the Wehrmacht to obtain the rest of its supply from Germany. But the weakness in the system was that there was no over-all allocation of labour. The Wehrmacht continued to attract whatever labour it wanted by offering higher wages.

The investigation into what burden should be imposed on Norway after May 1941 was carried out between 30 October and 12 November by Reichsbankoberinspektor Lehrer of the Volkswirtschaftliche Abteilung of the Reichsbank and by Dr. Bonus, an official of the Reichskommissariat für die Preisbildung. Their work represents the first German investigation of the possible limits to the exploitation of an occupied economy, limits which elsewhere were only to be explored after 1942—a striking testimony to the difficulty of the Norwegian problem. It had already become obvious that, whatever the strategic value of occupying Norway, it might well distinguish itself from the other territories so far acquired by becoming an economic liability and not an asset.

In fact the strategic question was at the root of the problem, for it was the difficulty of defending a coastline as long as that from the Skaggerak to the Pyrenees that necessitated so large an army of occupation. Even were that army reduced to 250,000 men that would still have been the equivalent, on a population basis, of an army of 7 million men in Germany proper. As an economic burden it would be far greater than this comparison would suggest. Little over 40 per cent of Norway's pre-war

[1] F.D. 5211/45, Rk., Abt. Wi., 'Führerbericht', 18 November 1940.

consumption came from internal production whereas over 80 per cent of Germany's did. If in fact Wehrmacht expenditure in Norway did reach the level of 200,000 million kroner by May 1941 and if this expenditure were wholly covered by Norwegian credits Germany would, within a year, have acquired and spent for military purposes about two-thirds of the national income of Norway for 1938. When it is recalled how high a proportion of that national income was accounted for by invisible earnings the impossibility of imposing such charges on the Norwegian economy is obvious.

Yet is was also obvious that there was less likelihood of any really effective reduction of expenditure in Norway than in countries where the *per capita* burden of occupation was less. Norway had been singled out for a capital investment programme, whereas in other occupied western territories the level of investment was initially intended to be lower than in peacetime. The economic programme was a political and economic necessity; given the assumptions behind the war, the airfields, barracks, and fortifications were a military necessity.

Lehrer and Bonus analysed the various constituent elements of Wehrmacht expenditure in an effort to predict its future behaviour. This type of calculation was never made available to the civil authorities in the case of other western occupied countries. Indeed, the Commercial Policy Committee of the Foreign Office which fixed the level of occupation costs elsewhere was simply provided with a lump sum demand by the Wehrmacht and told nothing of the basis on which this was calculated.[1] The breakdown of expenditure revealed that certain items might be included as necessary civil expenditure. Such were the building of barracks for those made homeless in Kristiansund and the building of barracks for 6,000 German police and S.S. men.[2] These deductions, however, only reduced the Wehrmacht expenditure by about 130 million kroner. Of the remaining total only 18 per cent was attributable to the pay and upkeep of the army of occupation whereas 57 per cent was attributable to construction projects.[3]

Such proportions might suggest that once the urgency of providing barracks in which the troops could last out the harsh Norwegian winter was over the level of Wehrmacht expenditure would drop. But the authors of the report drew attention to the fact that this gain would be nullified by the massive capital expenditure to be undertaken elsewhere. For the first time they calculated the actual cost of the economic programme and revealed how alarmingly high it was. The number of projects already

[1] A. S. Milward, *The New Order and the French Economy*, p. 287.

[2] The cost of the police barracks was 3,330 kroner per man. Wehrmacht expenditure on its own barracks was 700 kroner per man.

[3] F.D. 5212/45, Rk., 'Beanspruchung und Leistungsgrenze der norwegischen Volkswirtschaft nach dem Stande von Oktober 1940'.

decided on by various authorities was costed together for the first time. The more important proposals were:

(i) The Sørland railway. The railway track from Stavanger along the southern coast to the main network and to Kristiansand was to be completed. In all a total of 109 kilometres of track had to be built and the date for completion had been set for 31 October 1941. The total cost was likely to be 150 million kroner.

(ii) The Norland railway. This vast project was to carry the Norwegian railway system as far north as Narvik. The total length of new track between Mosjøen and Narvik would be 640 kilometres. In spite of the exceptional difficulty of the terrain completion was supposed to take only four to five years.[1] The total estimate of costs, including those for electrifying the line, was 700 million kroner. But there was one obstacle even greater than the cost, the quantity of material required. In 1941 alone 100,000 tons of steel would be needed. Such imports would represent almost a 50 per cent increase over Norway's steel imports in 1938.

(iii) The naval construction programme. Germany had already placed contracts with Norwegian shipyards between 75 and 100 million kroner in value to run to the end of September 1941. The navy already had plans for a further 20 million kroner of contracts to be placed after that date.

(iv) The naval harbour building programme.

(v) The construction of a cellulose factory at Sarpsborg. Twenty per cent of the capital for this works was being provided by the German firm Schlesische Zellwoll AG. The rest was to be provided mainly from private Norwegian sources. But the Norwegian state was contributing a sum estimated by the authors of the report at between 10 and 12 million kroner. The Reichskommissariat later estimated the total to be provided from state funds at 13 million kroner, 6 million kroner as secured mortgage loans and 7 million kroner as unsecured credits bearing no interest.[2]

(vi) The aluminium industry programme. An enormous industrial development was to be undertaken in the space of two years. The provisional cost was estimated at between 300 and 500 million kroner. About 225,000 tons of iron and steel would have to be imported over two years and 20,000 additional workers would be needed.

(vii) An increase in iron-ore output. Norway's productive capacity was to be doubled within three years to 3 million tons a year.

(viii) An increase in pyrites output. In this case the productive capacity was to be doubled within four years to 2 million tons a year.

(ix) An increase in the output of other metallic ores, in particular those of copper, nickel, lead, and molybdenum.

[1] It is still uncompleted.
[2] F.D. 5325/45, Rk., Generalbericht der Abteilung Finanzen für die Zeit vom 21 April 1940 bis 31 Dezember 1942.

(x) The building of new shipyards.

(xi) The construction of an autobahn from Halden on the southern frontier with Sweden to Trondheim. The straight distance was 500 kilometres and it was estimated that it would take one and a half years to build 100 kilometres and cost 150 million kroner for the same distance. Work would begin in spring 1941 and would require 20,000 workmen.

(xii) The provision of barracks for the workforce on the new autobahn.

(xiii) The plans of the German Labour Front to buy a bank, a shipyard, and several hotels.

(xiv) The reconstruction of the districts damaged in the war.

(xv) A programme of work creation by the Reichskommissariat to relieve the worst effects of seasonal unemployment.

(xvi) The construction of new power stations. Those already planned would cost at least 150,000 kroner and require about 15,000 tons of steel.

Of all these projects the report was most critical of the Norland railway. It would mean a 16 per cent addition to the Norwegian railway network which seemed unjustifiable on any economic grounds. In peacetime the ore it would carry would be too dear to compete with seaborne ores. As a wartime measure it was useless, for the war would probably be over long before the railway was finished. In military circles there were misgivings as to its strategic value because it was so exposed to enemy attack. But the building of the Norland railway was strongly supported by Hitler on other grounds. Whatever its economic value it was to be one of the greater monuments of the new Europe. The Sørland railway, which the report also suggested would not be completed until the war was over, was criticized for the method by which the contracts had been allocated. They had been awarded to a firm offering to halve the estimated two-year construction period but at twice the originally estimated cost.

The total cost of the whole investment programme for the financial year 1941–2 would be at least 1,000 million kroner.

Therefore, [the authors concluded] in the coming year further increasing inroads into the Norwegian economy should be reckoned with if these construction programmes are to be carried out within the estimated scale and time. But it is scarcely thinkable that Germany will be in a position to make available the huge quantities of iron which are necessary and they may even run into difficulties on the side of employment for already there are complaints over the increasing flight from the land and the fact that workers are leaving mines and industry.[1]

If the situation were not to fall into chaos some system of priorities over the allocation of resources was essential. But in this respect the report was pessimistic about the possibilities of achieving, even with controls,

[1] F.D. 5212/45, Rk., 'Beanspruchung und Leistungsgrenze'.

any useful system of distribution if such extensive programmes were maintained. The severe reductions in civilian food consumption did not overcome the general shortages of bread grains, fodder, and sugar. The bread ration was already only 60 per cent that of Germany. Almost all the iron and steel required by both Wehrmacht and civilian programmes would have to be imported from Germany but no effort had yet been made within the German economy to allocate these extra quantities. The coal and oil supply to the Wehrmacht had also to be imported on top of the normal Norwegian demand for these commodities. Almost the whole of what was left of the Norwegian merchant marine was already entirely engaged in transporting goods for the Wehrmacht. There were only three cement factories in Norway with a combined annual output of 300,000 tons. The whole of the existing stock of cement had been immediately seized for building airfields. Three-quarters of the current cement production was already being taken by the Wehrmacht and yet that quantity was insufficient, while at the same time war damage had to be left unrepaired. The huge demand for wood for Wehrmacht projects could not be met from Norway's own resources.

Bonus and Lehrer therefore drew three conclusions: (1) that the demands made by Germany on the Norwegian economy could neither be met in respect of commodities nor in respect of labour supply; (2) that a supply of goods from Germany and from other countries was urgently necessary; and (3) that a reduction in and some planning of the building projects according to their level of urgency and the available raw materials and labour was unavoidable.[1]

Were these recommendations to be accepted as changes of policy, the more fundamental problem of how much money and how many goods Germany could extract from Norway would still not have been solved. It would indeed have been posed in a more immediate manner. Had the investment programme been realistic it would have enormously increased Norway's capacity to provide goods and services. Or, if Germany had confined herself merely to demanding 'occupation costs', it would have greatly increased the amount which could have been requested through its effect on increasing the gross national product. Renunciation of parts of the programme, or even the spreading of the programme over a longer period of time, did not merely postpone the anticipated increase in supply of raw materials and services to Germany, it also postponed the increases in national product and made it more than ever necessary that a strict limit should be set even to the cash sums demanded.

In some ways the existence of the many investment programmes had been a substitute for real economic thinking. It had enabled the German administration to consider Norway in the same light as France, as a mine

[1] Ibid.

of riches to be exploited at will. Where there were obstacles to this exploitation they would be overcome by drawing on German resources. The realization that German resources were not available was a hard one. It was
possible with a large economy such as France's to demand an enormous
cash sum in occupation costs with very little economic calculation necessary. Given a strict control of monetary policy and goods the cash would
be found. In a small economy this was not so. The scope and range of
production was so much less, the possibilities of substitution so much more
restricted, that, once the investment programme was curtailed, there had
to be some hard calculation as to what could be paid.

The approach of the authors of the report to this question was not to
decide on a proportion of the Norwegian national income which could be
creamed off, but, having regard to the quite changed trading circumstances,
to decide what was the surplus actually produced by the Norwegian
economy. If the fishing season were a good one and it proved possible as
well for the mining industry to recapture its pre-war level of production,
a level of exports of about 500,000 million pre-war kroner might be attained,
about 600–700 million current kroner. That would be about three-
quarters the value of 1939 exports. The drop in consumption levels should
cause imports to decline by about 75 per cent. This would be offset to some
extent by the rise in import costs, partly because imports would no longer
be coming from the cheapest source of supply, and partly because the
general cost of all imports would be higher. Since the invasion the Norwegian wholesale price index had increased by 20 per cent for domestic
products and by 65 per cent for imported goods. If, as the authors
estimated, the import bill was about 400–500 million kroner there would
be a maximum possible export surplus, in the most favourable conditions,
of 200 million kroner. The contribution made to Germany could therefore
begin with this potential surplus.

In the event these calculations proved utterly mistaken for this surplus
never materialized, being based on the reduction of consumption in
Norway to a level much lower than it ever reached. Not only that,
Norwegian exports never attained the forecast level after 1940. In 1942
they were only 491·4 million current kroner.

What could be added to the 200 million kroner? In the first place the
shipping services performed by the Norwegian merchant navy for Germany. These were estimated at approximately 100 million kroner annually.
In the second place the employment of Norwegians for German purposes
in Norway. There the report demonstrated that if the 60,000 Norwegians
already employed by the Wehrmacht received the average wage, plus half
as much again for overtime and Sunday work, the Wehrmacht's wage
bill would be only half what it actually was. 'That the Wehrmacht's annual
estimates show more than twice that expenditure on wages demonstrates

the excessively high wages they pay. These wages must be brought back
to a reasonable size if the ore mines and industries which are important
in wartime are not to be brought to a standstill.'[1] The outside limit
for these payments was set at 200 million kroner. The total sum available
from the Norwegian economy therefore came to 500 million kroner
annually, or more or less exactly the sum on which the Reichskommissariat
and the Reichs Economic Ministry had insisted.

On 21 November Terboven and von Falkenhorst with their respective
experts met again in Oslo to discuss these conclusions. General Thomas
and State Secretaries Landfried and Kehrl travelled from Berlin. As
Terboven put it, the purpose of the meeting was to decide, firstly, what
was to be obtained from the Norwegian economy, so that the value of
goods due from Germany as compensation could be estimated, and
secondly to fit Wehrmacht supply into the German–Norwegian clearing
agreements and if possible to reduce it.[2] Somewhere between 1 July and
1 October the point had been reached, Kehrl declared, when the system
in Norway had to be changed. The burden of occupation in Norway
(doubtless what would have served as the minimum basis of occupation
costs in other occupied western territories) had increased from 60 million
kroner a month at the beginning to 200 million kroner a month. How much
of this could be recovered from Norway?

Kehrl's opinion was that as much as 780 million kroner *could* be obtained
in the first year but that on political grounds it might be better to accept
the figure of 500 million kroner.[2] The reality of the situation was that
limits to the cost of the occupation were not being imposed by the exchange
problem and the danger of inflation but by the shortage of shipping space.
In particular the level of activity in the Norwegian economy and the
feasibility of all these plans would be determined by the monthly quantity
of coal that could be shipped from Germany. The optimum level seemed
to be about 150,000–180,000 tons monthly. But Wehrmacht transport
needs were such that there was actually no Norwegian shipping space
available at all for transport for the civil economy and it could not be
denied that the supply to the Wehrmacht had top priority.

It was generally agreed that the constraints imposed by the lack of
shipping space must lead to a slowing down of the construction programmes, although the aluminium-industry programmes were exempted
because of their great strategic significance. When it came to the food
supply of the troops there was nothing but disagreement. The Wehrmacht
representatives were determined not to move from their original prog-
nostications of supply for an army of 150,000. In particular they sought to
maintain the rule that fats and potatoes should be obtained from Norway

[1] F.D. 5212/45, Rk., 'Beanspruchung und Leistungsgrenze'.
[2] *Aktstykker*, No. 16.

together with 40 per cent of the meat. Terboven was insistent that the 'frontier of production' had been reached in Norway and that there must be an absolute limit on Wehrmacht expenditure whatever previous decisions had been taken about the supply of the army. Finally, the meeting was able to agree that the only solution lay in trimming the economic programme so that it corresponded more nearly with the maximum sum available from Norway. There was one weakness in these decisions, namely that the major building projects could only be definitely postponed by a decision from the Führer.

November 1940 was thus a month of great significance for the fascist experiment in Norway. Before the Nasjonal Samling commissioner-ministers had taken a good hold of the reins of office, their hopes for a thorough social and economic change had been shattered. As far as the Reichskommissariat was concerned, German plans had priority over Norwegian. By November even the German plans were being postponed through financial stringency, of which the main causes were the disruption of the Norwegian economy and, even more, the size of the German armed forces in Norway. Before the German economy was itself brought face to face with the realities of military expenditure at home it was forced to face up to them in Norway. From November 1940 the fascist dream in Norway was fading in the harsh light of war and its impelling necessities. The plans of both fascist parties for a sweeping programme of economic reconstruction became from that time onwards less and less realizable.

One other thing was decided in November, the subjection in Norway of the military power to the civil. In the light of subsequent events it seems inevitable that this should have happened. The interest in making Norway an integral part of the Großraumwirtschaft rather than merely using its resources to further the German war effort implied from the outset that the country would be under civilian control, civilian control as finally expressed by the National Socialist Party. Although the existence of the army of occupation in Norway continued to be one of the most overwhelming facts of economic life until the German surrender and even after it, and although the Wehrmacht's activities continued to disrupt the economic policies of the Reichskommissariat, in all important matters the control of the economy had passed into civilian hands.

V

LATER FINANCIAL POLICY

THE pattern of economic existence in Norway determined by November 1940 survived with very few changes for the rest of the occupation. In particular the financial policy decided on by the Reichskommissariat was pursued with comparatively little difficulty until the end of the war. The accession of the Nasjonal Samling government to fuller powers in 1942 created some disturbance through their initial erroneous suppositions that this change of status would allow them to push through their own programmes. But Germany still controlled the purse strings and still insisted on a sound budgetary policy as a safeguard for the clearing accounts and occupation accounts which it never intended to pay back.

There was in German eyes the more reason for this financial orthodoxy as the threat of inflation remained always present. It had started before the invasion in the stockpiling boom and had received a boost from the rapid rise in the quantity and velocity of money circulation after that event. Since, to a certain extent, that had been planned by the invaders as a way of reducing real wages the question that has to be answered is why the economic controls then introduced were never entirely adequate to produce the stationary system which the German administration wished to achieve. First and foremost the blame must be laid on the continued dependence of the Norwegian economy on imports since for the whole period of the occupation the inflation continued to be import-led. Secondly, the social and economic policies of the Reichskommissariat demanded that the wages of certain groups and the prices of certain goods should be adjusted upwards. Thirdly, the failure to establish any sufficiently effective control over the labour market meant that the Wehrmacht continued to pay wages for construction work which were far above the regulation levels decreed by the Reichskommissariat.

Table 25 compares the relative increase in price of imports into Norway with those into Germany, and even allowing for the difference in the base of the two indices it is still clear that the relative increase in cost of imports into Norway was very high. The relative prices of exports from the two countries were closer, and allowing for the difference in base years of the index it may be that German exports increased in price relative to Norwegian, but hardly to such an extent as to represent the main reason for the increase in price of Norwegian imports.

Over the course of 1940 a set of agreements led to a much greater stability of the prices of Norwegian imports from Germany than they had shown immediately after the invasion. But the relative rate of increase in the price of imports from other countries does not seem to have slackened so much. Prices of goods from Germany showed a tendency to creep well beyond the levels of the 1940 agreements, leading in 1944 to a rash of

TABLE 25. *Indices of Foreign Trade Prices, Norway and Germany**

Year	Norway		Germany	
	Import prices	Export prices	Import prices	Export prices
	(1938 = 100)		(1936–8 = 100)	
1938	100	100	98·6	105·5
1939	102	96	96·8	101·7
1940	145	122	126·5	135·1
1941	218	159	143·3	161·0
1942	242	184	169·1	175·0
1943	287	201	193·9	188·3
1944	293	217	..	..

* For Norwegian index, Statistisk Sentralbyrå, *Statistisk-økonomisk utsyn*, p. 52. For German index, F.D. 5306/45, Beauftragte für den Vierjahresplan, Reichskommissar für die Preisbildung, 'Die Entwicklung der Ein-und Ausfuhrwerte von 1928 bis 1942'.

complaints from the Reichskommissariat. The difference in the price of grain in Norway and Germany, due to the exclusion of international price influences from the German grain market, meant a costly programme of price subsidization to prevent high prices of German exports driving up the price of Norwegian grain. Price supports of various kinds, and subsidies to keep down the price of grain imports, cellulose fodder, and fodder concentrates, committed the government to an expenditure of 33 million kroner in the 1940–1 budget, 127 million kroner in 1941–2, and 178 million kroner in 1942–3.[1] In January 1944 the Reichs Economic Ministry agreed to investigate numerous complaints from the Reichskommissariat about extensive price increases on German exports to Norway.

The negotiations with the Reichs Economic Ministry over the observed upward movement of the prices of German goods exported to Norway in the last year have resulted in the German side undertaking to do nothing to increase German export prices to Norway. It was agreed that the so-called Jahnke-agreement of 1940, which bound the export prices of both sides to the position on 8 April 1940 with relation to the individual costs, is still to be seen as binding for both parties.[2]

[1] F.D. 5325/45 Rk., Abt. Finanzen, 'Generalbericht für die Zeit vom 21 April 1940 bis 31 Dezember 1942.'
[2] F.D. 5362/45, Rk., Amt. Preisbildung und Preisüberwachung, 'Tätigkeitsbericht für die Zeit vom 4 Januar bis 3 Februar 1944', 3 February 1944.

As real wages fell, until by July 1941 they were one-third lower than they had been in May 1940, the Reichskommissariat pursued its social policy by giving compensatory adjustments to those sectors of Norwegian society which it particularly favoured. The consequence was a limited upward movement of some incomes and some prices. In spring 1941 agricultural workers were given a 12 per cent wage increase.[1] At the start of the next forestry year, forestry workers received a 10 per cent wage increase. The prices paid for agricultural products also reflected these social aims. Support was given by the Norwegian government to bread prices and milk prices, and the turnover tax on agricultural equipment was abolished. Meat prices and egg prices were increased in the hope of getting a bigger output. Dairy farmers were paid a sum of money in compensation for the ban on cream manufacturing. The price of wood was increased by 20 per cent to compensate for the higher wages paid to forestry workers and the increase in transport costs. These greater rewards were of course distributed to fishermen as well. The price paid for most fish was doubled by 1942 and fishermen's wages increased by a smaller factor.[1] Seamen's wages were increased by extra risk payments. Partly these wage and price increases were determined by the reality of the economic position; there seemed no other way of getting the necessary wood supply since felling depended on the seasonal attraction of casual labour. The cost of metal ores also tended to move upwards reflecting the urgent nature of German demand overriding the arguments in favour of price control. Such changes were often effected against the wishes of the price-control authorities.[2] There was a certain contradiction in price policy for the heavy increases in turnover tax also tended to bring about an upward movement of retail prices.

The attempt to fix prices for construction work began in 1940 but from the beginning ran into difficulties because of the Wehrmacht's firm persuasion that the work had to be done and that 'money didn't matter'.[3]

As long as the Wehrmacht offices cannot be convinced to submit themselves to a unified rule a great deal of work is in vain, and as long as a unified basis of wages is not created with the same rules for all no order can be introduced. As long as no tighter supervision of employment is possible and the Norwegians do what they want with the building offices and impose their own wishes on the German offices, after they have noticed that it can be done, we

[1] F.D. 5306/45, Rk., Gruppe Preisbildung und Preisüberwachung, 'Jahresbericht', 25 November 1941.
[2] F.D. 5362/45, Rk., Amt. Preisbildung und Preisüberwachung, 'Tätigkeitsbericht vom 16–30 September 1942', 30 September 1942.
[3] F.D. 5306/45, Rk., Abt. Preisbildung und Preisüberwachung, 'Tätigkeitsbericht für den Zeitraum von Mai 1940 bis Ende 1942'.

shall have these impossible circumstances. It might be considered whether it were not a good thing to send some of these unwilling Norwegians to Germany, perhaps to be mixed in German work columns and to learn to work.[1]

In October 1942 a survey of numerous building firms showed that the wages paid had 'scarcely any relationship to output'.[2] Wehrmacht contractors were tacitly allowed to pay piece rates for ordinary time work, thus concealing a 40 per cent pay increase. In addition they constantly over-reported the hours worked, with the acquiescence of the Wehrmacht. In Finnmark it had become customary, in order to attract labour, to pay a straight 40 per cent supplement on the hourly wage-rate. The survey found that in some instances the wages of building labourers had risen above those of skilled workmen. This was the more likely to have been the case as much of the building labour force was composed of casual labour, which also shared the higher rewards to fishermen and agricultural workers.

One consequence of these inflationary trends was the attempt to strengthen the machinery of price control by making it ever more repressive and dictatorial. In 1941 the chief executive force of the price-control authorities was still the Fylkesmann and the local price committees. The committees were strongly criticized by the German authorities for their tolerance of offenders against the price regulations. By the order of 28 January 1942 the whole structure of price control was taken out of the general administrative framework and transferred to the police administration. The consequence was a much more aggressive policy relying not on local notabilities but on an inspectorate responsible to the police. In May 1942 the local price committees were 'brought more in accord with the Führerprinzip'.[3] The chairman was made responsible for all decisions, the rest of the committee functioning merely as his advisers. These measures were still inadequate to stop the black-market trade. The price-control authorities wanted to have the penalties for black-market trade increased and became involved in an administrative dispute with the Norwegian Department of Justice and the German police administration to try to force Norwegian judges to impose maximum sentences on offenders.[4]

As Nasjonal Samling officials began to occupy positions in the price administration in greater numbers (by June 1942 10 per cent of the officials were party members), the authoritarian tone became still more pronounced.[5] But when Nasjonal Samling received its wider powers in

---

[1] F.D. 5306/45, Rk., Abt. Preisbildung und Preisüberwachung, 'Lagebericht', 5 September 1942.
[2] F.D. 5362/45, Rk., Abt. Preisbildung und Preisüberwachung, 'Tätigkeitsbericht für den Zeitraum vom 16.11–24.12.1942', 4 December 1942.
[3] Ibid., 'Tätigkeitsbericht für den Zeitraum vom 1–15 Mai 1942', 15 May 1942.
[4] Ibid., 'Tätigkeitsbericht für den Zeitraum vom 16 bis 31 Mai 1942', 1 June 1942.
[5] Ibid., 'Tätigkeitsbericht für den Zeitraum vom 1.6–15.6 1942', n.d.

September 1942 and began to try to initiate its own policies the efficiency of the price controls was again weakened by the open disagreements between Quisling and the Reichskommissariat on financial policy.

A sufficient understanding of a strict price stabilization policy is still quite lacking in the Quisling government. They are constantly trying to put through higher prices for single branches of production or firms. Therefore after 1 February 1942 a stronger influence in matters of detail and, unfortunately, a correspondingly greater amount of administrative work was necessary on the German side than would have been necessary in the case of a general unanimity on the lines of price policy such as previously existed.[1]

In particular the round of price increases in September 1942 met with the particular disfavour of the price-control authorities. 'Price Director Bjorheim turned down the desire of interested parties for price increases but finally had to concede them after repeated pressures. This overriding of the price directorate greatly hinders the implementation of the necessary price stabilization.'[2]

The effect of the constant inflationary threat was not so much to drive expenditure below the levels decided on in November 1940 but to cause the Germans to impose a rigid budgetary policy on the Norwegian government. In fact the main constraint on the Reichskommissariat's programme became, as Kehrl had indicated, one of the availability of materials rather than of money. The government's expenditure, for all the restraints imposed on it, increased in several areas to conform with the general policy of the Reichskommissariat. Extra expenditure above the pre-war level had to be laid out on new 'ministries' appropriate to the New Order. 'As in the previous year', wrote the Financial Department, 'the provisions go *far* beyond what the Norwegian state can support financially if it is to fulfil its obligations to the German Reich in respect of the occupation costs. Decisive cancellations will therefore have to be undertaken.'[3], Nevertheless the budget for 1942–3 included 11 million kroner for the department of culture and 41 million kroner for the labour department. At the same time the authoritarian nature of the regime resulted in much higher police costs. They rose from 16 million kroner in 1939–40 to 42 million kroner in 1942–3. To these extra administrative costs was added the cost of certain price supports decided on in 1940 and becoming increasingly burdensome during the occupation. Also the sums expended on subsidizing farming inputs increased. Subsidies on herring-meal and herring-oil

---

[1] F.D. 5306/45, Rk., Abt. Preisbildung und Preisüberwachung, 'Tätigkeitsbericht für den Zeitraum von Mai 1940 bis Ende 1942', n.d.

[2] F.D. 5362/45, Rk., Abt. Preisbildung und Preisüberwachung, 'Tätigkeitsbericht für den Zeitraum vom 16–30 September 1942', 30 September 1942.

[3] R.A., Rk., Haushalt Allgemein 2110, Abt. Finanzen, 'Staatshaushaltsplan 1942/43', 3 June 1942.

production, on cellulose fodder prices, and on imported artificial fodder amounted to 47·8 million kroner in 1942–3.[1]

Additional small sums were included in the budget for helping the Norwegian economy in its conversion to self-sufficiency. In 1942–3, 1·8 million kroner were made available for the adaptation of tractors and fishing-boats to propulsion by gas generators operated by wood fuel. The sums provided for A/S Norsk Cellullfabrikker at Sarpsborg should be considered in this light. German intervention in the affairs of the Notodden artificial-fibre works came under the same heading. When the owner of a considerable packet of shares in the company fled to London, Germany sequestrated the shares and used them as the basis of a capital-widening scheme. For this the Norwegian government provided a subsidy, as operations on the open market might have caused a fall in the value of the German shares. Subsidies up to 2·5 million kroner were included in the 1942–3 budget to carry out the plan for providing forcing houses in north Norway to increase the supply of vegetables there. In each of the first three years of occupation a subsidy of 33,000 kroner went to the pyrites mines in the Grong area. After 1941 a research company, partly formed by the Mansfeld firm, was set up to undertake a thorough exploitation and received an annual subsidy of 325,000 kroner, rising to 500,000 kroner in 1942–3.[1] Finally, there was the cost of repairing the war damage to certain Norwegian industries and towns.

All these additions to pre-war public expenditure take no account of the extra-budgetary expenditure. The financing of the aluminium industry programme was secured by a special account of 200 million kroner in Norges Bank, and the early debts piled up by the German army still had to be liquidated. The question of how much of the costs of the occupation Germany could include in the Norwegian budget was thus a question requiring constant finesse and discretion, especially as the precise status of those costs in international law remained so vague.

The decision in November 1940 to try to limit German expenditure in Norway to somewhere near the 'productive capacity' of the Norwegian state had more effect on the Reichskommissariat's economic programme than on Wehrmacht expenditure. By 1941 Wehrmacht expenditure had fulfilled the gloomiest prophecies. On 1 May the Wehrmacht account in Norges Bank stood at 1,950 million kroner.[2] The basic reason was the shortage of shipping space. The army of occupation continued to be supplied from Norway rather than from Germany because there was no other possibility. Part of this account could still be covered by contributions from the Norwegian government within the terms of the November

---

[1] F.D. 5325/45, Rk., Abt. Finanzen, 'Generalbericht für die Zeit vom 21 April 1940 bis 31 Dezember 1942', n.d.

[2] *Aktstykker*, No. 18.

agreement and the Reichskommissariat pressed for a further contribution of 150 million kroner but without specifying in which budget year the contribution should be shown. As a contribution to the total it was not too impressive and there began an anxious correspondence between Oslo and Berlin as to the implications of what had been decided in November. Who was ultimately the creditor to the Wehrmacht account in Norges Bank in respect of its excess above the Norwegian contributions, Germany or Norway?[1]

By the end of May the level of Wehrmacht expenditure had risen to 2,200 million kroner and it was obvious that the economic circumstances did not permit, nor would they permit in the future, a greater volume of goods to be supplied from Germany. Before the accounts for the second year of occupation were drawn up some permanent decisions about financial policy in Norway had to be taken in full acknowledgement that the decisions in November had now only a limited applicability. The Reichskommissariat, furthermore, believed that in April and May they could detect a quickening of the rate of inflation. They attributed this to the rapid growth of bank deposits with Norges Bank and the expansion of all other forms of credit.[2] It is most likely that what they were observing was the emergence of a state of full employment in the Norwegian economy after so many years of slack working. To place so large an army in the country and equip it with such relatively unlimited purchasing power was, in an economic sense, to impose a recovery programme on the country, and it was with the critical point of this recovery programme that the Reichskommissariat's officials were struggling in spring 1941. The effect of these economic changes and of the constantly mounting and largely uncovered Wehrmacht account in Norges Bank was such as to give them quite justified fears about the stability of the currency. Greater justification was given to these fears by the history of bank instability in Norway in the inter-war period when deposit banks, most of which were local rather than national and which were frequently heavily committed to the shipping industry, had often collapsed.

Terboven drew von Falkenhorst's attention to these fears on 31 May indicating that, should they be realized, they could seriously harm the economic programme and the Wehrmacht's ability to supply itself in Norway. Continued inflation would erode the price controls and the Wehrmacht would be obliged to purchase its supplies on the black market. To avert a disaster of this kind some absolute control over the Wehrmacht's expenditure was now essential as it was clear that the assumptions that had lain behind the decisions of the previous autumn were no longer valid.[2] At the same time, the question was raised in Berlin as to whether those decisions did not mean that Germany herself was responsible for the

[1] Ibid., No. 19.   [2] Ibid., No. 20.

Wehrmacht costs in Norway where they exceeded the agreed limit of 500 million kroner annually which had been held to represent the maximum level of exploitation possible in Norway given the political circumstances.

These initiatives by Terboven were the last moment at which a clearly defined financial policy could have been pursued in Norway. The failure of both left no alternative but for the Reichskommissariat to pursue the same policy as they had followed from November to May, that is to say to postpone all *ultimate* decisions about costs and to try to contain the situation by budgetary policy and by strictly enforced financial controls. Manœuvre, improvization, and a strict refusal to discuss the final question of costs with the Norwegian government had, henceforth, to be the orders for the day.

Von Falkenhorst replied to Terboven that in his opinion such economies as were possible would make no real difference to the situation. It might be possible to cut back expenditure on clothing and furniture but such reductions would scarcely be noticed by the side of the vast expenditure on construction. 'I am', he wrote, 'of the opinion that the problem cannot fundamentally be solved in this way. The only remedy here is a complete removal of the present currency system and the institution of the Reichs currency.'[1] In fact the solution proposed by von Falkenhorst, although it had been often proposed by *Großraumwirtschaft* writers in respect of other economies, had always been sternly rejected in official circles. It had, for example, been rejected by Funk in his celebrated speech of July 1940 which had first opened a public discussion between firms and the government on the nature of the New Order.

A currency union, however, demands generally comparable standards of living and these neither should be nor can be the same in the future in all the countries included in the European clearing, because the economic and social preconditions for that are lacking and the ordering of the European economy on this basis would be absurd in the foreseeable future.[2]

On Terboven's insistence a special Wehrmacht committee of inquiry visited Norway to examine ways in which expenditure might be reduced. The committee held that Terboven's fears for the currency and the banking system were quite justified, that the directors of Norges Bank might resign and that their public replacement would be a signal for the currency collapse to begin. The Wehrmacht could, of course, compel people to work in Norway even if inflation destroyed their willingness to do so, but this would be in flagrant contradition to the Führer's orders to Terboven on the 'conciliatory' treatment of the Norwegians.[3] The scope for reducing the 'personal' expenses of the Wehrmacht was very limited. It admitted of

[1] *Aktstykker*, No. 23.
[2] W. Funk, 'Wirtschaftliche Neuordnung Europas'.   [3] *Aktstykker*, No. 28.

one administrative reform which had already been instituted on 1 July 1941 when the transfer of army pay from Germany to Norway was stopped. In fact that measure meant considerable difficulty for the officials of the Reichskommissariat whose cost-of-living allowance for service abroad was paid in Germany. Some method now had to be found of transferring those sums to Norway.[1] The 'material' expenses of the Wehrmacht were mostly the sums spent on construction, by August 1941, 2,200 million kroner. The only possible reduction in the construction programme was the Norland railway. The committee rejected von Falkenhorst's currency proposals on the grounds of impracticability. Would the Norwegians accept German banknotes? And if they did would that solve the problem, which was not the type of currency but its quantity? They made a number of alternative recommendations. One was their own, that the financial expedients used in the German recovery programme after 1933 be tried in Norway and that Norwegian entrepreneurs be paid in future bills comparable to the pre-war German *Lieferschaftzanweisungen*. This suggestion was not received enthusiastically by the Reichskommissariat whose view was that Norwegian entrepreneurs would not accept such bills. Their other suggestions emanated from Sattler, and Keitel indicated that he would support their acceptance in Berlin.[2] The goods produced in Norway for Wehrmacht contracts, often from raw materials imported from Germany, should be regarded as Norwegian exports for the purposes of the clearing agreements. Those costs of the Wehrmacht in Norway which were not for long-term projects, as, for example, the expenditure on ships, aircraft, and some goods intended for immediate short-term applicability, rather than specifically for the occupation of Norway, should be separated from the genuine costs of occupying the country incurred by the armed forces. In this way Norway as a theatre of war might be financially distinguished from Norway as an occupied land. The committee also favoured the recommendation that at the very least there should be a monthly delimitation of the level of Wehrmacht demand so that even if it could not be substantially reduced it could be more effectively controlled over time.

While the committee was pursuing its inquiry the Reichs Ministry of Finance was considering Terboven's plan to have Germany categorically accept the responsibility for costs beyond the limit of Norway's agreed capacity to pay. Wehrmacht expenditure had in fact shown an upward trend after November so that if all were charged finally to Norway the *per capita* burden on the population would be 1·70 Reichsmarks a day. No other occupied territory was obliged to accept such a level of costs. In Belgium the *per capita* burden of the established 'occupation costs' was 0·40 Reichsmarks a day, in France, 0·38. But Sattler's conversations with

[1] F.D. 5227/45, Rk., 'Wirtschaftliche Übersicht', Finanz', 15 September 1941.
[2] *Aktstykker*, No. 28.

Oberregierungsrat Breyhan of the Ministry of Finance did not convince him of any necessity to change the system. 'It would be the first case where Germany has accepted final responsibility for the costs of occupation', wrote Breyhan.[1] Sattler had said that the responsible officials in Oslo would resign unless this were done. 'We regard Sattler's fears as exaggerated, at the moment, even as irrelevant.'[1]

The official decision was made at meetings on 15 and 16 August. The Ministry of Finance flatly declined any system by which the Wehrmacht accounts in Norges Bank should be taken over as part of the Reich debt. They also flatly refused to consider any division of the Wehrmacht costs in Norway into 'occupation' costs and 'non-occupation' costs. Such suggestions had already been made in the case of France and turned down. 'A covering of the account at Norges Bank could therefore only follow as a consequence of contributions from the Norwegian state.'[2] In a further conversation Breyhan said that these contributions should be 500 million kroner for the financial year 1941–2. The Norwegian contribution of 150 million kroner which it had been decided to request in May 1941 was now reckoned in the financial year 1940–1. On 8 December 1941 the Norwegian government was told that 500 million kroner to be paid according to these decisions would have to be provided in the budget.[3] Of this total, 100 million kroner would go to a special account to cover the development of the aluminium industry.

The Norwegian government asked for 100 million kroner of the total to be written off as compensation for the loss of agricultural land to the Wehrmacht. In reply Terboven hinted that the total payment might have to be greater in the following year if economic circumstances remained unchanged.[4] Since these payments were partly construed as an anti-inflationary measure much attention was paid to the question of how the tax revenue of the state could best be increased. The income tax was assessed with a special supplement. The assessment of company taxation on companies whose ships were thought to be engaged for Allied needs was also increased so that their profit level in 1940 was counted at one and a half times its level in 1938–9. The range of incidence of the turnover tax was widened. Taxes on tobacco and alcohol and on various luxury and 'colonial' goods were increased. In addition a range of new taxes was introduced. A steeply graduated war-profits tax was created which taxed the increase in profits over the level of the years 1937–9; a 20 per cent tax where the profit level had increased by 25 per cent, an 80 per cent rate where the profit had increased by more than 100 per cent. The anticipated yield from this one tax was from 50 to 60 million kroner.[5] A variety of other taxes

---

[1] *Aktstykker*, No. 25.
[2] Ibid., No. 29.
[3] Ibid., No. 31.
[4] Ibid., No. 35.
[5] F.D. 5227/45, Rk., 'Wirtschaftliche Übersicht, Finanz', 15 September 1941.

with much smaller yields, none previously known in Norway and some derived from German experience in the 1930s were also introduced. Taxes on matches, on confectionery, on luxury furs, and on lighting, all went to covering the record level of expenditure in the budget. So did a war supplement to the local income tax.

The subsequent increase in tax revenue may be seen from Table 26. If the increase in local taxes in 1941 is also considered the total tax revenue in that year to both local and central government was as high as 1,600 million kroner, over one-quarter of the gross domestic product of 1939. Taxation on so massive a level meant that the 500 million kroner was paid without difficulty. The Reichs Finance Ministry decided that in the next financial year the sum to be paid should be increased to 750 million kroner.[1]

TABLE 26. *The Revenue from Taxation in Norway, 1939–40 to 1941–2*

(000,000 kroner)

	1939–40	1940–1	1941–2
Income tax and wealth tax	157·3	218·7	242·3
War economy taxes	..	..	37·6
Turnover tax	44·2	269·0	500·3
Customs revenue	151·1	132·2	86·6
Other taxes	177·8	234·6	214·1
Total	530·4	854·5	1,080·9

Nominally, the result of a payment of 750 million kroner would be to bring the total contribution over the first three years of the occupation to 1,600 million kroner, one-third of the Wehrmacht's expenditure. In reality the contribution of the Norwegian state was greater than this. The use of state railways, of the postal service, of the telephone system, of the road network (when hardly any other users had the means to use it), all these appeared as official Norwegian expenditure in the budget and not even as a contribution to the costs. The Reichskommissariat estimated that for 1940–1 and 1941–2 the total contribution of the Norwegian state to the Wehrmacht costs was 1,750 million kroner out of a total of 4,955 million kroner.[2] Before the much heavier contribution for the financial year 1942–3 the proportion covered was already, therefore, larger than one-third. The average monthly level of Wehrmacht expenditure declined in the financial year 1942–3. In 1940 the monthly level was 150 million kroner; in 1941, 202 million kroner; in 1942, 190 million kroner.[3] Consequently the Norwegian state's contribution to the total in 1942–3

---

[1] *Aktstykker*, No. 36.

[2] F.D. 5325/45, Rk., Abt. Finanzen, 'Generalbericht für die Zeit vom 21 April 1940 bis 31 Dezember 1942', n.d.

[3] F.D. 5320/45, Rk., Beauftragter bei der Norges Bank, 'Bericht über die Finanzierung'.

approached more nearly to one-half than to one-third. Expressed on the basis of calendar years the increase in Norway's contribution over time seems even more striking. Political considerations aside, the Reichs Finance Ministry had had every justification for not changing their general policy.

TABLE 27. *The Provision of Finance for the Wehrmacht (including the Organization Todt) and the Reichskommissariat through Norges Bank**

(000,000 kroner)

	To 31 Dec. 1940	To 31 Dec. 1941	To 31 Dec. 1942
Wehrmacht withdrawals from Norges Bank	1,175	3,582	5,859
For redeemed Reichskreditkassenscheine	234	234	234
Total Wehrmacht withdrawals	1,409	3,816	6,093
Reichskommissariat withdrawals	33	139	214
Other entries	..	3	4
Total demand from German Administration	1,442	3,958	6,311
Norges Bank credits with the Chief Administration of the Reichskreditkassen	1,342	3,574	4,858
Contributions of Norwegian state to occupation costs in so far as they are entered in above account	100	250	1,300
Refunds for goods from Germany entered on clearing accounts but used by Wehrmacht, etc.	..	134	153
	1,442	3,958	6,311

* F.D. 5320/45, Rk., Beaufträgter bei der Norges Bank, 'Bericht über die Finanzierung'.

The secret of the success of these operations, Sattler claimed, lay in the undisclosed size of the credits to the Wehrmacht, undisclosed because they did not appear in the budget. The ambivalent nature of the Wehrmacht accounts sustained the hopes of leading Norwegians that Germany would eventually pay.

Even though this hope ought to have been somewhat dampened by the repeated German requests for the payment of Norwegian 'contributions to the German costs in Norway' (payment to date 1,500,000,000 kroner, new demand in February 1943 750,000,000 kroner), it is still, however, present today and has helped to lighten the responsibility of the leading Norwegians.[1]

Be that as it may, Quisling and his cabinet put up a stern fight in August and September 1942 against the higher demands. At a meeting with the

[1] F.D. 5320/45, Rk., Beaufträgter bei der Norges Bank, 'Bericht über die Finanzierung'.

financial officials on 3 September they tried to get the level of Norway's contribution retained at 500 million kroner. The Reichskommissariat blandly maintained that the increase was more an anti-inflationary device than an increase in occupation costs and although Quisling must have suspected the worst he had no alternative but to give in.[1] The pill was all the more bitter to swallow since Quisling and his Minister of Finance, Prytz, had no love for the directorate of Norges Bank which adhered to the Reichskommissariat's policy because of its anti-inflationary nature. In October 1942 the Reichskommissariat decided that in the next financial year the Norwegian contribution would be 1,000 million kroner.[2] The budget would be balanced at a further record high total of 1,900 million kroner, 1,200 million kroner from current revenue, and 700 million kroner from credit.

To what extent [wrote Breyhan] the excess amount of money in the Norges Bank credit should go towards the burden on Norway is a political question which does not need to be decided at the moment. In any case there is no cause on these grounds to change the present methods of financing and thereby to change unnecessarily the debt character of the Norges Bank credit.[3]

The high level of taxation already achieved in the budget for 1941–2 did not seem to hold out the hope of being further increased to meet these new demands. There now existed a whole range of previously unknown taxes in Norway, many of them bringing in a very small yield. German attention turned rather to reform of the basis of the system of taxation, something considered as early as 1940. In two respects it seemed capable of being changed to increase tax revenue, by altering the relationship between local taxation and central government taxation and by changing the method of collecting income tax. The rates at which local taxation had been levied varied very widely between areas. The central income tax had to leave room in its rate of assessment for the maximum level of local taxation, although many communities never approached that maximum level. The war had, however, changed completely the relative commitments of the localities and the central government by increasing central-government expenditure to hitherto unheard of levels while leaving the yield of the national income tax dependent on that of the local tax. The Reichskommissariat pressed that local and central taxation should be unified and that the cumbersome procedure whereby local taxation rates could restrict the rate of central taxation should be ended.[4] Local authorities might actually have a money surplus due to the taxation system and certainly its incidence was very inequitable between different local

[1] *Aktstykker*, No. 40.   [2] Ibid., No. 43.   [3] Ibid., No. 44.
[4] F.D. 5324/45, Rk., Abt. Finanzen [title and date of document missing]. (This and other documents in the same reference seem to be a separated part of the collection published in *Aktstykker*.)

authorities.[1] Such a reform should be combined with the payment of income tax at source, a reform already broached by a committee of the Norwegian government in 1936 but never implemented precisely because of the problem of local taxation assessments. There would then be one unified income tax and the localities would receive credits from the state on the basis of their expenditure in the financial year 1940–1. Otte wrote officially to Quisling on 27 November 1942 asking him to withdraw his reservations about these tax reforms. 'The natural maximum limits of income and expenditure taxes have been reached almost everywhere and that is also the opinion of Finance Minister Prytz, so that a further increase would lead to an over-tightening of the taxation screw.'[2]

The Reichskommissariat did not confine their anti-inflationary efforts solely to an attempt to change the basis of the Norwegian taxation system. Renewed efforts were made to force the Wehrmacht to accept a common tariff for construction work with the rest of the administration, for it was estimated that if only these costs could be brought into line with official guidelines, if, that is to say, the Wehrmacht could be forced to pay 'normal' wages and prices, a saving of 600 million kroner annually would result.[3] But what were 'normal' wages in a situation where the Wehrmacht was exceeded in importance only by the government as an employer? There was no hope of progress along these lines. In spring 1943 there consequently developed a determined administrative battle to force the Nasjonal Samling government to change its methods of taxation.

As far as Nasjonal Samling was concerned, their primary objective was to get the question of the uncovered credits in Norges Bank settled as soon as possible. Only when they knew to what extent they were to be liable for those debts could they effectively decide their own financial policy. Prytz took advantage of a private stay in Berlin to negotiate directly with the Reichs Finance Ministry on 1 April 1943. He was told by Dr. Berger, head of the Foreign Department of the ministry, that the Norwegian payments were necessary to maintain the value of the currency. 'The time, however, had not yet come to speak fundamentally about these matters. In any case, such a conversation would have to take place through the official channels of the Reichskommissariat.'[4] Prytz drew the conclusion that there would be no contribution from Germany until the end of the war.[5] Nor, according to Berger, was there any prospect that in return for its greater financial

[1] R.A., Rk., Haushalt Allgemein 2110, Abt. Finanzen, 'Künftige Finanzpolitik in Norwegen', 30 October 1942.

[2] F.D. 5324/45, Rk., Abt. Finanzen, Otte to Quisling, II/wi 54087/42, 27 November 1942.

[3] Ibid., Rk., Abt. Finanzen, 'Aktennotiz über die Rücksprache mit Oberregierungsrat Korff beim Rk.', 20 February 1943.

[4] *Aktstykker*, No. 46.

[5] F.D. 5324/45, Rk., Abt. Finanzen, 'Eingabe des Finanzministers an den Ministerpräsidenten über Richtlinien für die norwegische Finanzpolitik', 5 May 1943.

contribution Norway could be supplied with more goods. 'It was entirely out of the question that Norway should receive anything additional to the present quantity of goods without material counter-deliveries. Norway could do no better than to carry out the indicated measures of self-help.'[1]

The effect of these admonitions on Prytz was not to make him more amenable. He gave Quisling the impression that Norway would have to pay the whole cost. His conclusion was that, 'If Germany loses the war she would not be able to pay, and if she wins the war it is questionable whether she will want to pay.'[2] By the end of April the Reichskommissariat were aware that Nasjonal Samling would have to be compelled rather than persuaded to institute the taxation changes.[3]

The line of defence chosen by Nasjonal Samling was the inadequacy of the time available for such complicated arrangements. Payment of income tax at source meant that the year in which the tax was collected would be advanced by one year. In view of this it was not possible to institute the necessary arrangements in time for the 1943–4 budget. The Department of the Interior delayed the whole process of investigation into the tax reforms. For them the matter was one of great importance. Local tax rates could go as high as 20 per cent and the income from local taxation even in 1941–2 was almost twice as high, 467·8 million kroner, as the yield from the state income tax.[4] Since the demands on local expenditure were less controlled by German activity these local funds came to provide a source from which 'Norwegian' policies could be financed, as, for example, the reconstruction of areas damaged in the war. In order to defend these funds the Department of the Interior had introduced a law, without consulting the Reichskommissariat, on 23 July 1942, to increase the minimum level of local taxation from 12 per cent to 15 per cent, claiming it was to force the localities to spend this money.

The Reichskommissariat were determined against all opposition to introduce the new income-tax system on 1 July 1943. Urgency was lent to their manœuvres by the apparent impossibility of securing a revenue which must at the very least be at the 1941–2 level of 1,100 million kroner. In that year the turnover tax had accounted for almost half the tax revenue.[5] In the year 1942–3 the diminishing quantity of goods led to forecasts that its yield would not exceed 440 million kroner. Price policy forbade that its rate should be any further increased. The yield of taxes on luxury goods and of the other special wartime taxes, with the exception of the war profits tax, had not only reached its ceiling but had also begun to decline due to the growing scarcity of goods. Again, an increase in the rate of taxation was

---

[1] *Aktstykker*, No. 46. [2] Ibid., No. 50. [3] Ibid., No. 48.
[4] F.D. 5324/45, Rk., Abt. Finanzen, 'Vorschläge für die künftige Finanzpolitik in Norwegen' [n.d.]
[5] See Table 26.

ruled out on the grounds of price policy. There was no possibility of any increase in customs revenue. To increase the burden of direct taxation seemed the only way to produce the necessary budgetary income. The studies made by the Reichskommissariat showed that direct taxation in Norway brought in roughly 7 per cent of the hypothetical national income although the rate of assessment was, even in the Reichskommissariat's view, up to, and perhaps beyond, the bearable limit. In Germany, the income tax and poll tax brought in roughly 12 per cent of national revenue. Faced with these facts the Reichskommissariat's Finance Department was prepared to draft the necessary laws itself and force Quisling's hand.[1]

Nasjonal Samling was forced to acknowledge that there would be no further change in the system of financing German expenditure, certainly no further change in Norway's favour. On 27 May 1944 Sattler proposed terms to the Norwegian government which allowed the Reichskommissariat to dictate the taxation policy of that government without interference.[2] Terboven was advised by the Reichs Finance Ministry to close the account of the administration of the Reichskreditkassen at Norges Bank on a day to be declared. From that day onwards all Wehrmacht expenditure would be financed by the Reichskommissariat demanding the means directly from the Norwegian government.[3] Norges Bank resisted the proposals with such determination that the practices established in 1940 were maintained. But the necessity to prevent the exchange value of the kroner and Reichsmark from being revised meant that the attitude of the Reichskommissariat to the problems of Norwegian public finance became ever more dictatorial. In all essentials therefore the Reichskommissariat simply followed, after November 1940, the dictates imposed on them by the change of policy at that time. Although this meant that their own programme of economic and social reconstruction went ever more slowly and that of Nasjonal Samling was almost entirely suppressed, there seemed no alternative in face of the overwhelming need to keep the international arrangements of the New Order intact in face of the massive expenditure of the Wehrmacht.

When the Norwegian government paid its contribution of 1,000 million kroner on 29 July 1944, it paid it, not into the account of the Reichskreditkassen at Norges Bank, but into a separate account. This solution proved unacceptable to Germany and the Reichskommissariat insisted forcefully on maintaining the usual arrangements.[4] Germany wanted the money immediately in her own budget, as with the continual loss of territory the mechanism of war finance was being more and more deranged.

Experiences in other occupied countries have further demonstrated that it is urgently desirable in the interest of the Reich's finances as far as possible to

---

[1] See Table 26.   [2] *Aktstykker*, No. 56.   [3] Ibid., No. 57.   [4] Ibid., No. 59.

wind up the financial relationships between the Reich and the occupied territories since—quite apart from the military situation—circumstances could occur which could have an unfavourable effect on the capacity of the countries to provide finance.[1]

Norway was not immune from these circumstances; the evacuation of the northern areas in face of the Russian attack would surely have diminished the country's potential capacity. At negotiations in the Finance Department on 30 January 1945, the German authorities insisted on the dissolution of the new account.[2] Ultimately, they claimed, Norway's ability to pay would depend on her economic strength after the war. At the end of December 1944 the Wehrmacht withdrawals from the Reichskreditkassen account at Norges Bank had reached 8,163 million kroner.[3]

Whatever ambitions relative to Norway's place in the New Order had been entertained by either Nasjonal Samling or the National Socialists proved to be overweening. The demands of military strategy which had played so large a part in inspiring the occupation were not appeased by its successful completion. The overwhelming fact of Norwegian economic life for five years was the existence in the country of an army of occupation out of all proportion to the population or resources of the country. Its supply meant that there was never sufficient shipping space for the other German projects. The employment which it generated prevented any strict regulation of the labour market. The level of expenditure which it maintained meant that the Reichskommissariat's efforts had to be lent to the task of keeping the Norwegian currency sound and the kroner–Reichsmark exchange rate as stable as possible. The financial burdens ultimately imposed on Norway were harsher than those imposed on eastern European economies whose place in the New Order was in other respects much less honourable. Fulfilling these financial burdens while preserving the value of the kroner became a task which gradually excluded from consideration all the ambitions for the Norwegian economy with which Germany had begun the occupation. From the reconstruction of Europe German interests declined to the mere acquisition of cash.

The high cost of the occupation must be added to the dislocation of trade and shipping with the resulting shortage of goods, and to the opposition of the population, as the main reasons for the failure of German policy in Norway. In the short run German financial policy was ingenious, subtle, and successful. But in the light of Germany's wider aims, these short-term successes were symptomatic of a wider failure. A genuine integration of Norway into the New Order would have surely meant that the military burden would have been shared on a pan-European basis rather than being left to fall exclusively on Norway to the detriment of all other policy there.

---

[1] Ibid.   [2] Ibid., No. 62.   [3] Ibid., No. 59.

Nothing better reveals the intensely particularist nationalism at the heart of fascist thought than the failure to devise some more equitable way of bearing this burden. Under its weight all fascist economic policies in Norway, whether German or Norwegian, struggled and collapsed. In place of a dynamic reconstruction of the economy was substituted a series of financial and budgetary expedients designed to maintain the stability of the kroner and to allay the suspicions of the population. In Norway, as in other states under fascism, the regeneration of society came to mean the maintenance of social stability.

VI

FOREIGN TRADE

THE main physical constraint on German economic policy in Norway often seemed to be the shortage of shipping space. But this shortage did no more than aggravate the deeper problem of Norway's foreign trading relationships. The break-up of the pre-war pattern of Norwegian trade and the inability of the *Großraumwirtschaft* to compensate for this break-up was the main factor in the abandonment of Germany's economic plans for Norway. But even the revised version of those plans and the cautious policy pursued after November 1940 were based on a quite over-optimistic idea of the capacity of the *Großraumwirtschaft* to supply Norway and a similarly over-optimistic idea of what Norway herself could produce in a period of reduced trade.

There had never been any doubt that the immediate result of the invasion would be a violent disruption of trade, but at the end of 1940, taking stock of the situation, the German administration might well have felt relieved that this disruption had been less severe than might have been anticipated. The index of industrial production reached its average level for 1939 once more in September 1940. Indeed, it only fell a long way behind that level in the two months of fighting.[1] The index of consumer-goods production returned to its pre-war level one month before this. In industries producing for export production remained below its pre-war level, but in spite of this Norway was already moving from a period of severe unemployment to one of skilled labour shortage. Soon there was to be an absolute labour shortage.

The cessation of trade between Norway and the United Kingdom led, as had been expected, to a great increase in trade with Germany. In July, as may be seen from Table 28, the value of German exports to Norway again reached its 1939 level and then rose far above it by the end of the year as German exporters occupied markets whose demand had been met from elsewhere. The change of direction of Norway's exports took place even more quickly. In April and May 1940 Norway's exports to Germany were very low; in June they were twice the value of June 1939. In 1939 Germany had provided about 21·3 per cent of Norwegian imports by value and received about 16·7 per cent of Norwegian exports; from April to

[1] F.D. 5325/45, Rk., Hauptabt. Volkswirtschaft, 'Ein Jahr Reichskommissar für die besetzten norwegischen Gebiete'.

December 1940 she provided 55·4 per cent of Norwegian imports and took 69·8 per cent of Norwegian exports.

Nine bilateral trading treaties linking Norway to other economies in the *Großraumwirtschaft* had come into operation by the end of December. In particular agreements governing the trading relations between Norway and Sweden and Norway and Denmark had been established in which Germany admitted the importance of inter-Scandinavian trade by exempting this traffic from the Norwegian–German clearing agreements. Norway therefore had three foreign-trade balances during the war, an account with Sweden, an account with Denmark, and the central clearing account in Berlin through which her trade with all other European countries passed. That trade which, relative to the others, had never been large, dwindled. Germany, as she had intended, monopolized Norwegian foreign trade other than that which, essentially a continuation of pre-war trade, continued to flow to Denmark and Sweden. The ease with which German markets and German supplies initially adapted to these changes seemed also cause for congratulation, especially in view of the severe shortage of shipping tonnage for German-Norwegian trade.

But relief at these developments was premature. By December 1940 Norwegian foreign trade was already settling down at a much lower level than before the war. This also had been anticipated and the economic programme of the Reichskommissariat was in part designed to meet such a contingency. Even had that programme been carried out to the extent and at the speed intended, however, it could not have bridged the gap caused by such a fall in the value of foreign trade. The implications of the trading figures by the end of 1940 was that the production indices would not continue to show so rosy an aspect in 1941. Nor did they. Throughout the occupation Norway was short of those vital raw materials and manufactured products imports of which had sustained her production in previous years. Even in the heyday of the *Großraumwirtschaft* Norway could not be supplied; as it declined her situation became desperate.

The general picture of Norway's foreign trade in the occupation period is one of decline apart from a modest rally in 1943. The value of both imports and exports increased slightly in that year although the greater part of the increase is to be attributed to increases in prices. The total weight of exports from Norway declined in that year roughly in accordance with the over-all annual trend of the whole war period. There was, however, an increase in the weight of imports suggesting that their increase in value was not wholly attributable to rising prices. As far as the exploitation of Norway was concerned the fall in Norwegian exports represented a clear failure. In 1944, 81 per cent of Norwegian exports by value went to Germany.

The index of Norwegian foreign trade prices shows that the rise in the cost of imports by 1945 was almost threefold compared to 1938, that of exports rather more than twofold. Its value for measuring the figures in Table 29 is limited by the extent to which the shortages and restrictions of the occupation caused changes in the commodity structure both of total

TABLE 28. *Norwegian Foreign Trade by Value, April–December 1939 and 1940**

(000 current kroner)

Month	Imports 1939		Imports 1940		Exports 1939		Exports 1940	
	Total	From Germany	Total	From Germany	Total	To Germany	Total	To Germany
April	102,961	19,434	99,012	16,827	58,339	10,864	21,965	5,680
May	110,657	21,764	26,520	10,450	67,378	11,087	11,024	4,493
June	113,668	26,321	31,200	16,795	68,525	11,271	29,200	20,747
July	94,640	22,180	34,095	22,191	52,443	9,628	37,227	28,956
August	97,339	18,985	53,431	35,682	62,771	8,780	45,468	31,504
September	100,901	15,842	58,562	38,880	68,839	2,316	49,214	33,368
October	118,341	22,988	76,537	49,475	70,711	8,020	68,521	51,970
November	162,374	30,390	73,065	47,855	70,824	7,441	55,836	39,806
December	159,224	29,456	86,563	59,950	92,486	13,398	45,300	32,248

* F.D. 5325/45, Rk., Hauptabt. Volkswirtschaft, 'Ein Jahr Reichskommissar'.

TABLE 29. *Norway's Foreign Trade by Value and Weight, 1938–44**

	Value (000,000 kroner)			Weight (000 tons)	
	Imports	Exports	Import surplus	Imports	Exports
1938	1,192·7	786·5	406·2	6,597	5,358
1939	1,366·2	807·5	558·7	7,556	5,303
1940	948·0	612·0	336·0	3,656	2,499
1941	1,124·9	574·7	550·2	2,951	2,878
1942	943·8	491·4	452·4	2,758	2,302
1943	1,008·2	539·2	469·0	3,165	2,089
1944	721·5	517·2	204·3	2,410	1,706

* Statistisk Sentralbyrå, *Statistisk-økonomisk utsyn over krigsårene*, pp. 49, 115.

imports and total exports. In fact the various component parts of that index show considerable differences in behaviour. Over the same period of time, for instance, the cost of grain imports increased fourfold and that of 'colonial goods' over fivefold while the increase in price of manufactured goods was very slight.[1] The price of fatstuffs exported increased threefold, of hides, skins, and leather fourfold, while that of canned fish increased only 68 per cent. In spite of this range of variation in the Norwegian index the composite indices in Table 25 show something of the true implications of Table 29.[2]

[1] Statistisk Sentralbyrå, *Statistisk-økonomisk utsyn over krigsårene*, p. 52.
[2] See p. 122.

The fact that the increase in the price of exports remained well below that of the price of imports shows that, whatever the fears of inflation on the part of the German administration, they were more afraid of it in Germany than in Norway. The increase in the price level of Norwegian exports seems not to have differed significantly from the general increase in the price level of German imports in the same period. The prices of all Norwegian imports, however, increased much more steeply than the prices of all German exports and so much so as not to be explained by exceptionally high prices for Norwegian imports from countries other than Germany. Almost 70 per cent of Norwegian imports by value came from Germany in 1943. The conclusion that German exports to Norway increased in price considerably more than her exports to most other countries does not seem unwarranted. There were good reasons why that should have been so and the complaints of the Reichskommissariat that it was so appear to have some substance. Not only was Norway starved of imports but they were more expensive than the imports of other lands from Germany.

The rapid rise in volume of Norway's trade with Germany from the moment the fighting stopped tended to disguise the true nature of Norway's foreign trading position. Germany's ambition had been to fill the gap left by the sudden absence of British supplies to Norway. The two main British exports to Norway had been coal and textiles. It was perfectly possible to manage in wartime with a smaller quantity of the latter but no reduction in the supply of coal was thinkable if Germany's plans were to be carried out. In fact Germany was not able actively to fill the gap caused by the collapse of the coal trade with Britain and the export of coal in sufficient quantity to Norway became a serious economic problem. But behind the obvious fact of Germany's rising volume of exports to Norway in 1940 lay the decline in Norwegian trade with every other country, except Denmark, with whom it was still possible to trade.

The first of the bilateral trading agreements signed by the Norwegian government was with Sweden and ran from July to the end of December 1940. It covered imports to the value of 25 million Norwegian kroner, mainly iron and steel manufactures, machinery, and foodstuffs, and exports to the value of 29 million Norwegian kroner, mainly fertilizer, chemicals, pyrites, and molybdenum ore.[1] This level of trade represented roughly 65 per cent of the 1939 value of exports to Sweden for a comparable period of time and about 40 per cent the value of imports from that country. The first agreement with Denmark ran from August 1940 to the end of the year and was for imports to the value of 30 million Norwegian kroner, mainly foodstuffs and machinery, and exports to the value of 33 million Danish kroner, mainly fertilizer, fish, paper, cellulose, and wood pulp.

[1] F.D. 5325/45, Rk., Hauptabt. Volkswirtschaft, 'Ein Jahr Reichskommissar'.

These figures represented a substantial increase over the previous value of trade between the two countries. In fact in 1940 Norwegian imports from Denmark were less than in 1939, but this was exceptional, and the treaty ushered in a period of growing Danish-Norwegian trade. Agreements with other countries were based on the general level of pre-war trade. The first Norwegian-Finnish agreement for the period from August to December 1940 covered imports and exports each to the value of 6·5 million Norwegian kroner, the imports mainly wood and textiles and the exports fertilizer, fish, and sulphur. An agreement with Greece ran from September to December for imports to the value of 2,650,000 Norwegian kroner, mainly olive-oil and tobacco and exports to the value of 3,350,000 Norwegian kroner, mainly fish, paper, and cellulose.

Where the German armies had conquered it was a different story. The agreement with the Netherlands from December 1940 to 31 May 1941 was for less than a quarter of the pre-war level of imports from that country and more nearly one-quarter of the level of exports to it. The imports, worth 4·2 million kroner, would be mainly electrical goods, machinery, and syrup—and the exports, 3·3 million kroner, would be cellulose, wood pulp, and fish. An agreement with Belgium, to run from December 1940 to 30 April 1941, was for imports worth 5 million kroner, mostly machinery, machine tools, chemicals, and textiles, and exports worth 5·5 million kroner, mostly wood pulp and fish. Imports from Belgium were thus reduced to less than a fifth of their pre-war level and exports to Belgium to about one-third of the same level. Belgium had been the fourth biggest supplier to Norway in 1939, more important than Denmark. The effect of the New Order was to reduce Norwegian-Belgian trade to an insignificant amount akin to the level of Norwegian-Finnish or Norwegian-Spanish trade. The trade with the Netherlands declined similarly. As for France, from whom in 1939 43·8 million kroner worth of goods had been imported and who had been Norway's fourth most important market in 1939, no treaty had even been signed by the close of 1940. Although Norway continued to export to France on a lower level in 1941, imports from that country became quite insignificant for most of the war. Without any doubt Germany's capacity to increase her supply to Norway came in part from the enormous benefits she derived from the exploitation of France and the Low Countries. That same exploitation reduced the ability of France and the Low Countries to supply Norway. Germany was unable even by December 1940 to compensate adequately for the decline of most non-German branches of Norway's trade. A comparison of Tables 41 with Tables 31 and 32 shows that after 1940 the relative importance of non-German trade diminished. The effect of the New Order was to circumscribe Norway's trade even with other countries incorporated into the new system.

Only with Denmark, with whom it was possible to trade without going through the central clearing system, and with Hungary and Finland, with whom trade was very small, did the nominal value and proportion of trade increase. Denmark had been responsible in 1938 for 3·5 per cent of Norway's imports by value; in 1944 she provided over 8 per cent. Sweden's share dropped over the same period from 11·5 per cent to less than 7 per

TABLE 30. *Norwegian Trade with Continental European Countries,
1939 and 1940**

(000 current kroner)

Country	Imports		Exports	
	1939	1940	1939	1940
Belgium†	63,489	31,796	30,009	10,037
Bulgaria	878	176	68	17
Denmark	49,965	34,856	33,773	36,260
Finland	7,794	2,741	12,062	12,931
France	43,832	14,281	35,873	14,690
Greece	1,853	1,141	961	1,520
Hungary	5,617	1,668	1,351	1,232
Italy	23,712	17,489	20,937	10,551
Netherlands	35,232	12,628	27,099	9,784
Portugal	6,758	3,480	11,938	3,246
Romania	1,132	697	170	485
Russia	7,443	529	3,550	805
Spain	6,792	5,861	5,837	1,763
Switzerland	16,522	6,644	8,895	4,302
Sweden	139,508	94,616	85,704	78,658
Yugoslavia	1,740	990	296	214

* F.D. 5325/45, Rk., Hauptabt. Volkswirtschaft, 'Ein Jahr Reichskommissar'.
† Including Luxembourg to August 1940.

cent. These two lands and Germany together were responsible for 78 per cent of total Norwegian imports in the latter year. This is to leave out of account imports of crude oil and certain other oil products as the Norwegian Statistical Bureau did owing to doubts about the country of origin of such imports. Crude oil was only available by German releases from stocks and if it be counted as imported, in effect, from Germany the role of trade with countries other than Germany or the two immediate Scandinavian neighbours becomes even more insignificant. Crude oil is responsible for the greatest part of the entry under 'Source unknown' in Table 31. Imports from the Netherlands over the whole period were reduced to utter insignificance from a thriving trade and more or less the same was true for imports from France and Belgium. From a combined value of 116·8 million kroner in 1938 they fell to 11·9 million kroner in

1944, which represented in 1938 terms a value of approximately 4 million kroner. To all intents and purposes therefore the thriving Norwegian import trade from western Europe was completely eliminated.

Until 1942 Norwegian imports from Italy were able to resist the effect of the war on Italy's economy but to do no more than that. After that date as this source of imports also began to dry up the small increases in supply

TABLE 31. *Norwegian Imports by Value and Country of Origin**

(000,000 kroner)

Country	1938	1939	1940	1941	1942	1943	1944
Belgium†	41·8	63·5	31·8	7·8	8·9	9·5	5·1
Denmark	41·7	50·0	34·9	75·9	62·2	83·5	59·5
Finland	6·3	7·8	2·7	9·2	6·4	9·3	10·6
France	36·3	43·8	14·3	4·3	17·8	6·0	4·5
Greece	1·8	1·9	1·1	0·5	1·9	2·1	1·3
Hungary	5·5	5·6	1·7	2·5	7·4	13·6	9·5
Italy	22·7	23·7	17·5	24·8	15·2	9·1	2·5
Netherlands	38·7	35·2	12·6	9·6	9·1	5·4	2·3
Poland‡	22·9	22·3	0·5	..	1·2	2·1	1·3
Russia	19·3	7·4	0·5	7·5	0·3	2·7	2·1
Serbia ⎫ Croatia ⎭	1·8	1·7	1·0	0·1	0·2 / 6·5	0·3 / 4·2	.. / 0·6
Slovakia ⎫ Bohemia-Moravia ⎭	23·1	12·1	0·5 / 10·7	0·2 / 11·1	0·1 / 2·4	.. / 1·2	.. / 2·0
Spain	4·9	6·8	5·9	6·1	4·8	3·8	1·9
Sweden	137·0	139·5	94·6	72·7	60·2	66·5	48·1
Switzerland	12·0	16·5	6·6	12·9	4·6	1·2	1·9
Turkey	3·1	2·7	1·6	1·3	0·4	0·3	0·3
Germany	219·8	259·0	339·7	757·0	622·5	683·3	458·0
Source unknown	..	..	13·7	104·1	94·0	97·2	105·8
Other European countries	214·7	255·6	118·1	7·2	3·9	6·2	4·1

* Statistisk Sentralbyrå, *Statistisk-økonomisk utsyn over krigsårene*, pp. 94–100.
† Including Luxembourg to August 1940.
‡ After 1939 the General Government of Poland.

from Hungary and France were quite inadequate to compensate for it, especially as that from France was so temporary. The value of German exports to Norway reached its peak in 1941. As a proportion of total Norwegian import trade it remained more or less constant at between 66 and 67 per cent throughout the occupation and its fall to 63 per cent in 1944 was due to the severe difficulties of the last quarter of that year. Thus from 1941 onwards Germany's failure to remedy the deficiencies of supply caused by the failure of Norway's import trade with other countries became every year more marked.

Norway's exports to Denmark and Sweden moved in accord with the level of her imports from these countries, as they were now bound to do. Exports to Denmark rose from 4 per cent of total exports by value to almost

10 per cent. Exports to Sweden remained at roughly the same proportion of total exports by value, less than 9 per cent, to 1944 when they fell to less than 6 per cent of the whole. At the end of that year Norway's export trade had become monopolized by those two countries and Germany. Together they accounted for 96 per cent of Norwegian exports. The German share of Norway's exports rose throughout the occupation. From

TABLE 32. *Norwegian Exports by Value and Country of Destination**

(000,000 kroner)

Country	1938	1939	1940	1941	1942	1943	1944
Belgium†	26·3	30·0	10·0	7·2	7·4	7·4	2·8
Denmark	34·0	33·8	36·3	45·4	48·1	61·9	50·3
Finland	12·7	12·1	12·9	10·6	7·8	12·4	4·6
France	51·9	35·9	14·7	5·9	7·5	6·4	4·5
Greece	0·2	1·0	1·5	..	..	..	..
Hungary	1·8	1·4	1·2	0·9	1·5	3·5	2·3
Italy	23·4	20·9	10·6	20·2	3·8	3·8	0·1
Netherlands	20·7	27·1	9·8	21·9	6·6	3·2	1·1
Poland‡	11·2	11·6	0·1	..	0·1	0·2	0·3
Russia	9·6	3·6	0·8	0·3	..	..	..
Serbia } Croatia}	0·8	0·3	0·2	..	..	..	..
Slovakia } Bohemia-Moravia}	8·6	6·2	{ 0·3 { 6·3	{ 0·1 { 1·4	{.. { 1·5	{.. { 2·5	{ .. { 2·0
Spain	9·9	5·8	1·8	2·4	2·6	1·5	0·4
Sweden	69·2	85·7	78·7	55·2	47·1	47·9	29·7
Switzerland	6·4	8·9	4·3	1·6	0·7	0·5	0·8
Turkey	2·0	1·2	0·1	0·1	..	0·3	..
Germany	121·5	117·8	282·7	399·5	356·7	387·5	418·2
Other European countries	219·9	218·0	87·0	2·0	..	0·2	0·1

* Statistisk Sentralbyrå, '*Statistisk-økonomisk utsyn over krigsårene*', pp. 94–100.
† Including Luxembourg to August 1940.
‡ After 1940 the General Government of Poland.

46 per cent in 1940 it reached 73 per cent in 1942 and 81 per cent in 1944. Thus the failure to supply Norway was by no means counterbalanced by any relaxation of control over the destination of Norway's own produce. The German demands became greater as the war continued. Although Norway retained a small import trade with other European countries, her export markets were completely lost.

The most serious losses were those in western Europe, especially in France. Exports to France, Belgium, and the Netherlands totalled 98·9 million kroner in 1938. In 1944 they were worth 8·4 million kroner. To this should be added the complete loss of the trade to Italy after 1941. In many ways the New Order was only a continuation of the invasion which cost

Norway her markets outside Europe and in Britain. The loss of markets which began in April 1940 continued throughout the occupation and was still continuing in 1944. From being a country all the arteries of whose economy were fed by international commerce, Norway came to have a trading dependence on Germany as great as that of any colony on its possessor.

What made the situation worse for Norway was that, whatever the intentions of the National Socialist Party there, it was clear that in the trading framework of the New Order Norway was not even an important colony. Hitler's instructions about the 'conciliatory' treatment of the Norwegians have to be seen against their general lack of economic importance in the New Order as a whole and also the extreme importance of certain particular exports. The result was a constant pressure to acquire certain valued goods from Norway without making the same administrative effort to supply the country. The clearing balance between Norway and Germany remained moderately in Norway's favour throughout the occupation. Only in the last few months did the balance move in the other direction. The combined effect of supplying the Wehrmacht and the Norwegian population meant that Norway was the one occupied country which in every year of the war was an over-all drain on German resources. Whether the goods which Germany got from Norway were worth more in the circumstances than those she exported is another matter, impossible to cost meaningfully. But in *absolute* terms Germany was obliged to supply Norway every year with more than she obtained. The difference between Norway and all other occupied countries was therefore a very profound one in German eyes as the New Order became more and more a merely exploitative device.

Germany's clearing balance with the Netherlands oscillated violently and in 1941 was much more in favour of that country than ever the Norwegian balance was in favour of Norway, but by 1942 it had settled down to an equilibrium in which it moved little in either direction. After the monetary disasters in Greece, Germany was obliged to provide extensive help to that country in 1943. In the same year the clearing balance with the Protectorate of Bohemia-Moravia moved slightly against Germany. With Norway the problem was different for it could not depend on policy changes. In every year Norway had to be supplied as though she were an ally, not an exploited economy. The sums of money which were officially allocated by the Norwegian government from budgets to write down these costs never came near to doing so, although there can be no doubt that in fact Norway would have been ultimately left to bear the burden of the unregulated Wehrmacht accounts at Norges Bank.

Even if the total sum of those unregulated accounts is taken into consideration and considered as effectively reducing the Norwegian clearing deficit, indeed converting it into a substantial surplus, the sum of money which Germany would have gained by such a procedure is extremely small compared to the gains by both occupation payments and unredeemed clearing deficits from, for example, France. One brief calculation will suffice to show that the size of Norway's unredeemed contribution to Wehrmacht expenditure could not greatly affect German attitudes. At the close of 1944 the Wehrmacht account at Norges Bank stood at 8,163 million kroner, about 5,000 million Reichsmarks at the official wartime exchange rate. Germany's financial gain from France in 1943 alone, including occupation costs and the clearing deficit, was 13,680 million Reichsmarks at the wartime exchange rate.[1]

In terms of value Norway's main imports from Germany during the occupation were fuel and foodstuffs. In terms of significance for the functioning of the Norwegian economy these were also the most important categories of supply. Metal goods and machinery were scarcely less vital. It can be seen from Table 33 that the supply of foodstuffs from Germany declined after 1943. The exceptionally high figure for that year is due to the very large imports of German rye. Rye accounted for 127·9 million kroner of the total value of 255·5 million kroner, whereas in 1942 rye imports from Germany were only 34·4 million kroner and in 1944 38·8 million kroner.[2] Imports of fuel from Germany also reached their peak in 1943. The supply of machinery and metal products declined steeply after 1941 to a level by 1944 far below its pre-war level. In view of the plans for economic development in Norway this was particularly grave. There were numerous cases of Germany being unable to develop Norwegian mines of considerable strategic importance through a lack of the necessary machinery, and this also had its effect on the slow progress of the aluminium plan.

It was in these major items of trade that the future shortages in Norway were to occur. Many scarce materials were consumed in such small quantities in Norway that Germany was able to supply Norway's needs, after drastic controls on consumption, more easily than those of larger countries. Such was the case, for example, with rubber and with certain chemical products. Although there were problems with the supply of oil, they were much less in the case of Norway than in the case of France because it was possible to hold Norwegian consumption down to very small quantities. The only serious problem became the supply of oil to the fishing fleet and in part this was a distribution problem within Norway itself. What caused most trouble was the large items without which Norway could not function, especially when they were bulky cargoes like grain and coal. It has already been seen what a drain on the available shipping space the grain cargoes were. Coal was even more so and its supply in sufficient quantity to

---

[1] Milward, *The New Order and the French Economy*, p. 271.
[2] Statistisk Sentralbyrå, 'Statistisk-økonomisk utsyn over krigsårene', p. 101.

TABLE 33. Norwegian Trade with Germany by Value, 1939–44*

(000,000 kroner)

Commodity	1939		1940		1941		1942		1943		1944	
	Imports	Exports	Imports	Exports	Imports	Exports	Imports	Exports	Imports	Exports	Imports	Exports
Luxury goods, drink, foodstuffs, fats, tobacco	3·1	40·4	2·7	105·5	107·8	168·9	138·6	172·6	255·5	138·1	101·8	179·1
Chemicals	22·6	2·2	21·8	4·8	54·1	7·2	46·1	4·3	45·7	5·1	37·6	4·8
Fertilizer	2·2	..	3·9	..	8·2	..	7·4	..	9·3	..	11·4	..
Rubber	1·4	..	1·3	0·6	4·2	0·3	7·7	0·1	5·0	..	8·5	..
Timber	0·9	0·5	1·0	1·7	7·5	4·1	2·4	0·7	2·3	0·2	0·9	2·0
Pulp, paper, cardboard	3·8	2·1	4·4	54·7	10·3	58·4	4·8	15·1	5·0	27·9	3·9	18·9
Textiles and clothing	42·8	1·1	70·7	0·1	87·4	2·0	21·2	3·8	21·7	1·5	25·2	3·0
Fuel	7·6	0·1	55·0	..	106·5	..	118·2	..	137·7	..	116·2	..
Minerals, products thereof	10·9	1·2	19·7	5·3	42·3	8·7	28·8	11·3	26·2	19·4	25·2	20·9
Ores	1·4	28·1	7·9	19·1	6·6	39·8	6·3	47·2	18·6	46·4	15·9	52·0
Base metals	20·8	21·5	31·1	77·6	118·4	91·3	101·7	76·7	55·3	118·1	32·9	104·8
Metal goods, machinery	124·1	10·3	95·7	3·3	165·4	6·1	124·1	1·3	85·4	2·1	65·4	1·3
Other goods	13·6	0·9	17·1	1·4	32·1	3·0	14·6	4·8	15·2	6·9	12·7	10·5

* Statistisk Sentralbyrå, *Statistisk-okonomisk utsyn over krigsarene*, pp. 100–1.

Norway became one of the main problems of the New Order, worth considering at greater length. It was the commodity which made the biggest demand on shipping space and on the import of which the Norwegian economy was most dependent.

This problem had weighed with the German government before the invasion but while German thinking was still dominated by the Blitzkrieg strategy it seemed impossible that Germany would find herself short of a raw material with which she was so liberally endowed. In spite of this general optimism it was never intended from the moment the first controls on consumption were established to supply sufficient coal to Norway to maintain the pre-war level of consumption. In negotiations concluded on 11 May 1940 between the Reichskommissariat and representatives of the main Norwegian coal consumers, it was decided that only industries of particular importance to Germany would continue to receive their pre-war supply of coal. The industries selected were transport, mining, electrochemistry and electrometallurgy, herring oil and herring-meal processing, and fish canning. All other sectors of consumption would have cuts of up to 35 per cent.[1]

The quotas arrived at meant that 1,565,000 tons of coal would have to be provided annually as against the 3 million tons of pre-war years.[2] But the whole of this quantity, with the exception of the supply from Spitzbergen, about 300,000 tons in pre-war years, would have to be provided from Germany. In pre-war years German exports to Norway had been only about 250,000 tons annually. Coal transports from Spitzbergen to Norway stopped on 16 August 1941 when British troops landed on the island, burned the 130,000 tons of coal in stock there, blew up the loading machinery, and evacuated the inhabitants. From that date onwards Norway's dependence on imports was absolute.

The shifts in internal consumption of coal decided after the invasion may be seen from Table 34, where it will also be seen that the original plans had been considerably modified by 1942. The greatest burden was borne by small consumers and households. The reductions in bunkering coal reflect the declining importance of shipping and foreign trade. But the supply of fuel to industry also declined after 1940 thanks to the inability of Germany to maintain it at the agreed level.

It can also be seen from Table 34 that the German inability to sustain the agreed level of exports to Norway meant that Norway was living off accumulated stocks. Had Norway not still been obtaining supply from Spitzbergen in 1940 the situation might have been more serious. Even so the failure of imports from Germany to meet the agreed level meant that no effective reserves were built up in the winter of 1940–1. In February

---

[1] F.D. 5325/45, Rk., Gruppe Kohle, 'Generalbericht', 11 February 1943.
[2] Including 500,000 tons of coke produced in Norway itself.

and March 1941 there were serious supply problems, partly due to the German preparations for the war on Russia, which were not really solved until May. Some Norwegian industries had their coal supply cut by as much as 50 per cent for periods of up to three months. From August 1941 onwards the level of imports was again sufficient to meet consumption but not to build up stocks, so that in spring 1942 there was an even more serious situation. At the end of March stocks for industry were almost completely exhausted. The Wehrmacht released 30,000 tons of coal from its reserves and the Navy released a further 27,000 tons. In spite of this, in May there was insufficient coal to maintain the quotas and coal supplies had to be concentrated on certain sectors of the economy. There were no deliveries in that month to the construction industry, to iron and steel works, nor to textile factories.

TABLE 34. *Allocation of Coal within the Norwegian Economy, 1940–2*[*]

(tons)

Sector of consumption	Pre-war consumption level		Quotas for coal economic years[†]			
			1940–1		1941–2	
	Coal	Coke	Coal	Coke	Coal	Coke
Industry	1,010,000	190,000	855,000	325,000	707,000	261,000
State railways	210,000	6,000	270,000	..	300,000	..
Bunkering coal	650,000	..	370,000	..	310,000	..
Gasworks	115,000	..	..	..	..	..
Domestic and other small consumers	315,000	520,000	78,000	88,000	78,000	154,000
Total	2,300,000	716,000	1,573,000	413,000	1,395,000	415,000
Total coal and coke	3,016,000		1,986,000		1,810,000	
Actual total consumption	3,016,000		1,787,500		1,684,000	
Actual imports			1,358,100		1,442,100	

* F.D. 5325/45, Rk., Gruppe Kohle, 'Generalbericht', 11 February 1943, *passim*.
† Coal economic years ran from 1 May to 30 April.

The crisis of May 1942 led to changes in the system of coal exports and coal quotas which resulted, temporarily, in a marked improvement. But by that time it was clear that the ambitious programmes for Norway rested on yet one more insecure foundation. The quotas agreed on in 1940 implied a level of consumption of 165,000 tons a month. To secure this level the Statens Kullkontor, which since 1 August 1934 had had a central responsibility for negotiating the Norwegian coal-trade agreements with Britain, was transformed into the Brenselkontor so that the German suppliers and the Reichskommissariat would have a central authority to deal with in matters of allocation. No such simplification existed on the German side. The Army and Navy controlled their own allocation and formulated their demand for coal quite independently of the Reichskommissariat. In fact, there was no formal connection between the Reichskommissariat and the German coal-shippers nor any German shipping authority, and this administrative gap was certainly one reason for the failure of coal supply in Norway. Through personal connections in Berlin the Reichskommissariat was able to create the 'Reichskommissariat für die besetzten norwegischen Gebiete, Verkehrsstab', led by the same man, G. H. Teetzmann, who was Director of Abteilung Verkehr in Reichsvereinigung Kohle. After April 1941 one man was thus the essential intermediary between the administration in Norway and the German coal authorities, for he was the only man in a position to negotiate on the spot. Such *ad hoc* administrative arrangements, typical of the Blitzkrieg, did not measure up to the size or complexity of this particular issue.

From the start of June 1940 to the end of February 1941 imports of coal from Germany amounted to only 568,230 tons. Imports of coke in the same period were 190,717 tons. Imports from Spitzbergen were 240,000 tons. Only in September 1940 did the monthly level of coal imports from Germany exceed 100,000 tons. In January 1941 it was 15,000 tons. Were the agreed quotas to be maintained without drawing on stocks, the imports should have amounted to 1,160,000 tons of coal and 550,000 tons of coke.[1] Such a period was sufficiently long to indicate that German plans had gone wrong, but the existence of ample stockpiles in Norway postponed the moment of truth, although before that moment German plans in Norway had already suffered by the coal shortage. Stocks of coal and coke combined in Norway stood at 741,000 tons on 15 May 1940, at 437,000 tons on 30 April 1941, at 478,000 tons on 31 December 1941, and at 195,000 tons on 30 April 1942.[2]

With the rise to power of the Ministry of Munitions came a much greater centralization of control over German raw-material supplies. As a consequence it was possible, when Norwegian stocks fell to this extremely dangerous level of a little over one month's consumption, for Terboven's complaints to be acted on in a way that had not previously been possible. The previous two months had seen the establishment in Germany of the Central Planning Committee with power to allocate all raw materials within the economy of the Reich, of its chief planning organ, Planungsamt, and of Karl Kaufmann as Reichskommissar for shipping. In July Planungsamt carried out a survey of the Norwegian coal supply and Terboven was invited to a meeting of the Central Planning Committee to discuss what should be done.

[1] F.D. 5325/45, Rk., Hauptabt. Volkswirtschaft, 'Ein Jahr Reichskommissar'.
[2] F.D. 5325/45, Rk., Gruppe Kohle, 'Generalbericht', 11 February 1943.

The Planungsamt survey indicated that in the first six months of 1942 Norwegian coal imports had been a mere 382,547 tons, almost 200,000 tons less than in the first six months of the previous year. The monthly coal quotas within the Norwegian economy had been reduced in June to 95,000 tons and in July to 110,000 tons. The experiment had shown that with such quantities the maintenance of the economy was not really possible.[1] The level of stocks on 30 June was 170,000 tons. Planungsamt proposed a monthly allocation of 148,275 tons for the coal economic year 1942–3 for the civilian sector. To that had to be added a further 17,550 tons for construction plans including the extensions to the Heroen aluminium and magnesium plant, a grand total of 165,825 tons—approximately the amount originally decided on in 1940. Furthermore, an extra supply had now to be shipped to Norway to rebuild the depleted stocks. By 1 January 1943 Norway was to have at least four months' reserve to cater for the freezing of harbours, a factor which had meant a severe drop in supply in February and March of each of the two previous years. In north Norway the reserve had to be five months, enough to last until May, because, even if in April supply made up for its deficiencies in February and March, it had still to be distributed to those remote regions. The implication was that supplies must run at the level of 250,000 tons per month.[1]

Recognizing that so high a level might not be attainable, Planungsamt instituted a sliding scale of relationship between the amount of coal delivered monthly and the size of the total internal monthly allocation. A supply of 180,000 tons monthly, for instance, would mean a monthly quota of 120,000 tons. In this way the used stocks would be recouped. Certain essential services, however, had to be maintained. To maintain these meant a minimum monthly allocation of 112,700 tons. Although these plans did not differ significantly in the quantity of coal involved from those of 1940 they differed in the rigorous system of priorities which they embodied and also in the fact that they instituted definite machinery to allocate a sufficient supply of coal to Norway from Germany's own resources.

Terboven and Otte, Kaufmann, and the Reichs Coal Commissar, Paul Pleiger, all attended the meeting of the Central Planning Committee on 9 July 1942 at which these decisions were ratified. South Norway was to have in future a minimum four-month reserve of coal, north Norway a five-month reserve. For the civilian sector 250,000 tons monthly were to be delivered and for the military sector 80,000 tons monthly, a total of 330,000 tons monthly. Furthermore, the Reichskommissar in Norway was to be given an over-all control over the coal supply of both sectors,

[1] F.D. 5312/45, Rm.f.B.u.M., Planungsamt, 'Darstellung der im zweiten Halbjahr 1942 erforderlichen Kohlenlieferungen nach Norwegen und der Verteilungspläne', 8 July 1942.

a decision which he was to find very difficult to implement on his return. Such decisions meant that German coal output itself would have to increase and extra rations were accordingly allocated to German miners. Initially coal exports to those countries which could still be supplied at the normal level in the coming winter were reduced in order to build up the stocks in Norway.[1]

What success attended these decisive plans? There was a marked rise in imports but to nothing like the extent embodied in the Central Planning Committee's decisions. Pleiger, Kaufmann, and Körner, a member of Central Planning's triumvirate, met again in Skaugum on 14 September and reaffirmed the policy that Norway must have a level of coal stocks of 600,000 tons by the end of December.[2] On 23 October the Central Planning Committee complained that the Wehrmacht had prevented Terboven from unifying the coal quotas in Norway under one single allocation. The Wehrmacht objected that for their purposes in north Norway they needed coal stocks of ten months' capacity. The obvious hope of Central Planning was that, by a unification of the system of allocation, the consumption of coal by the Wehrmacht could be reduced temporarily in order to build up the promised stock in Norway.

Do you believe [Milch asked the Wehrmacht representative], that Terboven would let the troops freeze? What the troops need they will get. Only it would be ridiculous if the troops were to be warming themselves in two winters' time with the coal that we are now sending to them. I have been a soldier for too long not to know how the soldier thinks about the economy of supply.[3]

But the Wehrmacht stood firm. No reductions were possible and by the end of December coal supply, although much improved, was well short of its target.

Throughout 1943 and until autumn 1944 the monthly quotas remained at a much more even level than they had previously done. The monthly supply to the railway system varied between 22,000 tons and 30,000 tons and the amount of bunkering coal between 12,000 tons and 18,000 tons. This normally left between 120,000 tons and 140,000 tons of coal and coke available for other sectors.[4] The higher import figures for the calendar year 1943 show this situation of greater ease. The decline in 1944 shows how hard-won this situation was and how easily disturbed. There was a coal-allocation crisis in February 1944, before the final collapse of coal imports which began in the autumn.

[1] F.D. 3048/49, Folder No. 47, vol. vii, Rm.f.B.u.M., ' "Zentrale Planung" im Vierjahresplan, 9 Besprechung', 9 July 1942.

[2] F.D. 5325/45, Rk., Gruppe Kohle, 'Generalbericht', 11 February 1943.

[3] F.D. 3048/49, Folder No. 47, vol. vii, Rm.f.B.u.M., 'Stenographische Niederschrift der 16 Besprechung der Zentralen Planung betreffend Kohle am 23 Oktober 1942'.

[4] F.D. 5208/45, Rk., Gruppe Kohle, 'Kohlen und Koks-Plan für Gesamtnorwegen', 27 January 1943 onwards.

It would be wrong to suppose that the decisions in July 1942 had finally solved the problem of coal supply to Norway. The level of stocks did improve above its June 1942 position. By 30 September it was 465,000 tons of coal and coke and by 31 December 516,000 tons.[1] This was still 84,000 tons below the target level. What is more, the stocks had been built up by making available less coal to the economy than Planungsamt

TABLE 35. *Norwegian Coal and Coke Imports from Germany*
(calendar years, 1939–44)

(tons)

	1939	1940	1941	1942	1943	1944
Coal	486,000	548,000	1,052,000	1,185,000	1,380,000	1,132,000
Coke	73,000	200,000	283,000	242,000	329,000	287,000

had originally deemed desirable. The coal shortages which had governed Norwegian economic life since May 1940 were only partially alleviated. The question must also be asked as to how long those 1940 arrangements had been supposed to last. Even in 1943 the economy was functioning on about half the coal supply of pre-war years. August 1943 is a typical month of that period. There were no interruptions to 'normal' supply and the arrivals of coal and coke were about the average for the year. In that month the allocation to the railway system was 23,000 tons of coal, against a pre-war monthly consumption of about 17,500 tons. For bunkering coal 15,000 tons was allocated as against 54,000 tons pre-war. The amount available to industry was 51,000 tons, about half the pre-war level. Gasworks also received about half their pre-war level of supply.[2]

In February 1944 Terboven wrote personally to Speer to complain that coal deliveries had again failed to keep up to their promised size and that cuts in Norwegian production would once again be necessary.

The coal situation in Norway has undergone an extraordinarily critical development in recent months. In that respect my colleagues have in the past repeatedly drawn the attention of the relevant Reich offices to the fact that if there is no significant increase in the actual deliveries we must introduce cuts in production and closures even in those areas which are of particular importance for the Reich's armaments. Our recommendations have had no discernible consequence, so that I now see myself compelled to place the situation once more directly before you:

In November 1943 Norway was allocated a quota of 170,000 tons, instead of

[1] F.D. 5325/45, Rk., Gruppe Kohle, 'Generalbericht', 11 February 1943.
[2] F.D. 5208/45, Rk., Gruppe Kohle, 'Kohlen-und Koks-Plan für Gesamtnorwegen August 1943', 29 July 1943.

which only 108,300 tons were received. The quota for December was set at 160,000 tons while in fact only 101,800 tons were received.

In spite of this insufficient supply we continued in those months to allocate the necessary coal to fulfil the production programmes in the industries important for war and also in January 1944 in the expectation that an improved availability of wagons and a corresponding increase in the January quota would create a certain evening-up.

In fact the January imports have not exceeded the altogether derisory quantity of 50,000 tons.

Thus, the situation of which we warned has occurred, which henceforward compels us—if we do not wish to behave irresponsibly—to proceed to the most drastic cuts even in production important for armaments, for we have, due to the bad deliveries, but also in retrospect to the securing of better allocations to the important priority categories I and II in the interests of fulfilling the German war potential, lived off stocks in such a manner that we now have at our disposal a stock of only three months' duration.[1]

In May 1944 allocations were reduced so that the level of coal and coke stocks would not fall below 500,000 tons. This was a temporary device and in June the quotas were restored to normal. Crisis set in once more in September when allocations were again reduced to maintain stocks above the 500,000 tons limit. From July 1944 onwards the fall in imports became relentless and the limit had to be infringed anyway. At the end of December stocks were 352,000 tons.[2] The decline gathered momentum after October due to the loss of ships, the demands of Operation Northern Light, and sabotage. After the end of November, as Table 36 indicates, Norway was almost entirely dependent on accumulated stocks.

In November the situation was even serious enough to persuade the Wehrmacht to allow their supply to be imported and distributed in common with the civilian supply. In that month the forecast for imports in December was no higher than 30,000 tons.[3] The reality was much worse, less than 20,000 tons. The Ministry of Munitions altered the system of allocation in Germany and made 100,000 tons of coal from the eastern territories immediately available to Norway.[4] But there was no longer shipping available to move it even if it could have been brought to German ports. By February 1945 the Reichskommissariat admitted that Norwegian coal stocks would be exhausted in April.[5] The Wehrmacht practically forbade the use of coal for heating purposes and released its available stocks for

[1] F.D. 5359/45, Terboven to Speer, 2 February 1944.
[2] F.D. 5312/45, Rk., Abt. Binnenwirtschaft, 'Unterlagen für die Dienstleitertagung. Rückblick auf 1944—Ausblick auf 1945' [n.d.].
[3] F.D. 5217/45, Rk., Hauptabt. Volkswirtschaft, 'Bericht für die Zeit vom 1 bis 30 November 1944', 9 December 1944.
[4] F.D. 3045/49, section ix, Sc. 335, telegram, Speer to Kaufmann [n.d.].
[5] F.D. 5217/45, Rk., Hauptabt. Volkswirtschaft, 'Bericht für die Zeit vom 1 bis 31 Januar 1945', 15 February 1945.

the general economy. 'Since we can no longer count on further imports we must accustom ourselves to the fact that in the course of April Norway will have used up its total coal stock.'[1]

TABLE 36. *Monthly Imports of Coal and Coke**

(tons)

	Coal	Coke
1943		
September	125,000	10,000
October	101,000	37,000
November	142,000	35,000
December	98,000	21,000
1944		
January	45,000	8,000
February	106,000	16,000
March	116,000	38,000
April	129,000	25,000
May	175,000	10,000
June	132,000	32,000
July	130,000	32,000
August	79,000	21,000
September	84,000	11,000
October	73,000	16,000
November	80,457	
December	19,772	
1945		
January	11,824	
February	3,857	
March	3,374	

* Figures to November 1944 from F.D. 5308/45 and F.D. 5215/45, Rk., Binnenwirtschaft, 'Monatliche Rohstoffübersichten'. After November 1944 from F.D. 5217/45, Rk., Hauptabt. Volkswirtschaft, 'Monatliche Berichte'.

The general principles on which coal had been allocated within the economy were no longer applicable by February. The process of reducing every quota had begun to result in absurdities. The irreducible quota for any satisfactory functioning of the economy was set at 97,000 tons monthly and the quotas would continue to be drawn up on this basis until stocks were exhausted.[2] Along those lines, therefore, detailed allocation plans for March were drawn up as before.[3] The formal end of all planning of

[1] Ibid.
[2] F.D. 5364/45, Rk., Abt. Binnenwirtschaft, 'Erläuterungen über die Entwicklung des Kohlennachschubes', 22 February 1945.
[3] F.D. 5207/45, Rk., Gruppe Kohle, 'Gegenüberstellung Kohlenplan Februar und März 1945', 12 March 1945.

this kind, however, was pronounced by a telegram from Hans Kehrl, head of Planungsamt, to Otte on 17 March.

A thorough examination of the situation in the light of the present difficult transport situation in Germany has led to the result that, apart from Danish coal, imports of coal into Norway in worthwhile quantities can no longer be counted on. On that account Norway is until further notice solely dependent on the prospective imports from Denmark. According to my calculations on the basis of your memoranda the stocks will last until the middle of May, if a further reduction in consumption in the civil sector to about 35,000 tons follows. I order the quota for the railway to be cut to 10,000 tons and those for the stone and earth, iron and metal, chemical industry, electrometallurgical industry, and leather and textile sectors to be completely cancelled.[1]

The April allocation was therefore for 51,300 tons only.[2] As a consequence, most of Norway's manufacturing industry came to a halt.

Before the surrender of the German administration in Norway their position had become hopeless. But the deterioration of that position did not start only with the heavy fighting in Germany itself but before that date. Coal supply to Norway was only a part of the general problem of supply but it stands as an example of the failure of the *Großraumwirtschaft* to cope with that problem. The experiment of forcing the Norwegian economy to operate on a much smaller supply of coal did as much harm to German plans as to the Norwegian economy, but in the circumstances it was no doubt inevitable. Germany constantly failed, however, to maintain even the lower level of supply and from summer 1944 the whole Norwegian economy was plunged into an ever-deepening crisis.

It has already been shown that outside the links with Germany Norway's only substantial source of supply was through trade with Sweden and Denmark. Although both the Swedish and Norwegian governments went to considerable lengths to supply Norway with goods in the form of charity or relief outside the terms of the bilateral trading agreements the amounts that could be supplied in such a way were small and were confined to a limited range of products. The limitations of product on the more 'normal' trade were also fairly strict. Denmark's trade was closely watched by Germany and Sweden's by both Axis and Allies. Nevertheless, the links with both countries remained of great importance and provided Norway with a small amount of manœuvring space in her foreign trade denied to other countries in the New Order.

Norwegian trade with Sweden had a particular significance for it was only with a certain amount of co-operation from Sweden that Germany was able properly to provision her troops in north Norway. On 14 June 1940 the

---

[1] F.D. 5312/45, Rm.f.R.u.Kp., Planungsamt, telegram Kehrl to Otte, 17 March 1945.
[2] F.D. 5217/45, Rk., Hauptabt. Volkswirtschaft, 'Bericht für die Zeit vom 1 bis 31 März 1945', 16 April 1945.

German government first approached the Swedish government requesting certain transit facilities to Norway.[1] It was also from Norway that Swedish iron-ore exports to Germany were mainly shipped. The Swedish government could not wholly resist German demands even though the pressure brought on it by the Allies to do so was very strong. Owing to her geographical position Sweden was herself highly dependent on German supply and German markets. Since Sweden also occupied a very important strategic position in the defence of Norway the friendliness of German-Swedish relations depended a great deal on Swedish opinions about the fate of the New Order. Before 1943 Sweden frequently overstepped the bounds of strict neutrality to favour Germany. After 1943 her actions caused the German administration in Norway no little difficulty and annoyance.

The pattern of Norwegian-Swedish trade was firmly established by the trade agreement of 11 December 1940 which determined a fixed trade quota more effectively than the previous treaty.[2] The main Norwegian exports in value were fertilizer, salt herring, molybdenum ore, sulphur, pyrites, and fresh fish. This remained so for the duration of the war except that fish exports died away after 1940 as Germany's demand for fish became greater. It was Sweden's demand for more fish than was offered that led to the breakdown of the supplementary agreements in autumn 1942.[3] The size of all Norwegian exports to Sweden declined in 1944 as against other years but particularly those of molybdenum ore after the bombing raid on the Knaben mine.

Sweden's exports to Norway were supplemented by the charitable movement to provide relief for the Norwegian population. By November 1940 Norwegian and Swedish relief committees had already begun to co-operate in Stockholm on joint programmes.[4] Throughout winter 1941 and the following spring Swedish representatives negotiated in Oslo with German and Norwegian committees to arrive at a correct framework within which aid could be provided and finally signed an agreement on relief on 20 June 1942.[5] On 10 July 1942 American organizations to provide relief to Norway founded a joint committee with the Swedish committee thereby centralizing relief in Swedish hands. Other organizations, such as

[1] *Sveriges förhållende till Danmark och Norge under krigsåren. Redogörelser avgivna till utrikesnämnden av ministern för utrikes ärendena*, 1941–5 (Stockholm, 1945), p. 40.

[2] F.D. 5346/45, Rk., 'Ergebnisse der Besprechungen des deutschen und des schwedischen Regierungsausschusses von März/April 1941', and 'Grundlagen für den schwedisch-norwegischen Warenverkehr im Jahre 1941' [n.d.].

[3] R.A. Rk., Abt. Ausfuhrwirtschaft und Bergbau 122a, Pakke 2, 'Vermerk über das Ergebnis der am 26–27 Oktober 1942 in Stockholm geführten Besprechungen über Fragen des schwedisch-norwegischen Wirtschaftsverkehrs', 30 October 1942.

[4] *Norges forhold til Sverige under krigen 1940–45. Aktstykker utgitt av Det Kgl. Utenriksdepartement*, iii (Oslo, 1947), 475 ff.

[5] Ibid., iii. 533.

the Red Cross, tended to make their financial contributions through the same medium. There was good reason for this centralization for the Allies were reluctant to ease Germany's problems by allowing the foodstuffs and medicines purchased with these funds to be exported from Sweden freely and used as much pressure as they could to keep some control over these activities. The pressure on the American State Department to bow to the public opinion of American Norwegians was strong enough in December 1942 to cause them to take up the case with the British Ministry of Economic Warfare and in that month the Ministry permitted the re-export from Sweden to Norway of 100 tons of concentrated foodstuffs and vitamins.[1] It was always possible for Sweden to flout Allied controls and there is no doubt that the quantities of relief were greater than the Allies were prepared to sanction. The monetary measurement of the relief is necessarily a somewhat arbitrary business and some of it was not for the purchase of goods for Norway but for other help, such as aid to refugees or seamen.[2] By 1944, however, the foodstuffs passing as relief were beginning to make a significant impression on Norway's supply. In that year, for example, 6,000 tons of sugar, equivalent to one-fifth of Norway's total import of that commodity, and 1,000 tons of butter passed in this way.

A similar relief movement in Denmark also eked out the Norwegian food supply. In this case, as in the case of Sweden, the quantities had to remain small until the close of the war and were only really large in 1945. In this case it is even more difficult to be precise about the amounts involved as the relief seems to have been less centralized than in Sweden and it is impossible to know what passed in food parcels. Estimates suggest that the two most important items were flour and green vegetables, almost 3,000 tons of flour being sent as relief in 1944.[3]

Through the more normal trading mechanism Sweden's contributions to Norway's food supply were very fluctuating. Considerable quantities of canned meat were obtained in 1941 and 1944, of dried milk in 1944, of potatoes in 1943, and of other vegetables in 1941. The only year in which Sweden was able to make any contribution to Norway's bread-grain supply was 1941. The main items imported from Sweden were sawn timber, zinc ore, machines, and machine tools. In the first year of the occupation Norway was still receiving payment for ships commissioned in Swedish yards. If the value of these ships is omitted from the calculation the value of Norwegian imports from Sweden fell and the range of commodities imported shrunk.

On 1 October 1943 the Swedish government placed an embargo on the

---

[1] W. N. Medlicott, *The Economic Blockade*, ii (London, 1959), 280.

[2] See the calculations by J. Ihlen, 'Humanitär verksamhet', in B. Kugelberg and J. Ihlen, *Grannar emellan. En bok om sveriges förhållende till Norge under krigsåren 1940–1945* (Stockholm, 1945).

[3] N. J. Mürer (ed.), *Boken om Danskehjelpen* (Oslo, 1947).

transit to Norway of crude oil and extended this from 1 January 1944 to cover all products refined from crude oil.[1] In the negotiations for the new trade agreement between Sweden and Norway in January the Swedish government refused several German demands at first. The most troublesome of these refusals was that to supply mining machinery. The machinery was needed to restore production at the damaged Knaben molybdenum mine.[2] Only later, after much argument, was the export of the machinery permitted and then the machines never arrived because of delays caused by the producers.[3] In June there was a scare on the German side that the Swedes would stop the coal traffic through Sweden.[4] It was not unjustified in view of the pressure the Allies were bringing to bear. On 12 July Sweden claimed to have insufficient wagons to maintain the Norwegian traffic at the agreed level.[5] In September the transit of coal, coke, and cement to northern Norway was stopped. There were still 40,000 tons of coal and coke for Norway in the ports of Sundsvall, Härnösand, and Luleå.[6]

In fact Sweden had been very reluctant to conclude a further fixed agreement in summer 1944.

The negotiations were particularly difficult and unpleasant since the Swedes judged Germany's military and political position to be wholly unfavourable. . . . In spite of these impossible Swedish conditions both German and Norwegian sides finally declared themselves ready to seek a trade agreement on the basis of the Swedish proposals, since Norway is directly dependent on a range of Swedish goods and can also for her part stop the deliveries of goods to Sweden at any time if the practical application of the Swedish proposals is unsatisfactory for Norway.[7]

In effect the system of fixed commodity levels disappeared and Sweden and Norway agreed to trade in the same goods but without any definite stipulations as to quantity and length of time for the trade. It was the beginning of the collapse of the German trading and clearing system in Scandinavia.

In fact Norway's only really valuable bargaining counter in the negotiations was the high level of her fertilizer exports to Sweden. But Swedish

---

[1] F.D. 5312/45, Rk., Abt. Verkehr, 'Transitverkehr über Schweden', 28 July 1944.

[2] F.D. 5300/45, Rk., Abt. Ausfuhrwirtschaft, 'Beitrag zum Tätigkeitsbericht für den Monat Januar 1944' [n.d.].

[3] B. Kugelberg and J. Ihlen, op. cit., p. 67. The firms claimed they would be on the Anglo-American statutory list, equivalent to black-listing by those countries. See F.D. 5344/45, Rk., Hauptabt. Volkswirtschaft, 'Deutsch-schwedische Wirtschaftsverhandlungen', 6 July 1944.

[4] F.D. 5312/45, Rk., Abt. Binnenwirtschaft, 'Sitzung im Auswärtigen Amt am 30.6. über die Frage des Transit-Kohlenverkehrs durch Schweden', 29 June 1944.

[5] Ibid., Rk., Gruppe Kohle, 'Sperrung des Schweden-Transits', 12 July 1944.

[6] *Sveriges förhållende*, p. 259.

[7] F.D. 5344/45, Rk., Hauptabt. Volkswirtschaft, 'Norwegisch-schwedischer Warenverkehr im 2 Halbjahr 1944', 11 August 1944.

demand for this product was less than the Norwegian offer in 1944 and there was every likelihood that the fertilizer factories which Sweden had herself begun to construct at the start of the war would be in production by the end of that year. In 1943 the Reichskommissariat had still been proceeding on the assumption that these fertilizer imports were indispensable to Sweden. They had also banked very strongly on the widespread criticism in the Swedish press that the Swedish government was forcing the Norwegians to pay for their Swedish imports by exporting fish to Sweden.[1] The diversification of Norwegian exports to Sweden in 1943 had indeed been partly due to the effect of public opinion on the Swedish government, but that government was already free from all such pressures by autumn 1944. The impression is very strong that the collapse of the German system in Scandinavia really began in summer 1944 and that by that time the *Großraumwirtschaft* had already failed as far as Norway was concerned.

On 20 October Sweden stopped the movement of iron ore to Narvik, although by this time the shortage of shipping was so acute that it made little difference.[2] In December Germany suspended the export of certain Norwegian products to Sweden since it became clear that Sweden was prepared to issue very few export licenses for trade to Norway in 1945.[3] These were the final gestures in a play already ended. Sweden had never previously had any real possibility of refusing to co-operate economically with the *Großraumwirtschaft*. As soon as that possibility did present itself Sweden seized it. Her attitude was dictated throughout by the claims of objective economic reality, as it had to be. The surprising thing is that in a period of European history and in a trading system where such considerations had no place the Swedish population and government should have been able to insert any measure of humanitarian sentiment into their policy at all.

With Denmark the bargaining was, of course, more subject to general German plans. In view of the increasing demands made on that country by Germany during the occupation it was only understandable that the Danes should regard their surplus with a jealous eye. In this case, however, Norway's position was stronger, for her export of fertilizer was essential to Danish agriculture. In return Norway obtained flour, different types of grain according to the Danish harvest, eggs, meat, and, after 1941, butter.[4] The trade agreement of March 1943 stipulated a Norwegian export

[1] F.D. 5344/45, Rk., Abt. Ausfuhrwirtschaft, 'Vermerk betr: Norwegisch-schwedischer Wirtschaftsverkehr', 8 February 1943.
[2] F.D. 5217/45, Rk., Hauptabt. Volkswirtschaft, 'Bericht für die Zeit vom 1 bis 31 Oktober 1944', 10 November 1944.
[3] F.D. 5338/45, Rk., Abt. Wirtschaft, 'Dem Herrn Reichskommissar zur Vorlage über Herrn Senator Otte', 21 December 1944.
[4] F.D. 5357/45, Rk., 'Ergebnisse der Besprechungen der deutsch-dänischen Regierungsausschüsse von Sept.–Okt. 1941', etc.

of 38,180,000 kroners' worth of fertilizer to Denmark in the following six months, about 80 per cent of the value of all Norwegian exports to Denmark over the same period.[1] When the negotiations became particularly difficult in late 1944 Norway was able to use the threat of withholding her fertilizer supply from Denmark very effectively. Fertilizer exports to Egypt, the United States, and west European countries more or less stopped after 1941 although small quantities of cyanamide were exported to the Netherlands in 1942. After that date only Finland was allowed to receive supply apart from Denmark and Sweden. Although Norwegian fertilizer exports kept up quite well they became a bargaining counter in inter-Scandinavian trade and, as far as Germany was concerned, a way of sustaining the level of Danish agricultural exports to Germany.

The trading deficit on Norwegian-Swedish trade apparent from Tables 31 and 32 did not represent a substantial clearing deficit. Norway's invisible earnings in this case remained high because of the volume of Swedish ore carried on the Narvik railway and this enabled Norway to run an import surplus with Sweden. The original clearing account was wound up at the end of 1943 and a new balance begun in the next calendar year which tended to a Norwegian deficit.

The one other country with whom Norwegian trade substantially increased was Hungary, although it still remained very small. The first trade agreement with Hungary was signed in February 1941 to last until the end of July. The value of the trade covered was 1,115,000 kroners' worth of exports from Norway, mostly wood pulp and fish, and 1,710,000 kroner of imports from Hungary, almost entirely foodstuffs.[2] This represented a drop in the pre-war level of imports from Hungary but maintained the level of Norwegian exports. The composition of this trade did not change but the quantities increased. In the trade treaty signed in Berlin on 21 December 1942 for the year 1943 Norwegian exports were set at 4,800,000 kroner and Hungarian exports at the same level.[3] In this case Hungary was able to provide a market for one of Norway's more important exports which was of little use to Germany, wood pulp. The quantity which she took, however, remained far below the previous level of Norway's export to the United Kingdom. The supplements and additions to these treaties grew in 1943 and 1944 until Hungary became the most important supplier to Norway after Germany and the two Scandinavian countries.

The failure of the New Order adequately to supply Norway was not only a failure of production. As the war became increasingly desperate for

[1] F.D. 5300/45, Rk., Abt. Ausfuhrwirtschaft und Bergbau, 'Beitrag zum Tätigkeitsbericht für den Monat März 1943'.

[2] F.D. 5234/45, Rk., 'Grundlagen für den ungarisch-norwegischen Warenverkehr für die Zeit bis zum 31 Juli 1941' [n.d.].

[3] F.D. 5318/45, Rk., 'Protokolle nebst Anlagen über die Regelung des Warenverkehrs zwischen Ungarn und Norwegen im Kalenderjahr 1943'.

Germany, her demands on other economies under her control grew and the availability of surplus resources for Norway became less likely. But even by the end of 1940 the low level of supply was not only a function of the scarcity of goods in Europe but also of the lack of shipping space. Had there been more goods available for Norway it is not certain that the shipping resources at Germany's disposal could have carried them. A desperate shortage of shipping space existed from the moment of Germany's failure to get hold of the Norwegian mercantile marine. The Norwegian Trade and Shipping Association (Nortraship), formed in London by the refugee government with the bulk of the pre-war merchant fleet, was the biggest shipping company in the world, employing on its own account 30,000 seamen.[1] There were continued desertions to Nortraship by the ships remaining under German control during the occupation, but the more important factor in reducing the available Norwegian mercantile marine still further was the heavy losses. Even allowing for the fact that German naval strategists had advocated the occupation of Norway within the general framework of a short and relatively restricted war, it is impossible not to think that their plans were grossly over-optimistic. The shipping shortage became a crippling obstacle to all economic plans and even to a successful maintenance of the occupation.

There were about 800,000 B.R.T. of shipping capacity available in Norway after the invasion. About 300,000 B.R.T. were commandeered by the Wehrmacht by the end of May.[2] Of the remaining 500,000 B.R.T., 100,000 B.R.T. were employed solely as coastal shipping and a further 100,000 in regular liner traffic to Germany. Each of these categories was therefore mostly engaged in naval or military business of one kind or another. There were 260,000 B.R.T. available for general German-Norwegian cargo traffic. This volume of shipping was fully employed in the transport of pyrites and other metal ores to Germany and the return coal traffic. The use of German shipping was therefore essential from the start although this never seems to have been adequately understood.

The complaints of insufficient shipping space emanating from the Reichskommissariat appear to have had little influence on Hitler even though by early 1942 Norway's situation, especially in regard to food and coal, was becoming dangerous. It was only after the appointment of Speer as Minister of Munitions in February 1942 that the matter could really get to Hitler's attention. Even though Speer's first thoughts on Norway were to simplify even further the economic programmes there so that they demanded less material from Germany, shipping space beyond what was available was still necessary to get the essential quantity of exports

---

[1] F. Fjord, *Norwegens totaler Kriegseinsatz. Vier Jahre Okkupation* (Zürich, 1944), p. 4.

[2] F.D. 5325/45, Rk., Hauptabt. Volkswi., 'Ein Jahr Reichskommissar'.

from Norway. Besides, Hitler refused to abandon the construction projects which were extremely costly both in terms of ocean-going and coastal tonnage. On 19 April 1942 Speer was given clear orders to pursue the building of the Norland railway as energetically as possible.[1] It became at once clear that this was impossible without more shipping space, since lack of cement, building materials, and rail had been one of the primary reasons for the delays in construction. Speer hoped to use the opportunity to continue the series of administrative reforms in the economic administration by appointing a civilian committee to control shipbuilding and interested Hitler in a conference which might tackle this wider problem while providing more shipping for Norway.

Pointed out to the Führer the impossibility of carrying out the building programme in Norway as long as the position with regard to the supply of the necessary shipping space remains unresolved.

Informed the Führer of the impression from the last discussion with Minister Dorpmüller and Reichskommissar Terboven. The Führer wishes a date to be fixed soon for him to meet with Raeder, Dorpmüller, Blohm, Gauleiter Kaufmann, and Reichskommissar Terboven.

In connection with the question of providing the necessary shipping space for Norway the Führer started to discuss in principle the fact that he considers it correct to order for this purpose not large ships but a great number of small ships of about 1,000–2,000 tons capacity and that priority assistance should be given to producing them.[2]

Hitler's insistence on the Norwegian building programme was partly due to his reluctance to abandon the idea of a great naval base at Trondheim and this lent force to his Minister's demand for a civilian committee. On 13 May he insisted on a programme to reduce the turn-round time of ships in the Norwegian trade and to speed up the repair of damaged vessels.[3] Five days later he signified his approval of the appointment of Karl Kaufmann, Gauleiter of Hamburg, as Reichskommissar for shipping. Kaufmann had been an ally of Strasser and Goebbels in their attempt to build up the Ruhr National Socialist Party on different lines, an attempt which had also brought Terboven to the fore.[4] Kaufmann's appointment meant the centralization of shipping-space control in the Ministry of Munitions. This had both advantages and disadvantages for the Reichskommissariat; advantages in so far as there was now someone to deal with a problem over which the administration in Norway had never had any control, disadvantages in so far as the Ministry of Munitions imposed a strict programme of priority on economic plans for Norway.

[1] F.D. 3353/45, vol. viii, 'Führerkonferenz, 19 Avril 1942', 19 April 1942.
[2] F.D. 3353/45, vol., Powercase, 'Führerkonferenz, 6–7 Mai 1942', 8 May 1942.
[3] Ibid., 'Führerkonferenz, 13 Mai 1942', 15 May 1942.
[4] P. Hüttenberger, *Die Gauleiter. Studie zum Wandel des Machtegefüges in der NSDAP*, Schriftenreihe der Vierteljahrshefte für Zeitgeschichte, xix (Stuttgart, 1969), 27–9.

The immediate result of the change was an increase in the shipping tonnage allocated to the trade to Norway. 'The Führer orders that 10 per cent of the total merchant shipping tonnage in the hands of the navy, amounting to about 3 million tons, is to be placed at Reichsstatthalter Kaufmann's disposal for "Operation Viking". The Führer gives the necessary order to Admiral Kranke in an especially concise form!'[1] It was in fact the need to increase shipping space for the Norwegian trade that led to the curious experiment with building concrete ships. The impulse had come from the Führer's suggestion that the problem could best be solved by the construction of a large number of small ships. Although successful as a mass-productive device the concrete ship was less successful at sea and its development did not fundamentally improve the situation. As late as November 1944 Hitler ordered Kaufmann to provide the necessary shipping tonnage for the completion of the Norland railway.[2]

By this time other problems were emerging to make such an order even less feasible. The campaign in north Norway first led to a great increase in the demand for supplies to the Wehrmacht there, and then to the decision to evacuate the inhabitants and the capital equipment of the two most northerly provinces. This coincided with a rapid increase in losses in shipping. From September 1944 a complete failure of Germany's trade with Norway developed very rapidly which was very much due to shortage of shipping space. The system which had hung together from May 1940 broke down and the last eight months of the occupation form a period when Norway's foreign trade dropped steeply away and with it the availability of goods of all kinds whether for German or Norwegian purposes.

With the beginning of the evacuation of the northern provinces in autumn 1944, 'Operation Northern Light', Terboven had indicated by telegram to Kaufmann that the shipping situation as far as Norway was concerned was now too critical to guarantee shipping space for all the exports due to be shipped to Germany. The result was a telegram from the Planning Office of the Ministry of Armaments and War Production to Kaufmann insisting that the outward traffic from Norway to Germany must have first priority.

The importance of the Norwegian economy for the German war economy is known. I can spare myself longer disquisitions on this theme. This importance has currently increased with the loss of various other territories. The German war economy is dependent on these deliveries. At the present moment it is decisive that all production in Norway intended for Germany should be transported. This is especially so for ferro-alloys, where various production plants in the Reichs territory have been lost through enemy action, and for the most important raw materials and ores such as pyrites, iron ore, and so on. The

[1] F.D., 3353/45, vol. x, 'Führerkonferenz, 28–29 Juni 1942', 29 June 1942.
[2] Ibid., 'Führerkonferenz, 1–4 November 1944', 5 November 1944.

communication to me from the Reichskommissar for Occupied Norwegian Territory that, for example, the pyrites production will have to be cut by 50 per cent because of a lack of transport availability is, under the existing circumstances, intolerable. I know that the present relationships in the field of seagoing shipping are determined by Operation Northern Light. I would like, however, to address the urgent request to you, under consideration of the relationships indicated above, to provide as much empty tonnage for Norway as is possible in any way. I request you especially to make available sufficient shipping space for the transport of Swedish ore from Narvik because it is known that Sweden only permits ore-trains to run to Narvik to the extent that the ore can be taken away by ship.[1]

It is not possible to make any estimate of the amount of shipping required for the evacuation of north Norway. Like most retreats this one was carried out in a disorganized manner and the original intention of moving all fixed capital of any value out of the path of the invader was soon abandoned as impossible. But it is quite clear that the available shipping resources were never sufficient both to conduct this evacuation and to continue at an unreduced level the volume of German-Norwegian trade. The most serious factor leading to the shipping crisis was not, however, this extra demand on meagre resources but the rapid increase in losses of ships on the Norwegian run. Against these losses no policy could be successful and even before the evacuation the volume of shipping necessary to supply the Wehrmacht in north Norway had been reduced.

In September 1944 Hitler was persuaded to reduce the acceptable minimum period of stocks for the Wehrmacht in north Norway from nine months to between five and six months.[2] All economic projects in Norway which could not produce results before 1 April 1945 were also abandoned. Projects such as the Grong pyrites mines or the Skorovas and Gjersvik mines thus no longer needed shipping space.[3] Although Hitler was ready to reduce the Wehrmacht building programme in Norway, apart from submarine-pen construction, nothing would persuade him to abandon the Norland railway which made heavier demands on shipping than any other project. The Norwegian shipbuilding programme was simplified and twenty-five locomotives from the Hungarian railways were made available to Norway. Whatever happened in the northern provinces the rest of Norway had become economically more important to Germany than at any previous stage of the war. Nor could any further concessions be extracted from Hitler. It was therefore necessary after September to provide sufficient

[1] F.D. 3045/49, section ix, Sc. 335, Rm.f.R.u.Kp., Planungsamt, Der Leiter des Planungsamtes to Rk. f.d. See., 'Transporte aus Norwegen', 16 November 1944.
[2] Ibid., Planungsamt, Vermerk für Herrn Präsident Kehrl, 'Besprechung beim Führer über Tonnagebedarf für den Nordraum und Truppen in Nordnorwegen', 22 September 1944.
[3] Ibid., Planungsamt, telegram Baudisch to Otte, 9 September 1944.

transport to maintain trade while continuing to supply materials for what was left of the building projects. Since Terboven's suggestions in November that this was impossible were swept aside, no real modification of the plan took place from September 1944 to the end of the occupation.

At the end of September almost 30 per cent of the total shipping available to Germany was already undergoing repair. About 1,125,000 tons burthen were in use. The extraordinary difficulty of maintaining Norway in the New Order may be seen from the fact that 670,000 tons burthen monthly were required to sustain the programme of Norwegian shipping. Of this quantity 400,000 tons burthen were required for supply of coal and other goods to the Wehrmacht. A further 175,000 tons burthen were required for supplying coal to the civilian sector of the economy.[1] The only factor tending to reduce the commitment of so high a proportion of Germany's merchant fleet to this one route was the cuts in construction which Hitler had permitted. These had the effect of making the remaining construction projects capable of being supplied by the Norwegian cement industry. But all other factors tended to indicate that if Norway remained occupied it would continue to absorb as high or higher a proportion of available shipping space, not least the effect of withdrawing troops from Finland into Norway.

There was no other German trade which required a volume of shipping approaching in size that needed on the Norwegian run. Baltic shipping, including shipping to Sweden, demanded about 175,000 tons burthen permanently available. The rest of the stock was necessary to maintain coastal trade within the Reich itself. Consequently there was no room left for manœuvre by the end of September; any further losses meant a decline in trade. Since Norway was also much the most exposed shipping run to enemy action, it was also the most likely to suffer losses. The total net loss of German shipping in 1944 until the beginning of August had been 112,000 B.R.T., an average of 30,000 B.R.T. monthly.[1] Those losses were especially of the larger ships used for the Wehrmacht traffic and the coal traffic to Norway.

In October the demand on the dwindling shipping resources was increased when ships were sent in ballast from Germany in order to bring back the accumulating ore stocks at Narvik as the existing shipping space would have provided for only 70,000 tons of ore transport in that month, a situation which Planungsamt regarded as 'totally impossible'.[2] At the same time Norway's manufacturing plant began to accumulate stocks of raw material which could not be used for a variety of reasons. Whenever

[1] F.D., 3045/49, section ix, Sc. 335, Rm.f.R.u.Kp., Planunfisamt, Abt. Gesamtplanung, 'Transportage auf dem Gebiete der Seeschiffahrt und Dringlichkeiten', 28 September 1944.
[2] Ibid., Planungsamt, telegram, Baudisch to Otte, 9 October 1944.

such stocks could be used in Germany, shipping had to be provided to bring them there. The loss of the Petsamo nickel mines in north Finland to the advancing Russian army meant, for instance, that the planned increase in monthly output at the Falconbridge nickel plant could no longer take place. Since raw material had been accumulated there to cater for the much higher level of output, a certain part of that stock became surplus to the plant's future needs although it was still vital to German needs. In October shipping had to be provided to transport the metal and ore to Germany.[1] At the same time the evacuation of the German Twentieth Mountain Army southwards meant a demand for a further 100,000 tons burthen of shipping to supply them in new quarters. It these troops were to stay in Norway the demand for shipping capacity on the Norwegian run would be permanently increased to 750,000 tons burthen monthly.[2]

Shipping losses in August had continued at the same rate of 30,000 B.R.T. a month. At that rate, losses would have totalled a further 420,000 B.R.T. by the end of 1945, or roughly 650,000 tons burthen. The current shipbuilding programme, if fulfilled, would have meant an addition to the fleet of 279,000 tons burthen by October 1945. But if the current rate of wastage of ships on the stocks had been maintained, the total size of the available merchant marine by the end of 1945 would have been approximately what was needed to maintain the Norwegian traffic. Such calculations put the matter in its most optimistic light. Given that shipping losses were particularly in the category of ships of 5,000 tons burthen and above, that is in those ships most suitable for the bulk of the Norwegian traffic, Germany's prospects of maintaining supply much beyond March 1945 looked very gloomy.

In fact from October 1944 the level of shipping losses rose. Losses in November were 34,660 tons burthen. The amount of iron ore taken from Narvik actually fell to 11,000 tons.[3] Although in December losses were 28,390 tons burthen in January 1945 they rose to 40,716. Over that four-month period the chance of maintaining the shipping levels agreed on in September became impossible and both in the Reich and in Norway the German administration began to abandon all planning and simply to ship what it could when it could, while resigning itself to the fact that German industry could no longer be supplied regularly from Norway. 'The possibility of supplying the armaments industry with coal will have to be looked at again', wrote Planungsamt in December. 'Setting up a

---

[1] Ibid., Planungsamt, Rohstoffamt, 'Vorbereitungen zur Räumung der Nickelmaterialien im Werk Falconbridge im Ernstfalle', 12 October 1944.

[2] Ibid., Planungsamt, 'Schiffbauprogramm und Transportbedarf in der Seeschiffahrt,' 11 October 1944.

[3] F.D. 5217/45, Rk., Hauptabt. Volkswirtschaft, 'Bericht für die Zeit von 1 bis 30 November 1944', 9 December 1944. In May 1943, 223,000 tons of ore had been moved from Narvik.

production and delivery programme for a longer period of time under these circumstances is difficult henceforward.'[1] Conversely, Norway could no longer be supplied from Germany and her connection with the *Großraumwirtschaft* became very tenuous. In February the Reichskommissariat acknowledged this to be so.

Through the military events in the Reich, a decisive deterioration has set in in the Norwegian situation, where Norway has seen herself cut off practically overnight from the import of goods in bulk or even individual goods from Germany. As far as consumption is concerned, the following months will depend on the stocks at hand in the country and severe shortages will very soon appear in different areas, especially coal, iron, grain, and articles of all kinds.[2]

In such circumstances, German efforts were concentrated at the last on carrying away from Norway all valuable stocks of raw materials. Stocks accumulated for this purpose in January amounted to 85,000 tons of pyrites, 30,000 tons of iron ore, and numerous other metal ore and chemical stockpiles to a total of 150,000 tons. In addition, stockpiles at factories which would soon run out of coal had to be moved, a further total of 80,000 tons.[3] For stocks of especially vital materials, molybdenum, manganese, nickel, and so on, express transport arrangements were made. The Reichskommissar for shipping had been asked by the Ministry of Munitions to make 100,000 tons of shipping from the Baltic trade available for the extra Norwegian traffic in December after a special request from Terboven on 22 December.[4] From the start of the new year it would appear that Norway had been abandoned to its fate. 'In the month of March', the Reichskommissariat reported, 'the difficulties of supplying Norwegian industry increased still further as a consequence of the loss of raw materials and primary goods from the Reich so that the maintenance of industries necessary both for war and for existence was possible only in the most constricted way.'[5] It was no longer possible to maintain the trading links so arbitrarily created and the German and Norwegian population of the country alike was left to scramble over the remaining resources while what was still of use to Germany for armaments production was ruthlessly plundered.

---

[1] F.D. 3045/49, section ix, Sc. 335, Rm.f.R.u.Kp., Planungsamt, 'Situation in Norwegen', 11 December 1944.

[2] F.D. 5217/45, Rk., Hauptabt. Volkswirtschaft, 'Bericht für die Zeit vom 1 bis 31 Januar 1945', 15 February 1945.

[3] F.D. 3045/49, section ix, Sc. 335, Rm.f.R.u.Kp., Planungsamt, Baudisch to Arbeitsgebietsleiter, 23 January 1945.

[4] Ibid., Planungsamt, Baudisch to Otte, 4 January 1945.

[5] F.D. 5217/45, Rk., Hauptabt. Volkswirtschaft, 'Bericht für die Zeit vom 1 bis 31 März 1945', 16 April 1945.

VII

FASCIST PLANNING AND THE ALUMINIUM INDUSTRY

THE most remarkable German project in Norway, and one which is of extreme interest for the light which it throws on the nature of fascism as an economic system, was the plan to develop the Norwegian aluminium industry. The plan was vast in scope and far-reaching in its implications. It is convincing evidence of Germany's intention to attach Norway permanently to the sphere of German economic interest. Although the attempts to reduce Russia and Poland to the level of permanently under-developed agricultural colonies were projects of even greater immensity, in western Europe no other single project equalled the importance of the aluminium plan. The study of its details and its development is therefore not only central to the history of German occupation policy in Norway; it is also central to the history of German fascism, for no other wartime episode is so revealing about the nature of the relationship between the National Socialist government and the industrial circles which supported it, a relationship very much more complex than has usually been admitted by historians of fascism. The history of the aluminium plan shows the German industrialists as much more ardent supporters of most of the government's foreign economic policies than most western historians have been prepared to admit. But it does not show the government as a mere tool of monopoly capitalism. The general outlines of foreign economic policy, the creation of the *Großraumwirtschaft*, were actively supported by the German firms involved in Norway, but always with the attempt to modify the ultimate social purposes of the government, to reassert the independence of private capital within the framework of government protection and to strike off the shackles of military control. The ultimate social purposes of the National Socialists and the industrialists were different, but this difference only emerged in Norway, as in Germany, with the later stages of the development of fascism. Even in the early stages, however, it was occasionally apparent, and the general agreement to exploit the Norwegian economy for Germany's long-term plans was still punctuated by occasional sharp disagreements on the principles of *how* to do this.

The background to the plan was the tremendous expansion of the aluminium industry in Germany during the rearmament boom. After 1933 Germany developed into the world's leading producer, overtaking the

United States. From a total of 37,000 tons in 1934, German aluminium production reached 97,000 tons in 1936. The following three years saw an acceleration in the rate of investment and by 1939 production had reached 199,000 tons, 30 per cent of the world output. The basis of this extraordinary expansion was the creation in seven years of a large modern air force. So large was the demand from this source that although the level of aluminium production was a third higher than that of the United States, about 20 per cent of the total consumption was imported. Furthermore, the bulk of the production was based on imported bauxite. This expansion continued in the war. In 1942 German aluminium production was 260,000 tons.[1] The expansion of German aluminium firms into Norway should therefore be seen not as a new development but as the restless search for further production opportunities by an industry in full spate of development. In the course of this search they found that expansion in an area where they had previously little influence was dramatically opened to them by the action of the government. There is no evidence that, even in this case, there were any economic motives which immediately influenced military policy—the invasion of Norway was more than German industrialists could have hoped for. In spite of the obvious strategic value of aluminium there seem to have been no attempts by German aluminium manufacturers to seek government help in penetrating Norway. The conquest therefore came as an utterly unexpected reward for those industrialists who had supported the German government out of the general belief that they would gain from the creation of the *Großraumwirtschaft*—a sudden felicitous harmony of interest in an area not previously considered. As will be seen, this harmony was not too long sustained. The interests of the industrialists and the government were not precisely the same in the *Großraumwirtschaft*. At first, however, there was little time to consider these differences and the acquisition of Norway suddenly offered the solution to the extraordinary difficulties of maintaining the expansion of the German aluminium industry. For it was beyond doubt that such an expansion was necessary, so insatiable was the demand of modern war. In June 1941 the demand from the air force was for 30,000 tons of aluminium monthly. Plans for development of the air force meant that the demand would soon become 50,000 tons monthly, which, allowing for supplies to other users, meant a total monthly demand of 70,000 tons, or a yearly output of 840,000 tons.[2] The planned production of aluminium in greater Germany itself for 1943 was 350,000 tons, with a further 80,000 tons surplus available from France and Switzerland.[3] The bottle-neck could be removed

[1] D. Petzina, *Autarkiepolitik im Dritten Reich*, p. 182.
[2] R.A., Rk. Diverse, Pakke 82, 'Aktenvermerk über Sitzung in Stabsamt am 23. Juni 1941', 23 June 1941.
[3] R.A., Rk. Diverse, Pakke 82, Hauptabt. Volkswirtschaft, 'Besprechung des Reichskommissars mit dem Reichsfeldmarschall Göring', 26 June 1941.

by German manufacturers taking advantage of precisely the same advantages which had led other foreign entrepreneurs to produce aluminium in Norway, the relative cheapness of electric current. That they did so with such speed is remarkable evidence of the extent to which the integration of Norway into the German system was regarded as a fixed, finite affair. The qualms which beset German industrialists in other areas, qualms related to the ultimate political settlement and the consequent safety of their investments, seem to have been swept aside immediately in this case. The government must have given the impression at once that investment in Norway could be regarded as permanently safeguarded.

On the eve of the war Norway was the sixth largest producer of aluminium in the world and several of the firms there had plans for increasing their level of production. The total output in 1938 was 28,900 tons, although the capacity was considerably higher, about 37,000 tons. In one sense the capacity was even greater, for the power plants which supplied power to the aluminium smelters were capable as they stood of supplying a greater amount of current. The industry was very much a smelting industry, imported alumina being smelted into aluminium ingots which were then exported. Some companies, however, did produce their own alumina from imported bauxite. Only one company, the Norwegian Aluminium Company, produced finished products from the ingots; its subsidiary plants consumed in that way about 40 per cent of the aluminium smelted in its works at Høyanger. Otherwise the whole industry depended on unrestricted imports of raw material (bauxite) or semi-manufactures (alumina) and the unrestricted export of finished aluminium.

The smelters clung to the edge of the Norwegian coast and were mostly still controlled by foreign capital. The smelters at Tyssedal on the Sørfjord, and Eydehavn in south Norway, were owned by Norske Nitridaktieselskap, a company in which the majority capital holding was British and Canadian. The Haugvik plant on Glomfjord at the entrance to the Vestfjord was British owned and so were the two subsidiaries of the British Aluminium Company, the Vigeland works near to Kristiansand and the Stangfjord works on the Sunnfjord. The estimated productive capacity of these plants is shown in Table 37.

The fact that so much of the Norwegian aluminium industry was foreign-owned made it even more attractive to Germany. The practice and custom of 'belligerent occupation' bestowed certain rights of control over foreign property on the occupier. These were pushed to their furthest limits by the German administration in most occupied territories by the appointment of trustees (Treuhänder) for enemy property, usually German firms interested in the field.[1] In part this in itself accounts for the astonishing alacrity with

[1] For a rather disingenuous discussion of the powers of such trusteeships see O. Ulshöfer, *Einflußnahme auf Wirtschaftsunternehmungen.*

which the German firms acted, it was necessary to move quickly to get what were obvious pickings. Had they been allowed free rein, had the German government itself not had fairly precise interests in Norway, the pressure of German capital would soon have turned Norway into a colony. The metals subcommittee of I. G. Farben, meeting the week after the invasion of Norway, reported that 'in Norway all factories and mining

TABLE 37. *Estimated Productive Capacity of the Norwegian Aluminium Industry, 1940**

(tons per year)

Works	Aluminium capacity	Alumina capacity
Høyanger	8,500	18,000
Tyssedal	9,600	..
Eydehavn	5,400	..
Glomfjord	9,000	..
Vigeland	3,600	..
Stangfjord	700	..
Total	36,800	18,000

* F.D. 4870/45, Rlm., 'Leichtmetall Ausbau Norwegens'.

concessions owned by British or French nationals will be sequestrated and the Norwegian economy will be mobilized to work for us. The development of the Norwegian molybdenum deposits is to be started immediately. A discussion about this with Krupp is to take place on Monday.'[1] At the same meeting it was indicated that plans had already been formulated to ship German alumina to Norway so that the Norwegian aluminium works would be able to continue production.[2]

These discussions must have been based on the visit to the Norwegian aluminium producers of Director Koppenberg of the Junkers Aircraft Company. He arrived in Norway on 14 April, representing Reichsmarschall Göring in his capacity as Commander-in-Chief of the Luftwaffe, to negotiate with the Norwegian government and aluminium firms.[1] I. G. Farben's own reports on the potential structure of industry in the New Order declared that plans which were afoot to develop the manufacture of products out of aluminium in Norway should not be allowed to mature. Norway must be made to export the completed aluminium ingots to Germany for the next stage of production.

[1] F.D. 4870/45, Rlm., 'Die Aluminiumnot in der Luftfahrtindustrie und Maßnahmen zu ihrer Bekämpfung'.
[2] N.T.L.L. F.D. 2203/45, Supplement A, G2, I. G. Farben, 'Unser Interesse an der deutschen Einfuhr aus Norwegen', 1940.

If, also, the present capacity of the Norwegian chemical industry, as far as it disturbs our interests, were to be used in the first place to meet internal demand, we might express the opinion that a further development of the chemical industry in Norway should only be undertaken under agreement with the interests of the German chemical industry exporting to Norway and therefore with ourselves, something, for example, which has happened for years in the field of nitrogen and happens at present in the field of light metals.[1]

I. G. Farben's interest in Norwegian aluminium production was only a part of their interest in the Norwegian chemical industry as a whole. The interest of other firms was more exclusive, especially that of the German aluminium firm, Vereinigte Aluminiumwerke, a firm with close financial and personal ties to the governing groups. Koppenberg's connections were with the Junkers Aircraft Company and he and his staff were no experts on aluminium production.[2] But due to the fact that the manufacture of aluminium had played so important a part in the Four Year Plan, the head of which was also Göring, the Junkers corporation were in a strong position in any negotiations. The expansion of German aluminium production in the 1930s had been undertaken almost regardless of cost. Not only were the raw materials almost entirely imported but the cost of producing the large amount of electric current necessary in the electrolysis process was very high even for so large a coal-producer as Germany. The cost advantages of using hydro-electric power had been the main attraction for foreign firms producing aluminium in Norway. By a personal decision Hitler had decided that the stocks and the future production of aluminium in Norway should all be at the disposal of the Luftwaffe.[2] So urgent was their need that the first instalment of Norwegian stocks seized was actually flown to Germany.

In fact Koppenberg, in spite of his quasi-official position, had strong rivals in the German aluminium firms. In May representatives of Vereinigte Aluminiumwerke had visited Norway on a similar mission.[3] They had been forestalled by Hitler's decision, taken on 8 May, although their efforts were not to be without importance later. Göring had decided that the position of Vereinigte Aluminiumwerke had become dangerously monopolistic from the Luftwaffe's viewpoint and that for this reason the proposed developments in Norway should be entrusted to another firm.[4]

On 10 May Göring appointed Koppenberg his trustee under the terms of the Four Year Plan and on 23 July his powers were extended. Koppenberg was now given control over all stocks of aluminium and productive

[1] N.T.L.L., F.D. 2203/45, Supplement A, G2, I. G. Farben, 'Unser Interesse an der deutschen Einfuhr aus Norwegen', 1940.
[2] Innberetning til Oslo Politikammer. Vedrørende A/S Norsk Aluminium Company og Nordisk Aluminium Industri A/S.
[3] M. Skodvin, *Striden om okkupasjonsstyret i Norge*, p. 251.
[4] I.M.T. NI–8146, Case VI, Document Box 65.

capacity in France and over the stocks in Belgium and the Netherlands. At the same time he was charged with negotiations with the government of unoccupied France about the large aluminium industry and bauxite reserves which remained there outside the control of the German army. He was also empowered to conduct negotiations on a general development plan with the whole Norwegian aluminium industry, on a broader basis than his earlier discussions of 18 April. Throughout the summer of 1940 Koppenberg prepared his plan for the expansion of the Norwegian aluminium industry. On 1 October, with the plan prepared, he was invested with full powers as trustee of all foreign capital in that industry.[1] The Reichskommissariat reported that, due to Koppenberg's powers over the French and British interests there, 'the whole Norwegian aluminium industry now stands under German administration and will be able to be regulated and expanded according to German interests'.[2]

At the start of October Koppenberg revealed his plan. Norway had been chosen as the basis for the strategically necessary expansion in light-metal production. The grounds for this were both economic and technical. The new considerations relevant in a reconstructed Europe based on autarkic economic principles suggested that water power would be the best future source of electric current. The initial investment in producing hydro-electric power was greater than with coal-fired power stations but it was important to reserve coal for other purposes. Given this initial premise, Norway became an obvious choice. Firstly, there were a number of plans already available in Norway prepared by pre-war governments and on some of them work had already begun. Secondly, the ready availability of water power in Norway permitted large power stations of up to 100,000-kilowatts capacity to be built. Thirdly, these factors meant that the final price of the current would be cheaper than elsewhere.[3]

These premises are in themselves an interesting study. The availability of cheap electricity had certainly been the main reason why the aluminium industry had developed so successfully in Norway. To that should be added the freedom of entry for foreign capital, for the aluminium industry represented fully the liberal nature of Norway's economy. Within the area of the *Großraumwirtschaft* Norway would still be open to German capital, all too open in fact, and would also be open to imports of bauxite from Hungary and France. The price of these imports could easily be dictated by German interests. It is, however, curious to see how the development of these plans within the framework of the greater European economic area raised anxieties about the supply of coal, a raw material with which Germany proper was exceptionally well endowed.

[1] F.D. 4870/45, Rlm., 'Die Aluminiumnot in der Luftfahrtindustrie'.
[2] F.D. 5325/45, Rk., 'Ein Jahr Reichskommissar'.
[3] F.D. 4870/45, Rlm., 'Leichtmetall Ausbau Norwegens'.

Basically the plan assumed that extensive deposits of bauxite would be available to Germany in the future. These could only be in Hungary and in unoccupied France. Although it may not have been unreasonable to suppose that Hungarian raw materials would always be available since Hungary was inextricably a part of the fascist trading network, the plan was rather over-optimistic about the ease with which Germany would obtain raw materials from unoccupied France. This optimism, of course, was as nothing compared to the sweeping and ultimately unjustified assumptions made about the availability of shipping. Koppenberg indicated that Norway was particularly favoured with regard to sites because in every case it would be possible to bring the raw materials by sea!

The plan involved the development both of the alumina and aluminium industries. The former, however, was to be developed less than the latter and there would be an expansion of alumina-producing plants in southern France and south-eastern Europe whose production would be shipped to Norway for the final stage of conversion. The plan for increasing production was in two stages. The initial stage was the so-called emergency programme which would increase the output of alumina to 203,000 tons per year and that of aluminium to 119,900 tons per year. The time allowed for this stage in the plan was about one year. Included in the emergency programme was the construction of a magnesium factory at Herøen using sea water as a raw material and operating on the I. G. Farben electrolytic method of smelting.[1] The site in this case was chosen for its special proximity to Norsk Hydro whose surplus electric current it would be able to use. Its productive capacity would be 10,000 tons yearly. It will be seen that I. G. Farben had been not wholly excluded from this happy hunting. The second stage of the plan entailed an increase in aluminium production to 243,900 tons yearly on the basis of the previously developed alumina plant. No increase of alumina production was planned after the completion of the emergency programme.

The emergency programme was particularly dependent in its first stages on the import of alumina. Until the new Norwegian alumina plants came into operation, the expansion of aluminium production would have to depend on the import of alumina from France. In March 1942 a new alumina works constructed in Ludwigshafen by the firm of Giulini, whose output would be designed entirely for export to Norway, would have reached the stage of production. Until then the import dependence of the Norwegian aluminium industry on France would increase. In April 1942 the new alumina works in Norway would begin deliveries.

The additional power stations necessary to implement the second stage of the programme were to be built during the emergency programme. This,

[1] Magnesium was first used widely as the result of military developments in the thirties. It was a component of light alloys for aircraft engine casing and of the tubes used in incendiary bombs.

TABLE 38. *The Aluminium Programme**

Development of plant	Production			Cost (000 RM)			
	Power (kilowatts)	Alumina (tons per year)	Aluminium (tons per year)	Power stations	Alumina plant	Aluminium plant	Total
Existing productive capacity			36,800				
Extension of existing works		18,000	3,100				
1st Stage (emergency programme)							
Glomfjord (combined)	54,000		24,000	9,650		7,100	80,650
Eitrheim I			8,000			25,900	25,900
Heroen (Maare)†	124,000	50,000	24,000	85,000	33,000	91,500	209,500
Tyin	88,200	50,000	24,000	36,700	70,000	66,900	173,600
Sauda	42,000	85,000	24,000	16,000	67,400		83,400
Summary of emergency programme	308,200	185,000	80,000	147,350	170,400	255,300	573,050
Total including emergency programme		203,000	119,900				
2nd Stage							
Eitrheim II with Tysse II	76,600		16,000	44,000		40,000	84,000
Sundalsøra	159,200		60,000	111,400		160,000	271,400
Osa and Hardanger	181,200		48,000	154,800		135,000	289,800
Summary of 2nd stage	417,000		124,000	310,200		335,000	645,200
Total	725,200	203,000	243,900	457,550	170,400	590,300	1,218,250

* F.D. 4870/45, Rlm., 'Leichtmetall Ausbau Norwegens'.
† Plus 10,000 tons per year of magnesium.

and the need to provide a regular source of alumina, meant that the second stage of the Koppenberg Plan showed a much greater increase in aluminium production than the first. It is worth while reflecting on what was needed to guarantee the output of 243,900 tons of aluminium a year in Norway. An enormous increase in the capacity of hydro-electric plant and a great

TABLE 39. *Proposed Output of Individual Works in Aluminium Plan*

(tons per year)

Emergency programme	Aluminium	Alumina
Additional capacity to existing works		
Tyssedal	2,400	
Eydehavn	600	
Glomfjord	24,000	
Eitrheim I	8,000	
New works		
Herøen I	12,000	25,000
Tyin	24,000	50,000
Herøen II	12,000	25,000
Sauda		85,000
2nd Stage		
Eitrheim II	16,000	
Osa I (Ulvik)	12,000	
Sundalsøra (Aura)	20,000	
Osa II (Ulvik)	12,000	
Sundalsøra II (Aura)	40,000	
Hardanger (Ulvik)	24,000	

TABLE 40. *Proposed Power Production Programme*

(installed capacity in kilowatts)

Power station	Output
Glomfjord	54,000
Tyin	88,200
Sauda	42,000
Maare	124,000
Tysse II	76,600
Sundalsøra	159,200
Osa	81,200
Veigo	100,000

development in shipping were not all. The successful completion of the second stage also meant the building of alumina works in France and south-eastern Europe with a combined output of 250,000 tons a year. The bauxite in France was already being mined; in Greece and Croatia the mines had still to be developed. These plans would be completed by the middle of 1944. Since the Koppenberg plan was drawn up in autumn 1940 none of the bauxite deposits under consideration were as yet in German hands.

The production of electric power in Norway through the expansion of existing sources of power and the creation of new ones was to be increased to over 700,000 kilowatts. The total production of aluminium in Norway was to be increased from 30,000 tons a year to 240,000 tons a year. This was to be done over a very brief period of time. By 1 April 1942 the output of aluminium would be 60,000 tons a year, by 1 October in the same year, 120,000 tons, by 1 October 1943, 170,000 tons, and by 1 June 1944 the final total would be reached. To back up the first stage of the programme new alumina works would be built in Norway and a new works built in Germany by Italian capital which would be designed entirely for export to Norway. The Norwegian works would use labradorite, an ore found in Norway, but would also be capable of using bauxite if supplies were made available. In the second stage Norway would be supplied with alumina from works to be built in France and the Balkans. A factory for a yearly production of 10,000 tons of magnesium would be built. The total cost of this programme would be 1,450 million Reichsmarks, of which 1,200 million Reichsmarks were for the plans in Norway. It was therefore a plan involving a redeployment of the whole European economy to provide a German aluminium industry in Norway by a programme of capital investment over four years amounting to over one-third of the national income of Norway.

The scale of these plans meant that they could scarcely be the monopoly of the Junkers Aircraft Company. The officials of the Four Year Plan Department began discussions on the nature of the companies to be formed in Norway and the sources of their capital. In early October the plan was approved by the Luftwaffe and then by the Reichsmarschall, who added to the plan a note that it should be carried out as soon as possible. The Air Ministry, in its eagerness to get things moving, had already promised financial support for the early stages of the plan, but they were eager to recruit industrial capital for the next stages of development. In view of I. G. Farben's earlier interest in Norway, and because the plans closely involved their subsidiary, Norsk Hydro, it was understandable that that company should be approached. Karl Krauch, who more than any other director had linked I. G. Farben to the Four Year Plan, becoming himself one of the chief planning officials, was eager for I. G. Farben to extend its interests in Norway.

Among the series of proposals for the organization of the European chemical industry within the *Großraumwirtschaft* of the future, submitted by I. G. Farben to the Reichs Economic Ministry, exists a set of proposals for Norway.[1] The interest of I. G. Farben in metal-alloy production there was more than a merely defensive one. Its origins were connected with the early history of the Norsk Hydro firm. Two years after Norsk Hydro had erected its first plant at Notodden and begun the synthetic production of

[1] N.T.L.L.F.D. 2203/45, Bundle D, 'Chemische Erzeugung, Norwegen'.

nitrogen, it had entered, in 1907, into technical agreements with the Badische Anilin Fabrik. These early links were never broken, and after 1927, when the use of the Haber–Bosch nitrogen process began to develop more rapidly in Germany, Norsk Hydro entered into a twenty-five-year agreement to co-ordinate its exports with those of the German producers. The new factory at Herøen built in 1929 was designed with German technical help. In 1939 Norsk Hydro had signed an agreement with I. G. Farben to restrict its production of nitrogen. Although the inventive fertility of its engineers ensured its survival as a major industry on the Norwegian scale, on the European scale it was a small part of the cartel dominated by I. G. Farben. The Koppenberg Plan involved it directly, for the process of manufacturing alumina from labradorite was Norsk Hydro's own process and the initial expansion of alumina output was to take place at Herøen. In 1937–8 Norsk Hydro had plans to create its own plant based on using labradorite.[1] It was also to create a power station at Tyin from hydro-electric resources which Norsk Hydro had earmarked for its own development.[2]

Between 11 October and 16 October a series of discussions was held with I. G. Farben with Krauch apparently the main negotiator. The fluidity of Koppenberg's plan is indicated by the range of possibilities discussed with I. G. Farben. He was prepared to consider a target of 150,000 tons of aluminium yearly for the Emergency Programme if necessary. The expansion of the existing smaller works, such as Tyssedal, was envisaged on a rather greater scale than in the Air Ministry version of the plan. The production of alumina in the new Sauda Works was discussed as being as low as 80,000 tons yearly. The first stage touched I. G. Farben's interests in so far as it involved the production of 25,000 tons of alumina yearly at Herøen from labradorite by Norsk Hydro. The second stage involved them by embracing the Tyin developments which would be responsible for a further 25,000 tons of aluminium and 50,000 tons of alumina yearly. Krauch suggested to the directors of I. G. Farben that by participation in the new company they could acquire a controlling interest in it.

As is evident from the memorandum on the conference of the 11th inst. the Reich Institute for Research (RFW), Professor Krauch and Herr Koppenberg are extremely anxious for I. G. Farben to take over the technical co-operation in connection with the execution of the programme. Professor Krauch thinks that this is a unique opportunity in I. G. Farben's aluminium field.[2]

That Krauch was not alone in his interests may be seen from the remark of the company's Economic Policy Committee to the directors that,

as is known, we are greatly interested in the field of magnesium and aluminium production in Norway. We shall take the liberty of reverting to this subject and

---

[1] *Innberetning til Oslo Politikammer. Vedrørende A/S Norsk Aluminium Company og Nordisk Aluminium Industri A/S.*
[2] I.M.T., NI–8033, Case VI, Document Box 65.

presenting a special report at an opportune moment since the projects connected therewith have not as yet reached the stage in which it would be possible for us at this time to make special proposals and express requests.[1]

Meanwhile Koppenberg and Director Simmat of the Mineralöl-Baugesell-schaft had visited Norway to explore the sites, and Simmat's company, which had close financial ties with Göring and the Four-Year Plan Office had agreed to undertake the construction works.

Urgent letters to ter Meer and Weber, two of the absent directors of I. G. Farben, show the eagerness of German firms to join in this klondyke.

We do not know the extent to which other firms have already shown an interest in this project; however, we consider it quite possible that the Hermann Göring Works for instance, will enter the field if Farben does not take the opportunity offered now. If that happens, yet another large firm would enter the light metal field. We would once again experience the same situation which existed after the World War: Griesheim and Metallgesellschaft had built up the whole German aluminium industry before, and especially during the World War. As a result of the tendency towards socialization the Lautawerk, the largest foundry, fell to the state and the combine had to restrict itself to twenty per cent of the aluminium production. If another state-owned firm were to enter the field our share would be still further reduced.[2]

The proposals considered by I. G. Farben were that their participation should depend on having a 55 per cent controlling share in the capital of any new company. The Neuhausen Company, owing to its technical know-ledge of alumina production would have 20 per cent, the Metallgesellschaft 15 per cent, and, as a sop to Norwegian interests, Norsk Hydro would have to have 10 per cent. All this supposed that the Junkers Company would not want to participate. If it wanted to, its participation would be unavoidable. In that case its share should come equally from that of I. G. Farben and of Neuhausen.[2]

On 12 November 1940 Göring issued a special order to Koppenberg on the expansion of the Norwegian aluminium industry. 'On the basis of the conference held with myself I commission you to found the necessary company as Commissar for the building and production project in the Norwegian aluminium industry and with the help of that company to carry out the whole programme as quickly as possible.'[3] Koppenberg was to have control over the financial arrangements of the new company. The order breathed an air of optimism greater even than the plan itself. 'If, while construction is being carried out, it is learned that the building times may be lessened by special measures so that the annual production is possible

[1] I.M.T., NI–7784, Case VI, Document Box 65.
[2] I.M.T., NI–8034, Case VI, Document Box 65.
[3] F.D. 5515/45, Rlm., Göring to Koppenberg, 12 November 1940.

in a shorter period than foreseen, all available means must be brought to bear to achieve this result.'[1]

Such an exhortation had little effect on the industrialists. From their point of view the details were of extreme interest for their eyes rested on the peace-time prospects as much as on the wartime actuality. It was supposed that the financial arrangements which were being made were arrangements which would last for a very long time and the companies were not to be bullied quickly into so long term a settlement. The difficulties which I. G. Farben had met with were very small compared to the problem of controlling and financing the whole project. The main interests at stake were those of the German government, in particular that of the Air Force, the Norwegian government and manufacturers, the Reichskommissariat, the German aircraft manufacturers, represented by Koppenberg, and the aluminium manufacturers, represented by Vereinigte Aluminiumwerke, the firm which had been closely associated with the government in the pre-war expansion of the German aluminium industry. The aluminium industry was an international business and the power of the international con-nections of the manufacturers was well demonstrated by the fact that even the foreign interests in the Norwegian companies could not be ignored. The raw material supply had to come from abroad and many of the alumina-producing plants were also partly controlled by important foreign interests. The ramifications of the whole affair were extraordinarily complex and both Koppenberg and Göring were to find that their hasty methods could not produce the results they wanted, even in a war.

The discussion between Göring and Koppenberg which had taken place on the same day shows how few doubts there were about the whole plan and how urgent it was. Germany's aluminium output was still 100,000 tons less than the combined output of the United States and Canada. The formal constitution of the company to undertake the Norwegian programme did not matter, Göring indicated; there might even be two companies. 'What is important and decisive is that the building and production projects proposed by Koppenberg be carried out as fast as possible under the aegis of the most important and the biggest consumer, the Reichs Air Ministry. . . . Finally, energetic advice to create the enterprise as quickly as possible. Details are not interesting! ! !'[2]

In the first stage of the negotiations the Air Ministry got its own way over I. G. Farben, mainly because it was willing to bear the initial financial outlay of getting the programme going. A new company was formed on 3 December, with vague powers over the supervision of the plan, powers whose scope was later to be the subject of much argument.[3] Nordische

[1] Ibid.
[2] F.D. 5515/45, Rlm., 'Besprechung Herr Reichsmarschall Göring — Dr. Koppenberg', 12 November 1940.
[3] F.D. 4870/45, Rlm., 'Die Aluminiumnot in der Luftfahrtindustrie'.

Aluminium Gesellschaft, 'Nordag' as it was invariably known, had its initial share capital controlled by a majority holding by Bank der Deutschen Luftfahrt, a bank owned by the Air Ministry. I. G. Farben's role was limited to the participation in the plan of Norsk Hydro. To that extent their hopes of preserving the new developments almost entirely for private enterprise were disappointed, an outcome not entirely surprising in view of the strategic importance of the developments. But the degree of freedom to be allowed to private firms, the participation of the various interests in these plans, and the balance of power between these interests had still to be settled. The determining issues were two. What would the powers of Nordag be and by whom would the much larger sums of money needed for the detailed stages of the plan be provided?

Terboven and the Reichskommissariat wished to control the powers of Nordag so that Norwegian banks and entrepreneurs would play a greater part in the affair. He was afraid that the German interests would so combine as to make it impossible for the Norwegian industrialists to enter freely into the enterprise and he wished on political grounds to avoid any suggestion of compulsion. This was especially so in the question of financing the developments. The nature of the monetary policy which the Reichskommissariat pursued in Norway would have made any attempt at using Norwegian public funds on a large scale for these developments extremely dangerous. It would have worsened the inflationary tendency, unbalanced the budget further, and weakened the fragile public confidence in the currency, thus destroying all of Terboven's long-term projects. Accordingly, in January 1941, after the founding of Nordag, the Reichskommissariat insisted both that it should function as a holding company to control the finances of a set of independent companies each to undertake a particular part of the total plan and that it should be a holding company which would retain a majority of the share capital of those companies. General Udet, Quartermaster-General of the Air Force, was against any participation by the Reichskommissariat itself and very much in favour of the Luftwaffe keeping a controlling interest over the whole operation.[1]

Meanwhile the German firms pressed on with their claims and Koppenberg's plans, in spite of the delay in organizing them, became more ambitious. At the start of 1941, I. G. Farben came to an agreement with Norsk Hydro about the construction of the planned magnesium factory at Herøen. The participation would be 51 per cent by I. G. Farben and 49 per cent by Norsk Hydro.[2] This was yet another attempt by I. G. Farben to retain a control over developments which the government, in spite of its close ties to that firm, was unwilling to permit. On the very day that the

---

[1] F.D. 5515/45, Rlm., Generalluftzeugmeister, 'Ausbau der norwegischen Aluminium-industrie', 23 February 1941.

[2] I.M.T., NI–8079, Case VI, Document Box 65.

agreement was concluded a message arrived from Koppenberg pointing out that his proposals were much larger. They involved another aluminium factory at Herøen with a potential output of 12,000 tons a year, an alumina works with an annual output of 25,000 tons, and a plant for the production of cryolite.[1] Since the directors of I. G. Farben anticipated that they would have to provide some of the capital for the plant to be built at Sauda in order to be allowed to take part in the Herøen project, they were obliged to reopen their negotiations on a wider front. Basically they had no interest in the Sauda project and were concerned with ensuring that the expansion at Herøen did not bring other groups into their working arrangements with Norsk Hydro. They hoped to sign a further agreement for the wider project on the same ratio of capital participation, but facing up to matters realistically they agreed on a reserve plan which would accept a 40 per cent participation for I. G. Farben and Norsk Hydro in the expanded firm and a 20 per cent participation for the groups represented by Koppenberg. If the worst came to the worst I. G. Farben would even accept a 30 per cent participation each for themselves and the Koppenberg interests provided that Norsk Hydro retained a 40 per cent interest. But the less satisfactory arrangements presupposed 'that the problem of procuring capital can be solved as far as possible by a loan of Norwegian or other capital in some way that would be acceptable to I. G. Farben'.[2] Those presuppositions would inevitably be unacceptable to Terboven, although I. G. Farben may not have been aware of that as yet.

On 6 February Koppenberg and the representatives of I. G. Farben met to discuss the further expansion at Herøen in the Reichs Air Ministry. The I. G. Farben representatives defended the part played by Norsk Hydro who had surrendered their own expansion plans to take part in the general scheme which had obviously drawn heavily on the pre-war planning of Norsk Hydro. Ministerialdirektor Cejka, representing the Air Ministry, insisted that they, who were providing an assured market for the increased production, should have a share of at least one-third of the whole project.[3] Nordag would be a holding company to maintain the Reich's interests in the Norwegian companies and the Air Ministry could not find itself in a minority in that holding company. Before I. G. Farben settled for this, which was slightly worse than their worst fears, they received four assurances from the Air Ministry. One was that Metallgesellschaft, a company which had signed contracts with I. G. Farben to participate in the Herøen developments, would eventually receive an offer to take part in some later stage of the Koppenberg plan to compensate for the cancellation of its contracts in the Herøen plan. The second was that Norsk Hydro would be

[1] I.M.T., NI–8079, Case VI, Document Book XIIA.
[2] I.M.T., NI–8079, Case VI, Document Box 65.
[3] I.M.T., NI–8144, Case VI, Document Box 65.

compensated for its reduced share in the new developments by being invited later to participate in a new nitrogen works in Norway. The third was that the Reich would loosen its interest in the whole Herøen expansion as soon as the capital could come from other sources without endangering the success of the plan. The fourth was that the Air Ministry would grant temporary short-term credits to I. G. Farben in the first stages. For I. G. Farben, therefore, the terms were quite generous. Indeed, their determination to maintain their independence of public control even in wartime is very remarkable. For Norsk Hydro the terms were much less satisfactory.

The curious relationship between the National Socialist Government and the larger firms had dictated the whole course of the negotiation. Unwilling to see firms whose ideological soundness they suspected dealing with vital military matters, the Party was time and time again driven into their hands in order to get things done. Even a firm so apparently friendly to the Party as I. G. Farben was suspect. And not without reason, for, no matter how high the hopes its directors pinned on the economic aspects of National Socialist foreign policy, in the last resort they were businessmen and not fascist politicians. Their main aim was to emerge with a stronger position after the war than before, in Norway as well as in Germany. In the case of Norway that aim scarcely coincided exactly with the government's own interests. Tied to I. G. Farben by the Four Year Plan, the Party was unable to shake off those ties in the aluminium plan, although the settlement itself was far from what the company had wanted.

On 28 February two directors of I. G. Farben and two directors of Nordag met with Otte and the chief financial officials of the Reichskommissariat to discuss the settlement between themselves and the Air Ministry as the basis of foundation of the first of the development companies. The initial share capital, to be held in three equal portions by I. G. Farben, Norsk Hydro, and Nordag would be 40 million kroner. The ultimate need was 160 million kromer.[1] The difference was great enough to raise the whole issue of the financing of the industrial development plan in Norway.

As far as the Reichskommissariat was concerned, they hoped that the Norwegian contribution would come in the form of private capital investment, and to that end they wanted to devise the set of institutional arrangements which would least offend Norwegian sentiment. In particular they did not want to change Norwegian laws on concessions which insisted that the exploitation of Norwegian water resources could only be undertaken by companies with a majority Norwegian control. These laws were of great historical and social significance in Norway. They had been passed in their original version before the First World War at the height of foreign investment in the country. Subsequently the control of water resources had

<hr/>

[1] R.A., Rk. Diverse, Pakke 82, 'Besprechung im Reichskommissariat am 28.2.1941', 28 February 1941.

remained a fundamental issue in domestic policy. The directors of Nordag were only prepared to allow the Norwegian interests to have a 50 per cent interest in the new power companies to be formed, and they were strongly supported by the I. G. Farben directors. The agreement between the Air Ministry and I. G. Farben thus did not lead to any immediate action but to a direct clash with the Reichskommissariat.

There were other aspects of the Norwegian law on industrial concessions which Terboven was equally concerned to maintain so that the political situation would not deteriorate. The maximum period of time for which a concession over natural resources could be granted was fifty years, with the possibility of extension for a further ten, too short a period for the German firms. Power stations would return to the State at the end of that period of time. A certain proportion of the current produced had to be made available to local authorities. The laws granting such concessions had to be sanctioned by the Størting. That was of course no longer possible, but the powers and prerogatives of the Størting had passed to the new Ministers, so that the decision on whether to grant the concession would have to be made by the Ministry of Public Works. Norwegian law stipulated that companies exploiting concessions in Norway must be founded under Norwegian company law and must have their main seat in Norway.

Director Ilgner of I. G. Farben had proposed at the meeting in Oslo in February that one way around the difficulties was to found another inter-mediate holding company as well as the actual aluminium-producing company itself. The holding company would function as a subsidiary of Nordag but would be founded under Norwegian law in Oslo. On 2 May Koppenberg and Ilgner agreed to found two new companies. One, a further holding company, A/S Nordag, Oslo, would have a 51 per cent capital participation by the Air Ministry which insisted on this control. Only one-quarter of the capital would be Norwegian. The capital of the other company, A/S Nordisk Lettmetall would be divided in three parts between I. G. Farben, Norsk Hydro and the new holding company, A/S Nordag, Oslo.[1] The delegates of the Reichskommissariat agreed to this procedure although they clearly did not think it would work since the arrangements were not such as to attract Norwegian capital freely. Politically, the advantages of attracting direct investment by Norwegian firms were very great. But there was also the more obvious economic advantage. 'Furthermore, from an economic point of view, it is pointless for Germany to invest greater quantities of money in Norway than is necessary for the guarantee of German influence. This guarantee would be fully provided by a 51 per cent German participation.'[1] Terboven's advisers therefore suggested that he should personally deal with the two ministers concerned,

[1] R.A., Rk. Diverse, Pakke 82, Abt. Volkswirtschaft, 'Leichtmetallbauprogramm', 2 May 1941.

Funk and Göring, to change the arrangements. The change in the company arrangements had in no way diminished the Reichskommissariat's opposition to this method of proceeding.

Otte was advised by the monetary policy section of the Reichskommissariat that the 500 million kroner which would probably be needed to implement the 'emergency programme' would not be available on these terms. It would have to be produced by some compulsory measure and such a measure was not to be recommended. If it succeeded it would be a Pyrrhic victory for it could succeed only once and would endanger the whole monetary policy. The budget for 1941–2 already covered by loans 400 million kroner of the occupation costs, thus ruling out further loans, and an attack on savings would be politically disastrous.[1] This advice is what was submitted to Terboven on 28 May. Koppenberg had known after the Oslo conference on 28 February what the Reichskommissariat would agree to but he had failed to negotiate these conditions in Berlin. Nordag still refused even to agree to the separation of the aluminium companies and the power stations to supply them in order to circumvent Norwegian law. Their grounds were that the whole basis of the plan was the cheapness of electric current in Norway. The transport costs were extremely high and if the one advantage which Norway had as an aluminium producer was not to be under their control they considered the plan too risky on the grounds of price of the finished product. They were prepared to compromise only if the price of the current produced could be legally restricted to the actual cost of production, as though the separate companies were still one vertical concern, if the supply of current was guaranteed by long-term contracts stipulating a supply beyond the actual production needs of the smelters, and if the power plants helped as far as possible in the construction of the smelters.[1] There was a further difficulty. The proposals for founding A/S Nordag, Oslo allowed Vereinigte Aluminiumwerke only 26 per cent of the capital and it was still by no means clear that they would accept this. Terboven was therefore advised to reject the new scheme as useless. The truth of the matter was that both he and his officials had acquired a much sharper sense of the political realities in Norway than any of the other participants to the plan.

Had there been any harmony of interest between the Reichs government and the German firms on the details of what was to be done Terboven would no doubt have been overridden. But the firms themselves were engaged in bitter rivalry and were each supported in their rivalry by different branches of the government. Göring and the Air Ministry supported Koppenberg, whereas the Reichs Economics Ministry always pushed the case of Vereinigte Aluminiumwerke. I. G. Farben was

[1] R.A., Rk. Diverse, Pakke 82, Abt. Wirtschaft, 'Vermerk zur Vorlage für den Herrn Reichskommissar', 28 May 1941.

more ambivalent. Their seat of power was in the Four-Year Plan Office, but this meant they had to submit ultimately to Göring whose main interest remained the Air Force. This unseemly rivalry spread throughout Europe as the firms sought to gain a decisive influence in Norway in two ways, by securing control of the foreign capital invested there by the same means they would have used in peacetime, rather than waiting for the Reichs government to distribute rewards according to its own wishes, and by securing control of the raw-material supply. It is not surprising that the aluminium project in Norway should have involved such complicated manœuvres on a European scale, for the aluminium industry had been internationalist in its outlook from the start. In fact in such an international business the larger firms had many advantages because of their personal contacts and the complex ramifications of their pre-war legal agreements over the National Socialist government. That government's policy was to turn the industry into one of intensely national outlook serving a great national need and sacrificing many of its pre-war policies to the quite different needs and policies of the fascist government. In these circumstances clashes between industrialists and government were inevitable, and it is clear that not even I. G. Farben, so closely bound to the government as it was, could wholly accept the government's policy.

They hoped to circumvent Norwegian law and Terboven's obstinate refusal to modify it in their favour by a complicated intrigue. If they could secure the French capital holdings in the Norsk Hydro firm by more 'normal' business negotiations they would find themselves in a much stronger position in the new companies. They therefore initiated a series of negotiations with the two French directors of Norsk Hydro, evidently expecting that in the circumstances of the occupation of France, and having regard to the numerous surrenders of capital which the German government had forced on France through various official and unofficial means, their task would not be difficult.[1]

But while these negotiations were taking place, the Ministry of Economics, which supported the Vereinigte Aluminiumwerke, also tried to secure the French capital holdings for its allies. They helped an Austrian firm, Vergasungs-Industrie AG, to establish contact with the French stockholders and to make them an offer for the whole of the 10 million kroner of Norsk Hydro stock held in France through the Dresdner Bank.[2] The Swedish president of Norsk Hydro, Marcus Wallenberg, was given permission to travel to Paris to sign an agreement with the French directors on behalf of I. G. Farben. The two French directors agreed to the terms for the formation of the new company.[3] The Reichs government then

[1] I.M.T., NI–8089, Case VI, Document Box 65; I.M.T., NI–1278, Case VI, Document Box 65. [2] I.M.T., NI–8088, Case VI, Document Box 65. [3] I.M.T., NI–13194, Case VI, Document Box 65.

intervened and declared the terms to be unacceptable because they were against its own wartime interests.[1]

Without permission from the government the manœuvres could go no further because the clearing agreements imposed by Germany on both France and Norway allowed no possibility of transferring funds directly between the two countries and the government would not allow this principle to be breached so that the French shares could be bought by a French bank on behalf of the Norwegian company.[2] In fact I. G. Farben had misled the two French directors as to the ultimate consequences of the agreement by disguising from them exactly what proportion of the capital stock would be controlled by I. G. Farben once the agreement had been signed. There was every danger that if the transaction took place directly between France and Germany the French government, realizing the political consequences and perhaps having a better over-all view of the economic consequences, would invoke its own laws to prevent the capital transfer.[3] These laws could be overridden by German pressure at the Franco-German Armistice Commission at Wiesbaden, but the evidence of previous attempts was that the Reichs government had to have the most pressing and immediate reasons in order to act in this way because the French resistance at Wiesbaden was always extremely stubborn. Where the German government did act in this way it was always to further its own conception of the new Europe, not that of the industrialists. Eventually I. G. Farben's manœuvres were completed but only after they had been forced to come to a compromise agreement with all the other interests involved. On 4 September 1941 the French government gave its permission for a new agreement by which the Swedish Enskilda Bank bought the subscription rights of future Norsk Hydro shares from the Banque de Paris.[4]

Koppenberg's policies were more direct. He hoped to resolve part of the difficulty which Norwegian law raised to German majority control of the new Norwegian firms by using the occupation of France to extend German control over the bauxite and alumina producers there. The means would have also to be through the Franco-German Armistice Commission. Hans Hemmen, the chief German representative there, refused to bring such pressures to bear; like his government and like the Commercial Policy Committee of the Foreign Office from which he received his instructions, he was not prepared to break the armistice terms except for more important matters. The Vichy government were determined to protect their bauxite resources from German control and since almost all the mines were in

---

[1] I.M.T., NI–13207, Case VI, Document Box 65.
[2] I.M.T., Ilgner Document (defence), No. 220, Case VI.
[3] They are discussed by Y. Bouthillier, *Le Drame de Vichy*, ii (Paris, 1951), 112 ff.
[4] I.M.T., Ilgner document, No. 234 (defence), Case VI.

unoccupied France the terms of the armistice gave them considerable powers in this regard, powers which they exercised with great stubbornness.[1] Hemmen told Koppenberg plainly that he could not rely on the Wiesbaden committee to help him. 'I heard in the conversation that the demand to set up a German control bureau in unoccupied France had already been turned down by the French the day before and, further, that we do not possess the power to carry out our wishes other than by actually following the path of negotiation.'[2]

It was consequently decided to raise with the French Ministry of Finance the question of German financial participation in the French bauxite mines.[3] Koppenberg was concerned that such financial participation should represent the interests he favoured. At this stage of the proceedings a new company to manage German interests in the field first appeared in the negotiations, Hansa Leichtmetall AG. Hansa Leichtmetall was only formally constituted on 28 May.[4] It operated as a subsidiary of Nordag and was concerned with the acquisition and provision of suitable raw-material supplies in France and the Balkans. It occupied the headquarters of Nordag and took over most of its functions after the transfer of a lot of the personnel to the new Norwegian subsidiary A/S Nordag, Oslo. The French industrialists were asked to negotiate with Hansa Leichtmetall which would serve as an intermediary between themselves and the Norwegian firms, although of course the extent of French knowledge of the plans for Norway was very small.

Koppenberg laid before Hemmen a plan for the future negotiations at Wiesbaden. The French aluminium industry was to be fully utilized but 70 per cent of the monthly output of aluminium would be allocated to German purposes. The capacity for the production of alumina was to be increased and 90 per cent of the output was to be allocated for German purposes. A permanent German commission would be set up in unoccupied France to regulate the industry.[5] These proposals introduced a long period of bargaining in the Franco-German Armistice Commission at Wiesbaden between the representatives of Hansa Leichtmetall and the French firms.

In this bargaining Koppenberg was in a weak position thanks to the furious opposition of Vereinigte Aluminiumwerke, which had asserted its interests in occupied France before Koppenberg had approached Hemmen and had already secured certain liens on the use of French bauxite resources. Representatives of Vereinigte Aluminiumwerke had begun negotiations

[1] See the correspondence in *La Délégation française auprés de la Commission allemande d'Armistice*, ii (Paris, 1950), 338 ff.

[2] F.D. 5515/45, Rlm., Koppenberg to Udet, 31 March 1941; *La Délégation française*, iv 250.

[3] F.D. 5515/45, Rlm., Koppenberg to Udet, 4 April 1941.

[4] F.D. 4870/45, Rlm., 'Die Aluminiumnot'.

[5] F.D. 5515/45, Rlm., Koppenberg to Udet, 4 April 1941.

with the French bauxite companies as early as 9 July 1940 and had visited the French works on 11 July 1940.[1] The leader of the negotiations, whom Göring had asked on 23 July to inquire into the way the resources of occupied territories could be used for German purposes, was Dr. Westrick, the managing director of Vereinigte Aluminiumwerke.[2] This was on the same date that Koppenberg's own powers were extended to cover responsibility for aluminium stocks in all western occupied territories and for certain other aspects of the aluminium industry there. A clash was inevitable. When the French and German negotiators finally agreed on the detailed terms of a contract under which bauxite would be supplied to Germany the contract had to be transferred from Vereinigte Aluminiumwerke to the Junkers Aircraft Company.[3] To overcome their apparent loss of favour in government eyes, however, Vereinigte Aluminiumwerke signed an independent contract with the French Compagnie des Bauxites for deliveries of bauxite at prices below those agreed on by the two governments. This contract was in turn disallowed by the French delegation to the Armistice Commission until the price was increased. The French government did not issue export licences for this bauxite until 19 December 1940.[4] In spite of all difficulties it could still be said that Vereinigte Aluminiumwerke were entitled to a great deal of consideration in the disposal of French bauxite. And it was on French resources that the Norwegian plans had ultimately to depend.

At the same time it was evident that even if German negotiations were successful the total quantity of bauxite and alumina available from France would now be insufficient to meet the total demand from Norway if the Koppenberg plan was to keep to its proposed time-table. Another source of supply had to be found. The finger pointed to another newly occupied country, Yugoslavia.

There, extensive bauxite deposits had been developed in the inter-war period and the Yugoslav government had constructed an alumina plant in Moste near Ljubljana with a yearly capacity of between 6,000 and 10,000 tons. Near Schibenik in Dalmatia there was a small aluminium works of about 1,000 tons annual capacity.[5] Its source of power was two uncompleted power stations which were entirely owned by a French company, La Dalmatienne. In the attempts to secure control of the power stations in France, and the factories in Yugoslavia, Vereinigte Aluminiumwerke fought even more bitterly. They strongly disputed Koppenberg's right to act with full powers outside Norway although Göring had given him an

[1] *La Délégation française*, i. 149, 195.

[2] F.D. 288/45, Mbh. in F., Wi. Abt., Generalluftzeugmeister to Koppenberg, 23 July 1940.

[3] A. S. Milward, *The New Order and the French Economy*, pp. 86 ff.

[4] *La Délégation française*, ii. 342.

[5] F.D. 5515/45, Rlm., Koppenberg to Udet, 19 April 1941.

order on 30 April 1941 to develop a raw-material basis in south-eastern Europe for the Norwegian aluminium industry.[1] The disarray in government circles is shown by the fact that earlier, on 28 March 1941 at a conference in the Economic Ministry, Hans Kehrl had proposed a general plan of co-operation in which Vereinigte Aluminiumwerke would be allowed to participate in the Norwegian bonanza as soon as possible and in which they would, in the meantime, make their expert knowledge on aluminium production available to I. G. Farben.

So much for these attempts at peace-making by government circles. While they were taking place, Vereinigte Aluminiumwerke and Koppenberg were each intriguing with the Croatian fascist party in exile to get concessions in Yugoslavia. To make matters there more complicated, Italian firms were also intriguing for the same purpose, strengthened by the Italian government's desire to annex Dalmatia.[2]

On 1 May Koppenberg wrote to consul Neuhausen in Belgrade that it was essential for the Croatian bauxite deposits and the Moste alumina works to be available for Norwegian industry.[3] But it was not to be such plain sailing. Vereinigte Aluminiumwerke had signed a secret treaty with the Croatian Ustascha party, binding them not to erect any further alumina or aluminium works without the participation of Vereinigte Aluminiumwerke.[4] The treaty also reserved the future exploitation of bauxite deposits to such factories as the Croatian government and Vereinigte Aluminiumwerke should jointly construct. By the terms of the treaty the Croatian government had signed away a number of important powers. After three years from the signing of the treaty, Vereinigte Aluminiumwerke had the right to decide whether the correct conditions existed for the construction of an alumina and aluminium works, whereas the Croatian government had to co-operate with Vereinigte Aluminiumwerke in the immediate exploitation of its bauxite deposits. At the close of three years the German firm could therefore continue merely to take the bauxite if it so wished.

A draft of the treaty was obtained through espionage by Hansa Leichtmetall, and Koppenberg complained bitterly to Udet of Vereinigte Aluminiumwerke's 'colonial' methods.[5] Bitter reproaches aside, there was clearly only one solution, a compromise agreement between the two rival companies. On 2 July Koppenberg set out his views on such a compromise and prepared a draft agreement.[6] He had already decided to reduce the

[1] F.D. 4870/45, Rlm., 'Die Aluminiumnot'.

[2] L. Hory and M. Broszat, *Der kroatische Ustascha-Staat, 1941–45*, Schriftenreihe der Vierteljahrshefte für Zeitgeschichte, No. 8 (Stuttgart, 1964), pp. 43 ff.

[3] F.D. 5515/45, Rlm., Koppenberg to Neuhausen, 1 May 1941.

[4] Ibid., 'Vorvertrag, I Variant, zwischen dem Ministerium für Forst- und Bergwesen und den VAW. A.G.'

[5] Ibid., Koppenberg to Udet, 1 July 1941.

[6] Ibid., 'Zusammenenarbeit Hansa Leichtmetall Aktiengesellschaft/Vereinigte Aluminiumwerke A.G.'

volume of bauxite transported to Norway by increasing the quantity of alumina manufactured in France, so that to abandon his negotiations with the French firms Péchiney and Ugine would mean a retreat from his plan for Norway.[1] If Vereinigte Aluminiumwerke would stay out of these negotiations some bauxite for their purposes would still be available from France. As for Croatia, the only solution seemed to be a decision made between the two governments allocating spheres of interest to the two companies. This was the more necessary as disputes were already in sight over Romania and Hungary where both firms had plans to construct new factories.[2] Behind this lurked the still larger question of Russia. Terboven had been told on 23 June 1941 that the Kola peninsula and the area around Leningrad would come into the Norwegian sphere of influence after occupation. The implication was that Koppenberg's powers in Norway would automatically be extended to the same area and he would consequently become responsible for two of the larger Russian aluminium works and three alumina works. There were bigger fish to catch, and it might be worth while to leave the minnows for Vereinigte Aluminiumwerke.

The conversations of 23 June had led to certain decisions by Göring about the form of future co-operation, and Udet and State-Secretary Körner of the Four Year Plan had made a provisional allocation of interests in Croatia. On 3 July 1941 Koppenberg and Dr. Westrick of Vereinigte Aluminiumwerke met to discuss peace terms.

The conversation turned to Croatia and I put the question to Dr. Westrick whether he knew the phrase in a certain document. 'The Croatian state will erect no other alumina or aluminium factory and will become partner with no other company for twenty years.' Dr. Westrick was taken aback for a moment and said, 'How did you get the treaty? I am proud to have concluded this agreement and stand by it.'[3]

Udet and Körner had decided that there should be a working group of the aluminium industry under the chairmanship of Carl Krauch, to decide future policy. Westrick was not impressed by that arrangement. He refused to allow Krauch's committee to discuss 'things which had already been decided'.[3]

All attempts to win the competition in Norway by securing extra-Norwegian advantages thus produced only further stalemates. For the firms involved, some kind of co-operation was now essential since they all had one immediate objective in common, to persuade Terboven to modify Norwegian law in order to increase the safety of their investments. This

[1] I.M.T., NI–8146, Case VI, Document Box 65.
[2] F.D. 5515/45, Rlm., Koppenberg to Ploch.
[3] F.D. 5515/41, Rlm., 'Heutige Unterredung mit Herrn Dr. Westrick', 3 July 1941,

advice had been frequently given to them by the Reichs government but that government itself was so ideologically divided that its actions had tended only to increase the amount of industrial rivalry. Terboven's role had been a waiting one. He wished no infringement of his powers in Norway and no interference in his political and economic management of that country. The plan was to go ahead only on his terms and he appears to have been glad to use the rivalry between the firms as a way of postponing legal changes which their combined pressure might otherwise have forced him to make.

On 14 June 1941 General Udet wrote personally to him to beg him to give the aluminium negotiations the most urgent priority. The Air Ministry had already conceded that the holding company to manage the enterprise would be a Norwegian company with its seat in Oslo. Göring still insisted, however, that 51 per cent of its capital should be owned by the newly founded Hansa Leichtmetall which would supply the raw materials and purchase the finished products. Hansa Leichtmetall was itself owned by the Air Ministry. Both State-Secretary Körner and the Reichs Finance Minister Schwerin von Krosigk had personally asked Udet that Vereinigte Aluminiumwerke should be allowed 26 per cent of the capital in the new company. Each works would have its own managing company and there would be room in every case for a 49 per cent Norwegian participation. 'From which, dear Terboven, you will see that Norwegian capital will have more opportunities at its disposal than it can most probably use.'[1] Under certain conditions, however, the power stations could be left under Norwegian control. If the conditions imposed together with the preservation of a customs barrier were to make Norwegian aluminium dearer than German then the whole project might have to be abandoned.

The conditions were stipulated in a letter from Nordag to Terboven. The concessions must run for sixty-five years with the possibility of an extension for a further fifteen years. There could not be a Norwegian majority on the board of management. The restrictions on the employment of foreign materials and foreign labour must be lifted. There must be limitations on the provisions that 10 per cent of the current had to be made available to the state or to local authorities.[2]

Terboven accordingly travelled to Berlin to settle these problems personally and took part in a series of meetings there. On 21 June it was agreed that General Udet should be nominated as trustee for German interests in Nordag and administer 51 per cent of the Nordag capital. In the other companies German authorities would be content with a 50 per cent holding. The building projects should get immediate priority in Norway and Nordag, Oslo itself should have initial responsibility for the

[1] R.A., Rk. Diverse, Pakke 82, Udet to Terboven, 14 June 1941.
[2] Ibid., Nordag to Terboven, 11 June 1941.

first stages of the power development programme.[1] On 23 June Terboven met Göring, Schwerin von Krosigk, Körner, Milch, Udet, Krauch, Landfried, von Hanneken, and the rival industrialists. Göring opened the proceedings in his customary style and with fervent oratory declared that everything must be sacrificed to helping the Luftwaffe. Peacetime considerations could no longer play any part.

The Luftwaffe, which, in the Führer's own words, bore the chief weight in deciding the present war, had not been sufficiently considered in the past in the allocation of aluminium. In order to remedy this he had himself decided to develop the Norwegian aluminium industry exclusively as a kind of ministerial industry (*als eine Art Hausindustrie*) so that the approximate 37,000 tons of aluminium to be produced there should comprise a supplementary reserve in the supply for crisis periods.[2]

Originally Göring had thought the aluminium industry in Norway should be 100 per cent German owned, now he was prepared to accept that it should be merely 51 per cent German controlled.

Schwerin von Krosigk then asked for a guarantee that if the majority capital holding was released by the Air Ministry it should go to Vereinigte Aluminiumwerke. On that condition Westrick pronounced himself perfectly willing to renounce his demand for 26 per cent of the capital. 'At that the Reichsmarschall declared that the desire existed as soon as possible after the end of the war to return to private enterprise industrial holdings which were not absolutely indispensable.'[2] He was prepared to give the necessary guarantee, provided Vereinigte Aluminiumwerke should still be under government control.

Terboven did not agree to these terms at the meeting. On 3 July he decided that they were unacceptable and that in conformity with Norwegian laws there must remain a Norwegian majority in the companies to be formed.[3] Koppenberg was incensed at Terboven's attitude. He had proceeded throughout on the assumption that the law would be changed. So had the directors of Nordag. In their view, Terboven

in repeated conversations with Dr. Koppenberg had given unreserved assurances that legal obstacles in the way of the building programme, especially with respect to concessions, would be removed. On these assurances our whole previous planning was based and we had proceded, particularly in those ministries participating, on the basis that the conditions on the relevant concessions limiting German interests would be removed.[4]

[1] R.A. Rk. Diverse, Pakke 82, Hauptabt. Volkswirtschaft, 'Besprechung des Reichskommissars mit dem Reichsfeldmarschall Göring,' 26 June 1941.
[2] Ibid., 'Aktenvermerk über Sitzung im Stabsamt am 23. Juni 1941', 23 June 1941.
[3] Ibid., 'Gesellschaften mit deutscher Beteiligung', 3 July 1941.
[4] F.D. 5515/45, Rlm., 'Besprechung im Reichskommissariat am 4.7.1941', 5 July 1941.

In reply Terboven indicated that political considerations were the most important and they were all against any significant change in the law, especially as regards the nationality of the directors and the question of majority holdings. 'For Nordag itself the possibility exists that either the German members of the board of directors should take Norwegian nationality, which could be arranged at the moment without difficulty, or that corresponding Norwegian straw-men should become members of the board.'[1]

On 18 July Sattler, the Reichskommissar at Norges Bank, attended a joint meeting of the directors of Hansa Leichtmetall and Nordag at which Terboven was bitterly attacked for his attitude. Koppenberg exclaimed that Terboven himself had said that the financing of these projects would present no difficulty.

He told me there was enough money in Norway in the banks alone to cover the 1,400,000,000 kroner required.

Sattler: By this statement the Reichskommissar only intended to indicate the general monetary situation, not that these 1,400,000,000 kroner came into question for the purposes of investment, because this sum had been entrusted to the banks by depositors on short-term. Even in Germany we do not deploy savings deposits in long-term industrial finance. In Norway the banks do not have means of their own to dispose of in a sufficiently high quantity. . . .

Koppenberg: We shall get nowhere with these individualistic methods. Terboven promised me that he would provide the money in an emergency by compulsory measures. We must evidently enforce a compulsory loan.[2]

Sattler objected that a policy of forced loans would have to be part and parcel of the occupation costs. In that case it raised the whole question of the Norwegian budget and the extent to which the Norwegian public finances could be asked to bear the cost of such a project. Why should they meddle with a situation of surpassing difficulty and make it worse when, by changing the terms of the company foundation, private capital would be available in plenty in Norway? The industrialists insisted that the Norwegian Nordag should be founded with a 51 per cent German capital participation, although the directors would make a concession and take Norwegian nationality. To these terms Sattler agreed, as he wrote later, because there seemed no point in opposing them further there.[3] But he advised Terboven not to accept them.

There was one possibility of compromise. During his discussions in Berlin Terboven had agreed that although the Norwegian law on concessions must not be infringed in these operations, its validity could be raised in any future peace treaty. This concession to the demands of the Air

[1] Ibid.
[2] R.A., Rk. Diverse, Pakke 82, Hauptabt. Volkswirtschaft, 'Aufsichtsratsitzung der Hansa Leichtmetall A.G. und der Nordag', 18 July 1941.
[3] Ibid., Hauptabt. Volkswirtschaft, 'Gründung der Nordag', 18 July 1941.

Ministry was confirmed in a personal letter to Udet on 9 August 1941.[1] This loophole enabled Terboven to present the matter to the Norwegian government on 19 August. They were told nothing about the vast scope of the plans but simply that the Germans intended to pursue a programme of capital investment in the Norwegian aluminium industry, that there might have to be an infringement of the laws to get the programme going, but that the laws would not be changed. The Norwegian government asked that 2 per cent of the capital should go to a third party leaving Norway and Germany to participate on equal terms.[2]

If this represented a certain development in Terboven's thought it was doubtless a bowing to inevitability. The obdurate attitude of the German firms once they had really settled their quarrels over the terms of the investment meant that Terboven ran the risk of the matter being decided against him in higher circles. On 6 September he proposed terms to State-Secretary Hustad which represented considerable changes in the concessions laws. The concessions were now to run for 100 years, the Norwegian government was to renounce its right to the return of the investment, and the directors were not to be obliged to take Norwegian nationality. These had little chance of being accepted by the Norwegian government.[3] But Terboven appears to have taken a decision on 5 September to force the issue.[4]

In conformity with this burst of activity some small details of the plans for Norway were changed with the general idea of raising the targets. The main influence was undoubtedly the success of the campaign in the Balkans and the early victories against Russia. The general climate of optimism spread throughout the German economic ministries, for it seemed that the *Großraumwirtschaft* was within a hair's breadth of becoming a completed reality. The occupation of Greece put Greek bauxite resources at Germany's disposal and the first weeks of the Russian campaign opened the prospect of control over the great Russian aluminium works on the Dnieper.[5] In these circumstances Göring felt able to order the increase of European aluminium-producing capacity to 1 million tons by the close of 1943 at the latest.[6] In this further development Norway was to play a small part. The proposed increase in the annual productive capacity of the Eitrheim (I)

---

[1] R.A., Rk. Diverse, Pakke 82, Hauptabt. Volkswirtschaft, 'Vermerk über die Besprechung am 24 Juli 1941 im Hotel Adlon, Berlin, betr. Ausbau der norwegischen Aluminiumindustrie'.

[2] Ibid., Wi. Abt., 'Vermerk zur Vorlage für den Herrn Rk. durch Herrn Hauptabteilungsleiter Otte', 19 August 1941.

[3] Ibid., Hauptabt. Volkswirtschaft, 'Vermerk', 6 September 1941.

[4] Ibid., Wi. Abt., 'Vermerk', 8 September 1941.

[5] F.D. 5515/41, Rlm., 'Heutige Unterredung mit Herrn Dr. Westrick', 3 July 1941.

[6] RA., Rk. Diverse, Pakke 82, Der Gbm. für Sonderfragen der chemischen Erzeugung, 'Leichtmetall-Ausbau Norwegen. Besprechung mit Herrn Oberregierungsrat Dr. Baudisch am 7.7.1941', 10 July 1941.

works was increased by 2,000 tons to 10,000 tons. This meant that the first stage of the plan had a slightly higher target. The more remote targets were also raised by the proposed increases in the capacity of the Osa (Ulvik) works. Several of the proposed power stations were to be built to develop a greater kilowattage than originally planned. The orders given to Koppenberg by Milch on 16 September were more cautious in respect of the emergency programme but not in respect of the further stages of development. In addition they spoke of the erection of an alumina plant in unoccupied France with an annual production of 150,000 tons, and a plant in Croatia with similar capacity, both to be used to supply Norway.[1] Nevertheless these orders for the first time admitted that military events could change the details of the second stage.

Whether it was the military developments which also induced Terboven to change his mind about the Norwegian concessions law is doubtful. It is more likely that in such a climate of opinion he could not afford to seem to be the dog in the manger. The reasons given to Hustad were that the initiative for the programme was coming wholly from the German side, that the developments were in the interests of Norway, and that after the war the whole Norwegian economy would have been transformed by the creation of an industry much more important than any previous one, and the costs of such an investment programme in so short a time were beyond Norway's reach. 'In that respect—seen in the long run—the national interests of Norway will be better served than if the construction of the factories should rest dependent on the inadequate Norwegian money market.'[2] In short the concessions laws were never meant to deal with an economic transformation on this scale.

This may be compared with the decision that Terboven had passed on to Sattler, Berghold, Korff, and the other financial officials on 19 August.

The concession for Nordag is to be awarded on political grounds and with regard to the wish to recruit Norwegian capital according to the framework of the concessions laws, that is to say for sixty years and without surrender of the right of return to the home country. The question of the composition of the directorate is to be proceeded with dilatorily and a solution to be sought which, while formally observing Norwegian rules, ensures German leadership. The final demands over the German demands which exceed this should await the peace conference.[3]

The original negotiations on Norwegian capital participation had proceded on the basis of this earlier decision. Otte's memorandum to Terboven on 9 October suggested that it was not now possible to present Norwegian

---

[1] Ibid., 'Aluminium-Ausbau Norwegen', 16 September 1941.
[2] Ibid., letter to Hustad, 14 November 1941.
[3] Ibid., Hauptabt. Volkswirtschaft, 'Beteiligung der norwegischen Wirtschaft an der Finanzierung des Aluminiumprogramms', 15 December 1941.

industrialists and bankers with the changed terms and expect them to contribute, and urged the Reichskommissar to revert to his earlier decision. On 15 December 1941 he again urged Terboven to revert to his earlier decision.

One and a half years therefore passed without any final decision on the framework of German investment in the Norwegian aluminium industry, and those one and a half years of bargaining and rivalry constituted in themselves a very good reason for the slow start to the German plan and the relative lack of initial success. By December 1941 the plan was for most of its parts still a paper plan. It was impossible for coherent planning to take place without a coherent body to control it. Instead of such a body there was only the internecine ideological warfare of the Reich government and the German firms. Göring and Koppenberg signally failed to steamroller their plans through and became bogged down in a morass of economic and legal questions. But one good reason for this was the impracticable nature of the plans themselves.

It makes a sharp contrast to step from the world of aluminium planning in Norway to the world of actual aluminium production. A plan to increase Norwegian aluminium production sevenfold ended in production actually going down.

TABLE 41. *Production of Aluminium in Norway and its Export to Germany 1938–44**

(ooo tons)

	Production	Export to Germany
1938	29,035	3,386
1939	31,130	1,360
1940	27,780	18,185
1941	17,528	14,267
1942	20,498	15,911
1943	23,514	17,212
1944	20,035	15,154

* *Statistisk-økonomisk utsyn*; F.D. 5365/45, Hauptabt. Volkswirtschaft, 'Produktion und Lieferung in der Zeit vom 1 Jan.–31 Dez. 44'. Production figures from *Historisk Statistikk*, 1968.

The reasons for the utter failure of the plan are involved in the whole history of German economic policy in Norway, and with the general development of the war. But the fundamental nature of the shipping problem should be remarked. Only in 1943 was more bauxite imported into Norway than in pre-war years. The quantity of alumina never attained anything like pre-war levels. This cannot of course be blamed solely on the shipping shortage. It is also related to the problems of German occupation policy in France, in Hungary, in Greece, and in Yugoslavia. The output of alumina in France never reached its proposed level. Had it done so, however, the shipping problems would have been more acute.

TABLE 42. *Imports of Bauxite and Alumina into Norway, 1938–44**

(000 tons)

	Bauxite	Alumina
1938	25,942	43,737
1939	32,696	45,639
1940	4,824	29,769
1941	23,967	19,165
1942	27,239	29,365
1943	41,449	26,496
1944	28,558	15,256

* *Statistisk-økonomisk utsyn*; F.D. 5365/45, Rk., Hauptabt. Volkswirtschaft, 'Produktion und Lieferung in der Zeit vom 1 Jan.–31 Dez. 44'.

There was no attempt at modifying German plans until the end of 1941. Terboven received a confidential express memorandum from his representatives in Berlin on 9 December, the first official indication of cancellations.

Dr. Koppenberg informed me confidentially yesterday that under the chairmanship of State-Secretary Körner and with the participation of all the relevant authorities such as Field-Marshal Milch, Professor Krauch, the Economic Ministry and other ministerial offices and also the representatives of the aluminium industry in Germany, Berlin took the decision no longer to carry out the second stage of the Norwegian aluminium programme. It was General Thomas and Professor Krauch as well as the German aluminium interests who spoke against on all counts. The grounds are to be sought in the new military developments as well as in the transport problems and the constantly growing shortage of cargo space.[1]

The two power stations for the second stage on which work had already begun would be finished and the current used for other purposes.

Such a decision had no great impact on what was actually happening to the 'emergency programme', the first stage of the plan. But it was not long

[1] R.A., Rk. Diverse, Pakke 82, Hauptabt. Volkswirtschaft, 'Aluminiumprogramm', 9 December 1941.

before that, too, was called into question. The occasion was the changes in the economic administration in Germany and the development of a powerful Ministry of Armaments and Munitions with control over resource allocation and some power over the various competing economic agencies. At the end of April 1942 when the new ministry had been in control for only three months Speer, the minister, asked Koppenberg for a survey of Nordags's plans.[1] The Central Planning Committee, which had become responsible for the allocation of all raw materials within the economy, considered the report on 15 May.[2] As a result the existing aluminium programme was reduced and the surviving part turned into a 'Schwerpunkt-Programm' with top priority.

The first priority in respect of power supply and shipping space was to be given to the existing factories in Norway. Second priority was to be given to the successful completion of the Herøen factories. Their projected output, however, was reduced by more than one-half.[3] The process of manufacturing alumina from labradorite had proved so costly in electric power that it had more or less cancelled out the main reason for selecting Norway as the site of a large aluminium industry. Third priority was allocated to the provision of an alumina factory, for the manufacture of 3,000 tons a year at the Eydehavn works. No other priorities seemed feasible given the existing availability of raw material, labour, and transport. Not all the rest of Koppenberg's plan was discarded, however. The construction of the huge alumina plant at Sauda was earmarked for the next priority if conditions improved. The rest of the emergency programme was retained in remote stages of priority, perhaps so remote that revision was not worthwhile. The second stage disappeared from the scene. By fixing priorities so severely on the basis of what existed rather than what was planned the revised programme could be said to be almost an abandonment of the original plan.

Subsequent military events were to drive this revised programme even more rapidly in the direction of the disappearance of all priorities except the first, that is to say to the disappearance of the whole of Koppenberg's plan. A commando attack by British troops on 21 September 1942 brought the Glomfjord works to a standstill until the end of the year. That this event was less important than the problem of supply may be noted from the fact that the works was idle for a further three months after its repair

---

[1] *Innberetning til Oslo Politikammer*, p. 79.

[2] Only the brief record of subjects discussed at the Zentrale Planung meeting of 15 May seems to have survived. The question was discussed but the record of decisions taken is missing. Decisions taken in June by the Reichskommissariat are recorded as based on a meeting of Zentrale Planung. For the decision of 15 May see F.D. 3038/49, Sc. 246, Rm.f.B.u.M., Minutes of Zentrale Planung, 16 May 1949. The decisions are placed on 14 May by *Innberetning til Oslo Politikammer*.

[3] F.D. 5325/45, Hauptabt. Volkswirtschaft, 'Bericht der Hauptabt. Volkswi. für die Zeit vom 1 bis 15 Juni 1942', 17 June 1942.

because of the shortage of alumina. When it did begin production in April 1942, it only did so at 35 per cent of its productive capacity.[1]

In July 1943 an air attack destroyed the magnesium and alumina plant at Herøen. It would have taken over one year to rebuild it. Central Planning adjudged this to be too long to be worthwhile, especially as the works was very unfavourably situated for air defence.[2] The construction of the Maar

TABLE 43. *Revised Aluminium Plan, June 1942*

(tons per year)

Order of priority	Works	Proposed production			
		Alumina	Aluminium	Magnesium	Cryolite
1	Existing works	10,000	37,000	..	..
2	Herøen	23,000	12,000	10,000	3,000
3	Eydehavn	..	3,000	..	..
4	Sauda	85,000	..	..	..
	Eitrheim	..	8,000	..	..
5 (*a*)	Glomfjord	..	24,000	..	..
(*b*)	Tyin	50,000	24,000	..	..
Total		178,000	108,000	10,000	3,000

power station which had been intended to serve the extensions at Herøen was stopped forthwith. Terboven attended the meeting where this decision was made. In September the three partners in the Herøen enterprise appealed against this decision. Their appeal was personally rejected by Speer who accused them of making serious mistakes in their calculations about the necessary power supply for the enterprise.[3] The accusation was quite true. It had been entirely due to I. G. Farben's pressure that the manufacture of alumina from labradorite had been begun, for in 1940 no shortage of bauxite in Norway had been foreseen at all. The decision not to continue at Herøen left Norsk Hydro in a difficult position. It had invested nearly 90 million kroner in the works and power plant together and it seemed that I. G. Farben and the Bank der Deutschen Luftfahrt might have to give support. All three partners applied for compensation in November and the German partners gave Norsk Hydro an advance on the strength of the claims.[4]

---

[1] E.D. 5359/45, Rk., Hauptabt. Volkswirtschaft, Abt Ausfuhrwirtschaft und Bergbau, 'Bericht über die Durchführung der mit dem Reich für die Zeit vom 1 September 1942 bis zum 31 August 1943 vereinbarten produktionen und Lieferungen norwegischer Roh- und Grundstoffe'.

[2] F.D. 3048/49, Section II, Sc. 246, Rm.f.Kp., 'Ergebnisse der 46. Sitzung der Zentralen Planung am 30 Juli 1943', 1 August 1943.

[3] NI–8261, Case VI, Document Box 65.

[4] Ilgner Document No. 198, Case VI, Document Book XIIa

By August 1943 the shortage of alumina was acknowledged in the delivery programmes formulated by the Speer Ministry. Norwegian deliveries were now estimated on the basis of an annual production of 30,000 tons of aluminium, the first official acknowledgement that plant could not work at full capacity because of a shortage of raw materials.[1] In the same month the delivery of alumina to the Glomfjord works was stopped. By September the plant had used up its stocks and came once more to a standstill.[2] The end of the Koppenberg programme was merely a formality. Its death warrant was not officially signed until September 1944 when Speer ordered the cancellation of the alumina works at Tyin.[3]

TABLE 44. *Production of Alumina and Aluminium, 1943-4**

(average production in tons per month)

	1943	1st quarter 1944	2nd quarter 1944	Productive capacity at 1 April 1944
Alumina				
Germany	43,924	44,371	46,398	47,300
Norway	1,404	1,276	1,227	3,000
France	10,201	9,790	8,615	16,500
Italy	8,855	2,596	1,881	11,900
Hungary	1,100†	1,800†	1,800†	1,900
Aluminium				
Germany	20,839	18,267	22,533	27,300
Norway	1,950	1,857	1,818	3,000
France	3,872	2,269	..‡	8,200
Italy	3,849	2,422	1,169	4,400
Hungary	500†	800†	800†	1,000

* Milch Documents, vol. 50, pp. 28–31, Planungsamt to Milch, 21 July 1944.
† Approximately.
‡ No figures available.

The plan had made little difference in Germany's actual supply. France remained the biggest aluminium producer apart from Germany in the new Europe. Norwegian production remained far below, less than one-tenth of its German counterpart.

In so far as the aluminium plan was a plan to extend production for German purposes, and from Göring's words it is clear that this was its

[1] F.D. 5352/45, Rk., Hauptabt. Volkswirtschaft, Abt. Ausfuhrwirtschaft und Bergbau, 'Dienststellenleitertagung, 4 August 1943'.
[2] Ibid. 'Vermerk über das Ergebnis der Besprechung zwischen Herrn Staatssekretär Körner und Herrn Senator Otte', 11 August 1943.
[3] F.D. 3045/49, Section IX, Sc. 335, Rm f. Kp., Planungsamt, Baudisch to Otte, 9 September 1944.

purpose, it involved a diversion of effort from the main task. Exports of bauxite from Hungary, Croatia, and France continued to go to Germany although their level was never high enough to be satisfactory. The plan could have succeeded only if the capacity had existed for a great increase in imports into Norway over the pre-war level, not merely of bauxite and alumina, but of all the materials necessary to carry out such a vast investment programme. But every part of the plan had to compete at every stage for scarce resources with other claims on Norwegian economic capacity. It reflected the very weakest aspects of German economic administration and policy.

TABLE 45. *Total Aluminium at Germany's Disposal from Foundries, 1943–4**

(tons per month)

	1943	1st quarter 1944
Germany	20,839	18,267
Norway	1,451	1,485
France†	2,288	1,765
Italy†	485	4,608
Switzerland†	361	369
Total	25,424	26,494

* Milch Documents, vol. 1, Planungsamt to Milch, 21 July 1944.
† Imports of finished aluminium and semi-manufactured aluminium and deliveries of metal for German contracts in the countries concerned.

In a letter to Milch on 20 August 1941 Koppenberg explained that the original date for the first production from the new factories, January 1942, would have to be postponed by two or three months. He enumerated the reasons for this delay. The construction of the works had been delayed by the failure to obtain building materials, mainly due to the refusal of the responsible authorities to give the necessary materials a sufficiently high priority rating. The Reichs Economic Ministry had not given the necessary licences and foreign exchange to obtain machinery and wood from Sweden, the most convenient source of supply. The military construction projects in Norway, by paying illegally high wages, had attracted all the building labour. Only in the autumn, at the end of the building season, had the necessary building force of 1,400 men been first available for the aluminium building projects. Finally, the responsible authorities had been slow to permit the use of foreigners, especially important Swiss personnel.[1]

[1] Ibid., Koppenberg to Milch, 20 August 1941.

The difficulties of obtaining labour did not diminish with the simplification of the plan. In August 1942 special arrangements had been made to employ 3,000 construction workers and 2,000 metal workers for the aluminium programme, as labour could not be obtained on the open market in Norway because of Wehrmacht competition.[1] The measures proved inadequate and in March 1943 the first 'Ostarbeiter' were set to work on building the factories.

All these difficulties were, of course, only symptomatic of much wider problems in the management of the Norwegian economy over which Koppenberg did not have a proper view. Yet apart from the internal problems of the Norwegian economy and the failure of the Reich administration to give the necessary degree of priority to the details of the aluminium plan there were other problems which had existed from the start. Only with the full and unfettered achievement of the Großraumwirtschaft could there be any chance that the necessary quantity of bauxite and alumina would be available to the Norwegian factories. It was not really a plan for Norway which was under consideration but a plan for Europe. If there were so many political and economic obstacles to fulfilling the plan in Norway how many more were there to fulfilling it in Europe?

The bauxite deposits in France were in unoccupied territory, and Koppenberg was thwarted by the fact that his own powers there were insufficient unless backed up at every turn by his government. Here even stronger political considerations applied. The terms of the Franco-German armistice left France a great deal of power to obstruct German wishes at the Wiesbaden meetings of the Armistice Commission. In Croatia the feeble government of that country could still retain some independence by manœuvering between the German and Italian governments or between different German firms. Essentially the independence of governments and industrialists in both these countries depended on the same things that had caused Terboven to resist all pressures to ride roughshod over Norwegian law and institutions. There were only two possible ways of carrying out such an enormous project as the aluminium plan. One was to do it with the full and free consent of the conquered territory, the other to do it by ruthless and total subjection of it. If no powers of sovereignty at all were left to the conquered and if the conqueror did not care whether the conquered lived or died, few of the obstacles which actually arose would have been really formidable. But the very fact that in the middle of so ferocious a struggle it was possible to argue so long over the details of share ownership demonstrates that, whatever may have been the case in Russia or Poland, the German administration was not indifferent to the fate, or unconcerned about the loyalty to the new system, of the population of Norway. Although

[1] R.A., A/S Nordag, Box 18, '5,000 Mann-Aktion, Kurzer Überblick über die von der A/S Nordag getroffenen Maßnahmen', 22 August 1942.

they had every intention of bringing down the standard of existence of that population they still intended to give it a privileged position in the New Order compared to the Slavic populations of eastern Europe.

In western Europe the New Order was a series of politico-economic compromises which, partly due to the stubborn reluctance of the conquered territories to accept the new system, were often much less in the German interest than industrialists or economic planners had originally hoped. Indeed, even if the welfare of the inhabitants of western European countries had become a matter of *absolute* unconcern to the conquerors, broader economic considerations to do with diminishing returns due to diminishing productivity would have become important, for western European countries all had something to contribute to the German war effort. For all these reasons it was necessary to sacrifice a good number of ideological considerations. It is quite mistaken to suppose that in the case of the aluminium plan Terboven took the position he did because he was a pragmatist first and foremost. His whole existence was that of a most determined ideologue. But it was also that of a most skilful and determined politician. His political and economic aims for Norway were purely fascist, but they were long-term aims. He was not prepared to put them in jeopardy for short-term gains. Doubtless when the war was safely over it would have been a different story.

The relationship between the German government and its industrial supporters as revealed by the aluminium plan was a curious one. It bears out neither the bland liberal assumptions so common in western historical writing that there was no conspiracy or even community of interest between German business circles and the National Socialist government, nor the assumption so common in eastern historical writing that fascist governments were merely the expression of monopoly capitalism. The question in the mind of both industrialists and the government was 'what sort of Europe is Germany to create?' And they were by no means in agreement on the answer. Even a firm which gained so greatly from the fascist government as I. G. Farben tried to thwart the wishes of its own government and to change its policy. Vereinigte Aluminiumwerke also intrigued continually against the Four Year Plan Office in a vital strategic matter to defend its own position. All the industrialists involved were afraid that these developments would end up entirely under the control of the Reich government and thus weaken their position even further against the governing fascist politicians who took by no means the same view of capital and its deployment as they did. The industrialists wanted to emerge with bigger profits and in a stronger international position in the face of their pre-war rivals after the peace treaty, and they saw the Norwegian projects as an excellent opportunity to do so. The government's first interest was strategic, it had to have more aluminium for the Air Force. To this end it could not allow too much latitude to the industrialists. On the other hand, they were not only among its main supporters but they were indispensable to it in order to win the war. Finally, the industrialists knew well enough that their own purpose in creating a *Großraumwirtschaft* was not the same as that of their government. They wanted to create a unified economic area from which they could exclude all other rivals and on the basis of which they could pursue the aims of economic growth and higher profits. The National Socialists wanted to create such an area for opposite reasons, to enable their counter-revolution to achieve stability. The *Großraumwirtschaft* was an area sufficiently large to isolate its economy and social change and thus to permit the new society to maintain its hold in perpetuity.

These fundamental differences of outlook are the reason for the astonishing lack of co-ordination in the aluminium plan. It really had more of the nature of a dream than a plan. There was no intra-industrial co-operation or consultation, quite the opposite in fact. There was no over-all review of the economic possibilities of the *Großraumwirtschaft* for aluminium production or even of Norway's own potentialities. The competing firms had the support of different parts of the Reich administration which themselves held widely differing views about the nature of the *Großraumwirtschaft* according to the extent of their fascist convictions. In such circumstances planning was impossible. The targets of the aluminium plan were not precise figures, they were optimistic visions of a future Europe, their realization not depending on economic management but on military victory and faith.

VIII

AGRICULTURE, FOOD, AND WAGES

ALTHOUGH there has not been much literature on the subject of German agricultural policy in Norway, what there has been has tended to paint a picture of a common agricultural and rationing policy agreed between the German and Norwegian governments which, until the last six months of the occupation, was successful. The treatment of Norway is contrasted with the drastic rule imposed on agriculture in eastern Europe and, through this contrast, the impression is given that, in the circumstances, German policy was well conceived.[1] But German agricultural policy in Norway cannot be considered justly outside the context of general fascist economic policy. The aims of that policy were not solely to feed the Wehrmacht and the Norwegian population as best as could be in the inevitable circumstances of shortages of imported food. Rather they were to do that while carrying out a long-term programme designed to eliminate those shortages. As far as that long-term programme was concerned, it was a failure, and its failure was attributable to the same defects of historical and economic comprehension of Norway that may be seen in every aspect of German policy there. More than this, the failure of this programme of agricultural adaptation imposed considerable hardships on the Norwegian people, hardships which they might well have been spared had German policy been less ambitious, had it been confined more to administrative mechanics and less concerned with economic change.

The essential elements of German policy might be briefly recalled here. They were to increase the production of food in Norway, partly by a change in farming methods and in the final mix of goods produced, but mainly by an extension of the total area under cultivation.[2] In so doing it was hoped that the relative social and economic position of the food producers in Norway would be improved *vis-à-vis* that of other social groups, and that rural society would be stabilized and become a staunch support of the fascist New Order. The mechanism by which these objects would be achieved was a mixture of compulsion and price incentives.

There is no point in debating the success or failure of the political objectives in this policy; the Norwegian peasantry were not converted to

[1] K. Brandt, *Management of Agriculture and Food in the German-Occupied and other Areas of Fortress Europe* (Stanford, 1953).

[2] R.A., Rk. Diverse, Pakke 22, Abt. Ernährung und Landwirtschaft, 'Weidekultivierung in Norwegen', 27 February 1941.

fascism. Economically the policy was, in its early stages, successful, only to collapse into failure as the occupation became more prolonged. The will to effect changes, the imposition of central planning on a *laissez-faire* system, and the diversion of resources due to other causes led to a considerable degree of success by the end of 1942. But short-term changes in agricultural output in exceptional circumstances are fairly easy to achieve, a fact to which the agricultural history of almost every European country in the First World War bears ample testimony. In the long run such changes are much more difficult to sustain.

Between 1938 and 1942 the total area under the plough increased from 282,662 hectares to 357,667 hectares.[1] The areas devoted to grain and to potatoes both increased in size. Between 1939 and 1942 the area devoted to wheat farming increased in every Norwegian county except Troms and Finnmark (where wheat was barely cultivable), and Østfold. In Østfold, however, the area devoted to rye, the other bread grain, increased from 646 hectares to 1,209 hectares.[2] Over the same period every Norwegian county showed a substantial increase in the area devoted to potato cultivation. The increase in output, as is usually the case, was not commensurate with the increase in area cultivated. The policy implied the utilization of marginal land which, in Norway, was often very poor land. Nevertheless, output did increase and there was a general air of optimism in the Reichskommissariat reports.[3] The plan for 1941–2 was to produce 135,000 tons of grain in Norway. In spite of the late harvest, 131,804 tons were produced.[4] In April 1943 the Reichskommissariat still flattered itself that the trend was upwards and that its programme of heath conversion meant that the target for ploughed land had again been reached.[5] Although the subsequent potato harvest was the highest yet to be produced in Norway, the grain harvest remained at much the same level.[6] It will be seen from Table 46 that the planned expansion of arable farming failed to take place after 1942 and there was indeed a tendency to revert to the level of the immediate pre-war years. The area devoted to bread grain did not grow in size after 1942. The area devoted to fodder grains declined after 1941, to fall by the end of the occupation below its pre-war level. The area devoted to potatoes began to decline after 1943.

It should be taken into account in any consideration of these figures that

---

[1] F.D. 5360/45, Rk., Hauptabt. Volkswirtschaft, Abt. Ernährung und Landwirtschaft, 'Größe und Aufteilung der Ackerfläche Norwegens in den Jahren 1938–1942'.

[2] Ibid., 'Roggenanbaufläche in ha.'

[3] And elsewhere in Norwegian circles. See R.A., Rk. Diverse, Pakke 43, 'Vår kornproduksjon og matforsyningen. Foredrag av direktør Olav Hillestad i Selskapet for Norges Vels møte 5 mars 1941', 5 March 1941.

[4] F.D. 5202/45, Rk., Hauptabt. Volkswirtschaft, Abt. Ernährung und Landwirtschaft, Tätigkeitsbericht für die Zeit vom 16 bis 30 September 1942', 1 October 1942.

[5] Ibid., 'Tätigkeitsbericht für die Zeit vom 1 bis 30 April 1943', 5 May 1943.

[6] Ibid., 'Tätigkeitsbericht für die Zeit vom 1–31 Oktober 1943', n.d.

the trend towards a greater bread-grain area had actually been much more strongly upwards in the thirties so that the real result of German policy in this respect was to arrest these developments. In 1917 only 19·3 million hectares were devoted to the cultivation of bread grain.[1] In so far as this upward trend had been achieved at the expense of land devoted to fodder grain it could be argued that the temporary result of German policy was to continue to increase the amount of bread-grain cultivation while achieving a sharp rise in the amount of land devoted to fodder grains, but that after

TABLE 46. *Area Devoted to Different Crops in Norway, 1934–45**

(000 hectares)

Crop	1934–8 (average)	1939	1940	1941	1942	1943	1944	1945
Wheat	28	41	41	46	49	48	47	48
Rye	6	3	3	4	4	4	4	3
Feed grains (barley, oats)	152	139	142	156	152	150	142	132
Potatoes	51	51	57	63	79	81	73	65

* Statistisk Sentralbyrå, *Historisk statistikk, 1968*, p. 137.

1941 the effort was too great and bread-grain cultivation was only sustained at its 1942 level by allowing the amount of land used for fodder grains to decrease once more. The area devoted to fodder grain reached its 1929 level and even, in 1941, went well over that level. By the end of the war it had again sunk to the level of 1939. As far as potato cultivation was concerned German policy succeeded in greatly increasing the amount produced but was not able to sustain these high levels towards the end of the occupation.

That by 1944 everything was going wrong may be seen from the way in which the pattern of land utilization of that year failed to live up to the plans of the Reichskommissariat. The over-all plan was that 365,000 hectares of land should be used for arable cultivation for the 1943–4 harvest. Of these, 213,000 hectares were to be devoted to grain of all categories and 91,000 hectares to be devoted to potatoes.[2] The shortfall was therefore 20,000 hectares in the case of grain and 18,000 hectares in the case of potatoes, which must be adjudged nothing less than a complete failure. In fact the target level for arable area for the 1944 harvest was exactly that which had not been reached in the 1943 harvest. Even the record area devoted to potato farming in 1943 must therefore be regarded as a relative failure. The attempt to produce more vegetables in Norway

[1] Reichsministerium für Ernährung und Landwirtschaft, *Die Landwirtschaft in Norwegen.*

[2] F.D. 5202/45, Rk., Hauptabt. Volkswirtschaft, Abt. Ernährung und Landwirtschaft, 'Tätigkeitsbericht für die Zeit vom 1–31 Dezember 1943'.

appears as not very successful although better sustained than other aspects of German policy.

As late as May 1944 the Reichskommissariat believed that its planned food output would still be attained in spite of the lateness of the spring. 'By and large it can be estimated that the basic production plan will be fulfilled', was their verdict on 2 June.[1] Such optimism was quickly swallowed up in the profound supply difficulties which emerged with the smaller harvest of 1944. Not only was that harvest small, it was also late. So had the 1942 harvest been late but the quantity of grain bought by Statens Kornforretning by October in that year was greater than in October 1944.[2]

TABLE 47. *Arable Production in Norway**

(tons)

Crop	1939	1940	1941	1942	1943	1944
Grains and pulses	1,836,741	1,866,767	2,067,200	2,061,547	2,025,485	1,941,191
Potatoes	506,927	572,394	631,800	789,896	808,065	734,269
Other root crops	225,434	226,987	271,000	241,508	184,577	256,574
Other farm and garden produce	376,566	367,582	320,700	294,805	318,444	343,208

* Statistisk-økonomisk utsyn', p. 118.

By the end of the year it was clear that neither the grain nor the potato harvests would suffice. The potato harvest was estimated to be sufficient to last only until June 1945, after which imports from Denmark would become a necessity. Not only was the grain harvest smaller but the quality of the grain was much worse.[3] In March 1945 there was an effective reduction in the bread ration when the number of bread coupons required for a loaf was increased.[4] Earlier than this the land utilization plan for 1944–5 had been forced to take account of the failures of the previous two years. The area of arable land for grain cultivation was to be reduced to 210,000 hectares and that for potatoes to 80,000 hectares.[5] It can be seen from Table 46 that this first lowering of the targets scarcely represented any nearer approach to reality; they were missed in 1945 by an even wider margin. From autumn 1944 the dependence of Norway on overseas trade for her food supply became greater than ever, because the Wehrmacht had also to be supplied. This greater reliance on imports coincided with the period of the occupation when imports were least obtainable due to the loss of territory under German control and to the increasingly successful Allied raiding of German

[1] F.D. 5202/45, Rk., 'Tätigkeitsbericht für die Zeit vom 1–31 Mai 1944', 2 June 1944.
[2] Ibid., 'Tätigkeitsbericht für die Zeit vom 1–31 Oktober 1944', 7 November 1944.
[3] F.D. 5217/45, Rk., Hauptabt. Volkswirtschaft, 'Bericht für die Zeit vom 1 bis 31 Dezember 1944'.
[4] F.D. 5202/45, Rk., Abt. Ernährung und Landwirtschaft, 'Tätigkeitsbericht für die Zeit vom 1–31 März 1945', 9 April 1945.
[5] F.D. 5217/45, Rk., Hauptabt. Volkswirtschaft, 'Bericht für die Zeit vom 1 bis 28 Februar 1945', 14 March 1945.

shipping. From autumn 1944 Norway entered into a period of severe food shortage which, although prolonged well after the occupation, was directly attributable to the occupation.

Since the chief aim of German policy was to increase the product of arable farming in Norway, the question must be posed as to why this was not achieved. The failure is not to be attributed to any single cause but rather to a variety of aspects of occupation policy. The area of arable land itself did not significantly increase. In the first place the cost of ploughing new land in a country like Norway was very high. Farmers were not going to undertake such a heavy investment except in the most favourable circumstances. After 1942 they clearly regarded the circumstances as unfavourable. Their reluctance might have been overcome by a massive programme of public investment, but financial policy prevented such a development. The Reichskommissariat had, for the most part, to rely on price incentives and, although Norway's severance from the benefits of international specialization and the cheaper food which they implied made these price incentives fairly easy to operate, such a policy did not rest on a strong enough basis to overcome the Norwegian farmers' doubts as to what would happen after the occupation was ended. The farmer was most reluctant to make long-term changes in land use without an equally long-term guarantee of new markets and new prices.

The preference of farmers was to retain their grassland and livestock rather than make a wholesale switch to comply with what seemed, after 1942, to be only a transient state of international trade. Consequently, German policy was only a little more successful in this sector than in the arable sector and its failure in the one was directly related to its failure in the other. The aim, it will be recalled, had been to reduce the quantity of livestock depending on imported fodder and, through a policy of heathland revitalization, increase the number of livestock which could be sustained for a part of the year on domestic feed resources. It will be seen from Table 48 that the increase in the number of sheep was far less than intended; the stock should have reached 2·1 million by the autumn of 1941. If the Norwegian peasantry had played their part the number would have increased to between 4 and 5 million.[1] The reduction in the pig stock was what had been intended, that in poultry much more drastic. Both those reductions were easily effected, it was simply a matter of cutting off feed supplies. But cattle farming continued to be the standby and the bulk of the available fodder was consumed by cattle farmers. Rather than effecting any great change in agricultural policy in this sector, therefore, the result of the occupation was simply to reduce drastically the stock of pigs and poultry in the country.

[1] R.A., Diverse, Pakke 20, Rk., Abt. Ernährung und Landwirtschaft, 'Die Schafzucht in Norwegen', August 1940.

There were other, less important, reasons for the failure to extend the arable area by the desired amount. One was the increasing demands on land made by the Wehrmacht. Land used for airfields was often good farming land. In 1943 the Reichskommissariat conducted a census of Wehrmacht land. They discovered that the Wehrmacht had taken over one large estate and 1,253 medium- and small-sized peasant farms. By this time they had 6,369 hectares of good agricultural land and 5,032 hectares of previously unused land.[1] After this date their demand for land grew and a spate of

TABLE 48. *Norway's Livestock, 1939–45**

(000 head)

Livestock (summer stock)	1939	1940	1941	1942	1943	1944	1945
Horses	203·9	206·0	207·0	208·0	218·0	227·0	231·0
Cattle	1,455	1,400	1,280	1,250	1,220	1,255	1,220
Sheep	1,743·8	1,700·0	1,666·0	1,695·0	1,715·0	1,795·0	1,760·0
Pigs	362	400	270	220	145	220	195
Chickens	3,437	3,000	2,340	1,500	1,200	1,200	1,200

* *Historisk statistikk 1968*, p. 144. The figures for 1940 and later are estimates.

land seizures in January 1944 made the situation more difficult. 'In the month of January a large number of land confiscations by the German Wehrmacht became necessary for which the basis was a policy order of the Reichsmarschall. In Trondheim alone, for example, according to previously foreseen plans, 600 hectares of agriculturally utilizable land had to be made available to the Wehrmacht.'[2] In July there were more confiscations.[3]

Wehrmacht confiscations in other directions also had a harmful effect on the harvests. The shortage of oil meant a strict control of transport from 1940 onwards from which rural areas suffered particularly. In February 1943 the Reichskommissariat embarked on a plan to equip a third of the tractors in Norway with gas generators by the summer.[4] Shortage of fuel and of transport had a particularly serious effect on the 1944 harvest.

The availability of wagons has so far been completely insufficient to bring the grain from the peasants to the State collecting depots and, particularly, to the mills. Our efforts with the transport section, before whom we placed a grain transport plan for the Norwegian harvest going into small details, to bring about an improvement in the situation have remained practically without result. This is to be related to the fact that the Wehrmacht without regard for the transport

[1] F.D. 5202/45, Rk., Abt. Ernährung und Landwirtschaft, 'Tätigkeitsbericht für die Zeit vom 1 bis 30 Avril 1943', 5 May 1943.
[2] Ibid., 'Tätigkeitsbericht für die Zeit vom 1–31 Januar 1944', 4 February 1944.
[3] Ibid., 'Tätigkeitsbericht für die Zeit vom 1–31 Juli 1944', 4 August 1944.
[4] Ibid., 'Tätigkeitsbericht für die Zeit vom 1 bis 28 Februar 1943', 3 March 1943.

necessities of the civilian sector disposes of the stock of lorries in such a way as to leave scarcely anything for the civilian sector.[1]

The Wehrmacht also paid a high price throughout the occupation for good draught horses. In part this was responsible for the increase in their numbers, but the periodic large-scale purchasing of horses by the Wehrmacht damaged Norwegian agriculture in so far as such purchasing was unpredictably spasmodic. In August 1944 the purchase of 3,500 horses came at an especially inopportune time even though in return the Wehrmacht released petrol for tractors from its stocks.[2] In October a further 5,000 horses were purchased.[3] The loss of horses was felt more in forestry for they were still the chief means by which felled wood was transported.

Difficulties of supply meant that the availability of fertilizer in Norway, although very good in respect of nitrogenous fertilizer, was very poor for all imported fertilizer. This was particularly the case with phosphatic fertilizer. In 1943 only 800 tons of raw phosphate was used compared to 15,000 tons for a smaller arable area in 1939.[4] The increase in the use of potash, which even in 1945 remained well above its pre-war level, and a doubling of the amount of nitrogenous fertilizer used did not entirely compensate for the virtual disappearance of phosphates.

These restrictions in the employment of fertilizer are an indication of how far-reaching the effects of the foreign trade situation were. However true it was that agricultural policy was designed to eliminate as far as possible Norway's dependence on foreign supply, the period of transition still demanded unlimited access to certain commodities obtainable from abroad. For three categories of these commodities, bread grains, fats, and sugar, there was no intention of eliminating dependence for it was beyond the bounds of possibility to do so. In so far as there were shortages of these commodities, the effect was on the whole nation, not on the agricultural sector. But for a further category, animal feed, the shortage of imports did result in modifications of agricultural policy which were undesired. The plan to produce and use more cellulose fodder failed to progress beyond a certain point, imports of fodder concentrates declined, and the production of herring meal failed to come up to the required level, while Germany's demands on what was available increased. As the occupation progressed, protein fodder, such as herring meal, bran, and oil-cake, became very scarce and the consequence was a sharp decrease in the output of dairy products. The consumption of cellulose fodder rose from 89,000 tons in the year 1941–2 to 207,000 tons in the year 1942–3.[5] The planned increase

[1] Ibid., 'Tätigkeitsbericht für die Zeit vom 1–30 November 1944', 7 December 1944.
[2] Ibid., 'Tätigkeitsbericht für die Zeit vom 1–31 August 1944', 5 September 1944.
[3] Ibid., 'Tätigkeitsbericht für die Zeit vom 1–31 Oktober 1944', 7 November 1944.
[4] Ibid., 'Tätigkeitsbericht für die Zeit vom 1–31 Dezember 1943', 6 January 1944.
[5] The harvest year, for statistical purposes, ran from 1 December to 30 November.

for the following year was not successful and total output was reduced to 176,000 tons.[1] It was the demand from other areas for wood pulp that was responsible, and the decline in cellulose fodder production was a symptom of Norway's changed international system, for which it was supposed to be one of the remedies.

The decline in the production of herring meal began with the occupation and was related to the wider problems of the fishing industry, but also to the need to continue to specialize in other aspects of fish processing to keep up fish exports. Its production fell from 100,000 tons in 1940 to 23,800 tons in 1944. In April 1943 Germany began to demand a larger quota of Norwegian herring meal for her own use in order to increase the quantity of pig feed in the Reich.[2] The Reichskommissariat was reluctant to release a greater quantity in view of the continued fall in production. Finally, in June, Norway agreed to deliver 15,000 tons of herring meal to Germany in the following year in return for 15,000 tons of oats, 10,000 tons of sunflower seeds, and 8,750 tons of other feed.[3] German deliveries to Norway were to start in autumn 1943, but they could not compensate for the particular Norwegian deficiency in protein fodder. In the economic year 1942–3 herring meal production was 16,000 tons less than the estimated demand.[4] In January 1945 Sweden offered 5,000 tons of oil-cake. In February it was agreed to purchase that amount. By feeding it to specially selected herds the Reichskommissariat hoped to produce an increase in the supply of butter.[5]

In fact agricultural policy had never succeeded in sustaining the required deliveries of meat either to the Wehrmacht or to civilian consumption. In 1942 instead of the 16,500 tons of meat which should have been provided only about 13,000 tons were forthcoming.[6] The Reichskommissariat's response was to compel the Norwegian ministry to institute punitive legislation.

In negotiations which we have carried on with the Department of Supply in the last few days in this connection, it was requested by us that those producers who do not produce their deliveries of cattle for slaughter shall not only have to suffer significant fines but shall also be made aware that the cattle due to be

---

[1] F.D. 5202/45, Rk., Abt. Ernährung und Landwirtschaft, 'Tätigkeitsbericht für die Zeit vom 1–31 Dezember 1943', 6 January 1944.

[2] Ibid., 'Tätigkeitsbericht für die Zeit vom 1 bis 31 Mai 1943', 3 June 1943.

[3] Ibid., 'Tätigkeitsbericht für die Zeit vom 1 bis 30 Juni 1943', 2 July 1943.

[4] Ibid., 'Tätigkeitsbericht für die Zeit vom 1–31 Oktober 1943', 3 November 1943. Economic years ran from 1 December to 30 November.

[5] Ibid., 'Tätigkeitsbericht für die Zeit vom 1–28 Februar 1945', 5 March 1945; F.D. 5217/45 Rk., Hauptabt. Volkswirtschaft, 'Bericht für die Zeit vom 1 bis 28 Februar 1945', 14 March 1945.

[6] F.D. 5202/45, Rk., Abt. Ernährung und Landwirtschaft, 'Tätigkeitsbericht für die Zeit vom 1 bis 31 Dezember 1942', 11 January 1943.

delivered will be forcibly collected. The necessary measures will be immediately insituted by the Department of Supply.[1]

In spite of these measures, meat deliveries again fell below the quota in July and continued below the quota level until December.[2] In January 1944 a special effort was made to increase meat production, but by March deliveries were again below the quota level.[3] From June onwards until the end of the war meat deliveries in every month fell below the quota level. Furthermore the cattle delivered were in bad condition.[4] The reason was the lack of fodder. 'The meat deliveries are still unsatisfactory', the Reichs-kommissariat reported in March 1945.

In part transport difficulties are responsible, but an unwillingness to deliver on the part of the producers must also be indicated. The Department rests on the standpoint that without special measures a forced increase in delivery must begin because the peasants do not have enough fodder to retain the animals until such time as they can be transferred to the heaths.[5]

Milk deliveries fell in 1943–4 to 39,400,866 litres from their previous year's level of 44,405,522 litres.[6] From August 1944 the decline became so severe as to make the weekly milk ration scarcely worth the distributing. That import shortages should have such an effect on an area of agricultural

TABLE 49. *Milk Deliveries in Norway, August 1944 to February 1945**

(000,000 litres)

Month	Total full-milk deliveries to creameries
August 1944	34·2
September 1944	29·0
October 1944	21·7
November 1944	16·5
December 1944	14·9
January 1945	15·9
February 1945	15·9

* F.D. 5202/45, Rk., Abt. Ernährung und Landwirtschaft, 'Tätigkeitsbericht für die Zeit vom 1–31 März 1945', 9 April 1945.

[1] Ibid., 'Tätigkeitsbericht für die Zeit vom 1 bis 31 Januar 1943', 3 February 1943.
[2] Ibid., 'Tätigkeitsbericht für die Zeit vom 1–31 Dezember 1943', 6 January 1944.
[3] Ibid., 'Tätigkeitsbericht für die Zeit vom 1–31 März 1944', 3 April 1944.
[4] Ibid., 'Tätigkeitsbericht für die Zeit vom 1–30 Juni 1944', 5 July 1944.
[5] F.D. 5217/45, Rk., Hauptabt. Volkswirtschaft, 'Bericht für die Zeit vom 1 bis 31 März 1945', 16 April 1945.
[6] F.D. 5202/45, Rk., Abt. Ernährung und Landwirtschaft, 'Tätigkeitsbericht für die Zeit vom 1–31 Juli 1944', 4 August 1944.

production where Norway was so strongly favoured is an apt comment on the failure of the adaptation to a different international situation which Germany wished to bring about.

The final collapse of milk production in Norway, although it had a specific cause, the shortage of protein fodder, came at the end of a long period of falling output of dairy products and of meat. There is therefore one further comment that may be made on the policy of extension of arable cultivation. It seems to have been paid for very dearly in the failure to sustain the output of animal products. The figures recorded in Table 50 are figures for deliveries from farms. There is every reason to suppose that the actual level of production of all commodities was understated in wartime if only to avoid compulsory purchase of too high an amount, but also for patriotic reasons and also, of course, in order to have larger amounts to sell on the black market. With all these reservations, the record is still not impressive.

TABLE 50. *Deliveries of Dairy Products and Meat, 1939–45*[*]

(ooo tons; meat, ooo tons deadweight)

	Milk	Butter	Cheese	Meat
1939	793	17·6	21·0	63
1940	653	13·4	15·1	58
1941	525	8·4	13·6	16
1942	425	11·3	9·8	16
1943	376	9·0	6·2	12
1944	338	7·1	3·8	11
1945		4·1	3·9	15

[*] K. Brandt, *Management of Agriculture*, p. 332.

In one other area Germany had planned to increase production, that of vegetables. The most that can be said is that a general fall in the production of vegetables other than potatoes was avoided. The harvest of green vegetables was increased by about 20 per cent between 1939 and 1945.[1] The centre-piece of the German plan, however, had been the construction of forcing houses in north Norway in order to solve the especial difficulties of food supply there. That plan was abandoned in May 1942 on the grounds that there were insufficient materials available for the necessary construction.[2]

The failure to increase the production of almost all foodstuffs underlines the fact that the reasons for the failure to increase the product of arable farming were not confined in their effects to that sector alone. Whether a more determined or more ruthless policy could have extended the arable

[1] *Statistisk-økonomisk utsyn*, p. 118.
[2] F.D. 5325/45, Rk., Hauptabt. Volkswirtschaft, 'Bericht für die Zeit vom 16 bis 31 Mai 1942', 5 June 1942.

area within the generally unsatisfactory framework of agricultural policy as a whole is difficult to decide. In a country such as Norway there was little scope for making the economy more self-sufficient in agricultural produce; the cost of producing more bread grain was likely to be very high in terms of imports of animal feed. The percentage of the land actually farmed for any purpose was very small, the level of consumption of the inhabitants very high. In consequence the possibilities of flexibility in farming policy were very few. In the changed international circumstances flexibility became even more difficult; it was, for example, impossible to increase substantially the imports of animal feed or of fertilizer. Even on the more detailed level the specific reasons for the failure of the attempt to increase the product of arable farming were related to failures in other sectors. The costs of breaking up new land or changing the pattern of land use were relative costs, the rising price of inputs in all sectors led farmers to hedge their bets. Decisive changes could not therefore be expected, the sounder policy was to opt for the *status quo*.

After 1940 the food supply of Norway continued to depend as before on international trade. The extra amount of foodstuffs produced by the domestic economy could not compensate for the size of the army of occupation, nor could it alter the dependence on outside supply for grain, fat, and sugar. The rations of Norwegian consumers, given the demands which the Wehrmacht in Norway made on domestic supplies, were finally determined by the ability of the *Großraumwirtschaft* to sustain a level of exports to Norway satisfactory both to the population and to the army of occupation. But to all the agricultural experts of the *Großraumwirtschaft* it was clear that there was no possibility of an agricultural surplus until a successful attack on Russia.[1] Before that event the difficulties of supplying the western occupied territories were bound to be acute, particularly in Norway and Belgium.

The original plans for feeding the army of occupation, which were based on a smaller army than eventually existed, had stipulated the foodstuffs for which Norway was herself to be responsible for supplying the Wehrmacht. The development of so much greater an army of occupation than originally intended led early to anxiety for the Norwegian food supply, especially in the remoter parts of north Norway where so many extra mouths were a great threat.[2] Terboven wrote a personal letter to Darré, the Reich Minister of Agriculture, in September 1940, to explain his anxieties about the

[1] R.A., Rk. Diverse, Pakke 25, Abt. Ernährung und Landwirtschaft, 'Vermerk für Hn. Dr. Richert, Betrifft: Bericht über die Produktionslage im Reich', 21 November 1940.

[2] Partly solved by strict attention to the vitamin content of the soldiers' diet. Commissariat-Councillor Schweigert who was responsible for these successful experiments applied to be posted to Britain to carry out the same functions there after the occupation. RA., Rk. Diverse, Pakke 38, Abt. Ernährung und Landwirtschaft, Intendanturrat H. A. Schweigert to OKW., 9 August 1940.

situation. It was unreasonable, he argued, to expect Norway to obtain the same level of self-sufficiency as the Reich itself, even at a much lower standard of living, without a period of time similar to the seven years which the Reich's own agricultural investment programme had so far taken. The cuts in Norwegian food supplies, partly due to the Wehrmacht's presence, had driven living standards down dangerously near to the level of subsistence. The Reichs Food Ministry had stipulated that it should be a principle that supplies to the Wehrmacht from Norwegian sources should be replaced by an equivalent supply from the Reich to Norway. But the Wehrmacht demands were growing to a point where it was doubtful that such supplies would be available from the Reich. Up to 10 August 1940 the Wehrmacht had received 10,000 tons of fodder and 16,000 tons of foodstuffs at the very least estimate. The Reich had also agreed to provide potatoes to cope with the extra demand caused by the occupation army.[1] Now a further demand from 11 August 1940 to 30 April 1941 amounted to a total of 120,430 tons of food and fodder. The Führer's order that the Wehrmacht must also retain stocks for one year's duration meant that there should be an additional demand for a further 50,000 tons. Terboven therefore requested that the Reich should provide immediate help with three bottlenecks, fodder, sugar, and syrup, of which the most important was fodder.[2] It seems that this appeal led to a series of precise agreements with the Ministry of Agriculture. When Terboven heard, mistakenly, in November that there was to be no more food supplied to Norway, he protested to Darré in the sternest language.

The frontier of mobilization of the food sector in Norway in favour of the troops has been reached in the present situation where we are no longer in a position to fulfil the administratively indicated rationing quotas. We shall, however, go right up to this frontier. But to cross this frontier would have to be declined under any circumstances because the Norwegian people are indispensable as a labour force for the Wehrmacht and the tasks of the Wehrmacht in Norway would be endangered in all circumstances by a possible diminishing of the labour force. . . . It would interest me to learn if any other occupied territory has organized all these measures of help as early, as carefully and to the same extent as has happened in Norway. State-Secretary Backe and Ministerial-Director Moritz will confirm that in the food sector a whole row of precise and binding promises were made to us, all promises which laid down the utmost limits of what we had to have from the Reich as help in the individual sectors and whose non-fulfilment would endanger to the utmost degree our whole food plan.[3]

---

[1] RA., Rk. Diverse, Pakke, 22, Abt. Ernährung und Landwirtschaft, 'Vorlage für den Reichskommissar, Betrifft: Reisebericht Berlin', 2 May 1940.

[2] RA., Rk. Diverse, Pakke 70, Terboven to Darré, 17 September 1940.

[3] RA., Rk. Diverse, Pakke 60, Hauptabt. Volkswirtschaft, Abt. Ernährung und Landwirtschaft, Terboven to Darré, 21 November 1940.

The agreements between the Reichskommissariat and the military authorities had been based on the general principles underlying the Wehrmacht's original ideas. By 1943 these principles had had to be considerably modified to fit the reality of Norway's food situation. The basic quota of meat, 5,200 tons, which the Norwegian economy had been supposed to supply for the Wehrmacht, had been increased by 200 tons. To that quota, however, should be added the meat deliveries for Norwegian workers employed by the Wehrmacht. These additional quotas amounted to 600 tons annually after March 1942 and for the supply year 1943–4 were increased to 1,000 tons.[1] The main reason for the smallness in the increase over the original estimates was the far greater demand made on fish supplies. The original estimate of 3,700 tons of all types of fish annually was far exceeded. For 1943–4 the Wehrmacht quota was set at 7,000 tons of fresh fish, 1,000 tons of salt herring, and 500 tons of stockfish and *klippfisk*.

The original estimate of 26,000 tons of potatoes annually had swollen to 100,000 tons by 1942–3.[2] In the following supply year it was increased to 170,000 tons.[3] Half of the actual increase in potato production between 1939 and 1943 was therefore taken by the Wehrmacht, for whom in fact even the new quota proved too small. The quota of other vegetables stood at 15,000 tons. It had originally been planned that the Wehrmacht would require 4,500 tons, most of which in fact were to be supplied from Germany or Denmark. In only two cases were the original quotas reduced and neither of these could be said to have had any effect on actual consumption. The cheese quota had originally been estimated at 810 tons. In 1942–3 it was 1,200 tons. In 1943–4 it was cancelled as a response to the declining output of dairy products in the country. But the milk consumption of the Wehrmacht had grown to such a level as to be one of the main reasons for the decline in cheese production. The egg quota was set in 1942–3 at 1·2 million. However, it was already recognized that it could not be fulfilled at that level.[4] The shortage of eggs continued in 1943.[5] One of the main reasons was that the Wehrmacht were in fact supplying themselves locally as the stock of chickens dwindled. Finally, the egg quota was suppressed and this practice of local purchase was tacitly sanctioned.

Where these supply quotas could not be met it was the practice to add the missing amounts to the quota for the following year. In 1942–3, for

[1] F.D. 5202/45, Rk., Abt. Ernährung und Landwirtschaft, 'Tätigkeitsbericht für die Zeit vom 1 bis 31 August 1943', 4 September 1943; ibid., 'Tätigkeitsbericht für die Zeit vom 1–31 Mai 1944', 2 June 1944. The 'supply year' ran from 1 August to 31 July.
[2] F.D. 5325/45, Rk., Hauptabt. Volkswirtschaft, 'Bericht für die Zeit vom 1 bis 15 Juni 1942', 17 June 1942.
[3] F.D. 5202/45, Rk., Abt. Ernährung und Landwirtschaft, 'Tätigkeitsbericht für die Zeit vom 1 bis 31 August 1943', 4 September 1943; ibid., 'Tätigkeitsbericht für die Zeit vom 1–31 Mai 1944', 2 June 1944.
[4] Ibid., 'Tätigkeitsbericht für die Zeit vom 16–31.8.42', 31 August 1942.
[5] Ibid., 'Tätigkeitsbericht für die Zeit vom 1 bis 28 Februar 1943', 3 March 1943.

example, the missing quantity of meat from the Wehrmacht quota was added to the quota for 1943-4.[1] Similarly the quota of fresh vegetables, which was only 85 per cent filled, was proportionately increased for the following year.[2] This was not the case, however, with fruit where it had to be acknowledged that the quota was impossible to fulfil. From the beginning of December 1943 the task of supplying workers on Wehrmacht contracts and on the Nordag construction projects was transferred from the Wehrmacht to the Reichskommissariat.[2] As far as the total consumption was affected the difference was very slight, for in order to prevent the change from Wehrmacht to civilian rations causing too much disturbance among the workmen, they were all awarded heavy workers' rations.

The exact quantities of food supplied to the Wehrmacht obviously cannot be measured. The true size of the harvests is not known and for products like eggs the estimates of annual output are really the merest guesses. What the Wehrmacht obtained by local purchase, by confiscation, and on the black market must also be little better than a guess. On the whole, the estimates made by Aukrust and Bjerve have the air of being underestimates. It can be seen from Table 51, however, that even if the official records kept by the local supply offices of the quantity of food provided for the Wehrmacht are too low they are still high enough substantially to affect Norway's foreign-trade pattern.

One example alone will suffice. Although the output of potatoes in Norway reached record heights in 1943, by the end of the war Norway was obliged to import potatoes to meet the higher demand which this occasioned. In summer 1942 the Wehrmacht had demanded that its potato quota should be increased to 186,000 tons in the following supply year.[3] The size of the 1943 harvest was such that the Reichskommissariat felt able to meet this demand to a certain extent and the quota was fixed at 170,000 tons. In addition a further 20,000 tons was promised in the spring if there were still ample supplies.[4] In April, after much argument, the Reichskommissariat refused to provide the additional 20,000 tons, releasing only 8,000 tons for the troops in north Norway.[5] By May it was clear that stocks of potatoes in the larger towns were not sufficient and that Oslo itself might have to be supplied from Denmark or Sweden.[6] As the relatively poor results of the 1944 harvest became clear, the situation became much more serious. 'The delayed potato harvest and the generally-known bad harvest forecasts

[1] F.D. 5202/45, Rk., Abt. Ernährung und Landwirtschaft, 'Tätigkeitsbericht für die Zeit vom 1–31 Oktober 1943', 3 November 1943.
[2] Ibid., 'Tätigkeitsbericht für die Zeit vom 1 bis 30 September 1943', 4 October 1943.
[3] F.D. 5325/45, Rk., Hauptabt. Volkswirtschaft, 'Bericht für die Zeit vom 16 bis 30 Juni 1942', 4 July 1942.
[4] F.D. 5202/45, Rk., Abt. Ernährung und Landwirtschaft, 'Tätigkeitsbericht für die Zeit vom 1 bis 31 August 1943', 4 September 1943.
[5] Ibid., 'Tätigkeitsbericht für die Zeit vom 1–30 Avril 1944', 5 May 1944.
[6] Ibid., 'Tätigkeitsbericht für die Zeit vom 1–31 Mai 1944', 2 June 1944.

called forth a great tension in the population which spread to the Wehrmacht.'[1] The original supply quota of 150,000 tons to the Wehrmacht had to be reduced to 135,000 tons. The Wehrmacht itself organized commando groups to go into the countryside to obtain the necessary potatoes. Negotiations in Copenhagen led to the purchase of 20,000 tons of potatoes in Denmark.[2] By the end of January 1945 13,000 tons had arrived and were

TABLE 51. *Norwegian Trade with Germany in Foodstuffs and Requisitions by German Armed Forces in Norway, 9 April 1940 to 31 December 1944*[*]

(tons)

Commodity	Import	Export	German forces requisitions	Net import surplus (+) or deficit (−) including requisitions
Meat and meat products	..	..	29,700	−29,700
Canned fish	..	87,300	14,900	−102,200
Other fish products	..	756,400	10,300	−766,700
Grain, flour, and other cereals	707,700	..	12,800	+694,900
Cheese, milk, and eggs	..	..	60,300	−60,300
Vegetables and fruit	700	..	67,300	−66,000
Potatoes	2,100	..	509,500	−507,400
Sugar products and related goods	112,100	..	3,400	+108,700
Wine, liquor, beer, fruit juice, mineral water	2,900	..	104,200	−101,300
Fats	36,300	19,000	10,000	+6,700

* O. Aukrust and P. J. Bjerve, *Hva krigen kostet Norge* (Oslo, 1945), p. 34.

being used for the supply of Oslo, Kristiansand, and Stavanger.[3] From the start of 1945, therefore, Norway was becoming dependent on the import of even the one commodity of which the German agricultural programme had really succeeded in increasing the production and which had been to all intents and purposes not previously imported.

For those commodities, the import of which had always been assumed to be indispensable, the situation also deteriorated towards the end of the occupation. It will be seen from Table 52 that the imports of bread grain and sugar declined sharply after 1943 and that imports of fat, although they did not decline, remained far below their pre-war level. The gradual disappearance from the markets of imported fruit and 'colonial' goods meant an even greater impoverishment of the Norwegian diet. The erratic nature

[1] F.D. 5217/45, Rk., Hauptabt. Volkswirtschaft, 'Bericht für die Zeit vom 1 bis 31 Oktober 1944', 10 November 1944.
[2] Ibid., 'Bericht für die Zeit vom 1 bis 31 Dezember 1944', 16 January 1945.
[3] Ibid., 'Bericht für die Zeit vom 1 bis 31 Januar 1945', 15 February 1945.

of supply from abroad may also be noted. Essentially, Norway was dependent on the recurrent negotiations in Berlin with the Reichs Food Ministry and in Copenhagen with the Danish government. The only other large-scale supplier was Sweden. In so far as supply came from other countries, it could only be through the central clearing agreements and thus with the sanction of the authorities in Berlin.

TABLE 52. *Norwegian Food Imports, 1939–44**

(tons)

Commodity	1939	1940	1941	1942	1943	1944
Meat and meat products	3,655	1,917	4,078	1,221	265	1,742
Wheat	252,787	104,535	13,050	21,153	599	..
Rye	139,289	21,323	155,332	89,651	295,812	77,489
Wheat flour	39,319	16,581	39	7,600	99	222
Rye flour	162	8	2,000	41,975	251	884
Oats	2,336	705	8,463	6,811	20,207	14,975
Barley	24,603	6,052	9,945	23,330	39,895	..
Fruit	49,039	14,132	6,091	1,956	2,013	1,276
Vegetables	12,224	10,614	6,203	6,198	9,772	4,974
Sugar	99,916	66,117	71,997	50,388	63,398	29,939
Syrup	17,020	11,650	6,637	6,222	5,616	4,564
Fats	100,411	8,875	1,525	13,363	25,168	13,668

* Statistisk Sentralbyrå, *Statistisk-økonomisk utsyn'*, pp. 57 ff.

The first serious difficulties with grain imports were felt in 1942. In the previous year the high quantity of rye obtained had led to the supposition that this might be a substitute bread grain for the duration of the war. The grain imports from Germany in 1942, however, showed that Germany was able to release more fodder grain than bread grain. The provision of oats and barley was therefore far higher than the normal peacetime level while that of wheat and rye was much lower. Nevertheless, a change of procedure whereby Germany promised to deliver grain imports monthly in 1943 rather than irregularly made the situation much easier.[1] The situation was further eased by the large amounts of rye flour which Norway was able to import in 1943. Although the available quantity of wheat was much lower the serious depletion of bread-grain stocks which had threatened in 1942 did not take place.

In fact, although Germany was able to meet Norwegian bread-grain demands in 1943 by supplying rye rather than wheat, she was not able to meet the high demand for barley. Nevertheless, the combined imports of barley and oats into Norway in 1943 were such as easily to avert a crisis

[1] F.D. 5202/45, Rk., Abt. Ernährung und Landwirtschaft, 'Tätikgeitsbericht für die Zeit vom 1 bis 31 Dezember 1942', 11 January 1943.

even if not such as to permit the unhampered prosecution of the agricultural programme. In August 1943 the stock of rye for the following year was 130,000 tons as compared to the 15,000 tons available in autumn 1942.[1]

The German offer for 1944 was 180,000 tons of rye plus a supplemental 10,000 tons which could be used to increase the rations for young persons and workers with supplementary cards.[2] As this grain began to arrive, Norway was actually faced with a grain-storage problem.[3] Actual deliveries in the course of 1944 did not live up to the promise of the closing months of 1943. As the situation began to deteriorate again in Norway the Reich let it be known that for the next year the rye quota would be only 160,000 tons. Even if this quantity was to begin to arrive in the closing months of 1944 the deficiency on imports in that year meant that an effort had to be made to get extra grain from Denmark. In November negotiations were started in Copenhagen for 20,000 to 30,000 tons of rye.[4] It was hoped to offer Denmark higher quantities of fertilizer for the extra grain. By the end of January 1945 71,000 tons of the promised 160,000 tons from Germany had arrived, although the contract stipulated that by that date deliveries should have reached 100,000 tons.[5] There was no hope of further supply from the Reich and pressure was put on Germany to force Denmark to release 50,000 tons of rye.[6] At the beginning of March the Reich promised to release 30,000 tons of grain from Denmark, but not all of it would be rye.[7] The release of this rye by Denmark did not disguise the fact that the mechanism of grain supply had broken down. Of course the failure of the system was due to the hopeless position of Germany and on the whole the Norwegian need for grain imports was supplied with reasonable success until late 1944. Before that time, however, strains were beginning to appear. The bread ration was sustained by a shift from wheat to rye and the imports of fodder grains were not high enough to meet the demands of the Reichskommissariat's policy.

The drastic fall in fat imports into Norway between 1939 and 1941 left the food administration with a problem which the subsequent increase of those imports was not able to eliminate. The total imports of fat in 1941 were a mere 2 per cent of the 1938 level. Although in 1943 they reached a quarter of the pre-war level, Norway suffered throughout the war from a

[1] Ibid., 'Tätigkeitsbericht für die Zeit vom 1 bis 31 August 1943', 4 September 1943.
[2] Ibid., 'Tätigkeitsbericht für die Zeit vom 1–31 Oktober 1943', 3 November 1943.
[3] Ibid., 'Tätigkeitsbericht für die Zeit vom 1–31 Dezember 1943', 6 January 1944.
[4] Ibid., 'Tätigkeitsbericht für die Zeit vom 1–30 November 1944', 7 December 1944.
[5] F.D. 5217/45, Rk., Hauptabteilung Volkswirtschaft, 'Bericht für die Zeit vom 1 bis 31 Januar 1945', 15 February 1945.
[6] F.D. 5202/45, Rk., Abt. Ernährung und Landwirtschaft, 'Tätigkeitsbericht für den Monat Januar 1945', 13 February 1945.
[7] F.D. 5217/45, Rk., Hauptabt. Volkswirtschaft, 'Bericht für die Zeit vom 1 bis 28 Februar 1945', 14 March 1945.

serious fat shortage. Of all foodstuff categories, this was the one which the *Großraumwirtschaft* could least spare and Norway's deficiency in this regard tested it at one of its weakest points.[1] One reason for the early catastrophic fall in imports was that German planning had made no allowance for the elimination of Norway's whale-oil catch. The entire output of the 1940–1 expedition was sold to Britain and although Germany captured a certain amount of booty in the raids on factory ships and although from time to time a small effort at whaling was recommenced, to all intents and purposes Norwegian whale-oil production was lost for the duration of the war.[2] Added to this loss was the failure to produce the pre-war volume of herring oil. Even before the shortage of protein fodder began to result in a decline of dairy produce, domestic-fat production in Norway was already decreasing.

In 1942 the nominal fat ration could not be honoured and Germany, after lengthy negotiations, agreed to increase her supply to Norway.[3] As an immediate measure 1,000 tons of sunflower-seed oil were provided. The sunflower seeds were obtained from the Ukraine because Germany's own fat supply was such as to make it impossible for her adequately to respond to Norway's appeal.[4] In November Germany had agreed to provide 1,500 tons of pure fat and to release 1,000 tons of butter from Denmark, but the earlier promises from both these sources had not yet been fulfilled. The general support for the Norwegian fat ration to which Germany was now committed was very slow to arrive.

In March 1943 agreement was reached with Denmark for the import of 1,000 tons of butter by the end of July, but in the same month herring-oil production fell below its target by more than this amount. In May Norway requested that the coming 'fat year' should begin with a level of 2,000 tons monthly imported from Germany.[5] In fact if butter and herring-oil production each reached their target level, Germany would have to supply 12,000 tons pure fat to sustain the ration.[6] Neither butter nor herring oil did achieve their production targets after August. Between the start of August and the end of October the output of butter was 495 tons below target. Over the same period the output of herring oil was scarcely noticeable; instead of a planned output of 680 tons, 50 tons were obtained.[7] It had been hoped that an increase in the herring catch in December might lead to a further 2,000 tons of herring-oil output in that month but in fact

[1] K. Brandt, *The German Fat Plan and its Economic Setting* (Stanford, 1938).

[2] Idem., *Whaling and Whale Oil*.

[3] F.D. 5202/45, Rk., Abt. Ernährung und Landwirtschaft, 'Tätigkeitsbericht für die Zeit vom 16 bis 31 Oktober 1942', 31 October 1942.

[4] Ibid., 'Tätigkeitsbericht für die Zeit vom 1 bis 15 Oktober 1942', 15 October 1942.

[5] Ibid., 'Tätigkeitsbericht für die Zeit vom 1 bis 31 Mai 1943', 3 June 1943. The 'fat year' ran from 1 August to 31 July.

[6] Ibid., 'Tätigkeitsbericht für die Zeit vom 1 bis 31 August 1943', 4 September 1943.

[7] Ibid., 'Tätigkeitsbericht für die Zeit vom 1–30 November 1943', 4 December 1943.

there was no significant output.[1] By the end of February butter production since August was 6,000 tons against a planned level of 7,377 tons and herring-oil production 2,800 tons against a planned level of 6,720 tons. The implications were that margarine output had also fallen 3,300 tons behind schedule.[2]

Had this trend continued, Norway's reliance on imports would have been even greater and her situation more desperate. But in the later part of the fat year there was an improvement and when it closed, 11,517 tons of butter had been produced out of the planned 14,000 tons and 7,124 tons of herring oil out of the planned 11,000 tons.[3] Imports of butter from Denmark were 2,000 tons instead of the planned 3,000 tons so that in hard-fat units there was a total deficit of 7,747 tons over the fat year. Norway survived by using up the reserve of 4,917 tons of hard fat and leaving herself with only her own dwindling production and a precarious foreign supply.

For the fat year 1944–5 Norwegian estimates of minimum need were 17,800 tons of fat including 3,000 tons of butter. It seemed as though it would not be possible to get more than the previous year's quota of 2,000 tons of butter from Denmark so Germany offered to release 3,000 tons of bacon from Denmark. All in all promises from the Reich covered 17,040 tons of the fat required but those promises placed a heavy premium on Danish goods. In fact Germany exacted in return a promise from the Reichskommissariat that if the ration were reduced in Germany it would be reduced correspondingly in Norway.[4] Herring-oil production in Norway had meanwhile come practically to a standstill. 'The country's fat stocks', reported the Reichskommissariat in January 'have sunk to the minimum. They are on 1.1.1945 some 1,800 tons on a butter/margarine basis. It is easily seen how the situation has come to a head if it is considered that we need for the planned fat supply alone an inventory of 5,000 tons butter/margarine basis.'[5] Although the Norwegian ration did go down to correspond to the fall in the German ration, it still could not be honoured. German supplies of 1,500 tons of vegetable oil had been promised for February but their arrival seemed doubtful. In January and February herring-oil production was higher than for the corresponding months of the previous year but it could not compensate for the continued decline in butter production. Nor could it compensate for the failure of the vegetable-oil deliveries from Germany to arrive.[6]

Imports of sugar maintained a higher level compared to before the war

[1] Ibid., 'Tätigkeitsbericht für die Zeit vom 1–31 Dezember 1943', 6 January 1944.
[2] Ibid., 'Tätigkeitsbericht für die Zeit vom 1–29 Februar 1944', 6 March 1944.
[3] Ibid., 'Tätigkeitsbericht für die Zeit vom 1–31 August 1944', 5 September 1944.
[4] Ibid., 'Tätigkeitsbericht für die Zeit vom 1–31 Oktober 1944', 7 November 1944.
[5] Ibid., 'Tätigkeitsbericht für den Monat January 1945', 13 February 1945.
[6] F.D. 5217/45, Rk., Hauptabt. Volkswirtschaft, 'Bericht für die Zeit vom 1 bis 31 März 1945', 16 April 1945.

than imports of fat. But they declined very sharply in 1944 and in this case too the *Großraumwirtschaft*'s collapse left Norway in a serious position. By the close of 1942 Germany was already imposing strict limits on the quantity of sugar that could be spared for the Norwegian economy. When the Copenhagen negotiations in March 1943 produced a quantity which was not sufficient to sustain the ration, Norway was already looking to Sweden in the hope of obtaining the decisive quantity as 'relief'.[1] In the calendar year 1943 Sweden did in fact supply 9,000 tons of sugar; 23,000 tons came from Germany and 24,000 tons from Denmark.[2]

In September 1943 an attempt was made to obtain 35,000 tons from Denmark. The Danes were prepared to part with only 10,000 tons until they knew the state of their sugar-beet harvest more accurately.[3] In the following month they acceded to the request and Germany promised 20,000 tons. In early 1944, with the arrival of these quantities, the situation eased. By summer it was again acute, so much so that the Wehrmacht released 2,800 tons from its own stocks for the civilian ration.[4] In July there was a meeting with the Swedes in Stockholm at which the Germans and Danes were also present to try and solve Norway's sugar problems. Sweden offered 6,000 tons of sugar for the following year conditional upon Allied agreements to the deliveries. Denmark was forced to earmark 25,000 tons for export to Norway and Germany 20,000 tons. In addition part of the German supply to Bulgaria and Croatia which could no longer be delivered was diverted to Norway and so was a smaller quantity made available through the German-Swiss trade negotiations.[5] In the event, a significant part of the supply from Germany originated in the Protectorate, and transport over so long a distance proved difficult and deliveries were irregular.[6]

The Danes put up a stiff resistance to parting with more than the initial 15,000 tons at the December negotiations in Copenhagen. The Danish sugar ration was half as high again as the Norwegian but the Danes were naturally afraid that in view of Germany's difficulties the onus of supplying Norway would be shifted entirely on to them and prolonged the negotiations interminably. 'In this unbelievable way it went on from sitting to sitting.'[7] The Norwegian representatives only won by threatening to withhold fertilizer exports from Denmark. In fact the Danish negotiators had been holding back since September and in November had claimed that there

---

[1] F.D. 5202/45, Rk., Abt. Ernährung und Landwirtschaft, 'Tätigkeitsbericht für die Zeit vom 1 bis 31 März 1943', 3 April 1943.

[2] Ibid., 'Tätigkeitsbericht für die Zeit vom 1 bis 31 Juli 1943', 7 August 1943.

[3] Ibid., 'Tätigkeitsbericht für die Zeit vom 1 bis 30 September 1943', 4 October 1943.

[4] Ibid., 'Tätigkeitsbericht für die Zeit vom 1–30 Juni 1944', 5 July 1944.

[5] Ibid., 'Tätigkeitsbericht für die Zeit vom 1–31 Juli 1944,' 4 August 1944.

[6] F.D. 5217/45, Rk., Hauptabt. Volkswirtschaft, 'Bericht für die Zeit vom 1 bis 30 September 1944', 18 October 1944.

[7] F.D. 5338/45, Rk., Abt. Schiffahrt, 'Dem Herrn Reichskommissar zur Vorlage über Herrn Senator Otte', 21 December 1944.

would be no tonnage available for sugar transport in December.[1] In January 1945 Denmark offered to deliver a further 7,500 tons of sugar to Norway above the agreed 30,000 tons but only on condition that Germany would deliver an equivalent amount.[2] Finally, Denmark promised 4,000 tons above the agreed quota as 'relief'. In March 8,800 tons of the agreed quota from Denmark arrived, covering Norway's sugar needs until the end of June.[3] Had Denmark and Sweden not contributed both within the framework of the *Großraumwirtschaft* and outside it as 'relief', Germany could not have sustained the level of sugar supply to Norway. Effectively the level of imports in 1944 was too low to allow the Norwegian rationing system to continue to function.

The combined effects of the failure of domestic agricultural production to sustain higher levels of output and of the *Großraumwirtschaft* to provide anything more than a restricted and monotonous diet for the population, and after 1943 its inability even to do that, meant that the Norwegian rationing system never functioned as intended. Before the invasion coffee and sugar rationing had been introduced. Flour and grain rationing began in April 1940 and were made comprehensive in September. In November livestock slaughtering was subjected to control by licence and consumer meat-rationing cards were introduced in June 1941. The rationing of dairy products began early in June 1940. With the introduction of potato rationing in 1942, almost all food and animal feedstuff was rationed.[4]

The official Norwegian rations were lower than those in the Reich by about 100 to 200 calories a day for most categories of consumer. Children under five, for example, in December 1941 were allocated 1,619 calories daily in Norway and 1,770 in Germany; workers were allocated 2,045 calories compared to 2,200 in Germany.[5] This was after the law of 25 November 1941 which sought to place rationing on a more socially just foundation by increasing the rations for children, pregnant women, and heavy workers, a counterblast to the machinations of 'international Jewry', 'English plutocrats', and their 'bolshevik accomplices'.[6] The most favoured category, heavy workers, were allocated 600 calories daily less than in Germany, and after 1941 steps were taken in the interests of the German war economy itself to reduce this gap. The main method of providing extra

---

[1] F.D. 5217/45. Rk., Hauptabt. Volkswirtschaft, 'Bericht für die Zeit vom 1 bis 30 November 1944', 9 December 1944.

[2] Ibid., 'Bericht für die Zeit vom 1 bis 31 Januar 1945', 15 February 1945.

[3] F.D. 5202/45, Rk., Abt. Ernährung und Landwirtschaft, 'Tätigkeitsbericht für die Zeit vom 1–31 März 1945', 9 April 1945.

[4] F.D. 5218/45, Forsyningsdepartementet, Direktoratet for proviantering og rasjonering, *passim*.

[5] K. Brandt, *Management of Agriculture*, p. 344.

[6] Verordnung zur sozialen Gestaltung der Versorgung des norwegischen Volkes, in *Verordnungsblatt für die besetzten norwegischen Gebieten*, n. 15, 1941. There is a copy in R.A., Rk. Diverse, Pakke 27, classified as a 'Gesetz' not as a 'Verordnung'.

food for workers was in canteens and although in the later stages of the occupation workers' canteens were introduced under pressure from the Reichskommissariat, this ignored 'heavy workers' who could not be fed in this way. That the rationing gap between Norwegians and Germans was not closed may be seen from the subsequent surveys conducted by the Reichskommissariat whose results are shown in Tables 53 and 54.

TABLE 53. *German and Norwegian Rations in October 1942**

(calories per day)

Consumer group	Germany	Norway
Children 0–5 years	1,785	1,529
Children 6–14 ,,	2,100	1,991
Children 15–18 ,,	2,110	1,920
Normal consumers	1,797	1,734
Workers	2,583	2,356
Heavy workers	3,588	2,882
Self-supplied people	3,800	3,364

* R.A. Rk. Diverse, Pakke 43, 'Ernährungslage Norwegens', 31 October 1942.

TABLE 54. *German and Norwegian Rations in December 1942 and Autumn 1943**

(calories per day)

Consumer group	December 1942		Autumn 1943	
	Germany	Norway	Germany	Norway
Children 0–3 years	1,957		1,819	
Children 0–2 ,,		1,678		1,687
Children 3–6 ,,	1,870		1,740	
Children 3–5 ,,		1,684		1,625†
Children 6–10 ,,	2,003	2,007	1,949	
Children 10–14 ,,	2,328	2,007	2,225	2,021‡
Normal consumers	1,949	1,727	1,888	1,704
Heavy workers	2,651	2,364	2,594	2,704
Very heavy workers	3,386	2,723	3,331	2,956§

* F.D. 5325/45, Rk., Abt. Ernährung und Landwirtschaft, 'Jahresbericht 1942', 12 February 1943. figures for 1943 taken from K. Brandt, *Management of Agriculture*, p. 345.
† Children 2–5 years.
‡ Children 12–15 years.
§ Heavy workers with four supplementary ration cards.

Normal consumers would have been receiving a satisfactory diet from a merely nutritional standpoint in the long run had they been receiving between 2,200 and 2,500 calories a day. But no such long-term questions arose. On 1 October 1942 Dr. Karl Blankenagel replaced Dr. Richert as Head of the Food and Agriculture Department and in a general survey of the situation gave a most succinct account of the principles of German policy.

I can therefore only proceed in the future on the basis that as much as possible is to be removed from Norway for the Reich and the Wehrmacht and as little as possible is to be asked for from Germany. The deliveries from Germany are in accordance with the motivation that Norway's supply situation must be maintained just so far as is necessary to sustain the productive power of the people and especially the workers, in order to produce the necessary economic capacity for Germany and its armaments.[1]

The official rations say very little about what the consumers actually received. In the first place about 70 per cent of the population lived in rural areas and had access to undeclared food stocks and also to production above the official quotas to be delivered to collecting stations. About 40 per cent of the families were connected with farming or fishing activities in some way and the official ration for many commodities for them was meaningless. On the other hand, and increasingly towards the end of the occupation, the official ration could not be honoured. Urban inhabitants as a consequence very frequently got less than the official quota. The rationing quotas were reduced very sharply between September 1940 and June 1941, the coffee ration to one-eighth of what it had been in September, the tea ration by more than one-half, and the bread ration by 40 per cent.[2] The main reason was not the desire to delude the Norwegian population at the start of the occupation but the self-delusion of the Reichskommissariat. Supply from Europe was not adequate from the start to permit their high expectations to be realized.

One example will show that the problems were greater than the will or the ability to solve them. In the inter-war period, Norwegian margarine, which was manufactured domestically, was composed of 56 per cent vegetable fats, 27 per cent whale and fish oil, and 16 per cent dairy fats.[3] To continue margarine production in the occupation meant that the input of whale oil had to be replaced by greater inputs of herring oil or other fats. It also meant a constant supply of vegetable oils from abroad. None of these conditions were fulfilled even at the start of the occupation. When herring oil and milk production also declined the shortage of margarine became acute.

If German policy was a failure in its more immediate aims, if the trends of Norwegian agricultural production in the thirties were not sustained,

---

[1] R.A., Rk. Diverse, Pakke 43, 'Ernährungslage Norwegens', 31 October 1942.
[2] F.D. 5227/45, Rk., Nachrichtenblätter des Rk., nr. 10, 1 August 1941.
[3] D. Reppen, *Sjølberging. Hevning av bøndebefolkningens levestandard* (Oslo, 1941), p. 62.

much less accelerated, if the reorientation of Norwegian farming to meet the opportunities and needs of the *Großraumwirtschaft* did not take place, this was partly due to the failure of the policy on its deeper level. Although the Norwegian food producers suffered less than other sections of the community, and in some cases benefited, from the occupation, the proliferation of controls was sometimes a great inconvenience. The shortage of fertilizer and feedstuffs meant that the farmer's decisions had often to be taken from a range of possibilities which excluded his own particular preferences. The good prices paid by the administration were less than the black-market prices which could be obtained. The general aim of agricultural policy was to push agricultural output into directions which farmers were unwilling to follow without much longer-term guarantees than the circumstances of the war indicated. Finally, when prices proved inadequate, the administration resorted to compulsion. In the last two years Statens Kornforretning began forcibly to collect grain. In autumn 1942 and January 1943 there were compulsory slaughterings of livestock to accumulate a sufficient stock of meat to provide increased rations for heavy workers. Set about by difficulties in supply, by restrictions on marketing, by programmes designed to make him invest his small capital in ways with which he had little sympathy, the Norwegian farmer was not persuaded by his money income to give his allegiance to the new system.

In fact grain prices in Norway during the occupation were not allowed to rise to the level of Germany although the original reason for their lowness, international competition, had disappeared. Large subsidies were paid to keep down the price of grain from Germany, the government using for this purpose a tax on the alcohol derived from processing wood into cellulose fodder. Imported grain was therefore kept down to the domestic price. The domestic price increased by roughly 75 per cent during the occupation. The price offered for wheat always remained higher than that for other grains. The actual level of harvests during the war indicates either that prices were an insufficient means to effect the agricultural policy or that the price differentiation between wheat and other grains was insufficient. The differential between wheat prices and rye prices was eliminated between 1942 and 1944 in the hope of getting more bread grain of any kind. The increase in the price of potatoes was much greater than in the price of grain and this might indicate the reason for the relatively greater success of the potato-growing campaign. But the limitations of price policy in such a situation are shown by the failure of a similar increase in the price paid for milk by creameries to bring about an increase in milk production. Egg prices were more than doubled, but here, of course, the influence of black-market prices and local Wehrmacht purchasing meant that official price policy could have little effect. Farmers were prepared to respond to price policy within limits but those limits were too narrow for what both the Reichskommissariat and Nasjonal Samling hoped to achieve.

The use of price policy seems to have been less successful in Norway than in other occupied territories and this appears to be related to the structure of the Norwegian economy. The forcible surrender of crops and livestock was commoner in Norway than in France where the peasantry suffered a good deal less from the occupation than other social groups. There is evidence, as will be seen, that the peasantry of Norway benefited in many ways from the prices paid for their produce and from the sure markets, yet their response was more sluggish to the general policy of the occupying power. No doubt something must be explained by the simple wish to thwart the occupier. But the main reason lies in the backwardness of Norwegian agriculture. German policy seems to have been designed for an advanced economy, unlike the much cruder policies pursued in Poland.[1] However, the agricultural sector of the Norwegian economy, albeit that it existed within the framework of a highly advanced economy had been little affected by the factors which had changed the rest of the economy. Although French peasant farmers were scarcely distinguished for their modern methods they were, when compared to their Norwegian fellows, better supplied with fixed and liquid capital and with knowledge. Their average holding of land was also larger. Where the size of a peasant farm was as small as it was in Norway any departure from established farming practice needed a far stronger guarantee from the central government than was provided; price changes were too weak an instrument.

Price policy was supplemented by legislation derogating certain quasi-compulsory powers to the Ministry of Agriculture or its representatives. The Order on Special Measures to increase Agricultural Production (*Verordnung über Sondermaßnahmen zur Steigerung der landwirtschaftlichen Produktion*) of 7 January 1942 gave the Minister of Agriculture powers to stipulate in some cases the proportion of ploughland to be cultivated on the farm and the type of crops. The Ministry could withdraw the right to the use of the farm if it was cultivated in an unsatisfactory manner. The decision had to be sanctioned by the local peasant committee, but since that was organized on the *Führerprinzip* so that the leader took the decision and the other members served merely as advisers, the safeguard was not very strong.[2] The legislation was supplemented on 9 April by similar laws allowing the Ministry of Agriculture, through the same machinery, to direct the use of plough-teams, tractors, and other agricultural machines where they were most needed. Measures such as these were also supported

[1] H. von Streng, *Die Landwirtschaft im Generalgouvernement*, Studien des Instituts für Besatzungsfragen, No. 6. (Tübingen, 1955).

[2] R.A., Rk., Hauptabt. Volkswirtschaft, Pakke 35, 'Gesetzliche Maßnahmen zur Steigerung und Sicherung der landwirtschaftlichen Erzeugung in Norwegen', 26 January 1944.

financially through subsidies. It was possible to get subsidies for between one-quarter and one-third of the cost of the conversion of pasture to ploughland. Subsidies up to one-third of the cost were available for water regulation and control of drainage. Below a certain size of farm the peasant could get subsidies for the use of artificial fertilizers.[1]

This type of legislation often took on a distinctly threatening air. Legislative changes designed first and foremost to improve the peasant's position were far less than in Germany. There were certain obstacles to stabilizing the pattern of landholding in Norway according to the terms of the German *Reichserbhofgesetz*. The peasant farms created with a perpetual entail in Germany were usually between $7\frac{1}{2}$ and 10 hectares in size, the area of land supposed to be necessary to support a family and to function in the long run as a productive unit. Well over half the Norwegian farms were much smaller than that and, in terms of National Socialist ideology, would have been considered uneconomic units. There were some attempts to introduce a security of leasehold derived from German legislation on the protection of the tenant, in particular the legislative orders of 21 March 1941 (*Verordnung über Pachtverhältnisse für landwirtschaftliche Grundstücke*). But these decrees reserved to the Ministry of Agriculture the right to revoke long-term leases if the land was not cultivated to its satisfaction. Furthermore the local peasant committees had the right to review leasehold tenures on the request of either party to the lease.

Yet in many ways the increasing food prices achieved some of the social results which the unrealized programmes of agricultural reconstruction had been designed to achieve. Legislative plans for debt liquidation and for providing greater security of tenure for peasant farmers remained ineffective. In the absence of some concrete legislative gesture peasant allegiance was not diverted from the agrarian parties to fascism. But the burden of agricultural debt was nevertheless substantially reduced by these years of relative prosperity. In 1940 only 11·7 per cent of Norwegian farmers were free from debt; they owned 9·8 per cent of the total assets owned by landowners. In 1944 23·5 per cent were free from debt; they owned 19·9 per cent of the total assets. If those farmers who have less than 30 per cent debt are added in the same category as those free from debt, the total is 34 per cent of all farmers; they owned 37·3 per cent of gross assets and 11 per cent of the total debt. In 1944 such a category embraced 53·6 per cent of all farmers, 56·2 per cent of gross assets, and 21·5 per cent of the total debt. The percentages of landowners more than 70 per cent in debt dropped from 18·5 per cent of the whole in 1940 to 6·3 per cent of the whole in 1944.

Some indications of the way in which these movements of debt were

[1] R.A., Rk., Hauptabt. Volkswirtschaft, Pakke 35, 'Maßnahmen zur Steigerung der landwirtschaftlichen Erzeugung in Norwegen'.

related to the war economy in Norway may be derived from the changing composition of the gross assets of farmers. In 1940 57 per cent of those assets were represented by farms and buildings, 16 per cent by livestock and movable capital equipment. In 1944 the percentage represented by farms and buildings had declined to 52 per cent and that represented by livestock and movable capital equipment had increased to 20·3 per cent.[1] In the circumstances this must have been attributable wholly to increases in the value of livestock. The indications are thus that the period of occupation led to a considerable deterioration of the capital stock but that the accompanying inflation of food prices cleared a large proportion of the agricultural debt which had been such a dead weight in the inter-war period.

TABLE 55. *Movement of Agricultural Indebtedness in Norway, 1940–4**

(excluding Finnmark)

Degree of debt	Per cent of total number of landowners	Per cent of total assets	Per cent of total debt
Position on 1 January 1940:			
Debt free	11·7	9·8	..
Less than 30 per cent indebted	22·6	27·5	11·0
30–50 per cent indebted	22·0	23·3	22·9
50–70 per cent indebted	20·7	21·8	31·5
70–100 per cent indebted	15·0	13·8	27·1
100 per cent or more indebted	3·5	2·3	6·2
Position on 1 January 1944:			
Debt free	23·5	19·2	..
Less than 30 per cent indebted	30·1	37·0	21·5
30–50 per cent indebted	22·0	23·8	34·1
50–70 per cent indebted	12·8	12·9	27·4
70–100 per cent indebted	5·2	4·3	12·4
100 per cent or more indebted	1·1	0·8	3·3

* Statistisk Sentralbyrå, Norges offisielle statistikk, x. 183, *Bøndenes bruttoformue og gjeld* (Oslo, 1949), p. 23, 'Antall bønder, deres bruttoformue og gjeld delt etter gjeldprosenten'.

Whether Nasjonal Samling would have regarded this mechanical procedure as satisfactory is doubtful. Their propaganda was based on a change in the quality of life of the farmer, on a spiritual reawakening. In Germany

[1] Statistisk Sentralbyrå, Norges offisielle statistikk, x. 183, *Bøndenes bruttoformue og gjeld* (Oslo, 1949).

the means used to bring about this reawakening were in fact also mechanical. The simple act of placing a higher emphasis on the peasant farmer's vote in 1931, and the accompanying propaganda placing a higher worth on his life and manner of existence achieved the most startling successes. Nevertheless, the tenure reforms and the very high food prices in National Socialist Germany were sweeping political gestures cementing the alliance of peasantry and fascism. The only equivalent gesture that could be made in Norway under wartime conditions was to refrain from driving down wage-rates in the agricultural sector as brutally as in other sectors of employment. The aim of wages policy after the German occupation was to achieve a decrease in the high standard of living as quickly as possible through a reduction in wages, which in general were above the level of those in the Reich and could no longer be maintained due to the altered circumstances in Norway. Therefore certain price increases were consciously permitted straightaway while wages were decreased through a reduction in the cost-of-living bonus.[1] This process was regarded as over by the end of 1940. From that time on, the increasing shortage of construction labour led to great pressure for increased wages. It was the clear policy of the Reichs-kommissariat only to yield to such pressure where the most vital interests of the German war economy were at stake.

While all pressure to increase industrial wages was resisted the wages of agricultural workers were increased at the start of the occupation by 12 per cent, of forestry workers by 10 per cent, and of fishermen by between 10 and 15 per cent. This was 'on social grounds'.[2] An investigation in 1941 showed that the level of wages for workmen was still higher in Norway than in Germany while the wages of agricultural workers were lower. Norwegian wages, the Reichskommissariat concluded, had not developed 'organically'.[3] The level of wages in agriculture was 'under the existence minimum' and 'socially irresponsible'.[3] One task of fascist policy was, accordingly, to stop wage rates merely reflecting the strength of trade unions and cause them to reflect a broader social justice, supposedly embodied in the new fascist society. Even when, by 1942, the exigencies of the war caused the Reichskommissariat to refuse a further increase in agricultural wages the refusal still envisaged a further correction in their favour after the war.[4]

There were three reasons given for 'correcting' the level of Norwegian wage rates. Firstly, the need to maintain the German-Norwegian exchange rate. Secondly, the fear that bigger incomes amongst a class which was entirely food-consuming would cause a much more vigorous black market. Thirdly,

[1] F.D. 5211/45, Rk., Abt. Arbeit und Sozialwesen, 'Jahresbericht', 7 January 1942 .
[2] Ibid., 'Führer-Bericht für die Zeit vom 16/11/40–31/1/1941', 31 January 1941.
[3] Ibid., 'Jahresbericht' 7 January 1942.
[4] R.A., Rk. Diverse, Pakke 38, Abt. Ernährung und Landwirtschaft, 'Lohnerhöhungen in der Landwirtschaft', 25 July 1942.

the Reich is extremely interested, with regard to the coming greater European economic area (*grosseuropäischen Wirtschaftsraum*) and on labour utilization grounds also, that Norwegian wages, which, in spite of the wage reduction measures applied in 1940, remain generally high and above the comparable levels in Germany, should not increase further, but, on the contrary, should be little by little brought down to the level of those of the Reich. If this final aim seems impossible at the moment on political grounds having regard to Norway's present economic situation, this target must still be kept in view and its future attainment facilitated by maintaining the stability of current wages.[1]

TABLE 56. *Industrial Wage Rates in Norway, 1939–43**

(Hourly rates in kroner. Piece rates and overtime inclusive)

	1st quarter 1940	1940	1941	1942	1943	Per cent increase 1939–43†
Industry and mining in general	1·74	1·72	1·76	1·83	1·88	18
Of which mining and smelting works	1·63	1·60	1·71	1·85	1·93	29
Handicraft workers	2·27	2·23	2·13	2·15	2·17	4
Construction workers (total)	2·24	2·19	2·23	2·35	2·34	14
Of which:						
Eastern region	2·45	2·43	2·46	2·67	2·71	20
Western region	1·87	2·17	2·09	2·20	2·24	30
Trøndelag	1·77	2·04	2·03	2·00	2·08	28
Nordland, Troms, and Finnmark	1·82	2·17	2·59	2·81	2·36	41

* O. Aukrust and P. Bjerve, *Hva krigen kostet Norge*, p. 80.

† Reckoned under assumption that wages in autumn 1939 were 8 per cent lower than in the first quarter of 1940.

TABLE 57. *Agricultural Wage Rates (Exclusive of Overtime and Piece Work), 1939–40 to 1943–4**

(kroner)

	1939–40	1940–1	1941–2	1942–3	1943–4	Per cent increase 1939–40 to 1943–4
Agriculture						
Total yearly wage for servants (including keep and board)	637	706	892	1,093	1,237	94
Day wage for farm work (providing own keep)	6·05	6·70	9·01	10·39	11·28	86
Day wage for granite walling— summer half year	7·59	8·49	10·75	12·49	13·29	75
Forestry						
Forest workers—own keep, summer half year, day wage	6·18	7·02	9·20	11·02	11·59	88

* O. Aukrust and P. Bjerve, *Hva krigen kostet Norge*, p. 80.

[1] F.D. 5325/45, Rk., 'Gruppe Lohnpolitik und Arbeitsbedingungen, '3-Jahresbericht'.

The biggest obstacle to this policy was the short-term thinking of the Wehrmacht.

> It must, unfortunately, be recorded that the necessity for a determined implementation of the wages freeze does not find the required understanding in wide circles of industry and especially in the Luftwaffe who, understandably from this viewpoint, only have the immediate aims in front of them in view and thus overlook that there are other no less important tasks to carry out. . . .[1]

Norwegian workers and trade unions understood perfectly well the general drift of fascist economic policy. From the moment of the occupation a clash of interests was inevitable. The Reichskommissariat officials had never expected anything but opposition from the Norwegian labour movement but they were still surprised at so total a lack of 'corporate' feeling among both employees and employers. An initial meeting took place on 26 April 1940 between Dr. Marrenbach of the German Labour Front and Elias Volan, Chairman of the Norwegian Trade Union Conference, and a few days later Marrenbach met representatives of the employers' associations. But any hope of quickly creating an organization which would represent both parties to the wage contract seems to have been dashed. In September 1940 there began a widespread underground opposition to German measures in Norwegian trade unions which the Reichskommissariat regarded as 'not very dangerous'.[2]

The matter was brought to a head by Nasjonal Samling's attempts to exercise direct influence over the trade unions by forcing them into a body like the German Labour Front. Although this venture was marked by the political incompetence which seemed always to accompany Nasjonal Samling's own initiatives and although Terboven certainly wanted them to move more carefully, it was, in its general aims, supported by the Reichskommissariat.

> This intention could not, however, be carried out, because, due to the condition of the Party and to the still very Marxist outlook of the members of the worktakers associations, the danger of disturbing the associations with all the possible consequences of walk-outs, strikes, etc., was only too easily conjured up. Thus, in order to enable Nasjonal Samling in a given time to take over the associations, a National Socialist Factory Organization (similar to that before the take-over in the Reich) was set up whose task was specially to win the workers' world outlook for Nasjonal Samling and then to educate them sociopolitically.[2]

This, too, was a failure. In May 1941 forty unions sent a letter of protest to Terboven. Severe repression followed and four of the most prominent

---

[1] F.D. 5211/45, Rk., Abt. Arbeit und Sozialwesen, 'Jahresbericht'.
[2] F.D. 5325/45, Rk., Abt. Arbeit and Sozialwesen, 'Jahresbericht 1940/41/42', 22 February 1943.

trade-union leaders were put in gaol. In July Nasjonal Samling created its own Directorate for Labour Organizations to complete the take-over. Edvard Stenersen, its leader, proved so incompetent at the task that he was finally forced out by the German administration in November after they had expressed the strongest doubts about his political competence.[1] From the moment of his appointment there followed a spate of factory sabotage of a much more serious kind. On 8 September a complete strike began in the Akers shipyard in Oslo. The strikers went back as soon as they were threatened but on the day they did so forty other factories came out on strike. On 10 September a state of emergency was proclaimed in Oslo and a more violent repression began. The unions were put under the control of the leader of the Nasjonal Samling Trade Group Organization, Odd Fossum, and special commissars appointed to control each union. There followed the imprisonment of many union leaders and members, the execution of two of the leaders of the strike, and the eventual total subjection of the trade union movement.

Every measure [complained the Reichskommissariat] which ought to be carried out here in Norway, whether it be in the field of professional education, of the organization of leisure time, or in that of increasing productivity, founders, or can only be unsatisfactorily applied, because it must be negotiated with two organizations, the associations of work-takers and work-givers, which rival each other constantly or go about their aims from a hostile standpoint of class-war. Both organizations regard each other as enemies and even now co-operate only in the most necessary things.[2]

The enmity of the Norwegian working class was only to be expected. The aim of economic policy was to win the allegiance of rural wage earners. It was at this point that policy failed rather than in the violent disputes with the trade unions. To be *relatively* better off was a poor incentive for the bottom rungs of Norwegian rural society when they were often absolutely worse off. Where they were not absolutely worse off this was because they sold their labour to entrepreneurs engaged on the numerous military and transport construction sites throughout the country and did so at so high a rate as to ruin the carefully conceived wages policy of the government. No less than the peasants with more land they scorned the rewards of an anti-materialist government for the higher rewards which the labour market still offered in war time.

Norwegian peasants were left in a situation where the market economy still dictated policy but where an increasing number of controls, not all of them beneficial to the cultivator, hedged around their freedom to respond to the market. Superimposed on this situation was the firm impression that

[1] F.D. 5211/45, Rk., Abt. Arbeit und Sozialwesen, 'Jahresbericht'.
[2] F.D. 5325/45, Rk., Abt. Arbeit und Sozialwesen, 'Jahresbericht 1940/41/42'.

it was all temporary. The only adequate response was to make as much money as possible while the occupation lasted and keep a weather eye open for what would happen after the war. What more complete rejection of Nasjonal Samling's exhortations to abandon 'materialism' could there be? Had Nasjonal Samling been able to construct an economic framework in which 'materialism' could have been abandoned safely, it might have been a different story. But was that possible without complete subjection to Germany?

IX

THE FISHING INDUSTRY

WHAT is there to say about the German plans for the Norwegian fishing industry except that they were a complete failure? They were a failure on two grounds. In the first place, the scheme for a reconstruction of the industry which might turn it into the basis of a fascist society came to nothing. This could be blamed on the events of a prolonged war. Capital, raw materials, and time were all lacking so that the social dreams of both German and Norwegian fascist parties could never be translated into positive action. But there was another dimension to the German failure. It was also their intention that the Norwegian fishing industry should play a central role in the economic organization of the New Order. By increasing the export of fish from Norway the over-all protein deficiency which would still persist even in the diet of an autarkic European New Order stretching to the Urals could be remedied. As it was, in the course of the occupation, although Norwegian fish exports were concentrated very heavily on the German market the total volume of fish caught and exported declined. Both on ideological and on economic grounds, therefore, German policy was a failure. Since the connections between the ideological and economic aspects of this failure were so strong it is difficult to attribute the second aspect of this failure entirely to the war or entirely to exogenous circumstances, such as a temporary shortage of fish in the sea. Had the New Order been finally established, it does not seem that the potential weakness in its food supply would have been remedied by a greater availability of fish from Norway.

To understand the precise nature of Germany's economic hopes it is necessary to look briefly at the range of activities of the Norwegian fishing industry. Most Norwegian fishing was coastal. Thus the naval warfare after 1940 had not led the occupiers to suppose that the fish catch would suffer too much. It had been assumed from the start that the Spitzbergen, Iceland, and Greenland fisheries must close.[1] Their contribution was small, however, compared to the total catch in Norwegian coastal waters which, it was assumed, need not be disturbed by events. Within that coastal catch the preponderant role was played by two distinct fish, cod and herring. But the herring fishery itself was by no means a unified whole.

Cod were caught mostly in the first half of the year. It might even be said that they were caught mostly in three months of the year, for, of a

---

[1] F.D. 5325/45, Rk., Hauptabt. Volkswirtschaft, 'Ein Jahr Reichskommissar'.

total annual catch which tended to average around 130,000 tons, about 100,000 tons would normally be caught from January to April between Ålesund and the Lofoten Islands, the so-called Lofoten fishery. In April the boats followed the cod shoals north to Finnmark recording ever smaller catches. The bulk of this catch had always been exported, either dried or salted. The chief markets for these products were Italy and West Africa. Sweden, Portugal, and Spain were the only European markets, apart from Italy, to play a significant part in this trade. The demand from markets with higher *per capita* incomes was for fresh-frozen fish. Lack of capital in the cod fishery prevented it from responding to these demands. As far as the export of fish was concerned, the cod fishery thus had little dependence on the *Großraumwirtschaft*. It did not produce what was wanted there and its catch was too seasonal to make it the basis of any permanent transformation of the future diet of that area.

The by-products of the cod fishery were more specialized and valuable. Cod-liver oil, together with a smaller quantity of other fish-liver oils, had become an important export, amounting to over 100,000 hectolitres annually. Cod was also processed into fish meal for animal feed. The meal was processed from those parts of the fish rejected by the dryers of *klippfisk* and stockfish. Consequently, it was the by-product of the least-profitable part of the fishery.

Between January and April also took place the so-called 'spring herring' (*vårsild*) fishery. The spring herring were caught off the west coast between Stavanger and Ålesund. Like the cod fishery, the spring-herring fishery was both seasonal and regional. After April the herring fishery depended on 'small herring' (*småsild*) which, although caught thoughout the year, migrated northwards and in later months formed the shoals known as 'fat herring' (*fetsild*). Between November and January occurred another seasonal fishery, the 'large herring' (*storsild*) fishery. Large herring were caught mainly in the open sea rather than in the fjords and immediate coastal waters.

As with cod, the most valuable form of export for herring was as fresh or fresh-frozen fish and, as with cod, it was also the least developed. Salted herring, the traditional form of export, were still sold and about 38,000 tons were exported in 1939. Two markets were overwhelmingly important, Germany and Sweden. They accounted between them for almost 24,000 tons of the total export in 1939. Herring meal developed as an export with the increase in 'scientific' feeding methods in agriculture. Its export from Norway was especially tied to German agriculture. Of the total exports of fish meal over 60 per cent went to Germany. German plans for improving Norwegian agriculture by a greater consumption of fish meal there either implied a certain sacrifice on Germany's part or an increase in fish-meal production in Norway. Herring oil and canned herrings were also produced. The herring-oil industry was less valuable than the production of cod-liver oil but spring herring canned as 'kippers' or small herring canned as 'sild' had a considerable sale outside the confines of the *Großraumwirtschaft* to Britain and the United States.

As far as the export of canned herring was concerned, no problem was presented either to Germany or Norway. From the earliest date possible the canning factories worked on Wehrmacht contracts. The problem lay with the winter fishing. It was Germany's intention to increase the proportion of fresh fish in the total export of fish products to the other states within the *Großraumwirtschaft*.[1] This meant in particular an increase in the yield of the two seasonal herring fisheries, the spring-herring fishery and the large-herring fishery. The small herring hardly repaid the effort of installing quick-freezing plants in various centres. The bulk of the herring meal produced was also obtained from spring herring and large herring. The projected increase in protein supply to the *Großraumwirtschaft* and the projected increase in fodder consumption in Norway both required the same thing, a much greater success in two fisheries which were not only seasonal, and thus subject to the vagaries of climate and annual variations in the behaviour of fish shoals, but were also more demanding of capital and organized effort than the small-herring fishery. The other great source of the potential increase in fresh fish exports was the Lofoten fishery, as seasonal as the spring- and large-herring fisheries.

The increase in fresh fish exports to Germany could only be achieved by a large investment of capital in quick-freezing plants for the catches were landed at a multitude of points on the 1,100-mile-long Norwegian coastline. The level of fresh fish exports other than herring to Germany in the 1930s had been about 5,000 tons annually, less than half the weight of the export of salt herring. German efforts to shape the *Großraumwirtschaft* of the future, however, had been so unrelenting as to achieve success even with Norway. The German-Norwegian trade agreement of 20 February 1940 increased the level to 55,000 tons annually, an increase to be achieved by the installation of German refrigerating installations. The return to Norway was not merely the foreign capital thus attracted but the much higher price for exports. The first refrigerator ship, with an annual capacity of 25,000 tons, arrived in Trondheim in time for the invasion. This agreement was replaced on 1 August 1940 by an agreement between the German government and Norges Raafisklaget for an annual delivery quota of over 150,000 tons.[1] These deliveries included the deliveries to the Wehrmacht. A freezing plant was installed at Bodø and two additional plants stipulated for, a mobile factory ship and an installation at Hammerfest. In December the quota was increased to 200,000 tons.

[1] F.D. 5325/45, Rk., Hauptabt. Volkswirtschaft, 'Ein Jahr Reichskommissar'.

All herring products were also demanded in greater quantity by Germany except herring meal. In that case, it was recognized that agricultural plans for Norway meant that more fodder must be used there and that Germany must sacrifice some of the herring meal output to Norwegian purposes. In fact shortly before the occupation agreements had been signed to direct 40,000 tons of herring meal annually to Germany, but the first report of the Reichskommissariat indicated that it was unlikely that fulfilment of the terms of the agreement would be required. The increase in the export of fresh fish in no way indicated a decrease in the export of salt fish to Germany; rather the contrary, for Germany intended to divert to her own purposes all Norwegian salt-fish exports which had previously gone outside the boundaries of the *Großraumwirtschaft*. The attempt to get more small herring was given greater force by the timing of the invasion. Immediately after that event small herring were the only effective source of supply for the fish-canning industry which was employed on Wehrmacht contracts.

The general nature of German plans to revitalize the Norwegian fishing industry and to enable it to carry out its new role in Europe have already been indicated. It is scarcely worth examining them in detail since they proved merely pious hopes. The Fisheries Department of the Reichskommissariat blamed the failure of these plans to materialize on the shortsighted opposition of Norwegian authorities and, by implication, on the failure of the Reichskommissariat to force compliance with their wishes. The traditional Norwegian administration was certainly reluctant to further German plans, the more so as those plans seemed to involve an almost complete capital penetration of the processing part of the fishing industry. Nasjonal Samling was caught between a sympathy for German plans in their social and economic aspect and the determination of a nationalist party not to allow foreign capital to control the destinies of the industry which employed a greater number of Norwegians than any other and which had so much historical, cultural, and mythological significance in the history of the country.

Although the measures which the Fisheries Department wished to enforce were obstructed by administrative delays that is not the first reason for their non-enforcement. The complaints of the lesser departments of the Reichskommissariat were very much like the complaints of minor administrative departments everywhere, based on an extremely limited view of the situation. Terboven saw his first job as to get more fish to Germany. This could best be achieved by allowing the industry to operate initially in as undisturbed a way as possible while making sure by more conventional methods that a high proportion of its catch was made available either for the German forces or for export to Germany. This was secured by trading agreements of the kind that had been negotiated before the invasion. The difference now was that Germany was in an invincibly strong position in such bargaining, so strong as to be able to dictate her own terms, whereas before the war she had been able to exercise only a very limited influence on Norwegian trade and had consequently found it much more difficult to negotiate favourable terms with Norway than with most other European lands.

A theme which runs throughout the construction of the New Order seems to be particularly loud and clear in German dealings with the Norwegian fishing industry, the opposition between the social revolutionary aims of fascism and the more general economic aims of the *Großraumwirtschaft*. In some ways that opposition was no more than the expected opposition of violently nationalist parties when forced to construct an international economic system, especially when one of them was so dominant. The *Großraumwirtschaft* was constructed entirely in the German interest. It was a system in which Germany by military and economic force satisfied her own nationalist aspirations at the expense of others. Nevertheless, it was also the expression of a particular social and economic philosophy which was not confined to Germany, and an attempt to create a new European system on the basis of that philosophy. It was an attempt to bring some order into the chaos of economic relationships which had pervaded in Europe since the collapse of the gold standard. That order implied a very different order of society, akin to the new order of society in Germany.

The Norwegian fishing industry seemed to both National Socialists and Nasjonal Samling to be the best basis for such a social reconstruction in Norway. Their interest in it was far more than merely increasing the German protein supply, it was to be the spiritual root of a social regeneration in Norway. But to make the system work, during a war, and to make it work in Germany's interests, meant to prefer a policy of playing safe. The effort to convert Norway's fishermen to fascism was very small while that to secure their fish was very large. Propaganda cost money for which, in wartime, there was no shortage of alternative and more imperative uses. The construction of the *Großraumwirtschaft* was an unsatisfactory compromise bound to disappoint the hopes not only of fascists in non-German countries but of the more radical wing of the German party. For this no doubt the course of the war was partly responsible. Wars have to be won and the necessity for winning the war implied a cautious policy with regard to Norway's fishing industry. The events of the war itself, the growing demand for money, the growing shortages of goods, the long collapse of the *Großraumwirtschaft*, all made it more certain that German interest in the Norwegian fishing industry should primarily be to maintain the *status quo* and to increase the level of exploitation. In this way the *Großraumwirtschaft* became less an expression of a new European social and economic order than an obstacle to that order.

It is clear [wrote the Department of Fisheries about German plans for the Industry] that a thoroughgoing development of the Norwegian industry of that kind can only take place under German influence and German capital participation. The Norwegian economy cannot contribute sufficient capital to carry out thoroughly the great tasks of the future which grow before it. So far nothing has been undertaken on this side by the Norwegian government. It can even be said that the present economic policy for fishing has only hesitatingly confronted such a naturally necessary development. The present concessions law still in force obstructs from a narrow national-economic standpoint the necessary co-ordination between Germany, as the chief customer, and the Norwegian fishing economy. It is still to be remarked that more understanding prevails for these ideas in economic circles than among the Norwegian authorities. These authorities are particularly to be blamed for the fact that, in spite of our year's work, and in spite of all attempts to convince them of the basic correctness of these developments in economic policy, they have not yet done anything for the long term incorporation of the Norwegian fishing economy in the greater European area and have, rather, sought to impede this development by every means. They still hope that the present position will have changed after the end of the war.[1]

The transfer of fuller political powers to Nasjonal Samling on 1 February 1942 only meant that these aims of the Fisheries Department receded even further into improbability. By 1943 the events of the war had revealed the *Großraumwirtschaft* for what it had become, mere exploitation. 'It is,' the Department wrote, 'generally understandable that the Norwegian fishing economy must be so directed in the future as the tasks of war demand. It is to be hoped that the political preconditions in Norway will be so ordered that the Reichskommissar will have greater powers over the Norwegian authorities and the Norwegian fishing economy than has been the case since 1.2.1942.'[2]

Nasjonal Samling policy seems to have been to induce the German administration to concentrate more on the social aspects of their policy and to try to defend their 'national capital' against German intrusion. The confusion is evident in the text of a speech, presumably to be given by a member of the Norwegian government, submitted to the Reichskommissariat in March 1943. The speech is a frank attempt to reconcile the principles of independent economic enterprise, in which Nasjonal Samling believed, with the need for authoritarian control of the industry as a whole, a need now made imperative by Germany's weakened economic position.

[1] F.D., 5325/45, Rk., Hauptabt. Volkswirtschaft, 'Ein Jahr Reichskommissar'.
[2] F.D. 5325/45, Rk., Abt. Fischwirtschaft. 'Bericht für die Zeit vom 31.4.1940–31.12.1942', 14 February 1943.

That the Norwegian *Volk* had chosen fishing for an occupation was a sign of 'a healthy core'. Nasjonal Samling's policy was not to destroy this but to preserve it. 'I will not have it said that the government and its administrative machine does not *want* to support the fishing industry. Completely the opposite—I can assure you, ladies and gentlemen, that Nasjonal Samling is as strongly interested in no other branch of business except agriculture.'[1] German policy, which might seem to the independent fisherman to be a dangerous threat to his way of living, had to be seen as part of a historical trend which Nasjonal Samling would encourage and which must financially benefit the industry.

'It was already clear after the last World War that the old system with its unlimited freedom for states to pursue their own interests without regard for other states or for the welfare of the whole was not viable in the long run.' The political attempts at developing this system into something more coherent had failed, mainly because the internal economic policies of the constituent states had continued to be governed by a fierce economic individualism. The idea of a closer co-operation in economic policy between the various states had survived.

Germany, by the proclamation of the European *Großraumwirtschaft* has seized these ideas and placed them on a more realistic level than the high planes to which the fathers of the League of Nations so willingly surrendered themselves, and just for that reason the goals now to be pursued are more easily attainable. How this European greater space will be organized in its practical aspects it is still at the moment too early to decide. Today the war demands the concentration of all energies and the leading statesmen have only a little respite in which to tackle the practical aspects of the coming peace. So far only the principles have been laid down, but important clues may be derived from them. The first principle is that the war of all against all which formerly prevailed will be replaced by a planned order of European business life. An important precondition for that is the presence of a decisive power, an authority that can regulate the competing interests with regard to the welfare of the whole, and such an authority will be created in the form of a Germanic league. Within this bloc the branches of activity in the individual countries will be so developed as to serve in the best possible way the best interests of the whole. Since the policy of autarky is firmly founded in the wish to be independent of imports from other countries, a policy of autarky will be desired or necessary on the part of the individual states. In that respect the *Großraum* must be a totality in food and its processing and also in other ways as independent as possible of territories which it does not rule. The economic policy of the *Großraum* must therefore run in such a way that goods are to be produced where they may best and most cheaply be produced. This is the idea of absolute free trade which is realized within the European area under the direction of economic planning.[1]

[1] F.D. 5202/45, Rk., 'Probleme des Fischereigewerbes', 5 March 1943.

The weakness of this demonstration was that it was all too clear to the Norwegian fishing industry that on the practical level its exports were now confined to one market alone. The dangers of that situation, given the nature of that market, hardly compensated for a slight improvement in the quality of those exports and a higher price than in peacetime. Since the culminating failure of German policy was that the quantity of exports actually declined, the Norwegian fishing industry could regard itself as worse off in every respect. Nasjonal Samling did not regard the matter from so materialist a viewpoint.

Nasjonal Samling does not value an industry only on purely economic considerations. It is a known fact that we see the peasant estate as the basis of the life of our *Volk*—not only on the grounds that the peasant produces the food supply necessary for our life but because this vocation has the actual task of producing a healthy and strongly-living race. In the same way we do not evaluate the fishing industry solely according to its economic importance. We see it as a factor which educates the population and maintains and increases its health and its strength. The *Volk* which is directed to pursue a dangerous calling must necessarily also develop the capabilities and qualities to defy danger and overcome difficulties. The work on board fishing boats at sea demands and develops the capabilities and qualities which we especially esteem in Nordic peoples. These are courage and strength of performance as well as thoroughness, combined with a healthy power of decision. Anyone who glances at the population statistics in the statistical annuals can convince himself that the fisherfolk are a sound race. It emerges that the fisherfolk have the greatest number of children of all occupational groups. The poorest occupational group is here at the same time the richest, it is that one which gives the most to the nation.[1]

Whatever caused the high birth-rate among Norwegian fisherfolk it was not increasing incomes.[2] German policy actually worsened their position by reducing their sales. Of course this reduction was very much due to failures in other areas of the economy, to shortages of capital, for the number of freezing plants never reached the anticipated level, and to shortages of raw materials, such as oil for the boats, bait for the fishing, and salt for the curing; but the most disturbing factor was the warfare itself which imposed limitations on the areas which could be fished and the freedom with which fishing could take place. As the fish catch declined the German demand for a higher proportion of it rose. Far from the New European Order coming to depend on Norwegian fish to replace the extra-European protein which was no longer available, it was actually receiving less Norwegian fish by the end of the occupation. The fish supply became an indispensable part of German food supply and by 1944 Germany,

[1] F.D. 5202/45, Rk., 'Probleme des Fischereigewerbes', 5 March 1943.
[2] It is usually attributed in the literature to eating so much fish, a more scholarly fantasy.

not Europe, had acquired an absolute monopoly of Norway's main export.

The yield of each of the seasonal fisheries was apportioned in advance between Germany and Norway on a percentage basis and the same procedure used for the small-herring fishing. For example, in each of the economic years 1942–3, 1943–4, and 1944–5 the proportion of the fat-herring catch going to Germany was in each case 26 per cent of the total. Of the salted herring produced from fat herring 40 per cent were for export to Germany. The agreement for 1944–5 stipulated that if the total output of salted herring were over 100,000 hectolitres, 50 per cent of the extra output would be for Germany.[1] For small herring the proportion reserved for Germany in the year 1942–3 was 20·7 per cent.[2] If the total catch were greater than 1·4 million hectolitres this would rise to 22·5 per cent on the 'surplus'.[3] These proportions were unchanged the following year. The German quotas for other fish were much higher. In 1944 the quota for fish other than herring was 55 per cent.[3] In 1943 the Norwegian government made a determined effort to reduce the size of these quotas on the grounds that catches were so low that a greater absolute quantity of fish had to be made available to Norway. By claiming that the catches of the three previous years were exceptionally low the German negotiators insisted on maintaining the quotas. 'The experiences since 1941 have confirmed that the agreement on fixed quotas was completely correct and was in Germany's interests. The efforts on the Norwegian side to get away from fixed quotas and to undertake the division according to the actual landings will not therefore be considered.'[4]

The quota system was not in fact modified until October 1944. In that month a new system was introduced for the apportionment of the winter herring catch in the 1945 season, for the catch of other fish in the same season and for the division of the fish-meal output. In the first two instances Germany was at last obliged to admit the shrinkage of the fishery through allied action. The quotas would operate only up to a certain level of catch. Beyond that level a common stock was to be set aside which would be divided at the end of the season according to the respective needs of the two countries.[5] The same system was applied to fish-meal production except that there the idea of a fixed percentage quota was introduced for the first time on production up to a level of

[1] F.D. 5324/45, Rk., Abt. Fischwirtschaft, 'Vereinbarung über die Aufteilung der Fettheringsfänge 1942/43', 15 August 1942, etc.

[2] 15 May 1942 to 14 May 1943.

[3] F.D. 5324/45, Rk., Abt. Fischwirtschaft, 'Vereinbarung über die Verteilung von Kleinheringen 1942/43', 15 August 1942, etc.

[4] F.D. 5336/45, Rk., Abt. Fischwirtschaft, 'Material über die Aufteilung der Stor- und Vaarheringsfänge 1943/4 zwischen Deutschland und Norwegen', 16 September 1943.

[5] F.D. 5202/45, Rk., Abt. Ernährung und Landwirtschaft, 'Tätigkeitsbericht für die Zeit vom 1–31 Oktober 1944', 7 November 1944.

30,000 tons. The essential advantage of the quota system was that it was based on a putative catch. Germany's quota of the actual catch was therefore in many cases much higher.

Tables 58 to 61 show the results of the Norwegian fishing industry during the occupation. Estimates of the total fish catch are variable due to some doubt as to the quantities taken by the Wehrmacht and to confusion in the various 'statistical years' in which the Reichskommissariat tabulated

TABLE 58. *Total Catch and Number of Fishermen in Lofoten Fishery, 1934–44**

(tons)

Year	Total catch	Number of fishermen
1934	87,166	28,336
1935	55,098	28,772
1936	52,766	25,043
1937	82,493	23,559
1938	89,605	22,548
1939	115,318	25,803
1940	94,293	23,515
1941	85,067	14,984
1942	78,949	16,260
1943	57,863	16,170
1944	84,155	17,015
Average yearly catch, 1930–9	86,044	
Average yearly catch, 1941–4	76,508	

* F.D. 5336/45, Rk., Abt. Fischwirtschaft, 'Die Entwicklung der Produktion in den wichtigsten Fischereiarten'.

its information. Differences in reporting years are responsible for small discrepancies which occur between German figures and those of Statistisk Sentralbyrå. Tables 58 and 59 show that the two main hopes on which Germany's plans for an increase in the European fish supply were based, the winter-herring fishery and the Lofoten fishery, were most comprehensively deceived. The fall in the catch in the Lofoten fishery when compared to the average of the 1930s is small enough to be attributed to seasonal factors. But the extraordinary drop in the numbers taking part in this fishery in the first year of occupation should be noted. So great was the fall and so relatively successful the fishing in spite of it that it suggests that in that year seasonal factors were favourable rather than unfavourable. In 1935, for example, twice the number of fishermen employed caught only 60 per cent the quantity of fish. Only 1943 of the

occupation years seems to be clearly established as a bad season. The fall
in the catch of winter herring is too great to be accounted for by seasonal
factors alone.

TABLE 59. *Total Catch of Winter Herring, 1934–44**

(tons)

Year	Catch	
1934	110,771	
1935	401,012	
1936	483,227	
1937	318,981	
1938	496,428	
1939	412,426	
1940	409,220	(440,022)
1941	214,475	(230,062)
1942	253,404	(272,477)
1943	228,419	(245,612)
1944	300,085	(322,672)
Average yearly catch, 1930–9	(385,687)	
Average yearly catch, 1941–4	(267,706)	

* Statistisk Sentralbyrå, *Historisk statistikk*,
p. 175. Figures in brackets from F.D. 5336/45, Rk.,
Abt. Fischwirtschaft, 'Die Entwicklung der Produktion in den wichtigsten Fischereiarten . . .';
ibid., 'Gesamtfang in Norwegen', 22 March 1945.

Table 60 shows the fall in the total catch of fish during the occupation.
No single annual catch during the occupation approached the average
annual catches of the 1930s. The elements of this decline are easy to
identify. The increase in winter herring in 1944 was quite offset by the
catastrophic decline in small herring which set in in 1943 and in 1944
reduced the catch to one-quarter of its 1940 level. Had it not been for the
winter-herring catch of that year, 1944 would have been a disastrous fish
harvest. The fall in the catch of other fish reflects the same factors as the
fall in small-herring catches, the difficulties of supply, and the restraints
on activity of the smaller coastal fishermen.

The effects of this falling catch may be seen in Table 61. The production
of all fish products declined from the start of the occupation. The output
of herring meal in 1943 was one-third its level of 1940, of fish meal less
than one-third, of herring oil one-third, and of canned fish about 60 per
cent. All these products were of vital importance to German plans, all
were supposed to have their output increased.

To what extent was Germany able to increase the proportion of total
fish sold as fresh fish? In this instance considerable success met German

TABLE 60. *Norwegian Fish Catches, 1940–4**

(tons)

	1940	1941	1942	1943	1944
Fat herring	(47,828)	(76,876)	(55,652)	(51,341)	(14,296)
	44,283	71,509	51,756	47,767	13,296
Small herring	(298,467)	(233,375)	(156,474)	(114,364)	(74,456)
	277,575	217,039	145,520	106,447	69,365
Brisling	(14,689)	(4,826)	(15,561)	(12,414)	(8,201)
	12,486	4,102	13,227	10,552	7,005
Mackerel	(3,853)	(4,129)	(5,892)	(6,348)	(3,500)
	3,853	4,129	5,892	6,616	3,458
Total catch of North Norwegian fishery (cod, salmon, etc.)	(236,174)	(226,752)	(205,565)	(161,052)	(171,234)
Total catch of all fish including above	(1,081,091)	(810,896)	(754,883)	(629,184)	(641,073)
	1,023,846	772,111	718,364	611,587	618,087
Average annual total catch, 1930–9	(934,212)				
Average annual total catch, 1941–4	(709,009)				
	680,037				

* Statistisk Sentralbyrå, *Historisk statistikk 1968*, p. 175. Figures in parentheses from F.D. 5336/45, Rk., Abt. Fischwirtschaft, 'Die Entwicklung der Produktion in den wichtigsten Fischereiarten'; ibid., 'Gesamtfang in Norwegen', 22 March 1945.

TABLE 61. *Output of Fish-Processing Industries in Norway, 1938–43**

(tons)

	1938	1939	1940	1941	1942	1943
Herring meal	88,322	65,500	91,044	56,905	46,275	31,937
Fish meal	15,438	18,160	13,956	10,805	8,999	4,985
Herring oil†	282,311	208,091	258,307	129,950	100,364	80,296
Canned fish	43,280	43,073	39,622	34,385	27,077	24,429

* Statistisk Sentralbyrå, *Statistisk-økonomisk utsyn*, pp. 191 ff.
† Hectolitres.

efforts, or would have done so had the over-all yield of the fisheries not declined so much. The proportion of fresh fish to salted or dried fish increased in every year until 1944. In that year the freezing plants operated under special difficulties. The Hammerfest plant had to be dismantled in face of the Russian advance and partly reinstalled in Svolvaer in Lofoten while another part was repatriated to Germany. In the same year preparations were begun for dismantling the Øksfjord plant.[1] Until then, as may be seen from Table 62, the availability of this capital equipment effected a complete change in the marketing of the non-herring catch, a change which had been strongly advocated throughout the 1930s. The beneficial effects of this change should be seen in conjunction with the decline, in the same period, of the proportion of herrings processed by all methods.

TABLE 62. *Change in Proportion of the Codfish Catch and the Catch of the Lofoten Fishery Sold as Fresh Fish, 1938–44**

Year	Total cod fishery (%)			Lofoten fishery (%)		
	Proportion sold as fresh fish	Proportion sold as dried fish	Proportion sold as salted fish	Proportion sold as fresh fish	Proportion sold as dried fish	Proportion sold as salted fish
1938	5	42	53	..	..	..
1939	3	41	56	..	..	..
1940	21	30	46	10	40	46
1941	32	31	37	20	43	37
1942	47	20	33	37	25	38
1943	76	10	14	65	7	28
1944	64	12	24	54	14	29

* Statistisk Sentralbyrå, *Statistisk-økonomisk utsyn*. Figures for Lofoten fishery from F.D. 5336/45, Rk., Abt. Fischwirtschaft, 'Zahlen zur Lofotfischerei'.

The reasons for the decline in the total fish catch were related to general shortages in the economy as a whole. Since the fishing industry played so large a part in that economy and employed, if only on a part-time basis, so much of the labour force, it was inevitable that this should be so. The degree of importance of the various obstacles in the way of increasing the fish catch was indicated by Otte in a letter to the Four Year Plan Office in 1943.[2] The circumstances of the letter were Norway's failure to fulfil the fish-export quota imposed by the Four Year Plan Office in its decree of 15 August 1942, 500,000 tons fish products on a fresh-fish basis. At the time of the decree the Reichskommissariat had objected on the grounds that the quota was not fixed on a reasonable assessment of the previous two years' catches. In the second war economic year Norway had delivered 550,000 tons of fish products on a fresh-fish basis to Germany, but this had been due to the seizure as booty of large stocks of dried, salted, and canned fish and of fish meal.[3] In the war economic year ending in August 1942 exports to Germany on the same basis had been only 370,000 tons. In the

[1] F.D. 5217/45, Rk., Hauptabt. Volkswirtschaft, 'Bericht für die Zeit vom 1 bis 30 September 1944', 18 October 1944.
[2] F.D. 5336/45, Rk., Otte to Beauftragten für den Vierjahresplan, 'Lieferung der besetzten Gebiete', 15 September 1943.
[3] The war economic year ran from 1 September to 31 August.

war economic year 1942–3 it had been impossible even to approach the quota. Only 325,000 tons on a fresh-fish basis had been delivered, or 358,000 tons if Wehrmacht consumption is included.

The main reason for this shortfall was given as the general effect of Allied action, which closed fishing grounds, destroyed installations, and prevented the import of certain essential supplies. To this should be added the effect of combating that Allied action. Many rich coastal fishing grounds had to be reserved by the navy or by the artillery for defence purposes. Not only that but military demand had resulted in the confiscation of a significant part, and the more modern part, of the fleet of lorries serving the fishing industry. Where almost every coastal village took part in the industry and where the bulk of the catch was coastal the problem of collection and distribution was central to the organization of the whole industry. A shortage of lorries and a shortage of fuel for those that remained in use had an immediate effect on the willingness of peasants to take part in the fishery. The fuel shortage first began to have serious effects in autumn 1943 when it became impossible adequately to distribute the fish catch.[1]

After these effects, which were all due to the need to defend Norway, came the effect of specific bottlenecks due to the war economy. The general depreciation of the industry's fixed capital due to the low level of capital replacement was a force which operated on the fishing industry no less than on other industries. There were certain specific shortages which exaggerated this. One was the shortage of diesel oil and lubricating oil, which was, in its turn, exaggerated by the complicated distribution problem. Figures on the stock and allocation of diesel oil and the so-called 'solar oil' show that the problem was often not so much the inadequacy of the available quantity as the fluctuations in its supply.[2] Indeed, two-thirds of the fishing boats used had no motor, although these, of course, were the smaller craft for local inshore fishing.[3] For the 12,000 decked craft fitted with motors, supplies of fuel were especially short in 1941 and 1944. As the war continued, however, the narrowest bottleneck came in the supply of nets. Curiously enough the manufacturing capacity of the Norwegian fishing-net industry was very limited. So was that of the German industry. The biggest part of the imports before the war came from the United States and Britain. This bottleneck might be compared to one

[1] R.A., Rk. Diverse, Pakke 43, 'Ernährungslage Norwegens', 31 October 1942.

[2] F.D. 5336/45, Rk., Abt. Fischwirtschaft, 'Dieselözuteilung für die Fischerei in der Zeit vom August 1940–Dezember 1943', 23 March 1944; ibid., 'Solarölzuteilung für die Fischerei in der Zeit von August 1940 bis Dezember 1942', 30 January 1943; ibid., 'Dieselölzuteilung für die Fischerei in der Zeit vom August 1940–Dezember 1943', 23 March 1944.

[3] K. G. Wold, 'Ekonomisk och social utveckling', in W. Brandt et al., Norge ockuperat och fritt (Stockholm, 1943).

not mentioned by Otte, the growing scarcity of salt. The available stocks of salt declined by more than 50 per cent in the course of 1944 and the imports were about half the level necessary merely to maintain stocks.[1] To all these problems should be added the relatively poor food supply which rationing implied for the fishermen.

Such considerations were borne in mind to some extent when the total quota for Germany was reduced for the economic year 1943–4 to 400,000 tons on a fresh-fish basis. The true measure of the failure of German policy is best seen in Table 63. There it can be seen that there was no really significant increase in Norwegian fish exports to Germany after 1941. In some important respects there was a decline, in the export of herring meal and fish meal, for example, and in the export of canned fish. Compared to pre-war years of course the increase in the wartime years was extraordinary. But that was the main aim of German policy and when seen in that light the increase was obviously less than German planners must have hoped for. Not only that but it was achieved only by creating an absolute monopoly of Norway's exports. The geographical range of these exports in 1938 should be compared to their narrowing range during the war years when by 1944 there was no customer other than Germany. In 1943 there was still a tiny export of fresh herring and dried fish to Italy. When that ended, as far as the fish industry was concerned Norway became a colony of Germany.

The relative importance of Norway's fish supplies to Germany for German food supply may be judged from Table 63. One reason for the growth of the German monopoly was the severe drop in the German fish catch. A large part of Germany's fish supply came from deep-sea trawling operations. For this reason the German fishing industry was much more incommoded by the war than the Norwegian industry. Had Germany not had access to Norwegian exports, her total fish supply in the first four years of war would have been about one-third the peacetime level. With Norwegian supplies it was about two-thirds. After the invasion of Norway supply from that country was greater than the German domestic fish catch although its relative importance in respect of the total fish supply available to Germany declined after August 1941. As for fish meal German domestic production dropped even more than Norwegian. To extract as much as possible from Norway became a fundamental of policy, the more so as after August 1942 Norway was the sole foreign supplier. In the economic year 1942–3 supply from Norway, however meagre compared to its pre-war level, was twice German domestic production. One part of the failure of the agricultural plans for Norway may therefore be attributed to the low catches of fish in wartime Germany. Beginning with a

[1] F.D. 5303/45, Rk., Abt. Fischwirtschaft, 'Tätigkeitsberichte', November 1943 to January 1945.

TABLE 63. *Exports of Fish and Fish Products from Norway by Weight and Destination, 1938–44**

(tons)

	1938	1939	1940	1941	1942	1943	1944
Fresh fish (not herring)							
Germany	4,986	11,739	29,380	31,467	33,925	31,587	32,619
Belgium	1,115	1,206	418	24	..	..	..
France	882	928	24	..	..	..	..
Italy	591	362	..	1,184	653	..	..
Netherlands	714	612	126	214	..	..	..
Sweden	2,934	2,833	3,930	1,091	1,059	..	..
Switzerland	337	241	393	564	192	8	7
United Kingdom	11,480	13,961	9,549	..	..	..	..
Others	730	693	514	799	269	47	..
Fresh herring							
Germany	64,260	87,776	82,278	69,542	80,018	84,487	85,835
Belgium	1,498	1,855	830	..	377	81	..
Bohemia-Moravia	3,090	1,863	556	..	..	..	..
France	1,129	894	16	..	..	..	..
Italy	..	..	231	904	554	1,400	174
Poland	3,465	4,347	..	..	..	..	..
Sweden	2,404	2,898	3,559	314	155	..	..
United Kingdom	18,773	19,965	4,101	..	..	..	..
Others	1,497	1,876	2,011	25	16	55	6
Salt herring							
Germany	5,841	12,455	25,080	37,419	44,675	41,577	54,346
Denmark	955	1,197	1,804	346	..	..	..
France	2,138	1,680	720	1	..	..	..
Netherlands	1,048	1,020	1,352	1	..	20	..
Poland	6,239	4,107	353	..	..	..	..
Sweden	9,281	11,268	9,448	10,384	1,735	..	..
United States	3,138	3,149	993	..	..	..	..
Others	4,945	3,662	1,851	1,280	290	36	..
Salt fish (not herring)							
Germany	5	13	3,673	10,441	12,627	3,041	4,381
France	..	..	6,511	..	211	..	..
Italy	3,356	2,350	558	331	..	..	..
Sweden	737	766	1,076	1,185	558	..	..
Others	1,789	7,632	3,745	549	301	27	..
Dried fish							
Germany	441	955	12,809	15,107	4,314	1,489	1,834
Argentina	2,191	3,543	197	..	..	..	..
Brazil	517	1,648	439	..	..	..	..
Cuba	2,283	2,491	495	..	..	..	..
Finland	470	397	313	501	104	..	..
Italy	12,601	9,706	4,436	16,826	706	485	..
Sweden	1,573	1,710	1,903	596	305	47	..
United States	792	990	97	..	..	..	..
West Africa	9,525	6,840	341	..	..	..	..
Others	4,783	4,273	1,841	106	20	24	..

TABLE 63 (cont.)

	1938	1939	1940	1941	1942	1943	1944
Canned fish							
Germany	488	1,436	23,028	18,948	19,084	11,220	16,512
France	1,221	177	43	..	1	..	..
United Kingdom	7,389	11,546	3,514	..	..	..	..
United States	11,261	16,235	1,848	..	..	..	..
Herring and fish meal							
Germany	61,286	36,470	37,523	31,494	18,380	13,261	20,233
Belgium	1,555	857	565	..	..	..	..
Czechoslovakia	3,113	1,030	30	..	..	..	..
Netherlands	4,724	5,324	9,218	..	..	..	..
Switzerland	1,437	1,226	600	..	..	..	..
United Kingdom	3,143	3,540	462	..	..	..	..
Others	3,365	4,623	51	..	..	..	..

* Statistisk Sentralbyrå, *Statistisk-økonomisk utsyn.*

TABLE 64. *Supply of Fish and Fish Products in Germany, September 1938 to August 1943**

(tons)

	1 Sept. 1938 to 31 Aug. 1939	1 Sept. 1939 to 31 Aug. 1940	1 Sept. 1940 to 31 Aug. 1941	1 Sept. 1941 to 31 Aug. 1942	1 Sept. 1942 to 31 Aug. 1943
(a) Fish and fish products for human consumption					
German production	592,757	184,350	133,476	150,672	152,000‡
Imports from Norway	99,670	139,846	307,143	264,702	210,000†
Imports from Denmark	21,239	52,920	96,058	100,341	97,000†
Imports from other countries	164,963	66,621	36,194	50,347	93,000
Total imports	285,972	259,387	439,395	415,390	400,000†
Total supply	878,729	443,737	572,871	566,062	552,000
(b) Fish meal					
German production	80,314	10,454	7,433	7,778	7,125‡
(On raw material basis)	(401,570)	(52,270)	(37,165)	(38,890)	(35,625)
Imports from Norway	42,930	13,460	50,122	21,368	14,296†
Imports from other countries	19,777	3,848	287	498	..
Total imports	62,707	17,308	50,409	21,866	14,296†
(On raw material basis)	(313,535)	(86,540)	(252,045)	(109,330)	(71,480)
Total supply	143,021	27,762	57,842	29,644	21,421

* F.D. 5336/45, Rk., Abt. Fischwirtschaft, 'Seefischanfall (Produktion und Einfuhr) in dem letzten Friedensjahr und ersten bis vierten Kriegsjahr'; F.D. 5203/45, Rk., Abt. Fischwirtschaft, 'Einfuhr von Seefischen und Seefischerzeugnissen nach Deutschland (auf Rohstoffbasis)'.
† Figure for July and August 1943 estimated.
‡ Figure for August 1943 estimated.

programme of encouraging and extending the use of fish meal as fodder in Norway, Germany ended with a programme of extracting as much fish meal as possible from Norway for her own use. As for Norway, her fish exports to Germany were a serious drain on her food resources, already inadequate. But for the fish exports Norway would have had enough fats and protein to sustain the food rations at an adequate long-term level.

Taken all in all, German policy produced many such contradictions. Its one solitary success was in increasing the proportion of fish marketed as fresh fish. But even that success was of qualified value for Norway. The results of German policy were rather more satisfactory from a narrowly German point of view than from the point of view of the *Großraum-wirtschaft* and certainly than from the Norwegian point of view. Exploitation of the Norwegian fishing industry did prevent an acute shortage of fish in Germany. But this result was far short of the wide European expectations of the German planners.

X

THE CLOSING STAGE

MOST studies of German occupation policy in the Second World War, especially those which have dealt with particular aspects of that policy, have devoted more space to the later years of those occupations. This is not unreasonable, for to arrive at a considered judgement of German policy it has to be seen as a whole. Both in the political and economic field the grim developments associated with the closing years of the Third Reich need to be set against the imposing plans and propaganda of its spokesmen. There are other reasons also why studies have concentrated on the later years. It was in those years that the political oppositions emerged which were in most cases to form the Europe which has existed since 1945. This was no less true in the economic than the political field.

As far as German economic policy alone is concerned there is a lot more documentary evidence dealing with the economies of occupied territories after 1942 than before that date. This is mainly due to the internal changes in the administration of the German economy. The failure of the Blitzkrieg strategy necessitated a quite different economic approach to the war on Germany's part. For the first time it was necessary to organize the domestic war economy on the basis of a total mobilization. It became clear that the war was a struggle between the productive resources of massive industrial powers in which very few of the advantages were on Germany's side. This moment of truth in Germany arrived in the winter of 1941–2 and from January 1942 the work of reorganization and centralization of the domestic economy began in earnest.[1] It was inevitable that Germany should seek to neutralize the enormous productive resources of her opponents by drawing in a much more systematic way on the resources of the conquered territories.

The work of reorganizing the German economy itself to meet the new strategic basis of the war was sufficiently complicated for the effect of this development on the occupied areas not to be felt immediately. There were a large number of unutilized reserves available domestically to the German government in the first instance. The serious impact of these changes did not occur outside the frontier of the Reich until autumn 1942. From that time onwards the volume of documentation on economic policy becomes much greater. The economic administration both of

[1] A. S. Milward, 'The End of the Blitzkrieg', in *Economic History Review*, vol. xvi, no. 3 (1964).

Germany and the occupied territories became more efficient because it had to. The amount of statistical information collected became much greater and the vague ideas of planning which had existed in 1940 were replaced by more precise concepts of 'programmes' devised to fit in with reality rather than change it. As a consequence it is easier to say more about the later period of the occupations. But for the economic historian this later period is the less interesting. It is much harder to grasp what the ambitions of National Socialist planners were for they were temporarily in abeyance.

What in fact happened in Germany and abroad, on the economic front, was that broader plans for general reconstruction were sacrificed to the urgent and immediate task of fighting the war. In Norway, where very ambitious plans had existed, this change was bound to affect every aspect of economic policy. The instrument of the change of policy was the Ministry of Armaments and Munitions, later to become the Ministry of War Production. Its approach to economic questions was much more technical and detailed than that of the Four Year Plan Office, the Ministry of Food and Agriculture, the Reichs Labour Front, and the other agencies which had been mainly responsible for the formulation of plans for Norway. Ideological questions were pushed into the background and questions of production took their place. The Ministry of Munitions approached the Norwegian economy without any consideration of Norway's future racial and spiritual contribution to the New Europe but merely from the standpoint of an economic administrator trying to organize a war economy capable of resisting the economic strength of the Allies. 'What contribution can Norway make to increasing production in Germany?' was the first question they asked.

Thus, confining the issues within a narrow compass, it is not surprising that they should have found it a fairly simple matter to determine a strict list of priorities. As a part of the Nordic *Großraumwirtschaft* Norway had seemed of great importance to fascist theorists. Racially pure, economically advanced, strategically vital, sufficiently small to be digested, it sprang to the forefront of National Socialist policy. But once the occupied territories were arranged solely in terms of the contribution they could make to the German war effort Norway sank into unimportance. What raw materials and manufactured goods could Norway contribute to Germany's war effort? What was the minimum level of German investment and administrative effort necessary to secure this contribution? Such an approach rejected every assumption of the original plans for the Norwegian economy and was designed to rewrite them on a new basis. Combined with short-term planning dealing with the objective economic situation rather than creating a distant objective it meant that Norway sank to the economic status of a minor, although troublesome, administrative problem.

Of course the planned German investment in Norway had been far greater than the actual investment which took place. The impossibility of German plans while the war continued had been amply demonstrated by the financial discussions in autumn 1940. The stricter planning methods of the Ministry of Armaments could accordingly not be said to have greatly reduced the volume of that investment. Their immediate effect was twofold. Firstly, it was to change completely the goals at which German economic policy in Norway was aiming. Secondly, it was to make the exploitation of Norway in a narrowly defined area much more efficient and to disassociate this exploitation as far as possible from any corresponding contribution from the German side.

Once questions of European racial and economic organization were pushed into the background by questions of fighting the war on a sufficiently broad economic base it was inevitable that Norway should slip from an important position in German thinking to an utterly unimportant one. The new priorities acknowledged Norway for what she was, the supplier of a small range of valuable raw materials in relatively small quantities. As for the Germanic nature of her population and the Viking spirit of her society they were, after summer 1942, the subject-matter of Nasjonal Samling pamphlets but not the basis for German economic policy. That such an attitude was accepted by the National Socialist party was the price they paid for trying to save their revolution. Nasjonal Samling were not content with such a compromise. And why should they have been? Indeed, it was only accepted most reluctantly by the National Socialist party, and in summer 1944 the power of the Ministry of Armaments declined as the wider aims of the fascist revolution were again reasserted. But this reassertion had no impact on economic policy in Norway. It had simply become too unimportant a part of the New Order.

The basis of the new policies for the Norwegian economy was laid by *Planungsamt*, a committee serving the Central Planning Committee of the Four Year Plan and Ministry of Munitions. The Central Planning Committee (*Zentrale Planung*), a powerful triumvirate of Speer, the Minister of Munitions, Milch, of the Air Force, and Körner of the Four Year Plan, was set up in April 1942. Its function was to control the allocation of all raw materials within the German war economy. This function gave it relatively greater importance in the case of the smaller occupied economies whose importance to Germany was mainly as raw material suppliers. The history of the Ministry of Munitions is one of its development into a genuine Ministry of War Production, which title it eventually assumed, enabling it to control all aspects of economic life in occupied lands. In 1942, however, it was still a ministry, which, although having far greater powers than previous economic ministries, had still to operate within certain limits. Since the foundation of its power to centralize economic decisions lay in its absolute control over raw-material supplies it is all the more understandable that it should have taken a ruthless view on the Norwegian issue. Those aspects of Norwegian policy which did not come within its purview, social policy, road building, propaganda, and so on, were supported after 1942 by ministries which could not secure resources to carry them out because such resources came increasingly under the control of the Ministry of Munitions. The programme for which resources were available was the programme to obtain materials from Norway for the German armament industry.

It was this programme which was drawn up by *Planungsamt*. Hence it had many connections with that part of the economic programme for Norway which had been previously designed in the Reichs Economic Ministry. That ministry had had a general supervision until April 1942 over the availability of raw materials and a specific supervision over their importing. Its more general powers had been weakened by the semi-independent economic position of the three main branches of the Armed Forces, by the powers over the domestic economy of the Four Year Plan Office and, to a smaller extent, by the Ministry of Munitions in its earlier phase of existence. *Planungsamt*, when it was created to serve the Central Planning Committee, was in fact largely staffed by officials from the Reichs Economic Ministry. Its head, Hans Kehrl, continued to perform the same duties as he had performed in the Reichs Economic Ministry, but he was now backed with far greater powers and with a larger planning staff. Kehrl's had been one of the few voices advocating a more realistic approach to the Norwegian question in the early months of occupation.

Although the changes brought about by the development of the Ministry of Munitions might therefore seem in some respects to be less complete than on the surface they appeared, and although *Planungsamt* might seem the old Reichs Economic Ministry writ large, the measure of the changes which did take place can be taken in two ways. Firstly, after the creation of the Central Planning Committee, the raw materials delivery programmes from Norway were defined in a strict order of priority and this order of priority determined the allocation of resources to these programmes within the Norwegian economy. There was therefore much more likelihood that these programmes would be carried out. They became *the* object of economic policy in Norway, not one of its many objects. Secondly, and for this very reason, the demands made on Norwegian resources by these programmes increased. This may be seen in the changes effected in turning the Reichs Economic Ministry's programme in 1942 into the 'Production and Delivery Programme' of the Ministry of Munitions. The new programme was brought into being by Speer's order to von Hanneken, Under-Secretary of State in the Reichs Economic Ministry, on 30 June 1942. It was then implemented by discussions between the Reichs

Economic Ministry and the Reichskommissariat which were concluded on 28 August. The programme itself ran from 1 September 1942 to 31 August 1943.[1] There already existed such a programme of deliveries sketched out by the Reichs Economic Ministry as a continuation of its previous year's programme. The details of this programme may be seen in Table 65.

TABLE 65. *Reichs Economic Ministry's Delivery Programme for Norway, July 1942**

(tons)

Silicon	24,000
Molybdenum	420
Copper	17,400
Nitrogen	84,000
Aluminium	24,000
Silicon carbide	3,000
Ferrochrome	17,400
Zinc	16,800
Nickel	1,200
Carbide	75,000
Vanadium-pig-iron	4,200
Graphite	900
Sulphur	To be maintained

* F.D. 5325/45, Rk., Hauptabt. Volks-wirtschaft, 'Bericht für die Zeit vom 1 bis 15 Juli., 1942', 18 July 1942.

The Ministry of Munitions was not satisfied with the details of this programme as soon as *Planungsamt* came to consider them. In June they indicated their apprehensions over the supply of ferrosilicon. A standstill in the works processing silicon in Norway would have led to a drop of about 800,000 tons a month in the production of pig-iron in the Reich.[2] Because of this the Ministry of Munitions insisted on special arrangements being made for the supply of coal and coke to these works. This was symptomatic of the general unease about the state of the Norwegian economy. The transport difficulties due to the severe winter and the coal shortages which began to appear combined with the constant demands of the Wehrmacht to reduce the volume of output in Norway for export to Germany. The alarm about the production of ferrosilicon indicated how much more precise Germany's interests in Norwegian production were becoming. After all the programme for aluminium deliveries was far below the earlier proposed level and in view of the political agitation over the aluminium programme it might have been thought that the Ministry

[1] F.D. 5359/45, Rk., Abt. Ausfuhrwirtschaft und Bergbau, 'Bericht über die Durch-führung der mit dem Reich für die Zeit vom 1 September 1942 bis zum 31 August 1943 vereinbarten Produktionen und Lieferungen norwegischer Roh- und Grundstoffe'.

[2] F.D. 5325/45, Rk., Hauptabt. Volkswirtschaft, 'Bericht für die Zeit vom 1 bis 15 Juni 1942', 17 June 1942.

of Munitions would give priority to this. However, in the programme beginning in September ferrosilicon deliveries from Norway were accorded a degree of priority exceeded only by those of molybdenum, of which commodity Norway was Germany's sole supplier. Aluminium deliveries received only fifth priority. The relative size of the new programmes and their success can be seen in Table 66. The success seems to have been related to the degree of priority. In the first category of priority only the aluminium programme was conspicuously unsuccessful, although the results in copper mining were certainly disappointing. The silico-manganese programme was accorded priority only in April 1943. The reasons for the failure of the aluminium programme have been discussed elsewhere. They might be briefly summarized by citing the shortage of alumina due to the failure of deliveries from France and Germany and the damage done to the Glomfjord works by British troops in the raid of 21 September 1942. The advantages brought by such strict priority grading could be seen in the case of the Knaben molybdenum mine. Although it was put out of action by bombing raids on 3 March and did not resume production until 30 May nor full production until August, its output was greater than in the twelve months before the new delivery programme.

The commodities in the second category of priority tell a different story. The failure to improve significantly on the output and deliveries of ferro-chrome can be attributed to supply problems. Its output depended on the import of chromium ore from Germany to be processed by the Norwegian electro-metallurgical industry. Because of the failure of the raw material supply, deliveries of the processed material did not begin until December. The failure to achieve the targets for carbide production and for sulphur production was in each case due to a shortage of raw material, in the first case coal and in the second case quartz.

At the meeting of the Central Planning Committee on 30 July 1943 at which Terboven was present it was recognized that the supply of coal was the determining factor in implementing the Norwegian programmes and that in future planning some account had to be taken of the variations in this supply.[1] The general discussions on the programme between Otte and Kehrl and Schieber of Planungsamt were supplemented by a meeting between Otte and Körner, thus bringing the question directly to the attention of one of the members of the Central Planning Committee.[2] Körner promised to bring pressure to bear on the Reichs Coal Commissar to increase the coal quota to Norway so that industries not covered by the

---

[1] F.D. 3038/49, Section II, Sc. 246, Rm.f.B.u.M., 'Ergebnisse der 46 Sitzung der Zentralen Planung am 30 Juli 1943', 4 August 1943.

[2] F.D. 5359/45, Rk., Abt. Ausfuhrwirtschaft und Bergbau, 'Vermerk über das Ergebnis der Besprechung zwischen Herrn Staatssekretär Körner und Herrn Senator Otte. Betr: den norwegischen Produktions- und Lieferplan 1943/44 vom 7 August 1943', 11 August 1943.

production quotas, such as the cement industry, would still receive a satisfactory supply. Otte also made certain requests to which Körner acceded. One was that the production target for aluminium be reduced as

TABLE 66. *Delivery Programme for the Norwegian Economy, 1 September 1942 to 31 August 1943**

(tons)

Order of priority	Commodity	Previous year's deliveries (1 Sept. 1941 to 31 Aug. 1942)	German demand 1 Sept. 1942 to 31 Aug. 1943	Actual deliveries 1 Sept. 1942 to 31 Aug. 1943
(a) First category of priority				
1	Molybdenum ore	318·97	Maximum possible	392·56
2	Ferrosilicon	29,075	42,000	42,404
3†	Silico-manganese	8,392	4,200§	2,020†, §
4	Copper	14,219‡, §	17,400‡, §	15,406‡, §
5	Aluminium	14,415	30,000	16,625
6	Nitrogen	60,367	70,000§	80,235§
7	Silicon carbide	2,382	3,000	3,663
(b) Second category of priority				
8	Ferrochrome	3,179	10,400	4,400
9	Zinc	6,825	16,800§	15,558§
10	Nickel	884	850	875
11	Carbide	54,464	75,000§	60,933§
12	Pyrites	759,685	805,000	877,296
13	Sulphur	72,219	110,000§	85,465§
14	Graphite	2,404	4,500	2,761
(c) Third category of priority				
15	Vanadium-pig-iron	..	..	..
16	Cellulose for artificial fibre	..	84,000	41,698
17	Paper and cardboard	..	42,000	12,634

* F.D. 5359/45, Rk., Abt. Ausfuhrwirtschaft und Bergbau, 'Bericht über die Durchführung der mit dem Reich für die Zeit vom 1 September 1942 bis zum 31 August 1943 vereinbarten Produktionen und Lieferungen norwegischer Roh- und Grundstoffe'.
    † Priority ordered only in April 1943, production figure for April 1943 to August 1943.
    ‡ Cu-content.
    § Production figures.

the shortage of alumina was such that it was not worth while reopening the Glomfjord works. Another was that the Wehrmacht and the Organization Todt be forced to release all the skilled workers they were employing on construction sites so they might be available to Norwegian industry. Most importantly Otte asked that the Reichskommissariat be allowed to vary the order of priority in certain months if coal deliveries proved erratic.

The programme designed to operate from 1 September 1943 showed important increases of demand over the previous programme. There were also important changes of priority. For instance, iron ore was included in the programme for the first time and the importance of the Norwegian metallurgical industries was stressed more strongly. Everything, however, depended on the coal supply. To acknowledge this five separate targets were set for each commodity on the priority programme. The maximum target would apply if coal allocation was 165,000 tons monthly, the minimum target if it was 120,000 tons. There were three intermediate stages. The number of commodities on the list was increased to twenty-five.

Whether such optimism was justified by the results of the previous twelve-month programme was no longer a very relevant consideration. Germany was approaching an economic position where she had to have raw materials and semi-manufactures for her armaments industry to the maximum possible amount. The order of priorities in the September 1943 programme is more revealing than the planned production and delivery figures. The previous twelve months had been a period when the availability of coal in the Norwegian economy had been relatively greater than in other periods. This was itself due to the efforts at rationalization made by the Speer Ministry. But the size of stocks had not been built up to the desired level and any further interruption of coal supply would inevitably have its effect on this programme. In addition the loss of territory to the Allies and the increasing disturbance caused by Allied actions were also all too likely to create the same difficulties that had beset the previous programme, and were likely to do so to a much greater degree.

All this was realized by the Speer Ministry. But the situation demanded more goods in greater quantities and considerations of future difficulties had to be set aside. This was reflected in the greater priority given to ferrous-alloy production. Here was an industry which became so valuable a part of Germany's war economy, or, as the Speer Ministry preferred to call it, 'The European war economy', that it justified the transport of ore to Norway and the return transport of metal ingots for further processing in Germany in spite of the extreme shortage of shipping space. Similarly, the production of vanadium-pig-iron in Norway required the import of pig-iron ingots from Germany to be processed in Norway and then returned to Germany.[1]

The first six months of the operation of the new programme revealed how serious the difficulties were. The average monthly total of arrivals of coal in Norway between the inception of the new programme in September 1943 and the end of February 1944 was 124,034 tons. That is to say that coal arrivals were only such as to make available a sufficient coal quota for

[1] F.D. 5359/45, Rk., Abt. Ausfuhrwirtschaft und Bergbau, 'Dienststellenleitertagung', 4 August 1943.

TABLE 67. *Delivery Programme for the Norwegian Economy, 1 September 1943 to 31 August 1944**

Order of priority	Commodity	Maximum target	Minimum target
(a) First category of priority			
1	Molybdenum ore	1,000	1,000
2	Ferrochrome	7,200	7,200
3	Refined manganese	2,400	2,400
4	Ferrosilicon	40,000	14,600
5	Magnesium	Maximum possible	
6	Manganese	1,080	540
7	Silico-manganese	4,200	2,100
8	Silicon carbide	3,200	3,200
9	Copper	15,000†	15,000†
10	Iron ore (excluding Narvik and Sydvaranger)	250,000	250,000
11	Aluminium	30,000†	30,000†
11a	Alumina	35,000†	35,000†
12	Nitrogen	72,000†	70,000
13	Pyrites	805,000	805,000
14	Zinc	19,200†	16,800†
14a	Cadmium	11	..
15	Sulphur	110,000†	110,000†
(b) Second category of priority			
16	Graphite	3,600	3,600
17	Split mica	200	200
18	Whole mica	50	50
19	Vanadium-pig-iron	6,200	6,200
20	Electro-steel	Quantity to be exchanged for Thomas-steel	
21	Nickel	1,000	750
22	Carbide	65,000	40,000
(c) Third category of priority			
23	Cellulose for artificial fibre	42,000	0
24	Wood pulp (50% wet)	40,000	40,000
25	Paper	35,000	0

* F.D. 3043/49, Section VII, Sc. 194, Rk., Abt. Ausfuhrwirt-schaft und Bergbau, 'Produktion und Lieferung von Roh- und Grundstoffen von Norwegen nach Deutschland in der Zeit vom 1 September 1943 bis 31 August 1944'.
† Production figure.

the minimum target to be selected in the case of each industry in the pro-gramme. Arrivals in January 1944 had been such as to cause an almost general reduction in all aspects of Norwegian production. Otte asked

Speer to bring the matter to the Führer's attention as a threat to the war economy.[1] In fact, as Terboven's letter of 2 February to Speer makes clear, the Reichskommissariat had deliberately reduced its stocks of coal below the danger level determined by the Speer Ministry so that coal allocations of the right size could continue to be made to industries in the first and second categories of priority in the new programmes.[2] Only when the level of imports in January fell to so inadequate a level were cuts made in the quotas to industries in the priority programmes. To begin with the third category of priority, the pulp, paper, and cellulose industries, had their supply completely stopped. In the second category of priority the production target of vanadium-pig-iron was reduced by 1,400 tons. In the first category of priority the output of ferrosilicon was cut by 400 tons, the Nordag alumina plant was kept idle, and the production target for sulphur cut by 2,300 tons.[2] The only industry outside the production programmes to retain its coal quota was the cement industry.

Paradoxically the coal-supply situation was made easier by other difficulties in carrying out the production programmes. Bombing raids on 24 July 1943 closed down the Herøen magnesium works thus setting free 10,000 tons of coal for use elsewhere.[3] The north Norway fishery in autumn was so bad that the coal quota for processing the fish was substantially reduced and the coal reallocated. Shortages of other materials were more absolute. Chrome deliveries from Germany were insufficient to maintain ferrochrome production. Alumina imports were too low to achieve a production of 30,000 tons of aluminium. Zinc ore deliveries from Germany were too low to sustain the required production of zinc. The production of refined manganese which had been awarded priority in the new programme depended on the supply of electrodes from the Siemens factories in Berlin. These electrodes did not arrive as planned in October 1943 but in March 1944. In addition Allied action or sabotage were responsible for failures to reach targets in the production of molybdenum ore, silicon, carbide, alumina, and nitrogen. The Knaben mine was closed from 16 November 1943 to 3 February 1944 by air attack. At the end of March 1944 the aluminium production programme was 5,000 tons behind schedule. Finally, 21,500 tons were produced instead of 30,000.[4] Alumina production reached 20,096 tons instead of 35,000, nitrogen production 42,013 tons instead of 72,000, and copper production 11,447 tons instead of 15,000.

---

[1] R.A., Rk. Diverse, Pakke 17, Otte to Speer, 5 January 1944.

[2] F.D. 5359/45, Terboven to Speer, 2 February 1944.

[3] F.D. 3043/49, Section VII, Sc. 194, Rk., Abt Ausfuhrwirtschaft und Bergbau, 'Bericht über das Ergebnis der ersten sechs Monate des mit dem Reich für die Zeit vom 1.9.1943 bis zum 31.8.1944 vereinbarten Produktions- und Lieferprogramm', 11 April 1944.

[4] F.D. 5300/45, Rk., Abt. Ausfuhrwirtschaft und Bergbau, 'Produktions- und Lieferprogramm'.

Outside the first category of priority the general level of achievement was much lower.

In August the programmes were extended on a new basis for four months until the end of 1944. The order of priorities was not changed, and although a great deal of doubt must have prevailed about the wood-product industries in the third category, they also were included in the programme. In any case the fundamental order of priorities had been decided by the Führer order of 13 July 1944 which stipulated that the economies of occupied territories should be used for the armaments economy only.[1] The details of the programme are not worth reciting since it coincided with the acute period of coal and other raw material shortages. The actual details of the plan were more sophisticated than with previous programmes, whatever may be thought about the sophistication of continuing to plan on so general a basis at such a time.[2]

In fact plans of this kind were also drawn up for 1945 although whether they were intended to have any significance other than providing monthly target figures is difficult to tell. Even in February 1945 the effect of maintaining such strict priorities was that Norway was continuing to provide substantial quantities of material under these programmes for the German economy. In the first two months of 1945, 3,509 tons of ferrosilicon were delivered—well up to the target levels of 1944—56,448 tons of pyrites, 8,036 tons of sulphur, and 1,727 tons of nitrogen.[3] All the commodities having a priority grading continued to be delivered although many, such as zinc, in far smaller quantities than intended. The Norwegian economy continued to produce when production in the German economy was coming to a standstill. Indeed, where Norway stopped producing that was mainly due to deficiencies in supply from Germany.

Before turning to other aspects of the control of the Ministry of Munitions over Norwegian production it may help to give a more comprehensive view of the effectiveness of their narrow approach to the whole problem if some general survey of the volume of production of the industries covered by these programmes is given. The relative success of the first production programme of the new system may be judged from Table 66. Table 68 provides an over-all picture. If the failure to achieve the production targets in 1944 seems very marked it should be borne in mind that at the end of the second programme in August 1944 it was less marked and that

---

[1] R.A., Rk. Diverse, Pakke 11, Abt. Binnenwirtschaft, Gruppe Kohle, 'Einsatz der norwegischen Rüstungswirtschaft für Reichsinteresse', 4 November 1944.

[2] F.D. 5359/45, Rk., Abt. Ausfuhrwirtschaft und Bergbau, 'Neuplanung Produktions-u. Lieferprogramm für die Monate Sept.–Dez. 1944', 23 August 1944; ibid., 'Kommentar zum Produktions- und Lieferprogramm September bis Dezember 1944', 21 August 1944.

[3] F.D. 5217/45, Rk., Hauptabt. Volkswirtschaft, 'Bericht für die Zeit vom 1 bis 28 Februar 1945', Anlage I, 14 March 1945.

deliveries were still being maintained with a certain degree of success even at the end of February 1945. It must be admitted that this relative success did not justify the optimism in forming the entries in the 1945 column.

TABLE 68. *Output of Certain Raw Materials in Norway, 1942–4**

(tons)

Commodity	Output 1942	Output 1943	Planned output 1944	Actual output 1944	Planned output 1945
Iron ore†	347,458 (284,498)	217,783 (219,000)	226,664‡	266,238 (264,426)	387,900
Pyrites	827,442 (822,207)	809,270 (808,779)	793,666§	749,928 (750,405)	972,400
Copper ore (concentrate)	21,818 (22,238)	20,828 (21,216)	..	20,265 (20,260)	25,325
Lead ore (concentrate)	49	181	..	196	286
Nickel ore (concentrate)	21,561 (21,837)	16,093 (15,679)	..	14,000 (13,961)	12,880
Molybdenum ore (concentrate)	615·4	379·3	847·0	420·6	419
Wolfram ore	6·4	..	..	4·28	12
Mica	502	532	210‡	636	..
Quartz	105,000	238,057	..	198,500	..
Graphite	2,948	3,178	3,600	3,546	4,625

* F.D. 5217/45, Rk., Hauptabt. Volkswirtschaft, 'Bericht für die Zeit vom 1 bis 28 Februar 1945', 14 March 1945; F.D. 5365/45, Rk., Abt. Ausfuhrwirtschaft und Bergbau, 'Produktion und Lieferung in der Zeit vom 1 Jan.–31 Dez. 44'. Figures in parentheses from Statistisk Sentralbyrå, *Historisk statistikk 1968*, p. 221.
† Excluding Sydvaranger.
‡ Figure for delivery to Germany.
§ Delivery figure for unprocessed pyrites plus production figures for processed pyrites.

In some occupied economies, particularly in France and the General-Government of Poland, there was a further radical change of policy in autumn 1943 associated with the Ministry of Munitions and its transformation at that period into the Ministry of War Production. That change was the attempt to produce consumer goods for German purposes in the occupied territories so that their production might be reduced in Germany thus setting manufacturing capacity free for a still greater concentration of the German effort on producers' goods and armaments. Such a change required a fundamental redirection of economic policy in France and raised serious questions as to the basic nature of the New Order. The amount of consumer goods which the Norwegian economy could provide was not such as to cause these policy changes to have any great effect there. Norway was operated as a colony until the end of the war because its economy, in relation to that of the *Großraumwirtschaft*, was in fact colonial while the volume and nature of demand associated with the war persisted.

There were programmes for the manufacture of consumer goods in Norway, but the quantities, by the side of those contracted for and supplied in France, were very small. The Department for the Internal Economy recorded in February 1944 that, 'in agreement with the Ministry for Armaments and War Production, Norwegian industry shall be employed to a far greater extent than previously on contracts dispersed from the Reich. By that means branches of industry are to be drawn in which have hitherto worked only for the internal market.'[1] Already in that month contracts were being placed with the Norwegian furniture industry.

These contracts were finally settled in February. Norway was to manufacture 10,000 sets of bedroom furniture and 3,000 sideboards for the reconstitution of bomb-damage in Germany. In the same month contracts for export to Germany were awarded to all three Norwegian electric light-bulb manufacturers.[2] In May similar contracts were placed for the manufacture of pottery.[3] In July contracts were placed for bicycles to be supplied to the Wehrmacht.[4] The number of bicycles to be produced was 6,500. The pottery contracts stipulated quantities of 13,000 cups, 13,000 saucers, and 19,000 plates monthly.

At the outset these contracts were fulfilled. In July 20,000 plates and 21,000 cups were exported to Germany. But the shortages of raw materials which operated on the priority delivery programmes were bound to operate with equal or greater force on these contracts for consumer goods while they remained merely an addition to previous economic policy rather than a basic change in that policy. In May 1944 the Reichskommissariat had the greatest difficulty in placing a second round of contracts for furniture because the manufacturers did not have the necessary raw materials. A contract placed in July for 2 million electric light-bulbs could not be begun because the necessary raw materials had to be supplied from Germany. This diversion of effort in Norway does not appear to have had any effect on the operation of the delivery programmes. It competed with them for resources to only a very limited extent and in many ways, as far as Norway was concerned, it was merely a restatement of the problem of supplying the Wehrmacht in that country. For it was to the Wehrmacht

[1] F.D. 5307/45, Rk., Abt. Binnenwirtschaft, 'Tätigkeitsbericht für den Monat Januar 1944', 1 February 1944.
[2] Ibid., 'Tätigkeitsbericht für den Monat Februar 1944', 1 March 1944.
[3] Ibid., 'Tätigkeitsbericht für den Monat Mai 1944', 5 June 1944.
[4] Ibid., 'Tätigkeitsbericht für den Monat Juli 1944', 4 August 1944.

that a high proportion of the potato-peelers, coffee cans, and bicycles turned out were delivered.

Much more of a handicap to the delivery programmes was the survival of some aspects of the original plans for Norway outside the powers of the Ministry of Munitions. That Ministry's simplification of the economic programme for Norway was based in the last resort on the great personal powers of the minister, Speer. It was Hitler's personal confidence in and reliance on him which helped him so quickly to set aside the fantastic schemes of the Luftwaffe and the Four Year Plan Office for aluminium production in Norway and to starve to death the social experiments of the Reichskommissariat. But the same personal factors ensured that those programmes in which Hitler himself had a personal interest would survive. There were two such programmes in particular, the construction of a great naval base in the city of Trondheim and the completion of the railway to the north.

The frequency with which Hitler alluded to the Narvik railway in his conferences with Speer and Saur is an indication that its construction was not merely for the defence of Norway. It became a symbol of the new Europe which he hoped to create. The occupation of Norway was not intended to turn Germany into a great naval power, rather it was to strengthen her defensive position on the Continent. Aware that the Allied powers might try once more to strike at his position through Norway where their greater naval power could be brought to bear more effectively, Hitler wished to improve the ability of his troops there to withstand an invasion. Only an army supplied by rail could have an adequate supply to resist an invading army supplied by sea. These plans were a tacit admission of the fact that Germany was and would be a continental power; the northern railway served the same strategic function as the Westwall in France. The continental nature of the future *Großraumwirtschaft* was further emphasized by the readiness with which Hitler accepted the fact that the northern Swedish iron ores might have to be brought to Germany by rail, a method of transport which would have enormously increased their cost to German steel producers. A similar increase in transport costs for the Norwegian Sydvaranger ores would have probably eliminated them completely from the reckoning.

The plans for a naval base at Trondheim were more concerned with a future war. The deep water there meant that Trondheim could not be so effectively mined by the enemy as the main German naval bases at Wilhelmshaven and Kiel. Trondheim was to be a heavily fortified base for the big battleships which the German navy would have in the future. There would be a new town built separately from Trondheim itself to serve as an administrative centre and cater to the needs of the sailors. An autobahn would join Trondheim to Oslo. The immediate importance of the northern railway was much greater than that of the Trondheim project. But both plans testify to the fact that the occupation of Norway was not a temporary military expedient but intended as a permanent affair. Hence Hitler's insistence on the northern railway in the face of all economic objections was a reluctance to abandon his European plans even though the war had taken an unfortunate turn for Germany. The railway was an artery of the new Europe which could not be abandoned.

The economic problems were enormous. The shortage of labour which had developed in north Norway was emphasized by the competition for construction workers between the railway, the new aluminium-factory sites, and the new airfields. In such a difficult terrain, however, railway building required a fairly high proportion of skilled construction workers, miners, tunnellers, and so on, who were no longer available at any wage. The labour force had to be fed and housed in bleak and sparsely inhabited regions. Even worse was the problem of supply, requiring a fleet of ships to bring the raw materials to the right places. These difficulties, as much as the sums of capital involved, had always deterred previous Norwegian governments from attempting to extend their railway network as far as Narvik. They had been present in all minds when the decision to complete the northern railway had been taken in 1940 when the terms of the agreement had specifically placed the responsibility for supply on the Wehrmacht itself.

5. The Wehrmacht has to supply the whole raw material demand for the construction of the railway from its own quotas. The Norwegian quotas may in no case be used for this railway construction. Any agreements for the incorporation of Norwegian firms are to be approved from the raw material point of view.

6. The Wehrmacht has to supply the shipping space for the transport of the construction materials itself. The other overseas transports for the supply of Norway may not be influenced thereby.[1]

Hitler had conceived the idea from somewhere that the railway could be completed in one and a half years from the date of commencement. This was an idea to which Terboven's own experts did not subscribe.[2] It may have been possible at the complete sacrifice of every other project for Norway but, if these were to be continued, it was impossible to complete in so short a time. When the Ministry of Munitions became responsible for allocating supply to the railway project and when the minister himself, in his capacity as head of Organization Todt, became responsible for the building, progress was deliberately slowed down so as not to interfere with other economic priorities.[3] The price of such a policy was constant

---

[1] R.A., Rk., Hauptabt. Volkswirtschaft, Abt. Arbeit und Sozialwesen, Pakke 93, 'Aktenvermerk. Betrifft: Bahnbauprogramm der Wehrmacht', 14 December 1940.
[2] Information from Herr Willi Henne.
[3] Information from former Reichsminister Albert Speer.

harassment from Hitler who saw the railway from a much wider perspective than the merely economic one.

The Führer in fact made his opinions perfectly clear in his first official meeting with his new minister in February 1942. 'The Führer considers the extension of the railway network in Norway to be extremely urgent and states that failing this the coast cannot be defended from attacks indefinitely.'[1] Speer attempted to reduce the effect of so categorical an instruction. 'I pointed out to the Führer that first of all in Norway all building projects are to be co-ordinated with one another, the bottlenecks in transport facilities to be expected are to be ascertained and the whole programme is to be adapted to these bottlenecks.'[1] Hitler returned to the attack in April.

The Führer insists categorically on the railway construction programme. In this respect the stretch Mo–Narvik and cross-country connection with the polar coast is urgent. The two year period mentioned for the section Mo–Fauske is rejected by the Führer. Reichskommissar Terboven has promised that the section to Fauske will be completed during this year and has suggested a building time of $1\frac{1}{2}/2$ years for the whole railway. Reichsminister Speer therefore considers it only right that Reichskommissar Terboven should take over the responsibility for this building time by carrying out his own building.[2]

To show that this building time was impossible Speer had his ministry prepare comparisons with the time it had taken to build the trans-Alpine railways.[3] But to no avail. 'The comparable railway construction carried out in the Alps cannot, in the opinion of the Führer, form a standard for the task in Norway owing to the inferior technical resources and the smaller amount of power used in that period.'[4]

Hitler's interest in the construction programme was partly responsible for the alacrity and decisiveness with which he solved the shipping crisis in spring 1942, for Speer was able to represent to him that his railway projects were out of the question without a much greater availability of shipping. The intention of the Ministry of Munitions and perhaps that of the Reichskommissar also was to use the extra shipping in the end for programmes which they regarded as more essential. But Hitler ended his conference with Speer and Terboven on 13 May with a most explicit warning. 'The Führer very particularly calls attention to the fact that the building programmes promoted by him in Norway are of extraordinary importance. Their execution or non-execution could decide the war and

---

[1] F.D. 3353/45, vol. i, Rm.f.B.u.M., 'Besprechungspunkte über Reise zum Führerhauptquartier', 19 February 1942.

[2] F.D. 3353/45, vol. viii, Rm.f.B.u.M., 'Führerkonferenz, 19 Avril 1942', 19 April 1942.

[3] Information from former Reichsminister Speer.

[4] F.D. 3353/45, vol. viii, Rm.f.B.u.M., 'Führerkonferenz, 19 Avril 1942'.

at the same time tonnage would be economized to a considerable extent once the railway building was completed.'[1]

In June he repeated his warning. 'The Führer underlines again the special importance of "operation Viking" and particularly of the railway construction. He points out that the railway building plans are of decisive importance for the war.'[2] One reason for this insistence may have been Hitler's revelation at the conference with Speer and Terboven in August that once the great naval base at Trondheim had been completed, a further one would be built at Narvik.[3] Terboven tried to restrict building on the northern railway so that it did not have to penetrate as far as the Arctic Ocean. 'The Führer, however, definitely demands the construction of the Mo–Fauske–Narvik and Nordreisa–Kirkenes lines as well. He consents, however, to give preference to the Nyborg–Karasjok section.'[3] In order to complete the work foreign labour was to be drafted into Norway for the first time on a significant scale. Six thousand Russian prisoners of war were to be organized into building battalions and set to work on the Mo–Fauske stretch at the rate of 500 extra workers a week. Not only was the railway to be completed but it was also to be fully fortified along its whole length against a possible Allied or Swedish attack, with fortifications which were to be fully up to the standard of the Westwall.

No note of realism came into these plans until February 1943. In that month the idea of the railway through Lappland to Kirkenes was abandoned. But no modification of the specifically Norwegian project was allowed, except that Hitler allowed some consideration of whether the final stage of the route to Narvik might not have one ferry connection in order to avoid the construction of a stretch of funicular railway.[4] 'The construction of the stretch Mo–Fauske is to be carried out with great emphasis.'[4]

The problem of providing sufficient raw materials, especially cement, confined the progress north of Mo to a very slow pace. If that could not be solved at least the shortage of labour could. When the Russian prisoners of war were first drafted to Norwegian railway building Hitler had also considered sending Serbian prisoners to work alongside them. At the time he had insisted on extra rations for the prisoners so that they could withstand the Arctic weather. By February 1943 his ideas were more punitive. 'Besides the prisoners-of-war to be additionally allotted by Gauleiter Sauckel, the Reichsführer S.S. is to prepare persons in preventive

[1] F.D. 3353/45, vol. xi, Rm.f.B.u.M., 'Führerkonferenz, 13 Mai 1942', 15 May 1942.

[2] F.D. 3353/45, vol. xviii, Rm.f.B.u.M., 'Führerkonferenz, 28–29 Juni 1942', 29 June 1942,

[3] F.D. 3353/45, vol. xxi, Rm.f.B.u.M., 'Führerkonferenz 10–12 August', 19 August 1942.

[4] F.D. 3353/45, vol. xxxi, Rm.f.B.u.M. 'Führerkonferenz 6–7 February 1943', 10 February 1943.

custody (Punishment Drive in Holland) and Jews. Molly-coddling by additional rations is to be pursued before transportation to Norway.'[1]

In April 1943 the mountain route to Narvik was abandoned in favour of the coastal route in spite of the greater danger of enemy action against the coastal route. The advantage was the quicker completion of the railway, although Hitler also consoled himself with the thought that the mountain route was more susceptible to attack by Sweden.[2] On 28 April von Falkenhorst informed Speer that he regarded the road-building programme and the fortification of the ports as of much greater strategic importance than the completion of the northern railway.[3] Even these objections were swept aside by Hitler. From that moment onwards his insistence on the northern railway became almost monomania; the railway was to be built against the advice of all advisers and despite the impossibility of completing it without an effort so great as to disrupt every other aspect of economic policy in Norway. 'The Führer reiterates the importance of railway construction in Norway; those who are not taking the necessary steps now will bear a heavy responsibility for the future.'[4]

The reasons for this insistence seem to have belonged to Hitler's own conception of the New Order. Saving what was left of German conquest while abandoning the fascist Europe of his dreams did not interest him. His refusal to compromise on such a matter was a realism greater than that of his advisers. Whether that can also be said of his strategic conceptions seems very doubtful. It can certainly not be said of his economic conceptions. In so far as he had economic reasons for persisting with the railway they were very bad ones.

The Führer is gratified at the progress and situation of the work but mentions that the completion of the line in the shortest possible time may become of paramount importance and must therefore be pushed forward by all available means. . . . Aim of the railway is to transport the greatest possible quantity of Swedish ore to the south (Oslofjord) by rail. The increase in capacity of the line to the south is to be carried out in conjunction with the initial war-time construction of the track to Korsnes. As a guide, a traffic figure of 200,000 tons per month can be assumed, if possible more than the quantity of ore at present being shipped from Narvik.[5]

Hitler seems to have envisaged a New Order in a state of perpetual defence against a potential Allied invasion and in which sea routes whose flanks

[1] F.D. 3353/45, vol. xxxi, Rm.f.B.u.M., 'Führerkonferenz 6–7 Februar 1943', 10 February 1943.
[2] F.D. 3353/45, vol. xxxiii, Rm.f.B.u.M., 'Führerkonferenz, 3 Avril 1943', 3 April 1943.
[3] F.D. 3353/45, vol. xxxix, Rm.f.B.u.M., 'Führerkonferenz, 13–15 Mai 1943', 15 May 1943.
[4] F.D. 3353/45, vol. xlvii, Rm.f.B.u.M., 'Führerkonferenz, 4–5 August 1943', 8 August 1943.
[5] F.D. 3353/45, vol. lii, Rm.f.R.u.Kp., 'Führerkonferenz 13–15 November 1943', 16 November 1943.

were exposed to naval attack must be for ever eschewed. Nothing else could make so long a haul necessary for so heavy a commodity as iron ore. What would have been the price of such iron ore in the German market? And what would have been carried in the wagons in the other direction?

Even at the end there was no relaxation. In November 1944 Speer still recorded that 'Hitler orders that the railway building in Norway is to be continued with urgency. He decrees that Field-Marshal Keitel is to inform the Reichskommissar for shipping, Gauleiter Kaufmann, of this so that the necessary tonnage may be provided.'[1] Whatever the tonnage was needed for by that date there was no longer any point in providing it for railway building.

After 1942 this one remnant of the original economic plans for Norway therefore existed side by side until the end of the war with the priority exploitation programmes of the Ministry of Munitions which discounted all investment in Norway except where it could strictly be shown to provide some benefit for the German armament industry. Such a state of affairs demonstrates far more than Hitler's obstinacy. It demonstrates also the strange ambivalence of the New Order itself; on the one hand a scheme for a revolutionary reordering of the European continent, on the other hand an administrative device for strengthening the German economy by exploitation.

After the failure of the Blitzkrieg it was inevitable that questions of economic organization, the necessity to organize a total war economy not only in Germany but in Europe, should cause the more narrowly exploitative aspect of the New Order to come to the fore. That is what happened in Norway with the introduction of the Planungsamt programmes. But the conception of an economic revolution was never lost sight of. No doubt for a country like Norway these longer-term aims of fascism were even more threatening than exploitation in the interests of 'The European war economy'. The survival of the railway building project in Norway is good evidence that the rise to power of the Speer Ministry, with its technical viewpoint and its insistence on the primacy of the economic argument, was regarded by Hitler, and by his Party, as a temporary expedient.

The dream of a fascist Norway as an integral part of the new Europe therefore never died and on Hitler's part it was certainly the greater realism that he should have acted on the assumption that a Norway in any other form was not worth considering if fascist Europe was to survive. The development of the war economy in Germany may have precipitated the more colonial aspects of Norway's relationship to Germany by stripping off any fancier aspects of German planning leaving only the

[1] F.D. 3353/45, vol. lxxii, Rm.f.R.u.Kp., 'Führerkonferenz 1–4 November 1944', 5 November 1944.

bare facts of German needs and her determination to satisfy them. It did nevertheless create a purely economic nexus between the two countries and thus introduced a quite new element into the situation. Germany's original interest in Norway had not been an economic one. It seems to be the case that this primacy of economic affairs was only unwillingly tolerated by Hitler. For him the idea of a fascist reconstruction remained paramount.

XI

CONCLUSION: NORWAY AND THE NEW ORDER

THE fascist New Order has often been described as having had no objective existence other than as an empty phrase. Those who have taken this attitude have usually done so because of particular assumptions they have made about the nature of the fascist creed itself. Some interpretations of fascism have seen it as an utterly nihilistic and self-contradictory movement and the New Order as windy verbiage designed to camouflage the lack of all order, an exercise in propaganda scarcely worth the studying.[1] Others have seen fascism as nothing but old nationalism writ differently and the New Order as the entirely traditional diplomacy of the aggressive nation state. Academic works on the diplomacy of National Socialist Germany often strain officiously to consider it as one European country like any other.[2] It is even possible still to discover arguments in which fascism itself is supposed to have had no genuine existence as a governing principle. None of these standpoints has received much reinforcement recently. To accept any of them would be to reject any study of the New Order as a worthwhile scholarly enterprise and to substitute for it simply a study, in traditional mould, of a number of distinct 'belligerent occupations'.

The study of German occupation policy in Norway shows that without full recognition of the existence of the New Order as a political, economic, social, and ideological conception, German policy in Norway cannot be at all understood. The main reason for the occupation of Norway was originally strategic. Had Germany had no intentions other than strategic ones, a study of German economic policy in Norway would be simply a study of how the German forces in Norway were maintained. In fact, once the invasion had taken place the German administration bristled with social and economic plans for Norway, some of which, like the aluminium plan, were extraordinarily grand in conception. How far can these plans be regarded as an incident of Germany's wartime economy? To what extent were they conceived merely as a way either of reducing the cost to Germany of an occupation necessary on other grounds or of making the occupation

[1] This strain of thought has a most respectable lineage originating with H. Rauschning, *Die Revolution des Nihilismus* (Zürich, 1938), trans., *The Revolution of Nihilism* (London, 1939). But the family has now degenerated into a nightmare brood of conservative bogeymen.

[2] No doubt hoping that its history can continue to be written in the same way.

of Norway more profitable and thus permitting Germany to increase the degree of exploitation of the Norwegian economy to the benefit of her war effort?

If the plans for Norway had worked they would, of course, have had both these effects. But, leaving on one side the long-term nature of many of them, such as the food-production plan or the aluminium plan, which contrasted so blatantly with Germany's own short-term war plans, it is still clear that their aims were much more far-reaching than the more limited ones of helping the German war effort or merely reducing the burden on it imposed by strategic necessity. In economic terms the occupation of Norway was scarcely of any value whatsoever to Germany. It can be understood only as part of a much wider scheme.

This was in no way because Germany could not exploit the Norwegian economy successfully. On the contrary, the German exploitation of occupied Norway, like that of occupied France, was successful to a degree which most western economists would have denied was possible. The level of exploitation in each case was very similar and in each case very high. The standard of living of the occupied country was drastically reduced and its resources, capital, land, and labour were all ruthlessly diverted to German use. Seen in this light, German policy in Norway was a remarkable example of how far such policies can be carried out.

Aukrust and Bjerve have calculated the total loss to Norway arising from the German occupation.[1] This is not the same as the total gain to Germany, although, since so large a proportion of the loss to Norway was a direct financial loss in the form of the occupation payments, the difference cannot be very great. It has usually been considered that Norway was one of the heaviest-burdened of all occupied countries. In one sense this is true. The calculations of the Bank for International Payments in Basel estimated the burden of the occupation payments from Norway to Germany in the first two years of the occupation at 1,842 kroner per inhabitant. The Netherlands was the only western country on which the occupation costs lay so heavy; the burden on France in that period was 779 kroner per inhabitant and on Denmark 579. In other ways, however, the loss to Norway was less than elsewhere and the gain to Germany comparably less. No calculation need be made for the value of Norwegian labour lost to Germany. If a financial value be ascribed to the French or Russian prisoners of war in Germany and other workmen and women later forcibly deported, the relative gain to Germany begins to look different. Similarly, because the scope and variety of Norway's industrial capital was less than that of France, the amount of it to be used wholly for German purposes was correspondingly less. Finally, it should be remembered that whereas Norway, until 1944, had an import surplus from Germany, most other

[1] O. Aukrust and P. Bjerve, *Hva krigen kostet Norge*.

TABLE 69. *Direct Occupation Cost Balance for Norway, 1940–5**

(000,000, 1939 kroner)

Year	Net payments from Norges bank to occupying power	German requisitions without payment	Norwegian import surplus (+) export surplus (−) with Germany on clearing†	Balance of direct occupation costs
1940	1,257	521‡	+27	1,751
1941	2,413	330‡	+344	2,399
1942	2,335	316§	+228	2,423
1943	2,333	318§	+293	2,358
1944	2,332	300§, ‖	−23	2,655
31 Dec. 1944 to 30 Apr. 1945	623	..	−108	731
	11,293	1,785	761	12,317

* O. Aukrust and P. Bjerve, *Hva krigen kostet Norge*, p. 28.
† Not corrected for advanced or late payments of imports or exports.
‡ Total 851·11 million kroner for period 9 April 1940 to 31 March 1942 is approximated between year 1940 and 1941.
§ 1 April of year in question to 31 March ensuing year.
‖ Estimate.

TABLE 70. *Norwegian Resources Diverted for German Purposes, 1939–44**

(000,000, 1939 kroner)

	Actual national income	Loss due to occupation	Occupation costs	Total loss of national income
1939	4,800	..	..	..
1940	4,373	527	1,328	1,855
1941	4,478	522	1,534	2,056
1942	4,305	795	1,454	2,249
1943	6,218	982	1,451	2,433
1944	4,000†	1,300	1,548	2,848
1 Jan. to 30 Apr. 1945	1,300†	500	499†	999
Total	22,674	4,626	7,814	12,440
Yearly average	4,251	868	1,465	2,333

* O. Aukrust and P. Bjerve, *Hva krigen kostet Norge*, p. 48.
† Estimated.

occupied territories had an import deficit. In 1942 Norway had an import surplus of 130 million current Reichsmarks from Germany; France, for example, had an export surplus of 858 million Reichsmarks.[1] None of that is intended to play down the loss to the Norwegian economy but only to emphasize how limited was the gain to Germany.

[1] A. S. Milward, *The New Order and the French Economy*, p. 283.

In fact the difference between the loss to the Norwegian economy and the gain to the German economy is hardly worth bothering about since the gain from Norway was, however calculated, statistically no great addition to German resources. It appears that, as in the case of France, the burden of the occupation costs was greater than the burden of other losses due to the occupation, although in both cases the latter showed an increasing tendency to catch up with the former. Payment of occupation costs averaged about one-third of national income for each year of the occupation, in either case. The total share of national income in Norway lost to the country rose from about 25 per cent in 1940 to about 40 per cent in 1943 and may have been much higher in 1944. In France, Germany was taking for her own purposes about one-third of national income in the first year of the occupation and about one-half in 1943.[1]

One-fifth of Norway's pre-war capital stock was destroyed, although a significant proportion of that was shipping losses against which the earnings of Nortraship ought to be set. The coal-mines in Spitzbergen were destroyed and the iron-ore plants of Syd-Varanger, even by 1949, were not back to their pre-war capacity. The destruction in north Norway was catastrophic. Most of all, Norway's trading position seriously deteriorated, imposing severe post-war strains. A combined surplus of both visible and invisible exports in 1939 of 41 million current kroner was converted into a combined deficit of 747 million current kroner in 1946. Net receipts from shipping paid for one-third of Norway's pre-war imports but only for one-sixth after the war. Norway's claim for compensation against Germany amounted to 21,000 million kroner.[2] That sum was of course not supposed to be the equivalent of the gain to Germany for much of the loss to Norway was also loss to Germany. Capital depreciation, for example, would come in that category once some allowance had been made for the percentage of it that was caused by German use of capital resources. But even if the whole sum were to stand as the equivalent of Germany's gain, it would only amount to about 60 per cent of the value of just the goods and services obtained by Germany from France by payment to the end of 1944, omitting the value of French labour in Germany and taking no account of the greater part of the financial burden on France, the unpaid clearing deficit, and the occupation costs.

A total loss to Norway of 12,440 million pre-war kroner, to which might be added a further 5,000 million pre-war kroner for lowered capital formation, made only the most marginal difference to the German war effort. How much of the estimate for lowered capital formation should be properly

[1] A. S. Milward, *The New Order and the French Economy*, p. 273.
[2] *Preliminary Report on Germany's Crimes Against Norway*. Prepared for use at the International Military Tribunal by F. Palmstrøm and R. N. Torgerson (Oslo, 1945), p. 29.

credited to Germany is a statistical problem of infinite complexity, but supposing the whole sum so credited the total gain would still be very little. It would amount to approximately 6 per cent of the German Gross National Product for 1944 using the wartime exchange rate as the basis of the calculation. It may be objected that the wartime exchange rate grossly undervalued the kroner against the Reichsmark. Its undervaluation, however, was considerably less than that of the French franc and using the war-time franc–Reichsmark exchange rate as the basis of the calculation, the total payments from France to Germany in 1944 alone, that is to say the occupation costs plus the clearing deficit, amounted to 5·9 per cent of the German Gross National Product in that year.[1] The sum estimated, in Norway's case, as gain to Germany is an overestimate whereas the sum estimated for France is a flagrant underestimate. It may therefore be said that Germany's gain from Norway throughout the occupation, expressed financially, was less than her gain from France in one year of the occupation of that country.

Of course, the goods and services which Norway provided are not satisfactorily measured in financial terms. This may be easily shown by trying to establish the true value to the German war economy of certain rare metallic ores. Their price, although inflated out of all recognition, was still no indication of their importance to the working of the war economy. Many goods were indispensable to Germany, for it was a question of survival. But if this argument is used the value of the Norwegian economy to Germany relative to other occupied European economies is not enhanced but diminished. Although Norway did produce certain commodities which were particularly valuable to Germany they were few. Her industry was limited in scope and the substitutability of her fixed capital much less than that of other western industrialized economies. The larger and more varied the economy the easier it is to exploit. In Norway the range of exploitable sectors was strictly defined and the margin for error or for change of policy very small.

This may be seen by considering the trading pattern which actually arose in Europe during, and as a result of, the war. The whole trend of German pre-war trading policy had been designed to penetrate into south-eastern and central Europe and turn that area into a bloc of states with a semi-colonial trading relationship to Germany. Its success meant that the volume of German trade with those countries rose every year at the expense of German trade with western Europe. The events of the war completely reversed this trend, not merely because of the occupation of western territories, but because only certain western countries were actually capable of catering for the extremely wide-ranging and sophisticated demands of a mass-productive war economy. In this sense Norway's

[1] A. S. Milward. *The New Order and the French Economy*, p. 271.

capacity was neither sufficiently wide-ranging nor sufficiently sophisticated. It was the tremendous import surplus of goods, not subsequently paid for, from France, Belgium, and the Netherlands which was the outstanding aspect of Germany's war-time trade. By comparison the trade with the Balkan countries became insignificant. While those western states with a more sophisticated economic structure were feeding goods into the German war economy, Norway, in the first few years of the occupation, imported more goods from Germany than she sent.

From a trading point of view Norway was more in the situation of a German ally, like Italy, Romania, and Finland, needing to be supplied with goods to be kept in the struggle, than an occupied territory contributing to the conqueror's economy. In a financial sense this is covered in the foregoing calculations. Or, to put it another way, the occupation costs which Norway paid covered only too amply the commodities which Germany supplied to keep her going. Not only was this so in a strictly financial sense, but the terms of the clearing agreements by which Norway was bound to the New Order presented all manner of advantages to Germany. The original German policy to force all other European powers to conduct their trade on the basis of a central clearing institution in Berlin, had to be relaxed for Scandinavia. Norway was permitted to sign bilateral trading agreements both with Sweden and Denmark so that the financing of much inter-Scandinavian trade was not controlled in Berlin, although of course, the German government kept the strictest watch over the Dano-Norwegian trade treaties. With these two exceptions, all Norwegian trade was directed through Berlin and trade treaties between Norway and all other lands stipulated that each party should clear its accounts separately with the German clearing institutions rather than on a bilateral basis between themselves. The advantage of accumulating enormous clearing deficits which this system permitted to Germany was less applicable in the Norwegian case than in that of other occupied lands. But all the other advantages which such a system gave were equally marked. The timing of payments, the type and quantity of goods to be exchanged, the timing of those exports, all presented Germany with great opportunities for raising temporary credit on favourable terms. And in such circumstances, credit gains to Germany were credit losses to Norway, the more so as Germany could raise credit on Norwegian goods temporarily under German control although destined for other lands. Furthermore the prices of goods traded could be heavily influenced and in some cases decided by the central control over quantities traded which Germany now possessed.

These disadvantages had been accepted by many south-eastern European countries in the decade before the Second World War because they received in return an advantage which was particularly important in such a period, a guaranteed market at a selling price above world prices. But for a more industrialized land with a range of exports much wider than the exports of the less-developed European countries, most of whom depended on massive sales of a limited range of raw materials for their export earnings, the advantages of such a system did not compensate for its massive disadvantages. Before the invasion, Norway already had separate clearing agreements with Germany, Italy, Turkey, Greece, and Spain but elsewhere her trade was still open to the movement of international prices rather than to arbitrarily stipulated prices and exchange rates in guaranteed markets. Once the country was occupied by Germany, German control of internal prices was very strict and there was no possibility of any price agreements favourable to Norway being embodied in the bilateral trading agreements now forced upon her.

The Trade Policy Department of the Foreign Ministry advised strongly against allowing Germany to force Norway into trading agreements with other parties which would stipulate central clearing in Berlin.[1] The original members of the Directorate of Foreign Trade in the Department of Supply and of the Clearing Committee enumerated all the financial disadvantages which would accrue to Norway from such a system even earlier.[2] But Germany's political power was too strong to resist. It is, of course, a hypothetical issue as to how far the price policy which Germany pursued during the war may have meant that an apparent Norwegian clearing deficit with Germany at wartime prices represented an actual surplus at world prices. There were no genuine international prices during the war and even before the war a substantial part of Norway's trade had already passed at agreed exchange rates. Nevertheless, Germany did take the opportunity of pursuing a price policy highly favourable to herself by trying to keep the price levels in the peripheral countries of the *Großraumwirtschaft* below that in Germany. Nor did the prices stipulated in the trading agreements faithfully reflect the price levels within the two countries concerned.

Even so, the German liability to Norway was still considerable. The Norwegian economy could not function without fuel, food, and fodder. The occupation meant that all those commodities had now to be supplied from Germany or other occupied territories, in either case from where they were already in desperately short supply and carefully rationed or otherwise allocated. It has been seen that these supplies were only provided with great effort and in insufficient quantities and that, towards the close of the occupation, Germany could no longer provide them at all. Norway was therefore a liability of a peculiar kind on the German war economy.

---

[1] R.A., Bilag II til Faktaregister for okkupasjonstiden, 'Varebyttenemndas referatprotokoll fra møte', 12 August 1940.

[2] Ibid., 'Utskrift av varebyttenemndas referatprotokoll fra fellesmøte 28 mai 1940 kl. 11¼ av varebyttenemnda og nemnda for industri og omsetning'.

The only other occupied territory in an apparently similar trading position was the General-Government, but, in reality, its situation was very different because its import surplus from Germany was a surplus of goods imported from those areas of pre-war Poland actually annexed by Germany and therefore appearing in the German trade figures.

There is a further point to be made in this regard. Had Germany's capital investment plans in Norway developed as they were intended the gain from Norway, over the period of the war, would have been even less. If the aluminium plan had been carried out in its full scope according to the proposed time-table there would have been extremely heavy investment before there was any actual return in the form of aluminium for the German air force. It has been seen that if the plan had gone ahead in any of its early forms very little of that investment could have come from Norwegian sources (although that was not so clear to the framers of the plan).

Although, therefore, the occupation of Norway was a remarkably successful case of economic exploitation, it makes remarkably little sense without reference to the wider framework of German plans in which it was set. Norway's contribution to the German war effort can obviously not be discounted, but it was of very little importance compared to that from other occupied areas. And there were particular problems of supply and transport involved in maintaining this contribution which suggest that as an exercise in economic exploitation the occupation of Norway, in striking contrast to that of France, was hardly worth while. What was at issue was not Norway's economy as an adjunct to the German war economy but Norway's society as an adjunct to the New Order. The fascist economy in Norway has to be seen as an integral part of the fascist New Order and the history of its development testifies to the existence of that New Order as more than propaganda.

More than that, it throws considerable light on the nature of the New Order and thus on the nature of fascism itself. There has, in recent years, been a noticeable revival of interest in defining the nature of fascist politics. This interest has meant that the various views in which fascism, and hence the New Order, was regarded as not serious, or not consistent, or not definable, or even non-existent have fallen very much from fashion. Unfortunately this spate of scholarly interest in fascism, which has greatly advanced our historical knowledge of recent history, has not extended itself into an examination of the economics of fascism, let alone into the more specific problems of the New Order. Any interpretation of the New Order must depend upon a prior interpretation of the nature of fascism. It will not have escaped the reader that in this matter I have openly taken sides in favour of one such interpretation. I have done so because it seems to me that the study of the National Socialist economy, both in its domestic and foreign aspects, lends a great weight of evidence to support this one particular interpretation. If I may be permitted a personal note it is not the view of fascism to which I originally subscribed but rather the result of an accumulation of historical evidence.

The concluding chapter of so specialized a book is not the place to survey accurately and in detail the innumerable interpretations of fascism which historians have proposed.[1] At the unavoidable risk of offending many of the large number of those who have contributed to this debate it is necessary to classify their views and thus to simplify them sometimes, no doubt, beyond recognition. The basis of this classification is one merely of convenience for any study of the New Order. How many different views of the nature of the New Order may be derived from studies concerned with the more general problem of fascism as a whole? A fair answer to the question seems to be five, with the proviso that they are by no means mutually exclusive.

Firstly, there is the hypothesis that fascist movements were not governed by any but the loosest bonds of ideological similarity. A loose association of despotic, militaristic, and nationalistic governments subjected their own people and those of neighbouring states to a kind of institutionalized violence in order to make their policies effective. Such movements were usually called 'totalitarian' and it was often assumed that they reflected developments inherent in modern society in so far as modern society provided them with more advanced technological means for subjecting the population to mental and physical violence.[2] This interpretation was the offspring of an outraged liberalism. Its weakness is in its inability to distinguish fascism from any other anti-democratic creed, even from its diametric opposite, communism. In its more subtle and intelligent form it takes the more reasonable viewpoint that every fascist movement was a unique historical event requiring its own interpretation. Starting from these general assumptions the New Order could be seen as the concatenation of a series of unique historical phenomena rather than the superimposition of a generalized social and philosophical concept on European society.

It is perfectly possible, however, to accept the uniqueness of these historical events without rejecting the idea of a common ideology linking them together and a broadly common purpose motivating those who shaped them. This has been the standpoint of the four other general interpretations of fascism which need to be considered here. One of these is the hypothesis

---

[1] There are three good historiographical accounts, R. de Felice, *Le interpretazioni del fascismo* (Bari, 1969); W. Sauer, 'National Socialism: Totalitarianism or Fascism?', in *American Historical Review*, lxxiii (1967); and E. Nolte, *Theorien über den Faschismus* (Cologne, 1967). See also, E. Nolte, 'Zeitgenössische Theorien über den Faschismus', *Vierteljahrshefte für Zeitgeschichte*, xv (1967).

[2] C. J. Friedrich (ed.), *Totalitarianism* (Cambridge, Mass., 1945) is most typical of this interpretation.

that fascism represented, or was typical of, or likely to occur in, a particular stage of capitalist development. It was already formulated in the twenties in Italy although in a much less rigid fashion than it has subsequently often assumed. It then became refined into the theory that fascism was the last stage of monopoly capitalism.[1] As capitalism passes into its last stage it is forced to adopt political methods to defend itself, left to fight it out on the purely economic field it would be defeated by falling profits. The necessary level of profits has to be maintained by securing control over the government and turning it into a tool of the business interests. Seen in this light the New Order was the superimposition by military violence and ruthless force on European markets of the business interests of the larger German firms. It was a kind of German imperialism in which the markets to be conquered were not under-developed countries with primitive forms of government but developed states with sophisticated governmental systems only to be smashed by the exercise of tremendous violence.

This particular interpretation of the New Order is not without support from the events of the German occupation in Norway. It should be remarked that each of the interpretations here dealt with has some foundation in observed historical reality, for fascism was an extremely complex movement. The argument in favour of fascism as a stage of monopoly capitalism has been strengthened by some of the few studies to concern themselves with the economic history of fascism.[2] The behaviour of the larger German firms in Norway, in the affair of the aluminium plan and in other mining and industrial fields, lends some credence to this view. That German industrialists hoped that the foreign policy of their government would benefit them enormously and supported it accordingly cannot be doubted. Their actions in Norway fit that pattern, as they do elsewhere. What can be doubted is whether the conception of the New Order, *in the long run*, was the same among German industrialists as among the more ideologically committed members of the National Socialist Party. It is not merely a question of particular disagreements about particular policies. There is plenty of scope in this hypothesis of fascism for disagreements between government and capitalists to take place. Rather it is a question of whether the ultimate vision of human society of the greater capitalists and the fascists was a common one. The evidence of the aluminium plan

[1] For the history of this development see T. Pirker, *Komintern und Faschismus. Dokumente zur Geschichte und Theorie des Faschismus*, Schriftenreihe der Vierteljahrshefte für Zeitgeschichte, No. 10 (Stuttgart, 1965).

[2] For a review of some of these see W. Schumann and G. Lozek, 'Die faschistische Okkupationspolitik im Spiegel der Historiographie der beiden deutschen Staaten', in *Zeitschrift für Geschichtswissenschaft*, xii (1964). The most comprehensive work based on this interpretation is D. Eichholtz, *Geschichte der deutschen Kriegswirtschaft, 1939–1945*, vol. i (Berlin, 1969).

combined with that of the rest of German economic policy in the occupation seems to suggest that it was not.

Thirdly, there is the hypothesis that fascism is an aspect of the more general problem of industrialization and economic development. The history of fascism in Italy had suggested that it was not obviously the product of so-called 'mature' capitalism, but rather of the need of capitalism to achieve a breakthrough in industrialization.[1] Since then this viewpoint has widened until fascism has been seen as an attempt by countries to develop rapidly whether by purely capitalist means or no. One advantage of this interpretation has been its ability to assimilate events in Latin American countries, such as the Peronist movement in Argentina, to European experience.[2] Indeed, in general it is a far less Eurocentric hypothesis since its advocates obviously expect it to have a certain predictive as well as historically interpretative value. The normal workings of the political system are suspended so that the necessary transition to a higher rate of economic development can be achieved without having to trouble about the agreement of most of the population. Alternatively, the new arrangements might permit a harmony of agreement which would not be possible under the previous political system.

From this point of view, therefore, the New Order would be seen as an attempt to speed up the pace of economic development in Europe in the interests of two states. But the problem in accepting this view is that the New Order was most earnestly and actively supported in most European countries by those whose domestic economic policies were very much against an increasing rate of industrialization and whose supporters were most usually either petty-bourgeois or peasants. Furthermore, there are the many questions posed by the great differences in levels of economic development in the countries subjected to fascism within the meaning of this particular definition of the word.

Fourthly, there is the categorization of fascism as a stage in political development and participation. Its origins are in the extremely rapid transition between the introduction of more democratic constitutions in European countries during the First World War and the advent of new forms of quasi-dictatorship with broadly popular support in a way which earlier despots had never needed except in France where universal suffrage had come early. The precision with which the word fascist is used has never been very fine in this school of thought and the emphasis has

---

[1] This interpretation was not always so far from the previous one. See A. Gramsci, *Opere*, vol. ii, *Socialismo e fascismo: l'Ordine nuovo, 1921–1922* (Turin, 1966).

[2] A. F. K. Organski, *The Stages of Political Development* (New York, 1967); B. Moore, Jr., *Social Origins of Dictatorship and Democracy. Lord and Peasant in the Making of the Modern World* (Cambridge, Mass., 1966).

always been on the origins of fascist governments rather than their intentions.[1]

Its advantage in formulating a hypothesis of the New Order lies in this wide scope of meaning which it has attributed to fascism. These new forms of political society could embrace a wide range of economic and social viewpoints and reconcile them in new structures. Thus the apparent contradictions and conflicts in the New Order can be explained as only to be expected. But in Norway, as in all other occupied countries, the New Order was a German construction. The indigenous population, even those who were in favour of it, like Nasjonal Samling, had no say in the matter. They accepted this humiliating position because their outlook, although nationalist, was not confined to the nation-state. The nation-state was too impregnated with the idea of society (*Gesellschaft*) to be any longer a suitable vehicle for the idea of community (*Gemeinschaft*). If fascism were to triumph as a political creed it had to triumph beyond the bounds of the nation-state.

Each of these hypotheses about the New Order has a certain value and none of them is exclusive of others. Fascism was a most complex phenomenon related to peculiar national needs and problems in every European country. Like all such large-scale political movements it embraced many groups, often quite important, which wanted to change its policy and alter the direction in which it was going. Also it embraced many supporters who did not accept entirely the ultimate implications of the movement or did not fully understand the difference between their own aims and those of fascism but hoped to gain some of their own ends along the way. In that sense none of these categories can be seen as more than a literary convenience of historical writing. Nevertheless, the evidence from German policy in Norway argues for none of these hypotheses, but for the fifth and last.

This is that fascism was a profoundly anti-liberal and anti-communist movement, in a word, anti-materialist. As far as Norway was concerned the New Order was an attempt to force a particular philosophico-economic view of the world on to her as on to other European states. That view of the world was anti-materialist, antagonistic to economic growth, concerned with the creation of a society which would be stable enough to resist the hitherto relentless pressures of social change. Fascism was, as many contemporaries argued, a counter-revolutionary movement. Its immediate target was communism, because communism was the most widespread and potent modern revolutionary force. But all fascist ideologists saw communism, not as a comparatively new phenomenon, but as the logical result of the development of liberal thought. To overthrow the Russian

[1] G. Germani, *Sociología de la modernización* (Buenos Aires, 1969). See also A. Tasca, *Nascita e avvento del fascismo* (Bari, 1965).

revolution without extirpating the cast of mind that had given rise to the French Revolution was useless. It was only to delay revolution. In an age of mass politics and proletarian revolution the counter-revolution must also concern itself with the whole of society. Society not just government, must be cast in a form of social stability which would endure. That change needed one final revolution, the revolution of fascism. Of that revolution and reconstruction the New Order was the expression.

The New Order existed as a definite and necessary concept for the defence of the fascist revolution. Confined to two countries such a revolution could not long survive, the more so as both in Germany and Italy it was an incomplete revolution subject to all manner of humiliating compromises. It could be completed only on a European scale. Not all its protagonists, even its leading protagonists, always accepted this, for the implications of its acceptance were such as to give the boldest pause for thought. That those who did, amongst whom Hitler must clearly be numbered, have been justified by subsequent events is almost universally admitted by leaders of present-day European fascist parties. From 1951 onwards they have always couched their policies in pan-European terms, and even allowing for the obvious advantages such terms have as an anti-communist gesture, the New European Order which many of them now advocate derives, socially and economically, from that which the Third Reich imposed on Europe. They have even adopted the phrase 'The New Order' to designate in certain cases their party and in others their newspaper. The idea of a social and economic reconstruction of Europe, both anti-liberal[1] and anti-communist, has survived more strongly than any other aspect of fascist policy from the heyday of the movement.

The starting-point of this reconstruction for the fascist parties of the thirties was the necessity for a spiritual and psychological rebirth of man. The man they wished to create was the direct antithesis of the 'economic man' of eighteenth-century liberalism, whose origins they traced, quite rightly, to the Renaissance and to ancient Greece. They therefore faced themselves with a task of superhuman proportions, to create a type of human being different from that which two centuries of European society had increasingly tended to produce. To achieve this required nothing less than the social and economic reconstruction of the continent. The ultimate aim was not, of course, economic, but the new society had to have an economic base different from that of the old society and it is for that reason that the New Order is so revealing about the ultimate political nature of fascism.

The implications for Norway were extraordinarily serious. Although already at a high level of personal incomes, even if, perhaps, not so high

[1] In modern language, 'anti-American'.

as the *per capita* national income figures suggest, and with much of the apparatus of the modern industrial state, Norway was still a country in the full spate of economic development when it was incorporated into the New Order. The German plans for the industrial development of Norway followed in their main essentials the path of Norway's previous development. They were concerned with utilizing the same kinds of resources for the same kinds of industries where such resources still remained undeveloped. That there were great possibilities based on the development of still unutilized resources of water power and metal ores cannot be denied. Since 1945 Norwegian development has continued very much along the same lines. The German plans for the aluminium industry therefore had a respectable lineage in the plans of other foreign investors before 1939 and a respectable progeny in the plans of the Norwegian government itself after 1945. The expansion of the electro-chemical and electro-metallurgical industries, the development of unexploited low-grade iron-ore deposits, and the creation of a large steelworks at Mo i Rana, the exploitation of the pyrites deposits which Germany had intended to develop, and the improvement of both road and rail communications have all played important parts in Norway's continued successful economic development since 1945.[1]

But the framework in which these plans were set was completely different and it is this which singles out the fascist period as one of peculiar danger to Norway. Although there were no plans to dismantle Norwegian industry, and although Germany recognized that Norway was in certain limited respects a valuable addition to the German war economy and to the industrial strength of the New Order, it is in the German plans for the more backward sectors of the Norwegian economy that the essential difference between fascist policy and the preceding and succeeding periods can be seen. The plans for the aluminium industry resembled a development plan. For Germany they had a singular strategic significance. It was the importance of Norway's aluminium industry for the future strength of the German Air Force that over-rode all objections to further industrialization in what *Großraumwirtschaft* planners hoped would be part of the agricultural periphery of Europe. In its setting, however, the German development plan was very different.

The difference did not lie in the subjection of Norwegian industry and resources to German capital and German interests. The British, French, and Canadian interests which had previously developed the Norwegian aluminium industry had been no more concerned about Norway than were the Germans. Rather the differences lay in the general attitude to economic

[1] A. Bourneuf, *Norway: The Planned Revival*, Harvard Economic Studies, cvi (Cambridge, Mass., 1958), 6: United States, Economic Cooperation Administration, *European Recovery Program. Norway. Country Study* (Washington, 1949), p. 57.

growth. Pre-war and post-war plans were concerned with exploiting hydro-electric resources as a stage in the economic growth of the country; the new factories would solve the problems of Norway's relatively depressed peasant sector by attracting people increasingly from the poorly rewarded occupations of fishing and farming, where productivity was very low, into the high-productive and well-paid industrial occupations. It is this movement of people from the land into industry which has been the biggest measurable factor in economic growth in almost every European country since 1945; at least it has been the biggest factor in increasing the measured rate of growth. Fascist policy was specifically designed to stop this happening. Although in the case of Norway, for strategic reasons, some further industrialization had to be accepted, it was accompanied by a concerted effort to depress industrial wages relative to those in agriculture and fishing. Norway's role in the *Großraumwirtschaft* was, like that of all of the peripheral states, to be that of a primary producer. She could not export agricultural produce to Germany but she could export fish and at the same time become less dependent for her food supply on other economies. These objectives could both coincide with policies designed to better the position of those employed in agriculture and fishing. The New Order's economic needs were best served by retaining Norwegian labour in these sectors of employment and their retention there also strengthened the barriers to social change in the new society.

It is in that framework that German plans for the industrialization of Norway should be seen. Ultimately the intention was to exploit the country in Germany's interests while arresting, in the name of the fascist revolution, its future economic growth or changing the purposes for which such growth was normally fostered. It has been seen that the hectic events of the war often prevented the details of German policy from coinciding exactly with its general outlines. Nevertheless, the real wage rates of agricultural and forestry workers and of fishermen fell less in wartime Norway than those of industrial workers. They even fell less than those of construction workers, although because many construction workers were paid illegally high wages by the Wehrmacht their total earnings and standard of living probably fell less than those of agricultural workers. In fact the high wages earned by construction workers were the chief cause of the shortage of seasonal forestry workers.

The movement of wage rates in favour of agricultural wages is the more striking testimony to the determination with which Germany pursued an overtly fascist policy when it is considered that industrial labour, especially skilled labour, was at as great a premium in Norway as in any of the occupied territories. There were attempts in the early stages of the occupation to use Norwegian labour in Germany. The first transport consisting of 500 unskilled construction workers left on 15 January 1941 and a further transport of 400 on 6 February.[1] Such policies were soon given up. They were flying in the face of reality even at that stage, for in early 1941 it was estimated that at least 30,000 extra construction workers and 9,000 forestry workers would be needed in Norway that year.[1] By summer 1941 the Organisation Todt had begun its plans to import Danish building workers to undertake the enormous construction projects in Trondheim.[2] There were still 33,556 socially-insured workers registered as unemployed in April 1941 but after that the number became quite insignificant.[3] German plans to use Norwegian labour in Germany were tacitly abandoned and in that sense Norway made no contribution to Germany's war economy, in contrast with France whence over half a million workers left for Germany between September 1942 and June 1943 to join the 1 million prisoners of war already there. As far as Norway was concerned the movement was to be the other way. The Danish building workers at Trondheim were followed by 800 Russian workers for the fish-freezing plant at Bodø and 100 for that at Hammerfest.[4] Subsequently, Russian workers were used to build the northern railway and autobahn and were employed there in the most cruel and atrocious conditions. At the height of the Sauckel actions there were further attempts to obtain labour from Norway but even Sauckel himself was soon persuaded that such efforts were pointless.

That the German administration was faced with much hostility from Norwegian labour had serious consequences for the exploitation of the economy. The level of productivity per man was lower in wartime Norway than before the war and part of this no doubt was due to their unwillingness to work for the enemy. That Norwegian labour was right to see fascism in this light is beyond doubt. But it was not only in the field of labour relations and employment that German policy in Norway revealed itself in consonance with the basic tenets of the fascist New Order. Every aspect of economic policy there was consonant with the aims of the social and spiritual reconstruction to which fascism subscribed.

Norway had a special importance as being a repository of that Nordic stock which National Socialist thinkers supposed to be more suitable for producing the aristocratic élite of the future. It was this that Rosenberg meant when he wrote of the 'Nordic community of fate'. Instead of the mongrel conception of 'pan-Europa' he upheld the idea of a pan-Teutonic domination of Europe. Foreign political conflicts were, truly seen, a projection of the conflicts of blood, for the blood carried with it man's divine

---

[1] F.D. 5211/45, Rk., Abt. Arbeit und Sozialwesen, 'Führer-Bericht für die Zeit vom 16/11/40–31/1/1941', 31 January 1941.

[2] Ibid., 'Führer-Bericht für die Zeit vom 1/2–31/5/1941', 24 May 1941.

[3] Ibid., 'Jahresbericht', 7 January 1942.

[4] F.D. 5325/45, Rk., Gruppe Lohnpolitik und Arbeitsbedingungen, '3-Jahresbericht der Gruppe', 17 February 1943.

essence. The myth of the blood and subservience to it was the true foundation of European society, not the ratiocinatory inheritance so lauded by
liberals. In the new racial system of states Norway had a particular value.
Peoples endowed with a sound stock of blood should be exempt from all
nebulous illusions of individualism.[1]

The corruption of Western liberalism was a disease powerful enough
to have ruined for all useful purposes large sections of Norwegian society.
But that could not deter fascist ideologues, for Germany's battle against
liberalism had been equally long. Liberalism was a wound on man's
inner nature. Only a slow healing process was possible, a healing process
which would begin in those social groups where the trauma had been less
profound. The healing of Norwegian society would spread from the
peasants and fishermen. 'The working master-race of the towns will be
refreshed by the blood of the country nobility, the working race of knights
in the towns by peasant blood.' In that way the ideological values of the
race would triumph over imported sophistries.[2]

The exaltation of Norwegian rural society above urban, the attempts to
produce more food and to catch more fish, had their practical economic
side as well as their socio-psychological aspects. But it would be quite
mistaken to regard this practical economic side as being just an incident
of the war economy. The extra supply of food was to make Norway less
dependent on foreign trade and thus more suitable for incorporation in
the *Großraumwirtschaft* and the extra supply of fish was destined, ultimately, to lessen the dependence of the new Europe on imported protein.
Unless an economic area with a sufficient degree of autarky could be
created in Europe, infection from the more materialist systems was bound
to penetrate the new world, 'the spirit of profit', in Feder's language,
would contaminate 'the spirit of want-supplying'.[3] Norway was in many
ways peripheral to this *Großraumwirtschaft* which was to be created in
the south and east, but once incorporated, her economy had to be adapted
to fit. Hence side by side with the encouragement of agriculture and
fishing had to go the encouragement of mining, smelting, the production
of electric power, the production of aluminium, and the processing of
wood products. Taken as a whole, Norway would always have to be
supplied by the *Großraumwirtschaft*, but in each of these particular areas
she had peculiar advantages and resources to offer. The intention, therefore,
in developing particular aspects of primary and secondary production in
Norway was not to develop Norway, but to develop the new Europe. If

[1] A view most clearly (if such a word is permissible with respect to Rosenberg's writing)
expressed in A. Rosenberg, *Der Mythus des zwanzigsten Jahrhunderts; eine Wertung der
seelisch-geistigen Gestaltenkämpfe unserer Zeit* (Munich, 1930).

[2] F. Haiser, *Die Judenfrage vom Standpunkt der Herrenmoral; rechtsvölkische und linksvölkische Weltanschauung* (Leipzig, 1926), p. 76.

[3] G. Feder, *Das Manifest zur Brechung der Zinsknechtschaft des Geldes* (Munich, 1919).

the Norwegian economy had still to develop in some ways, these changes would be harmless to the massive stability of a new continent. Submerged in the larger whole Norway would sacrifice all control over her own destiny and over the purposes of her own development.

In doing so she would be turning her back on the very philosophical and economic forces which had been responsible for her development. It is worth pausing to consider the strength of these forces, worth considering how poor a country Norway had been in the memory of persons by no means old at the time of the German invasion, worth considering how meagre her resources, in order to comprehend the magnitude of this change of policy. An economic philosophy derived from the long history of German economic development was to be foisted on to a society whose whole history had been quite different. An economic system which was certainly neither inappropriate nor impractical for a large and centrally situated power fitted very strangely on a country whose almost every resource was lapped by the waters of the sea.

Hardly any of these wider plans for the Norwegian economy were successful. Many had begun to show the marks of failure before the New Order itself collapsed under military pressure. There was in any case no agreement on the details of economic policy between Nasjonal Samling and the National Socialist Party. On the rejection of the past with its corrupt values and on the creation of a new European system both were agreed. But Nasjonal Samling, for instance, had advocated as one way of doing this the establishment of a cheap-money policy with guaranteed credit for small businessmen and peasants in Norway. Indeed, that had been almost the only specific economic proposal in their party manifesto. Such a policy came into direct conflict with the cautious monetary policy of the German occupiers. So too did many other Nasjonal Samling schemes for social regeneration. The relationship between the two parties was such that Nasjonal Samling always had to accept the verdict of the conquerors so that their own policies were sacrificed both to the needs of the war and to the opposition of the National Socialist Party.

The persistence with which they tried to force their policies on Terboven even in 1944 revealed how politically naïve were the Nasjonal Samling ministers. Terboven, faced with their naïvety, deliberately spelt out German policy to Minister Lippestad in May 1944 in one of the frankest documents to bear his signature. Lippestad had pressed on Terboven his department's policy of increasing industrial wages over a wide range of occupations. Terboven enumerated the reasons why this could not be done

1. The government of a country in the grip of war which, out of its socio-political responsibility, is disposed to protect and secure the existence of the broad masses, will always quickly seize on the decisive measure of a concurrent

wage and price stop, because at that moment in which wages and prices begin to compete without the economy being in the position to produce a quantity of goods sufficient to satisfy the ever more rapidly increasing purchasing power which is the result, the collapse of the exchange would automatically start. The resulting catastropic effects would fall particularly on the broad masses, that is to say on the workers and on the middle classes. In spite of this clear situation I did not, when I began my task as Reichskommissar, proceed immediately with this measure, but first—both in the area of wages and in that of individual prices—undertook a wide-ranging basic readjustment. This readjustment was necessary because the renegade emigrant government had left in certain sectors socio-political conditions which were a blow in the face to every social conception and on the other hand, especially in the peasant sector, had pursued a price policy which could only lead to the death of the peasantry and in effect would surely have done so.

Out of many examples from the social sector, I will only draw attention here to the particularly important one, the increase in wages for agricultural and forestry workers. . . .

2. In time of war when all the necessities of life are rationed, the absolute level of wages is no longer the generally decisive measure for the high or low socio-political position of the broad masses. The three decisive measures are far more:

(*a*) that the rationing of everything be handled in a socially just way, that is to say that the financially stronger secure no advantage over the weaker;

(*b*) that the rationing quotas on paper are also available for those who receive the rations;

(*c*) that the income of one who dutifully fulfils his work is such that he can actually buy the quota set aside for him.

I believe I may say that all three points, in spite of recurring acute difficulties, in general have not only been and will be taken into account in the fullest manner, but that the present supply to the workers in Norway is far better than was the case in 1917 and 1918, at a time when transport with the rest of the Continent was open to Norway.

3. After the big basic readjustment had been carried out in 1940, and more particularly in 1941, it should not be overlooked that henceforward every further wage increase would release an immediate pressure on prices, a danger that is the greater because the Department of Agriculture on its own account has striven continually, in spite of the basic readjustment carried through in agricultural prices, to push through further price increases.

4. It is therefore my intention, in order to supervise with all means what is the most decisive task for us, to contain prices and where they have been broken against the will of the government to force them back again.[1]

Terboven was not flattering himself unfairly, Norway was better governed than most other occupied territories. Terboven and the Reichskommissariat were an efficient government and by their own lights a

[1] R.A., Quislings arkiv, unumerierte kasse (Quislings private korrespondanse), Terboven to Lippestad, 12 May 1944.

just one. But this very efficiency reduced the role of the Nasjonal Samling ministers even more. Eivind Blehr, after his resignation as Minister of Trade and Supply, wrote privately to his cousin in Germany that he had found himself 'treated like a puppet minister'.[1] Quisling's and Lippestad's view of Terboven's refusal to increase the pay of parish employees was that 'the employees of 500 parishes curse the Ministry of Social Affairs, the Minister of Social Affairs and, in the long run, the whole New Order for so much inconsistency and lack of understanding'.[2]

The construction of the new Europe receded into the background in 1942 and was replaced by the immediate necessity to organize a European war economy. Reminders that this was now the central task of the German administration had to be delivered with increasing sternness. When Minister Fuglesang twice published articles in the summer of 1944 in favour of Nasjonal Samling's cheap-money policy, once in the Nasjonal Samling monthly and once in Norsk Arbeidsliv, Otte pointed out to him all too clearly what the position of a Norwegian minister was.

Apart from the fact that the raising of such problems at the present moment is extremely critical and detrimental to the government, this paper of Minister Fuglesang transgresses against an instruction given to the Nasjonal Samling Press at the beginning of the year on account of a similar article in the Nasjonal Samling monthly, that the handling of questions of financial and exchange policy should only be pursued after previous soundings of opinion in the Reichskommissariat.[3]

Yet the original hopes of a New Order survived beneath the reality of the short-term exploitation of the country. The purpose of the European war economy remained a fascist one, however much the administrative details of its organization might cause the postponement of fascist aims. In any case there was no inherent contradiction between the idea of the New Order and the idea of exploitation. The new fascist order would be derived from the order of the animal world, an order not distorted by false sentimentality or morality. As the struggle in the animal world was for food so was that between peoples for Lebensraum. As one form of human society which could succeed materialism was cannibalism so could economic co-operation be replaced by exploitation.

The most obvious immediate cause of the failure of the fascist economy in Norway was the inability of the New Order to provide so satisfactory a framework for Norway's foreign trade. That is not to say that, given time, Norwegian foreign trade could not have been forced to adapt totally to the

[1] R.A., Kasse II, avl. UB, okt. 1970 (Eivind Blehr arkiv), 8 February 1945.
[2] R.A., Quislings arkiv, unumerierte kasse (Quislings private korrespondanse), 'PM. über das Verhältnis des Sozialministeriums zum Reichskommissariat', 17 January 1944.
[3] R.A., Løse dok., Næringsdepartementet, Otte to Whist, 1 September 1944.

fascist system since German economic policy was to reduce very substantially the standard of living of the Norwegian people and, consequently,
the demand for imports. At this point the question must be raised as to
whether or not the final successful integration of Norway into the New
Order would not have drastically reduced her productive capacity as well.
There are many indications that this would have been so. This could have
been overcome if all the German economic policies there were brought
to a complete fruition. But this achievement, in its turn, was dependent
on a huge programme of capital investment which was beginning to be
abandoned even in autumn 1940.

If the programme of investment had turned Norway into a bigger
producer of food, of electricity, of raw materials, and into a much more
significant aluminium producer, many of the difficulties presented by the
extraordinarily high level of imports in her economy would have been
eliminated. But the evolution of German monetary policy in Norway
prevented these developments. As long as Germany was in the war and
the political situation in Norway did not improve, monetary policy had
to remain extremely cautious. These restraints could have been removed if
Germany's military and economic strength had enabled her to crush the
military opposition or if the moral force of fascism had converted the
Norwegian population to a loyal support for the social and economic
principles of the New Order. Neither of these things took place. The cost
of the military occupation ruled out the additional costs of economic
reconstruction; the Norwegian people provided as flagrant an example of
opposition to the new system as could be found in Europe. Norway was
but an insignificant power, yet the history of the fascist economy there
shows not only the existence of the New Order as a concerted and radical
idea of social and economic reconstruction but also its greatest weakness,
the disproportion between its ambitions and its strength.

Had the final result of the war been different, could the Norwegian
economy have been successfully integrated in the long run into the New
Order? Given the fascist criteria of success there is no reason to suppose
that it could not have been. In wartime the integration could proceed only
half-heartedly and with many interruptions. Many of the worst problems,
such as the shipping shortage and the shortage of cash for investment,
were the result of the war rather than inherent in the economic situation.
Had the war ended in a victory for the fascist powers there would have
been a permanent rather than a temporary revolution in the Norwegian
economy. Norway had been able to exercise until 1940 an unusual degree
of choice for so small an economy within the international economy. This
relative freedom would have been exchanged for subservience to the
demands of central Europe for raw materials, foodstuffs, and strategic
materials. The high level of income within the country would have been

brought down below the level of Germany in the 1930s. All future economic development would have been dictated by factors operating within a much more rigidly defined economy. The greater consistency of demand which might have ensued would not have compensated for the fact that economic development and political life would have been entirely subjected to German interests. There was very little in fascist economic policy in Norway which offered much chance of converting the population to support for the fascist regime and much that made their conversion unlikely. Norway may never have become a genuinely fascist state, but it would have become an insignificant part of a European autarky, a country with neither political nor economic independence.

NOTE ON SOURCES

Unpublished

THE archives of the various departments for economic affairs of the Reichs-kommissariat für die besetzten norwegischen Gebiete were left in what seems to have been a relatively complete state to the Allies. They were then subjected to a curious process of division. An Anglo-Norwegian team of investigators went through them separating some files, and in certain cases single documents, for temporary transfer to Britain. It was the administrative practice of most of the German departments and sub-departments to compile monthly and annual reports of their activities for use within the administration itself. Mostly it was these reports which were taken to Britain, although some remained behind in Norway. The bulk of the correspondence and memoranda on which these working papers were based was left in Norway. There it subsequently passed into the care of the Riksarkivet.

This habit of dividing up archival collections was only too common in 1945 and 1946, a result of the hunt for useful political and economic evidence and of the desire for loot. Normally it was done with an absolute disregard for archival propriety or history. In this case, however, it was done with considerable skill, all too well, indeed, in the light of subsequent events. The documents trans-ferred to Britain, after an adventurous life some of which still remains in obscurity, ended up in a collection of German ministerial papers in the care of the Air Ministry. Thence they passed to the Foreign Documents Centre of the Imperial War Museum. By this time the Norwegian authorities and most British authorities had lost all trace of where they were. The catalogue of the Foreign Documents Centre revealed their presence but they seem not to have been noticed, perhaps because they were so small a part of a very large collection which was almost entirely composed of rather different materials. There was no real reason to suspect the importance of so relatively small and extraneous a part of a larger collection, and I was myself for some time equally misled until I inspected their contents.

By the time this book is published the archive will have been reconstituted in Oslo and it may be that the reference system for those documents in the Foreign Documents Centre will have been incorporated into that of the Riksarkivet. At the moment I have no alternative but to refer to the documents in Britain by the F.D. numbers which they have in the catalogue of the Foreign Documents Centre and to give a reasonably full account of the document where that could make indentification easier. The documents in Norway have of course been referred to by the file numbers of the Riksarkivet catalogues. In both cases the reference is to a file of documents in which the particular document is identified by title and date.

From time to time I have cited documentary evidence from other German sources, particularly from the Reichsluftfahrtministerium, the Reichsministerium für Bewaffnung und Munition, the Reichsministerium für Kriegsproduktion, the Reichswirtschaftsministerium, and Interessengemeinschaft Farben. The present location of these documents is indicated by the initial letters of the citation. Thus 'F.D.' indicates that the document is in the Foreign Documents Centre, 'F.D. (N.T.L.L.)' that it is in the National Technological Lending Library at Boston Spa, Yorkshire, 'B.A.' that it is in the Bundesarchiv at Koblenz, and 'R.A.' that it is in the Riksarkivet. The numbers are those in the current catalogues of the Foreign Documents Centre and the Riksarkivet and the Findbücher of the Bundersarchiv.

In addition I have occasionally referred the reader to documentary evidence relating to the trials of war criminals at Nuremberg. To signify the origin of such documents I have used the code 'N.D.'. That does not necessarily mean, however, that the document is published in the trial proceedings, whether the *Trial of the Major War Criminals before the International Military Tribunal, Documents in Evidence* (Nuremberg, 1947–9), or the proceedings of the lesser trials. I have included in each case the so-called 'Nuremberg number' allocated to the document at the trial and where the document is a document for the defence I have indicated that also.

Published

There are two published collections of particular usefulness. *Aktstykker om den tyske finanspolitikk i Norge 1940–1945* (Oslo, 1958), ed. S. Hartmann and J. Vogt, is a selection from a collection of documents of the greatest possible importance in the possession of Norges Bank. While it is much better that they should have been published than not, the editing of the volume leaves a great deal unexplained, not least the principles according to which the documents were selected. Norges Bank's own reports on wartime policy are also especially interesting, particularly *Virksomheten i hvert av årene, 1940–1944* (Oslo, 1945).

The publications of Statistisk Sentralbyrå are a source of information on the war years in Norway far superior to comparable materials existing for most other occupied countries. Those that have been referred to in the text have their full titles below in the list of published documentary sources. The list is not intended to be in any way comprehensive but simply to serve as a supplementary guide to the footnotes in the book.

BJONER, O., *Mot lysere tider. Artikler og taler* (Oslo, 1943).

La Délégation française auprès de la Commission allemande d'armistice, 5 vols. (Paris, 1947–).

Documents on German Foreign Policy 1918–1945, Series D (1937–1945) (London, H.M.S.O. 1949–).

EIDSIVATING LAGSTOLS LANDSSVIKAVDELING, *Straffesak mot Vidkun Quisling*, (Oslo, 1946).

HARTMAN, S., and VOGT, J. (eds.), *Aktstykker om den tyske finanspolitikk i Norge 1940–1945* (Oslo, 1958).

Hitler's Table Talk 1941–44 (London, 1953).

NASJONAL SAMLING, *9 april 1940. Førerens tale i Colosseum den 8 april 1941.* (Oslo, 1941).

—— *Die nationale Revolution in Norwegen. Reden von Vidkun Quisling und Gulbrand Lunde* (Oslo, 1944).

—— *For Norges frihet og selvstendighet. Artikler og taler 9 april 1940–23 juni 1941* (Oslo, 1942).

—— *Ministerpresident Vidkun Quislings tale i Oslo den 14 mai 1944* (Oslo, 1944).

—— *Mot nytt land. Artikler og taler av Vidkun Quisling 1941–43, Quisling har sagt* — iv (Oslo, 1943).

—— *Nasjonalt forfall og nasjonal gjenreisning. Quislings tale i Colosseum 12 mars 1941* (Oslo, 1941).

—— *NS Årbok.*

—— *Quisling har sagt* — *Citater fra taler og avaisartikler,* i (Oslo, 1940).

—— *Quisling har sagt* — *ii. Ti års kamp mot katastrofepolitikken* (Oslo, 1941).

—— *Ved terskelen til det avgjørende år. Tale av Vidkun Quisling 1 januar 1945.* (Oslo, 1945).

—— *Vidkun Quislings tale på førertinget 25 september 1942* (Oslo, 1943).

—— *Vidkun Quislings tale til norges håndverkere 9 september 1941* (Oslo, 1942).

NORGES BANK, *Beretning om den økonomiske stilling i de forskjellige landsdeler for årene 1940–44. Rapporter innhentet av Norges Bank* (Oslo, 1945).

—— *Virksomheten i hvert av årene 1940–1944* (Oslo, 1945).

Norges forhold til sverige under krigen 1940–45. Aktstykker utgitt av Det. Kgl. Utenriksdepartement, 3 vols. (Oslo, 1947).

NORSK ARBEIDSTJENESTE, *Årbok 1941, 1942, 1943.*

OSLO POLITIKAMMER, *Innberetning til Oslo Politikammer. Vedrørende A/S Norsk Aluminium Company og Nordisk Aluminium Industri A/S.*

PICKER, H., *Hitlers Tischgespräche im Führerhauptquartier 1941–1942. Im Auftrage der nationalsozialistischen Zeit geordnet, eingeleitet und veröffentlicht von G. Ritter* (Bonn, 1951).

SERAPHIM, H. G. (ed)., *Das politische Tagebuch Alfred Rosenbergs aus den jahren 1934/35 und 1939/40.* Quellensammlung zur Kulturgeschichte, No. 8 (Göttingen, 1956).

STATISTISK SENTRALBYRÅ, *Bedriftstelling i Norge.*

—— *Foreløbige resultater av folketellingen i Norge, desember 1930. Historisk Statistikk 1968.*

—— *Norges handel.*

—— *Norges industri. Produksjonsstatistikk.*

—— *Norske skip i utenriksfart.*

——*Økonomisk utsyn 1900–1950. Samfunnsøkonomiske studier,* No. 3 (Oslo, 1955).

—— *Statistisk Ørbok.*

—— *Statistisk-økonomisk utsyn over krigsårene* (Oslo, 1945).

SVERIGE, UTRIKESDEPARTEMENTET, *Sveriges förhållande till Danmark och Norge under krigsåren. Redogörelser avgivna till utrikesnämnden av ministern för utrikes ärendena 1941–1945* (Stockholm, 1945).

TERBOVEN, J., *Nyordingen i Norge. Reichskommissar Terbovens tale 25 september 1940* (Oslo, 1940).

BIBLIOGRAPHY

This bibliography, includes those books referred to in the text and certain others of immediate relevance. Entries are arranged according to the Norwegian alphabet.

ANDENAES, J., RISTE, O., and SKODVIN, M., *Norway and the Second World War* (Oslo, 1966).

ASKELUND, B., 'Nortraships hemmelige fond', in *Norge og den 2 verdenskrig: Mellom nøytrale og allierte*. Studier i norsk samtidshistorie (Oslo, 1968).

AUKRUST, O., and BJERVE, P. J., *Hva krigen kostet Norge* (Oslo, 1945).

BERGSGÅRD, A., *Frå 17 mai til 9 april. Norsk historie 1814 til 1940* (Oslo, 1958).

BJERKE, J., *Some Aspects of long-term Economic Growth of Norway since 1865*, paper presented to the 6th European Conference of the International Association for Research in Income and Wealth (Portoroz, 1959).

BOEHM, H., *Norwegen zwischen England und Deutschland. Die Zeit vor und während des zweiten Weltrieges* (Lippoldsberg, 1956).

BOURNEUF, A., *Norway. The Planned Revival*, Harvard Economic Studies, vol. cvi (Cambridge, Mass., 1958).

BOUTHILLIER, Y., *Le Drame de Vichy*, 2 vols. (Paris, 1950–1).

BRANDT, K., *Fats and Oils in the War*, War–Peace Pamphlets no. 2, Food Research Institute, Stanford University (Stanford, 1943).

—— *The German Fat Plan and its Economic Setting*, Fats and Oils Studies No. 6, Food Research Institute, Stanford University (Stanford, 1938).

—— *Whaling and Whale Oil during and after World War II*, War–Peace Pamphlets No. 11, Food Research Institute, Stanford University (Stanford, 1948).

—— et al., *Management of Agriculture and Food in the German-Occupied and other Areas of Fortress Europe. A Study in Military Government*, vol. ii of *Germany's Agricultural and Food Policies in World War II* (Stanford, 1953).

BRANDT, W., *Kriget i Norge. 9 april til 9 juni 1940* (Stockholm, 1941).

—— et al. (eds.) *Norge ockuperat och fritt* (Stockholm, 1943).

BREVIG, H. O. *NS — fra parti til sekt* (Oslo, 1970).

BRØYN, P. 'Den svenske malmeksport fram til okkupasjonen av Narvik i april 1940 — med særlig tanke på utførselen til Tyskland', in *Norge og den 2 verdenskrig: Mellom nøytrale og allierte*, Studier i norsk samtidshistorie (Oslo, 1968).

DARRÉ, W., *Das Bauerntum als Lebensquell der nordischen Rasse* (Munich, 1929).

DELEGATIONS FOR THE PROMOTION OF ECONOMIC COOPERATION BETWEEN THE NORTHERN COUNTRIES, *The Northern Countries in World Economy*, 2nd edn. (Helsinki, 1939).

DERRY, T. K., *The Campaign in Norway*, History of the Second World War, United Kingdom Military Series (London, H.M.S.O., 1952).

EICHHOLTZ, D., *Geschichte der deutschen Kriegswirtschaft 1939–1945*, vol. i, *1939–1941*, Forschungen zur Wirtschaftsgeschichte, ed. J. Kuczynski and H. Mottek, No. 1 (Berlin, 1969).

EMMENDORFER, A., *Geld- und Kreditaufsicht in den von Deutschland während des zweiten Weltkrieges besetzten Gebieten; eine völkerrechtliche Untersuchung über die geld- und kreditwirtschaftlichen Maßnahmen deutscher Besetzungsbehörden*, Institut für Besatzungsfragen, Studien zu den deutschen Besetzungen im 2 Weltkrieg, No. 12 (Düsseldorf, 1957).

EVANG, K., *Norway's Nutrition Problem* (London, 1942).

FEDER, G., *Das Manifest zur Brechung der Zinsknechtschaft des Geldes* (Munich, 1919).

FEDERAU, F., *Der zweite Weltkrieg. Seine Finanzierung in Deutschland* (Tübingen, 1962).

FELICE, R. DE, *Le interpretazioni del fascismo* (Bari, 1969).

FEN, A., *Nazis in Norway* (London, 1943).

FJORD, F., *Norwegens totaler Kriegseinsatz; vier Jahre Okkupation* (Zürich, 1944).

FORSVARETS KRIGSHISTORISKE AVDELING, *Norges sjøkrig 1940–1945*, 6 vols. (Oslo, 1954–63).

FRANKENBERG, R., 'Norwegen' in *Jahrbuch der Weltpolitik, 1944*, Deutsches Auslandswissenschaftliches Institut (Berlin, 1944).

FRIEDRICH, C. J. (ed.), *Totalitarianism* (Cambridge, Mass., 1954).

FUGLESANG, R. J., and KOLBY, O., *Nasjonal økonomisk nyordning* (Oslo, 1944).

GEMZELL, C.-A., *Raeder, Hitler und Skandinavien. Der Kampf für einen maritimen Operationsplan*, Bibliotheca Historica Lundensis, vol. xvi (Lund, 1965).

GERMANI, G., *Sociología de la modernización* (Buenos Aires, 1969).

GRAMSCI, A., *Socialismo e fascismo: l'ordine nuovo, 1921–1922, Opere*, vol. ii (Turin, 1966).

HAISER, F., *Die Judenfrage vom Standpunkt der Herrenmoral; rechtsvölkische und linksvölkische Weltanschauung* (Leipzig, 1926).

HARTMANN, S., *Nytt lys over kritiske faser i Norges historie under annen verdenskrig* (Oslo, 1965).

HAYES, P. M., 'Quisling's Political Ideas' in *Journal of Contemporary History*, vol. i (1966).

HEECKT, H., *Strukturwandlungen und Nachkriegsprobleme der Wirtschaft Norwegens*, Kieler Studien, Forschungsberichte des Instituts für Weltwirtschaft an der Universität Kiel, No. 8 (Kiel, 1950).

HERDEG, *Grundzüge W., der deutschen Besetzungsverwaltung in den west- und nordeuropäischen Ländern während des zweiten Weltkrieges*, Studien des Instituts für Besatzungsfragen in Tübingen zu den deutschen Besetzungen im 2 Weltkrieg, No. 1 (Tübingen, 1953).

HEWINS, R., *Quisling. Prophet without Honour* (London, 1965).

HILDEBRANDT, F., *Nationalsozialismus und Landarbeiterschaft*, Nationalsozialistische Bibliothek, vol. xvii (Munich, 1930).

HILLGRUBER, A., *Hitlers Strategie. Politik und Kriegführung 1940–1941* (Frankfurt am Main, 1965).

HORN, M., *Norwegen zwischen Krieg und Frieden* (Innsbruck, 1941).

HORY, L., and BROSZAT, M., *Der kroatische Ustascha-Staat 1941–1945*, Schriftenreihe der Vierteljahrshefte für Zeitgeschichte, No. 8 (Stuttgart, 1964).

HUBATSCH, W., *Die deutsche Besetzung von Dänemark und Norwegen 1940*, Göttinger Beiträge für Gegenwartsfragen, No. 5 (Göttingen, 1952).

HÜTTENBERGER, P., *Die Gauleiter. Studie zum Wandel des Machtgefüges in der NSDAP*, Schriftenreihe der Vierteljahrshefte für Zeitgeschichte, No. 19 (Stuttgart, 1969).

IRVING, D., *The Virus House. Germany's Atomic Research and Allied Countermeasures* (London, 1967).

JACOBSEN, H.-A., *Nationalsozialistische Außenpolitik 1933–1939* (Frankfurt am Main, 1968).

JÄGER, J.-J., 'Sweden's Iron Ore Exports to Germany, 1933–1944', *Scandinavian Economic History Review*, vol. xv, Nos. 1 and 2 (1967).

—— *Die wirtschaftliche Abhängigkeit des Dritten Reiches vom Ausland dargestellt am Beispiel der Stahlindustrie* (Berlin, 1969).

JANSSEN, G., *Das Ministerium Speer. Deutschlands Rüstung im Krieg* (Berlin, 1968).

JERNECK, B., *Folket utan fruktan. Norge 1942–1943* (Stockholm, 1943).

KARLBOM, R., 'Sweden's Iron Ore Exports to Germany, 1933–1944', *Scandinavian Economic History Review*, vol. xiii, no. I (1965).

KJELDSTADLI, S., *Hjemmestyrkene* (Oslo, 1959).

KNUDSEN, H. F., *Jeg var Quislings sekretær* (Copenhagen, 1951), trans. *I was Quisling's Secretary* (London, 1967).

KOHT, H., *Norsk utanrikspolitikk fram til 9 april 1940* (Oslo, 1947)

—— *Norway, Neutral and Divided* (London, 1941).

KOMMISSION DER HISTORIKER DER DDR. UND DER UdSSR., *Der deutsche Imperialismus und der zweite Weltkrieg*, Materialien der wissenschaftlichen Konferenz der Kommission der Historiker der DDR. und der UdSSR. vom 14 bis 19 Dezember 1959 in Berlin, 5 vols. (Berlin, 1960–).

KUCZYNSKI, J., *Studien zur Geschichte des deutschen Imperialismus*, 2 vols. (Berlin, 1948, 1950).

—— *Studien zur Geschichte des staatsmonopolistischen Kapitalismus in Deutschland 1918 bis 1945* (Berlin, 1963).

KUGELBERG, B., and IHLEN, J., *Grannar emellan. En bok om Sveriges forhållande till Norge under krigsåren 1940–1945* (Stockholm, 1945).

LEHMKUHL, D., *Journey to London. The Story of the Norwegian Government at War* (London, 1945).

LOOCK, H.-D., *Quisling, Rosenberg und Terboven. Zur Vorgeschichte und Geschichte der nationalsozialistischen Revolution in Norwegen* (Stuttgart, 1970).

—— 'Zeitgeschichte Norwegens' in *Vierteljahrshefte für Zeitgeschichte*, vol. xiii (1965).

LORENTZEN, Ø., *Norway, Norwegian Shipping and the War*, America in a World at War, No. 25 (New York, 1942).

LUFFT, H., *Die Wirtschaft Dänemarks und Norwegens. Gestalt — Politik — Problematik* (Berlin, 1942).

LUNDE, G., *Kampen for Norge. Skrifter, foredrag og avisartikler 1933–1940* (Oslo, 1941).

—— *Kampen for Norge* — II. *Foredrag og artikler 1940–1941* (Oslo, 1942).

MEAD, W. R., *An Economic Geography of the Scandinavian States and Finland* (London, 1958).

MEDLICOTT, W. N., *The Economic Blockade*, History of the Second World War, United Kingdom Civil Series, 2 vols. (London, 1952, 1958).

MILWARD, A. S., 'Could Sweden have Stopped the Second World War?', *Scandinavian Economic History Review*, vol. xv, Nos. 1 and 2 (1967).

—— 'The End of the Blitzkrieg', *Economic History Review*, vol. xvi, No. 3 (1964).

—— 'French Labour and the German Economy 1942–1945', ibid. vol. xxiii, No. 2 (1970).

—— *The German Economy at War* (London, 1965).

—— *The New Order and the French Economy* (Oxford, 1970).

MJØEN, J. A., *Germanen oder Slaven? Die Mongolisierung Europas. Eindrücke eines Neutralen von einer Reise an die Ostfront und zu Hindenburg*, veröffentlicht als Artikelserie in *Dagbladet*, Kristiania, *Nya Dagligt Allehanda*, Stockholm, und *Bergens Tidende*, Bergen (Berlin, 1917).

MOORE, B., JR., *Social Origins of Dictatorship and Democracy. Lord and Peasant in the Making of the Modern World* (Cambridge, Mass., 1966).

MÜRER, N. J. (ed.), *Boken om Danskehjelpen* (Oslo, 1947).

NASJONAL SAMLING, *Boken om Vidkun Quisling* (Oslo, 1940).

—— *Hva du bør vite om den nye tid* (Oslo, 1943).

—— *Nasjonalverket. Det nye Norge* (Oslo, 1941).

—— *Norges nyreising. Artikler om kulturelle og politiske sporsmalholdt som foredrag i serien 'Norges nyreising'* (Oslo, 1942).

NOLTE, E., *Theorien über den Faschismus* (Cologne, 1967).

—— 'Zeitgenössische Theorien über den Faschismus', *Vierteljahrshefte für Zeitgeschichte*, No. 15 (1967).

NORDISCHE GESELLSCHAFT, *Deutschland und der Norden. Gemeinsame Wege zur Kontinentalwirtschaft*, No. x, ed. W. Zimmermann (Lübeck, 1941).

—— *Die Wirtschaft der nördlichen Länder*, ed. W. Zimmermann (Lübeck, 1939).

—— *Nordeuropa und das Reich kriegswirtschaftlich gesehen*, ed. W. Zimmermann (Lübeck, 1940).

—— *Nordisches Schicksal Europas. Beiträge zum nordischen Gedanken und zur deutsch-nordländischen Arbeit*, ed. W. Zimmermann (Lübeck, 1939).

ORGANSKI, A. F. K., *The Stages of Political Development* (New York, 1967).

PAULSEN, H., 'Reichskommissariat og "motytelsene" under riksrådsforhandlingene', *Norge og den 2 verdenskrig: 1940-fra nøytral til okkupert*, Studier i norsk samtidshistorie (Oslo, 1969).

PETZINA, D., *Autarkiepolitik im Dritten Reich. Der nationalsozialistische Vierjahresplan*, Schriftenreihe der Vierteljahrshefte für Zeitgeschichte, No. 16 (Stuttgart, 1968).

PIRKER, T., *Komintern und Faschismus. Dokumente zur Geschichte und Theorie des Faschismus*, Schriftenreihe der Vierteljahrshefte für Zeitgeschichte, No. 10 (Stuttgart, 1965).

POLL, H., *Norwegen. Land — Menschen — Schicksal* (Oslo, 1942).

QUISLING, V. A. L. J., *Russland og vi* (Oslo, 1930), trans. *Russia and Ourselves* (London, 1931).

RADANDT, H., 'Die I. G. Farbenindustrie und Südosteuropa 1938 bis zum Ende des zweiten Weltkrieges', *Jahrbuch für Wirtschaftsgeschichte*, No. i (1967).

—— *Kriegsverbrecherkonzern Mansfeld. Die Rolle des Mansfeld-Konzerns bei der Vorbereitung und während des zweiten Weltkrieges* (Berlin, 1957).

REICHSMINISTERIUM FÜR ERNÄHRUNG UND LANDWIRTSCHAFT, *Die Landwirtschaft in Norwegen*, ed. H. Svensson, *Berichte über Landwirtschaft, Zeitschrift für Agrarpolitik und Landwirtschaft*, Neue Folge, Sonderheft 155.

REPPEN, D., *Sjølberging. Hevning av bøndebefolkningens levestandard* (Oslo, 1941).

RISTE, O., *The Neutral Ally: Norway's Relations with Belligerent Powers in the First World War* (Oslo, 1965).

ROSENBERG, A., *Der Mythus des zwanzigsten Jahrhunderts; eine Wertung der seelisch-geistigen Gestaltenkämpfe unserer Zeit* (Munich, 1930).

RUDOLPH, M., 'Geographie der Landstraßen und Eisenbahnen von Norwegen', Ergänzungsheft 206 zu *Petermanns Mitteilungen* (Gotha, 1929).

SAUER, W., 'National Socialism: Totalitarianism or Fascism?' *American Historical Review*, vol. lxiii (1967).

SCHRODER, R., 'Die Ausschußprotokolle der I. G. Farben als Quelle zur Betriebsgeschichtsforschung über die Zeit des Kapitalismus', *Jarbuch für Wirtschaftsgeschichte*, No. i (1967).

SCHUMANN, W., and LOZEK, G., 'Die faschistische Okkupationspolitik im Spiegel der Historiographie der beiden deutschen Staaten', *Zeitschrift für Geschichtswissenschaft*, vol. xii (1964).

SKAR, A., *Fagorganisasjonen under okkupasjonen 1920–1945* (Oslo, 1949).

SKODVIN, M., 'Norges plass i Hitlers militære planer etter 7 juni 1940', *Historisk Tidsskrift*, vol. xxxv (1951).

—— 'Norsk okkupasjonshistorie i europeisk samanhang', ibid., vol. xxvii (1951).

—— 'Norsk utanrikspolitikk 1939–1941 med særlig tanke på forholdet mellom die nordiske land', Studier i norsk samtidshistorie, *Norge og den 2 verdenskrig: Mellom nøytrale og allierte* (Oslo, 1968).

—— *Striden om okkupasjonsstyret i Norge fram til 25 september 1940* (Oslo, 1956).

SPEER, A., *Erinnerungen* (Berlin, 1969).

STEEN, S. (ed.) *Norges Krig 1940–1945*, 3 vols. (Oslo, 1947–50).

STRENG, H. VON, *Die Landwirtschaft im Generalgouvernement*, Institut für Besatzungsfragen, Studien zu den deutschen Besetzungen im 2 Weltkrieg, No. 6 (Tübingen, 1955).

STUDIER I NORSK SAMTIDSHISTORIE, *Norge og den 2 verdenskrig: Mellom nøytrale og allierte* (Oslo, 1968).

—— *Norge og den 2 verdenskrig: 1940 — fra nøytral til okkupert* (Oslo, 1969).

TASCA, A., *Nascita e avvento del fascismo* (Bari, 1965).

TIMM, E., 'Wirtschaft und Verkehr im nordeuropäischen Raum', H. F. Blunck (ed.), *Die nordische Welt. Geschichte, Wesen und Bedeutung der nordischen Völker* (Berlin, 1937).

ULSHÖFER, O., *Einflußnahme auf Wirtschaftsunternehmungen in den besetzten nord-, west-, und südosteuropäischen Ländern während des zweiten Weltkrieges insbesondere der Erwerb von Beteiligungen (Verflechtung)*, Institut für Besatzungsfragen, Studien zu den deutschen Besetzungen im 2 Weltkrieg, No. 15 (Tübingen, 1958).

UNITED KINGDOM, NAVAL INTELLIGENCE DIVISION, *Norway*, 2 vols., Geographical Handbook Series, B. R. 501 (London, 1949).

UNITED STATES, ECONOMIC COOPERATION ADMINISTRATION, *European Recovery Program. Norway. Country Study* (Washington, 1949).

VIGNESS, P. G., *The Neutrality of Norway in the World War*, Stanford University Publications in History, Economics and Political Science, vol. iv, no. i (Stanford, 1932).

WOOLF, S. J. (ed.), *The Nature of Fascism*, Reading University Studies on Contemporary Europe, vol. ii (London, 1968).

WYLLER, T. C., *Fra okkupasjonarenes maktkamp* (Oslo, 1953).

—— 'Hovedtrekk av Nasjonal Samlings idées om stat og samfunn' *Statsvetenskaplig Tidskrift* (1953).

—— *Nyordning og motstand. En framstilling og en analyse av organisasjonenes politiske funksjon under den tyske okkupasjonen 25.9.1940 — 25.9.1942* (Oslo, 1958).

ØRVIK, N., *Norge i brennpunktet fra forhistorien til 9 april 1940*, vol. i, *Handelskrigen 1939–40* (Oslo, 1953).

ØSTENSJØ, R., 'The Spring Herring Fishery and the Industrial Revolution in Western Norway in the Nineteenth Century', *Scandinavian Economic History Review*, vol. xi (1963).

AALL, H. H., *Er Norge et fritt land?* (Oslo, 1941).

—— *Nasjonalt livssyn og verdenspolitikk* (Oslo, 1942).

—— *The Neutral Investigation of the Causes of Wars. An Essay Concerning the Politics of War of the Great Powers and the Policy of Right of Small Nations* (Oslo, 1923).

—— *Nordens skjæbne* (Oslo, 1917), trans. *Das Schicksal des Nordens* (Weimar, 1918).

—— *Norges politiske nyreisning* (Oslo, 1941).

—— *Verdensdespotiet og havets frihet* (Oslo, 1939), trans. *Weltherrschaft und die Rechtlosigkeit der Meere* (Essen, 1940).

INDEX